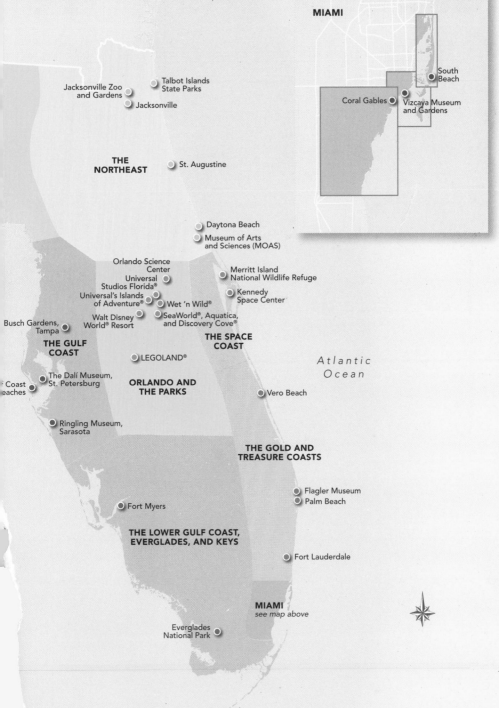

MIAMI

South Beach

Coral Gables

Vizcaya Museum and Gardens

Jacksonville Zoo and Gardens

Talbot Islands State Parks

Jacksonville

THE NORTHEAST

St. Augustine

Daytona Beach

Museum of Arts and Sciences (MOAS)

Orlando Science Center

Universal Studios Florida®

Universal's Islands of Adventure®

Wet 'n Wild®

Merritt Island National Wildlife Refuge

Kennedy Space Center

Walt Disney World® Resort

SeaWorld®, Aquatica, and Discovery Cove®

Busch Gardens, Tampa

THE GULF COAST

THE SPACE COAST

LEGOLAND®

The Dalí Museum, St. Petersburg

ORLANDO AND THE PARKS

Atlantic Ocean

Coast Beaches

Vero Beach

Ringling Museum, Sarasota

THE GOLD AND TREASURE COASTS

Flagler Museum

Palm Beach

Fort Myers

THE LOWER GULF COAST, EVERGLADES, AND KEYS

Fort Lauderdale

MIAMI
see map above

Everglades National Park

Key West

EYEWITNESS TRAVEL

FAMILY GUIDE
FLORIDA

Kids playing in the sand on the beach at Sand Key Park, Clearwater

Art Deco facade of a landmark hotel on Ocean Drive, Miami

How to Use this Guide

This guide is designed to help families get the most from a visit to Florida, providing expert recommendations for sightseeing with kids along with detailed practical information. The opening section contains an introduction to Florida and its highlights, as well as all the essentials required to plan a family vacation (including how to get there, getting around, health, insurance, money, restaurants, accommodations, shopping, and communications), a guide to family-friendly festivals and a brief historical overview.

The main sightseeing section is divided into areas. A "best of" feature for every chapter is followed by the key sights and other attractions in the area, as well as options for where to eat, drink, play, and have more fun. At the back of the book are detailed maps of Florida and Miami.

INTRODUCING THE AREA

Each area chapter opens with a double-page spread setting it in context, with a short introduction, a locator map, and a selection of highlights.

Locator map locates the area in the region.

Brief highlights give a flavor of what to see in the area.

THE BEST OF...

This planner shows at a glance the best things for families to see and do in each area, with themed suggestions ranging from history, art, and culture to gardens and games.

Themed suggestions for the best things to see and do with kids.

AREA MAP

Introductory text describes the key characteristics and geography of the area, and gives information on the transport infrastructure.

The map shows the area covered and all the sights in that chapter.

The Lowdown gives all the practical information you need to visit the area. The key to the symbols is on the back jacket flap.

SIGHTSEEING IN FLORIDA

Each area features a number of "hub" destinations (see below): pragmatic and enjoyable plans for a morning, afternoon, or day's visit. These give adults and children a real insight into the destination, focusing on the key sights and what makes them interesting to kids. The sights are balanced by places to let off steam, take cover options for rainy days, suggestions for where to eat, drink, and shop with kids, ideas for where to continue sightseeing, and all the practicalities, including transport.

The "hub" destinations are the best places to visit in each area, and use lively and informative text to engage and entertain both adults and children.

Key features uses illustrated artworks to show the most interesting features of each sight, highlighting elements likely to appeal to children.

Letting off steam suggests a place to take children to play freely following a cultural visit.

Eat and drink lists recommendations for family-friendly places to eat and drink, from picnic options and snacks to proper meals and gourmet dining.

Kids' Corner is featured on all sightseeing pages (see below).

The Lowdown provides comprehensive practical information, including transportation, opening times, costs, activities, age range suitability and how long to allow for a visit.

Find out more gives suggestions for downloads, games, apps, or movies to enthuse children about a place and help them to learn more about it.

Next stop... suggests other places to visit, either near the key destination, thematically linked to the sight or a complete change of pace for the rest of the day.

Further sights around each hub destination, selected to appeal to both adults and children, are given on the following pages.

Places of interest are recommended, with an emphasis on the aspects most likely to attract children, and incorporating quirky stories and unusual facts. Each one includes a suggestion for letting off steam or taking cover.

Kids' Corner is designed to involve children with the sight, with things to look out for, games to play, cartoons and fun facts. Answers to quizzes are given at the bottom of the panel.

The Lowdown provides comprehensive practical and transport information for each sight.

The Where to Stay section has a wide range of recommendations for places to stay with families, from hotels and B&Bs that welcome children to resorts and self-catering apartments.

Easy-to-use symbols show the key family-friendly features of places to stay.

Price Guide box gives details of the price categories for a family of four.

The Colony Hotel and other classic Art Deco establishments, lit up in colorful hues, on Ocean Drive, Miami Beach

Introducing

FLORIDA

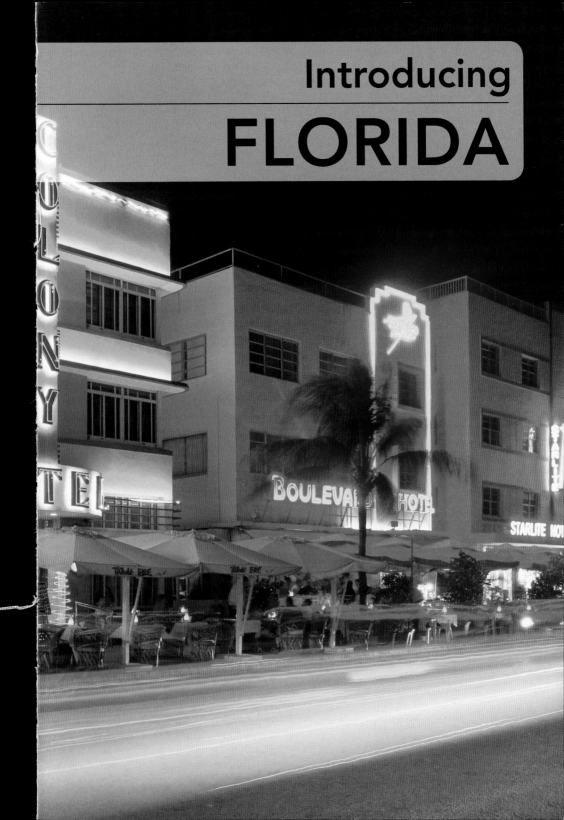

The Best of Florida

Famously known as the "Sunshine State," Florida is one of the most popular travel destinations in the world, drawing some 75 million visitors a year, including many families. With over 600 miles (970 km) of world-class beaches, and numerous waterways, Florida offers dozens of activities, from yachting and kayaking, to fishing and snorkeling. Nature-lovers can discover exotic flora and fauna in a host of nature preserves, or explore glorious scenery on the many biking and hiking trails. In addition, there is an array of world-famous theme parks, plus excellent museums that hold a special appeal for kids.

Beach bonanzas

The first decision is: which coast? Families can choose between the exciting Atlantic Ocean waves on the east coast or the soft sand and calm waters of the Gulf of Mexico on the west coast and in the northern Panhandle. **Miami Beach** *(see pp66–7)*, **St. Pete Beach** *(see p212)*, or **Fort Lauderdale** *(see pp80–1)*, with miles of accommodations on the sand, are very convenient for families. For a beach with plenty of room to toss a beach ball or build a sand castle without competing for space, head to **Anna Maria Island** *(see p212)* on the Gulf Coast, or the secluded **Virginia Key Beach Park** *(see p64)* on Key Biscayne in Miami. **Bradenton Beach** *(see p212)*, on the Gulf Coast, offers several restaurants and shops, and mini-golf a short stroll away, but those who prefer beaches that are quiet, undeveloped, and ringed with scenic dunes or sea pines will be happy on the **Gulf Islands National Seashore** *(see p194)* or the **Canaveral National**

Seashore *(see p148)* on the east coast. **Sanibel Island** *(see p238)* is a good place for kids to hunt for cockles, conchs, clams, and other prize shells, but even better beachcombing may be found at **Venice Beach** *(see p213)*, or by taking a boat to **Caladesi Island State Park** *(see p212)* near Clearwater, or **Shell Island** *(see p193)* off the Panhandle.

Right The Kilimanjaro Safari in Disney's Animal Kingdom®
Below Kids playing on Venice Beach, on the Gulf Coast

Above The high-speed thrill ride Kumba at Busch Gardens, Tampa Right The unique entrance to The Body Within exhibit in the Museum of Science and History, Jacksonville

Scream machines

"Roller Coasters 'R' Us" could be the motto of central Florida, and for many families, theme parks are Florida's biggest lure. If you have only a day for a park, consider **Busch Gardens** *(see pp214–15)* in Tampa, which has a choice of half a dozen world-class thrill rides such as Kumba.

Most kids would love to spend days in Orlando's theme parks, where competition is fierce for the best of the rides. Harry Potter™ fans will not want to miss the Wizarding World of Harry Potter™ and its Dragon Challenge™ roller coaster at **Universal's Islands of Adventure®** *(see pp120–21)*. The Hollywood Rip Ride Rockit® in **Universal Studios Florida®** *(see pp118–19)* is billed as the most high-tech coaster in the world.

The biggest theme park of them all, **Walt Disney World® Resort** *(see pp106–117)*, continues to excite with countless attractions such as the Rock 'n' Roller Coaster® Starring Aerosmith at **Disney's Hollywood Studios®** *(see pp114–15)*, and the perennial favorite, Space Mountain® in **Magic Kingdom®** *(see pp108–9)*, which does its swoops and swings in the dark. **Disney's Animal Kingdom®** *(see pp112–13)* provides a thrilling mix of rides, an animal safari, and several exploration trails. Don't forget Orlando's **SeaWorld®** *(see pp122–3)*, where the Kraken coaster dives underground three times, and Manta, the flying roller coaster, lets riders spin, glide, skim, and fly like a giant ray. At **LEGOLAND®** *(see pp132–5)*, Coastersaurus is a wooden coaster that curves and dips through a prehistoric jungle of animated and life-size dinosaurs made of LEGO® blocks.

Be warned, however, that the lines for major rides at all the theme parks can be long. See individual entries for tips on cutting the line.

The great indoors

Family fun is weatherproof in Florida, even for children who do not usually enjoy museums. The **Ringling Museum** *(see pp224–5)*, in Sarasota, is the place to see the world's largest miniature circus. Children of all ages will enjoy the large collection of wacky art by Salvador Dalí in **The Dalí Museum** *(see pp220–21)*, in St. Petersburg, devoted to the Surrealist. The **Morse Museum** *(see p130)* in Orlando's Winter Park features one of the world's most comprehensive collections of amazing glass creations by Louis Comfort Tiffany, including a chapel of glimmering glass tiles. At the **Cummer Museum of Art and Gardens** *(see p160)* in Jacksonville, Art Connections introduces kids to art by inviting them to "walk" through a painting, "listen" to a sculpture, or "paint" with a virtual paintbrush.

Miami, St. Petersburg, and Tampa are among several cities with terrific museums designed specifically for younger kids. Others, including the **Museum of Arts and Sciences** *(see pp176–7)* in Daytona Beach and the **Museum of Science and History** *(see p160)* in Jacksonville have separate museum wings filled with a variety of hands-on science activities geared to kids.

Butterfly, bird, and flora gardens

Florida's tropical climate fosters fabulous exotic plants, and the state's exceptional gardens allow kids to work off energy while their parents savor the scenery. Children will enjoy Miami's **Fairchild Tropical Garden** (see p56), which is the largest of its kind, with rare plants and 11 lakes, as well as a colorful butterfly garden. The **Marie Selby Botanical Gardens** (see p226) in Sarasota, home to over 6,000 orchids, is where kids can run on the lawn and feed fish in the koi pond. The **Morikami Museum and Japanese Gardens** (see p87), in Delray Beach, is a Japanese cultural center, with six gardens inspired by the most famous gardens of Japan. Visitors can stroll the zigzag bridges and picnic at the Lake Biwa and Saki Pavilion. The **Harry P. Leu Gardens** (see p130) in Orlando are known for their camellias and the best rose gardens in Florida. The **Alfred B. Maclay Gardens State Park** (see p201) in Tallahassee is also famous for its camellias, which begin blooming as early as January, while early spring is peak time for the prize azaleas here. The lush grounds of **Bok Tower Gardens** (see p135), south of Orlando, are beautiful year-round.

Something fishy

Florida's waters are filled with fantastic and colorful sea life. At Tampa's **The Florida Aquarium** (see p216), the showstopping Coral Reef Gallery is a colossal coral grotto in which more than 2,300 fish can be seen. Other favorite exhibits are the sea horses and the Penguin Promenade, where black-footed African penguins waddle their way through the lobby in daily parades. If kids get restless, **Explore A Shore** (see p216), an outdoor water adventure zone, lets them play among slippery slides and gushing geysers while parents relax in the shade. **The Aquarium at Mote Marine Laboratory** (see p226), in Sarasota, is the place to see sharks, manatees, and tropical fish, and to peep into the labs to see scientists doing research on sea life. Kids can swim with dolphins at **Marineland Dolphin Adventure** (see p172) in St. Augustine, **Miami Seaquarium®** (see p64), or **Dolphin Research Center** (see p249) in Marathon. Snorkeling opportunities are plentiful, but the best place to see colorful fish is at **John Pennekamp Coral Reef State Park** (see p251) in Key Largo, the country's first underwater preserve. Go underwater without getting wet at the floating underwater observatory at **Homosassa Springs Wildlife State Park** (see p219), where visitors can look at the resident manatees and the hundreds of fish that are free to come and go.

Right Snorkelers at John Pennekamp Coral Reef State Park
Below A leaping dolphin at Marathon's Dolphin Research Center

Florida through the Year

With its subtropical temperatures, southern Florida is most popular in the winter high season, from mid-December to mid-April, while northern Florida's beaches draw larger crowds in spring and summer. Avoid heading to the Panhandle or Daytona Beach in March when colleges are on spring break and hordes of young people visit the beaches. Each season brings its own share of fun and festivals that add excitement to a visit anywhere in Florida.

Spring

Spring celebrations salute everything from shells and strawberries to tall ships and motorcycles, while sports go into high gear with baseball spring training and traditional Scottish Highland Games.

MARCH

The **Big Bay Area Renaissance Festival** in Tampa features armor-clad knights sword-fighting on horseback. Another part of history comes to life as the 1668 **Sack of St. Augustine** is re-enacted.

Baseball brings cheering fans to spring training games all over the state, while motorcycle enthusiasts head for the annual **Bike Week** at Daytona Beach. The two-week **Festival of States** in St. Petersburg includes a special KidsFest and even a Festival of Pets to celebrate animal friends.

More March favorites include the treasures on display at the **Sanibel Shell Fair**, the **Florida Strawberry Festival** *(see p211)* in Plant City, near Tampa, and **Springtime Tallahassee**, a weekend festival that includes a parade of costumed floats.

APRIL

Kids will love the **Zoo Miami's Great Egg Safari**, where besides hunting for eggs, the fun includes face painting, rock climbing, bouncy castles, and visits from the Easter Bunny. The amazing underwater **Easter Egg Hunt** in Key Largo is open to divers and snorkelers of all ages.

Military musters are part of the festivities at the annual **Conch Republic Independence Celebration** *(see p234)* in Key West, while the weeklong **Scottish Festival** on the Gulf Coast features Highland Games, with competitions between colorful kilted bands, Highland dancers, and athletes having a go at the throwing of the hefty Dunedin Stone.

MAY

SunFest *(see p78)* in West Palm Beach calls itself "Florida's largest waterfront music and art festival," with more than 100 artist booths, food stands, and three stages of entertainment on the tree-lined walkways along the Intracoastal Waterway. A Family Activities Tent offers games and fun for little ones. Folk songs, crafts, and the chance to feast on gumbo and barbecue have drawn families to the **Florida Folk Festival** at Stephen Foster Folk Culture State Park, about an hour's drive west of Jacksonville, for more than 60 years. Jacksonville is the place to be on **Memorial Day** weekend, when musicians perform

Below left *Kids at Fort Walton Beach's annual Billy Bowlegs Pirate Festival, which pays tribute to a local pirate legend*
Below right *Costumed participants at the Big Bay Area Renaissance Festival, Tampa*

Above *Spanish-style houses on the extensive, picturesque grounds of Mission San Luis, Tallahassee*

Arresting architecture

Florida's architecture can help bring to life different phases of the state's history for kids. Tallahassee's **Mission San Luis** *(see p200)* has a reconstructed thatch-roofed council house, used by the Apalachee Indians, alongside small thatched houses built by the early Spanish settlers in the 1600s. The **Oldest House** *(see p168)* in St. Augustine is the state's oldest surviving Spanish Colonial home, dating to the early 1700s. Florida's vernacular style is exemplified by Cracker houses, built by the early pioneers. Although only a few survive, they have influenced local building styles for centuries.

The Gilded Age brought lavish mansions such as Henry Flagler's 1902 Beaux Arts-style Whitehall, now the **Flagler Museum** *(see pp90–91)*, in Palm Beach, and James Deering's Italian Renaissance **Vizcaya** in Miami *(see pp60–61)*, along with grand hotels such as the **Don CeSar Beach Hotel** *(see p228)* on St. Pete Beach. During this same period, Art Deco hotels were setting the style in Miami's **South Beach** *(see pp68–9)*, while lavish Spanish Revival homes were being built in other parts of southern Florida. Find examples of these in Addison Mizner's home in **Palm Beach** *(see pp88–9)* and in George Merrick's brilliant designs in **Coral Gables** *(see pp52–3)*.

On the road

Pleasant day trips from a base can be more fun for families than long drives that try the patience of young kids, and smaller roads may often offer more accessible pleasures than the super-highways. The Everglades Parkway (I-75), also called Alligator Alley, is the expressway through the **Everglades** *(see pp242–3)*, but the route following US 41 west from **Miami** *(see pp44–73)* to **Naples** *(see p240)* allows for more interesting stops along the way, and offers stunning views.

Head west on Route 40 from **Daytona Beach** *(see pp174–5)* to Ocala, driving through the green **Ocala National Forest** *(see p178)* and the rolling horse country that inspired Marjorie Kinnan Rawlings' book, *The Yearling* (1938).

To appreciate the variety of Florida's beaches, spend a day following Highway 789 from **Sarasota** *(see pp224–7)* through posh **Longboat Key** *(see p212)* to lively **Bradenton Beach** and the more secluded **Anna Maria Island**. On the east coast, Route A1A hugs the shoreline of the barrier beaches all the way from **Miami Beach** *(see pp66–71)* to **Fernandina Beach** *(see p166)* near the Georgia border. This allows for either a short outing or a multiday tour of the state taking in **The Gold and Treasure Coasts** *(see pp74–99)*, **The Space Coast** *(see pp138–53)*, and **The Northeast** *(see pp154–83)*.

Left *Colorful Art Deco buildings along Ocean Drive, South Beach's famous strip*

DK

LONDON, NEW YORK,
MELBOURNE, MUNICH AND DELHI
WWW.DK.COM

MANAGING EDITOR
MadhuMadhavi Singh

EDITORIAL MANAGER
Sheeba Bhatnagar

DESIGN MANAGER Mathew Kurien

PROJECT EDITOR Shreya Sarkar

EDITORS Shobhna Iyer,
Sushmita Ghosh

PROJECT DESIGNER Vinita
Venugopal

DESIGNER Meghna Baruah

PICTURE RESEARCH MANAGER
Taiyaba Khatoon

SENIOR PICTURE RESEARCHER
Sumita Khatwani

SENIOR DTP DESIGNER
Azeem Siddiqui

SENIOR CARTOGRAPHIC MANAGER
Uma Bhattacharya

ASSISTANT CARTOGRAPHIC MANAGER
Suresh Kumar

CARTOGRAPHER Zafar-ul-Islam Khan

PHOTOGRAPHY Steven Greaves

CARTOONS Julian Mosedale

OTHER ILLUSTRATORS Arun Pottirayil,
Richard Bonson, Richard Draper,
Chris Orr & Assocs, Pat Thorne,
John Woodcock

DESIGN CONCEPT Keith Hagan at
www.greenwich-design.co.uk

Printed and bound by South China
Printing Co. Ltd., China

First published in Great Britain in 2013 by
Dorling Kindersley Limited, 80 Strand,
London WC2R 0RL. A Penguin Company

12 13 14 15 10 9 8 7 6 5 4 3 2 1

**Copyright 2013 © Dorling
Kindersley Limited, London**

Contents

Swimming with the dolphins at the Dolphin Research Center, Marathon

EYEWITNESS TRAVEL

FAMILY GUIDE
FLORIDA

DK

downtown for the **Jacksonville Jazz Festival** (see p158). Kids love watching the stately ships sail in for Sail Jacksonville on the waterfront.

Summer

The crowds thin out in summer, but the fun carries on with festivals featuring food favorites. July 4 brings fireworks, the rodeo promises Old West excitement, and the Blue Angels aerobatics fill the skies with thrills.

JUNE

The **Monticello Watermelon Festival**, near Tallahassee, offers arts and crafts, a bed race, and cool, juicy watermelon for $1 a slice. More sweet treats await at the **Pollywoggle Watermelon Music Fest** (see p188) in Panama City, along with music, rides, and a kids' area with slides, bounce houses, and water fun. Not far away, in Fort Walton Beach, pirate gangs skirmish at the **Billy Bowlegs Pirate Festival**, which has a whole bunch of activities for young buccaneers.

At Anastasia State Park, the **Beach Bash** challenges the imaginations of sand-castle builders, and offers scavenger hunts and nature walks for families. For a change of pace, the **Silver Spurs Rodeo** in Kissimmee,

4½ miles (7 km) south of Gatorland, offers a chance to sample Western thrills such as bareback riding, bronco riding, and barrel races.

JULY

Independence Day on July 4 is celebrated all over the state, but Miami has the biggest events of all. The festivities begin at 11am in Key Biscayne, and feature a parade with marching bands, stilt dancers, floats, and bagpipers. Head to Bayfront Park for **America's Birthday Bash**, a full day of fun and food, including an afternoon Kids' Zone and fireworks starting at 9pm. Miami Beach offers free blues and jazz concerts and nighttime fireworks.

More than 100 stocky, bearded Ernest Hemingways show up in Key West for the Papa Hemingway Look-Alike Contest, a highlight of the **Hemingway Days Festival**. Don't miss the mock "running of the bulls," in which bulls on wheels are pushed around with Hemingway look-alikes perched on top.

All eyes are on the sky when the Blue Angels, the US Navy Flight Demonstration squadron, perform their famous aerial stunts. The **Blue Angels Air Show** (see p188) is held in Pensacola. Arrive early to get a seat in the bleachers at the National Naval Aviation Museum viewing area.

AUGUST

In Key West, the end of summer means the opening of the lobster season and cause for a party, **Lobsterfest**, with free concerts, a street fair, and lots of lobster to eat. A 45-minute drive north of Panama City, in Wausau, an all-American small-town parade, arts and crafts vendors, and great food make the **Wausau Possum Festival** (see p188) a much-loved tradition.

Fall

More seafood feasting, medieval jousting on horseback, lavish Latin parades, Halloween, and the American Sandsculpting Festival add flavor and fun to a fall visit. Late summer and early fall are the least crowded times in the theme parks.

SEPTEMBER

The oldest city in the US, dating from 1565, celebrates the **St. Augustine Founding Anniversary** with a re-enactment of the Spanish landing near the spot where it took place. More historic hi-jinks take place on **British Garrison Day** at the Castillo de San Marcos when Colonial re-enactors portray the British troops who occupied St. Augustine in the late 18th century.

Below left A diver in rabbit costume hunting for underwater Easter eggs at the Easter Egg Hunt, Key Largo
Below right Ernest Hemingway look-alikes on fake bulls at the Hemingway Days Festival, Key West

OCTOBER

Carnival Miami is a giant Latin party in Little Havana, known for its fabulous costumes and calypso bands. Across the state, in Tampa, costumes come out in the Cuban neighborhood of Ybor City for **Guavaween**, a Latin celebration of Halloween that includes live music, a costume contest, and a full day of Halloween activities.

Fort Lauderdale International Boat Show is one of the world's largest displays of boats, from skiffs and canoes to super-yachts. Shuttles, water taxis, and riverboats take visitors to the show's various venues. Hook the Future fishing clinics for kids teach young anglers how to catch the big ones.

NOVEMBER

The entries in the **American Sandsculpting Festival** at Fort Myers Beach boggle the imagination with sand sculptures ranging from statues of Venus to giant butterflies. The **Florida Seafood Festival** in Apalachicola has oyster shucking and eating contests, blue-crab races, and the chance to explore a charming historic nautical town.

The **Medieval Fair** (see p211) in Sarasota takes visitors back to 11th-century England where jousters in armor tilt at each other on horseback. The **North Florida Fair** in Tallahassee has more contemporary lures, such as livestock contests, rides, pig racing, and magic shows, plus lots of food and music.

Pirates in Paradise, in Key West, includes a carnival, walking tours, a kids' pirate costume contest, and sailing trips with the "pirates."

Winter

Boats brighten the harbors with holiday lights, art shows abound, pirates parade, and the circus and state fairs delight in the busy winter season. Note that Christmas and New Year vacation weeks are the most crowded at theme parks; plan to arrive early to avoid crowds.

DECEMBER

Holiday parades on the water dazzle, as boats compete for best displays. The biggest and brightest parades are the **Winterfest Boat Parade** in Fort Lauderdale, with over 100 boats competing for the best decorated, and the **Jacksonville Light Parade**, which ends in a blaze of fireworks.

Millions of tiny lights create a magical scene during **Nights of Lights** (see p169) in St. Augustine, a two-month-long celebration. Night tours led by storytellers in period garb, train and trolley tours, and art walks through the narrow brick streets add to the festive feel.

JANUARY

The New Year means football championships in Florida, with the **Orange Bowl** in Miami, the **Gator Bowl** in Jacksonville, and the **Outback Bowl** in Tampa hosting top college teams and attracting fans from near and far.

Epiphany, also known as Three Kings' Day or Twelfth Night, brings a gala Three Kings Parade, featuring the costumed Three Wise Men, in Miami's Little Havana. All ages will enjoy a stroll along Las Olas Boulevard in Fort Lauderdale to see life-size sculptures, colorful paintings, jewelry, and photography at the **Las Olas Art Fair**.

Pirates invade Tampa in late January or early February, tossing beads to the spectators from lighted floats at the elaborately costumed **Gasparilla Pirate Festival** (see p211), which is followed by a lively street fair. Meanwhile, the Alachua County Fairgrounds are transformed into a medieval marketplace, with another chance to see knights in armor jousting on horseback, for the **Hoggetowne Medieval Faire** (see p158), on weekends at the end of January and into February.

Below left *Stunning sand sculpture at the American Sandsculpting Festival, Fort Myers*
Below right *Jousting tournament at the Medieval Fair, Sarasota*

FEBRUARY

A favorite among children, **Circus Sarasota** (see p37) pitches its tent for most of the month of February each year, bringing world-class international circus talent to thrill the crowds, while engines roar for the fabled **Daytona 500** (see p158) race in Daytona Beach.

The 12-day **Florida State Fair** in Tampa is a chance for the state's farmers to show off their best animals – from sheep and cows to pygmy goats, exotic pigeons, and rabbits. The fairgrounds overflow with rides, music, food booths, a colorful horse show, a dog show, and plenty of free country-western entertainment.

The **Swamp Cabbage Festival** in La Belle, east of Fort Myers, has some unique entertainment on its agenda, including an armadillo race. The festival also features a parade, a rodeo, food stalls, arts and crafts, and the crowning of Miss Swamp Cabbage Festival.

The **Coconut Grove Arts Festival** (see p51) in Miami is one of the best and most colorful outdoor fine arts shows, a place where people get the chance to meet and talk to artists and enjoy good food and music. Children can have a go at creating their own works of art.

The Lowdown

Spring

Big Bay Area Renaissance Festival www.renfaire.com

Bike Week www.officialbikeweek.com

Easter Egg Hunt www.amoray.com

Festival of States www.stpetersburg.com/festivals

Florida Folk Festival floridastateparks.org/folkfest

Sack of St. Augustine oldpowderhouse.com

Sanibel Shell Fair sanibelshellfairandshow.com

Scottish Festival dunedinhighlandgames.com

Springtime Tallahassee www.visit tallahassee.com/events

Zoo Miami's Great Egg Safari miamimetrozoo.com

Summer

America's Birthday Bash www.bayfrontparkmiami.com

Beach Bash www.visitflorida.com

Billy Bowlegs Pirate Festival www.billybowlegspiratefestival.com

Hemingway Days Festival www.keywestvacationguide.com

Lobsterfest www.keywest lobsterfest.com

Monticello Watermelon Festival monticellojeffersonfl.com

Silver Spurs Rodeo silverspurs rodeo.com

Fall

American Sandsculpting Festival fmbsandsculpting.com

British Garrison Day staugustineinfo.com

Carnival Miami miamicarnival online.com

Florida Seafood Festival floridaseafoodfestival.com

Fort Lauderdale International Boat Show www.showmanagement.com

Guavaween www.cc-events.org/gw

North Florida Fair northfloridafair.com

Pirates in Paradise piratesinparadise.com

St. Augustine Founding Anniversary www.staugustineinfo.com

Winter

Florida State Fair floridastatefair.com

Gator Bowl www.gatorbowl.com

Jacksonville Light Parade makeascenedowntown.com

Las Olas Art Fair artfestival.com

Orange Bowl www.orangebowl.org

Outback Bowl www.outbackbowl.com

Swamp Cabbage Festival swampcabbagefestival.org

Winterfest Boat Parade winterfestparade.com

Public Holidays

New Year's Day Jan 1

Martin Luther King, Jr.'s Birthday 3rd Mon in Jan

President's Day 3rd Mon in Feb

Memorial Day last Mon in May

Independence Day July 4

Labor Day 1st Mon in Sep

Election Day 1st Tue in Nov

Veterans Day Nov 11

Thanksgiving 4th Thu in Nov

Christmas Day Dec 25

Below left *Participants showcasing their animals at the Florida State Fair, Tampa*
Below right *Race cars on the track during the Daytona 500, a famous NASCAR event*

Sports and Outdoor Activities

Florida's sunny climate means that families can enjoy outdoor activities and sports year-round. The state's excellent nature parks and preserves attract hikers and cyclists, while its numerous beaches and rivers offer opportunities for boating, fishing, sailing, surfing, snorkeling, and swimming. There are also tennis courts and the well-developed golf courses that Florida is so famous for. Fans of all ages can enjoy cheering on some of America's top sports teams.

Biking

Cyclists will find bike paths in nature preserves, parks, state forests, and on beaches. **Rails-to-Trails**, former railroad routes that are now paved for bikers and hikers, are ideal for family outings. The 14-mile (23-km) Jacksonville–Baldwin Trail near Jacksonville (see pp160–61) winds beneath a leafy canopy. The Myakka River State Park (see p229) offers miles of bike trails through scenic landscapes. The state's official **bike trails guide** can be found online.

Above Cyclists exploring a picturesque trail in the Myakka River State Park

Hiking

Florida's many state and national parks offer excellent hiking. The **Florida Trail**, stretching over 1,500 miles (2,500 km) across the state, has options for short hikes. In Ocala National Forest (see p178), trails take hikers through pine and hardwood forests, and prairies. The 10-mile (16-km) trail from Clearwater Lake Recreation Area to Alexander Springs includes one of the region's largest natural springs. Park websites have maps and suggestions for hikes.

City trails

The path through Sarasota's Bayfront Park (see p227) borders Sarasota Bay, while Tampa's (see pp216–19) 4.5-mile (7-km) Bayshore Boulevard is called "the world's longest continuous sidewalk." Jacksonville's Arlington Lions Club Park offers a path and boardwalks along the St. Johns River (see pp162–3), and Miami's mile-long Riverwalk through Bayfront Park has shops, cafés, and

art galleries. The trail in **Matheson Hammock County Park** (see p52) offers a taste of wilderness in the city.

Kayaking and canoeing

Most parks, nature centers, and wildlife refuges on the coast or on rivers offer paddling; John Pennekamp Coral Reef State Park (see p251), and Everglades National Park (see pp242–3) are all scenic. The **Suwannee River Wilderness Trail** in the Panhandle has multiday paddling trips with conveniently spaced river camps.

Fishing

Islamorada (see p250) in the Florida Keys is the state's sport-fishing capital, while the Panhandle's Destin has its largest charter boat fleet. The **Destin Fishing Rodeo** has big money prizes, and categories for kids and teens too. Lake Okeechobee, inland from the Treasure Coast, is the choice spot for freshwater fishing.

The Lowdown

Biking guides dep.state.fl.us/gwt; railstotrails.org
Datura Avenue Snorkel Trail fillexpress.com/library/datura.shtml
Destin Fishing Rodeo destinfishingrodeo.org
Florida Panthers panthers.nhl.com
Florida Trail floridatrail.org
Golf doralresort.com; stpete.org/golf/ mangrove; lpgainternational.com
Hiking floridastateparks.org; floridahikes.com
IMG Bollettieri Tennis Academy imgacademies.com/nick-bollettieri-tennis-academy
Jacksonville Jaguars jaguars.com
Miami Heat nba.com/heat
Miniature golf golflink.com/ miniature-golf/state.aspx?state=FL
National Parks www.nps.gov
Parasailing cocoabeachparasail. com; daytonaparasailing.com
Ron Jon Surf School www.ronjon surfschool.com
Sailing schools windwardsailing. com; offshoresailing.com
Suwannee River Wilderness Trail floridastateparks.org/wilderness
Tampa Bay Rays tampabay rays.mlb.com

Above Spectacular view of the TPC Blue Monster golf course at the Doral Resort, Miami Below left Surfing in Sebastian Inlet State Park, Vero Beach

Snorkeling and diving

The Keys are almost surrounded by America's largest living coral reef and the Biscayne National Park is rich with colorful coral. The Keys Shipwreck Heritage Trail features nine sites to explore. The **Datura Avenue Snorkel Trail**, near Fort Lauderdale *(see p80)* is an artificial "shipwreck," and shallow-water snorkeling can be enjoyed on Siesta Key's Crescent Beach, or around the rock jetty at St. Andrews State Park *(see pp192–3)* on the Panhandle.

Watersports

The calmer waters off the Gulf Coast, and the Intracoastal Waterway, are ideal for sailing. The Fort Lauderdale area offers 300 miles (480 km) of inland waterways and Sebastian Inlet State Park *(see p94)* offers great surfing opportunities. Short sailing courses are available at **Windward Sailing** at Fernandina Beach *(see p166)* or at the **Offshore** Sailing School® at Fort Myers *(see pp236–41)*. Cocoa Beach *(see p150)* is the state's undisputed surfing and parasailing center, and the **Ron Jon Surf School** offers lessons.

Golf and tennis

The golf courses at the **Doral Resort** in Miami and the **Mangrove Bay Golf Course** in St. Petersburg are well known. There are miniature golf courses in almost every Florida town, and no experience is required. Tennis enthusiasts will find public courts in most towns, many offering lessons, and tennis programs at most resorts. In Bradenton *(see p211)*, the **IMG Bollettieri Tennis Academy**, where top pros train, offers teen programs.

Spectator sports

In the fall, the Miami Dolphins, Tampa Bay Buccaneers, and **Jacksonville Jaguars** provide football action. Late fall and winter are best to catch the **Miami Heat** and Orlando Magic basketball teams, and ice hockey competition gets fierce for Miami's **Florida Panthers** and the Tampa Bay Lightning. March brings the Grapefruit League, the chance to see 15 baseball teams prepare for the season. The **Tampa Bay Rays** and Miami Marlins are in action from April through October.

Above left Snorkeler near coral reefs in Key Largo Left An ice hockey match in progress between the Florida Panthers and the Tampa Bay Lightning

Going Wild

Florida is a paradise for spotting wildlife, from alligators, dolphins, and manatees to pelicans, egrets, and great blue herons, and there are plenty of preserves where sightings are almost guaranteed. In addition, guided walks to see sea turtles are offered by nature centers all along the Atlantic coast in June and July. Be still so as not to frighten the birds and animals away, and observe the signs about not feeding them.

Everglades National Park

The only subtropical preserve in North America, the Everglades (see pp242–3) are teeming with wildlife, from tiny frogs to full-grown alligators. Covering 1,562 sq miles (4,047 sq km), and accessible from both east and west coasts, the park is home to birds such as the roseate spoonbill, wood stork, and great blue heron, and is the only place in the world where alligators and Florida crocodiles coexist. National Park Service rangers offer tours from the park's many visitor centers.

Myakka River State Park

This park (see p227) is home to 57 sq miles (148 sq km) of untouched wetlands, prairies, and woodlands. Walk along a canopy parallel to the tree tops, or spot alligators, turtles, and birds on hiking trails, on airboat rides that skim over the water, or by canoeing or kayaking in the Myakka River.

Lion Country Safari

A 4-mile (6-km) drive-through safari in this extensive preserve (see p92) in West Palm Beach offers the chance to see more than 900 animals from around the world living freely in the open. They are divided into seven home regions, from the pampas of South America to the forests of India and the Serengeti of Africa. Spot lions, tapirs, tortoises, llamas, zebras, giraffes, chimpanzees, and hippos, to name just a few. The safari is sure to be a hit with kids, and tickets include an amusement park with rides and a water "sprayground."

J.N. "Ding" Darling National Wildlife Refuge

Named for a conservationist who was instrumental in preserving the area, this Sanibel Island preserve (see p239) boasts an enormous bird population. Endangered manatees, sea turtles, and Florida

The Lowdown

Crystal River National Wildlife Refuge www.fws.gov.crystalriver

Everglades National Park www.nps.gov/ever

Homosassa Springs Wildlife State Park www.floridastateparks.org

J.N. "Ding" Darling National Wildlife Refuge www.fws.gov/dingdarling

Lion Country Safari www.lioncountrysafari.com

Merritt Island National Wildlife Refuge www.fws.gov/merrittisland

Myakka River State Park www.myakkariver.org

Wakulla Springs State Park www.floridastateparks.org

Below left Alligator in the Everglades National Park **Below center** Impala deer at Lion Country Safari **Below right** Birdwalk in Myakka River State Park crocodiles shelter here as well. See the refuge on a 5-mile (8-km) self-guided driving trail, on a guided tram tour, or by hiking, biking, or canoeing.

Wakulla Springs State Park

Turtles, alligators, deer, and many birds are just a few of the many wild animals at home in these environs (*see p202*) near Tallahassee. Riverboat tours are offered daily, while glass-bottom boat tours over the springs, in late winter and early spring, give a chance to spot the fossilized remains of mastodons at the bottom. Well known as the location of three Johnny Weissmuller-starring Tarzan movies, the park's wooded area has nature trails, and a playground, too.

Crystal River National Wildlife Refuge

The Crystal River is one of the state's largest manatee wintering grounds, home to about 200 of these unusual creatures. The refuge (*see p221*), established in 1983 to protect the endangered manatee, is accessible only by boat. Several operators at the marina in the town of Crystal River offer glass-bottom boat tours, and snorkeling tours that allow the whole family to swim with the manatees.

Merritt Island National Wildlife Refuge

This vast refuge (*see pp148–9*) has coastal dunes, and saltwater and freshwater marshland, with habitats for over 1,500 species. Explore the area on a 6-mile (10-km) drive, nature trails, a manatee observation deck and boardwalk, or canoe waterways.

Homosassa Springs Wildlife State Park

Watch manatees swim in the upper Gulf Coast's Homosassa Springs (*see p219*) and see fish up close from the Fish Bowl, a floating underwater observatory – only in this case people are inside and the fish are outside the bowl!

Getting to Florida

Among the most popular destinations in the US, Florida attracts millions of visitors each year. The state is served by two major international airports and several important secondary airports. It is a good idea to read up on entry requirements and be ready with all necessary credentials, including passports for children, to ensure a hassle-free entry. Advance planning will also help to get the best fares.

US entry requirements

Nationals of 36 countries, including most European nations, do not need a visa to travel to the US for stays of less than 90 days, but travelers must apply in advance for authorization to travel via the **Electronic System for Travel Authorization**. Note the authorization number and keep a print-out for reference. Citizens of all other countries need a valid visa. The **Transportation Security Administration** provides information on security regulations for travelers. Before landing, all visitors must complete a **US Customs and Border Protection** agency I-94/I-94W form with passport, arrival and departure details, a US address, and Declaration Form including the value of any gifts. On arrival, the forms will be inspected by CBP staff. Keep the departure half of the I-94/I-94W safe – it must be presented when leaving the US.

Arriving by air

The airports at **Miami (MIA)** and **Orlando (MCO)** serve most international flights and have frequent connections from other US cities. Major airlines, including **Air Canada**, **Air France**, **British Airways**, and **Virgin Atlantic**, arrive at both airports. **Aer Lingus** flies to Orlando, and Miami also has services on **Air Berlin** and many South American airlines. British Airways also has flights to **Fort Lauderdale (FLL)** and **Tampa (TPA)**. Tampa is the major airport for the Gulf Coast destinations, while **Jacksonville (JAX)** is the main gateway to northern Florida. Several domestic airlines, such as **American Airlines**, **Continental**, and **Delta**, offer frequent services to Florida.

Air fares are lowest between April and mid-November, except for holiday periods. For those traveling with children, direct flights are more convenient, although expensive.

Airport transfers

All major airports have counters that arrange onward transport, but do check with your hotel in advance about an airport shuttle service. Car rental companies (see p24) have booths at all airports.

The **Airport Flyer** express bus costs $2.35 from MIA to downtown Miami or Miami Beach. A taxi fare for one to five people averages $22 to downtown and a $32 flat fee to Miami Beach. Shared rides such as the **Super Shuttle** average $55 for the first person to downtown or the beach, and $22 for each extra person.

MCO is about 16 miles (25 km) from Walt Disney World® Resort, and the 30–45-min taxi ride costs $40–60.

Below left Travelers in the departure lounge of Orlando International Airport
Below right The six-lane MacArthur Causeway connecting downtown Miami and Miami Beach via Biscayne Bay

Shuttle buses charge $21 per person, $34 for a round trip. The local bus is slow but cheap at $4 per person.

Arriving by rail

Amtrak is the national rail system in the US, with stops in Jacksonville, Orlando, Tampa, and Miami. These are not high-speed trains, may require a night on board, and are pricier than airplanes. Check Amtrak website for family rates and frequent specials.

Arriving by bus

Greyhound is the largest intercity US bus line. Its newer buses have ample leg room, and electrical outlets. Book tickets online in advance and check for family discounts and other offers.

Arriving by car

Florida has a great road system and welcome centers offering information along the main highways. I-95 serves the east coast and I-75 covers central Florida, with connecting roads to the west coast. The main west coast artery, Route 41, is not an expressway and is slow, so it is better to use I-75 and consult a map. The expressways from east to west include I-10 across northern Florida and I-4 connecting Orlando to Tampa. In the south, I-75

goes through the Everglades. The Bee Line Expressway, between Orlando and the Space Coast, and the Florida Turnpike, from Orlando to south of Miami, are the only toll roads. I-95 becomes congested between Fort Lauderdale and Miami and is best avoided during the morning and evening rush hours.

Arriving by sea

Florida has America's most popular cruise ports, with excellent facilities, porters to help with baggage, and plentiful taxis. Several cruises from South America, the Caribbean, and Europe sail to Florida ports. **Seabourn**, **Holland America**, and **Royal Caribbean** are well-known cruise lines. Most cruises come into Fort Lauderdale, the largest and busiest port, and also the most convenient for air connections to other cities. The **Disney Cruise Line** ships arrive at Cape Canaveral. The two other major ports, Miami and Tampa, have connections from the cruise docks by taxi or shuttle to downtown or the airport.

The Lowdown

US entry requirements
US Customs and Border Protection, ESTA www.cbp.gov
Transportation Security Administration www.tsa.gov

Arriving by air
Airports
FLL www.fll.net
JAX www.airport-jacksonville.com
MIA www.miami-airport.com
MCO www.orlandoairports.net
TPA www.tampaairport.com
Airlines
Aer Lingus www.aerlingus.com
Air Berlin www.airberlin.com
Air Canada www.aircanada.com
Air France www.airfrance.com
American Airlines www.aa.com
British Airways www.britishairways.com

Continental www.continental.com
Delta www.delta.com
Virgin Atlantic www.virgin-atlantic.com

Airport transfers
Airport Flyer www.miami-airport.com/bus_and_rail_info.asp
Super Shuttle www.supershuttle.com

Arriving by rail and bus
Amtrak www.amtrak.com
Greyhound www.greyhound.com

Arriving by sea
Disney Cruise Line disneycruise.disney.go.com
Holland America www.hollandamerica.com
Royal Caribbean www.royalcaribbean.com
Seabourn www.seabourn.com

Below left Boarding a Greyhound bus at a rest stop
Below right The Royal Caribbean cruise ship Enchantment of the Seas docked at the Key West cruise terminal

Getting around Florida

While train and bus connections are available between major cities, it is more economical and convenient for a family to rent a car. Florida is an easy state to navigate, with excellent roads and good signage. Larger cities have public transportation and many towns offer sightseeing trolleys, but the routes are limited and having a car will allow you to be flexible. RVs are also a good way to travel, especially since campsites blanket the state.

In-state connections

Miami, Fort Lauderdale, Orlando, and Tampa airports (see p22) offer connections to smaller cities around the state, usually on small commuter planes. Amtrak trains connect Jacksonville, Orlando, Tampa, and Miami, while Greyhound buses (see p23) serve many smaller destinations, with an express service between Fort Lauderdale, Tampa, and Jacksonville. However, fares can be costly for a family, making it more economical, and quicker, to travel by car. Most of the popular tourist destinations are within a 4- or 5-hour drive of each other. The exceptions, distances that may be worth the cost of a flight, are from south to north, from Miami to destinations such as Tallahassee (466 miles/750 km), or Panama City (558 miles/898 km).

By car or RV

Car rental agencies, including **Avis**, **Budget**, and **Thrifty**, are found at all airports and in larger cities around the state. Rates vary with the seasons, but are generally less than $200 for a week's rental of a small car. Agencies require the driver to be over 21 (or 25 in some cases), with a valid driver's license and a major credit card. All US and most foreign licenses are accepted, but getting an international license is a good idea if your license is not in English. If your home auto insurance does not cover travel, consider buying insurance when renting. Note that state and local taxes can add up to 20 percent to the bill. Reserving in advance saves money. Travel sites such as **Expedia** also give a good overview of the car rental rates in an area. Gas stations are plentiful, but many are closed at night. Florida's population centers have heavy traffic from 7 to 9am and 3:30 to 6pm, so avoid these times if possible.

DRIVING REGULATIONS

All US traffic travels on the right-hand side of the road. Speed limits are 20–30 mph (32–48 km/h) in commercial and residential areas, and 55 mph (88 km/h) on highways except Interstate expressways, where the limit goes up to 70 mph (112 km/h). Most road signs are clear and easy to understand. Right turns are allowed at a red stoplight, unless signs indicate otherwise. Florida law requires all occupants to wear seat belts, and a federally approved infant carrier or car seat must be used for kids of 5 and under. The **Florida Highway Safety and Motor Vehicles** website is the best source for driving regulations.

Below left Cars cruising past Art Deco hotels on Ocean Drive in South Beach, Miami
Below right The Walt Disney World® Resort Monorail plying between Disney parks and resorts

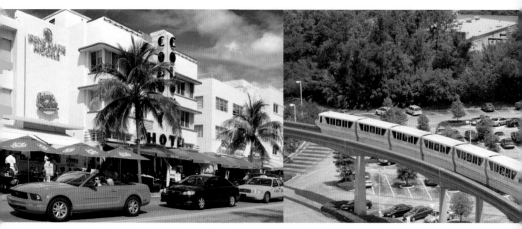

RV TRAVEL

Recreational vehicles (RVs), or mobile homes, can be great for families, providing comfortable quarters as well as transportation. Companies such as **Cruise America** and **Florida RV World** offer rentals in a variety of sizes to fit all budgets. Many RV campgrounds are mini-resorts, with plenty of amenities (see p31).

Public transportation

Most of Florida's cities have bus services, but the need is small and the time between buses can be an hour or more. Miami Beach is well served by two routes of the **South Beach Local** bus, and **Walt Disney World® Resort** (see pp106–17) is also blanketed by buses, trams, boats, and a monorail. Beach towns such as Bradenton and Sarasota have tourist trolleys connecting town and beach, and the **Suncoast Beach Trolley** connects all the beaches from Clearwater to St. Petersburg.

By bike

Florida is very bicycle-friendly and cycling families will find lanes almost everywhere to help them get around town, though pedaling on busy thoroughfares may be a bit intimidating. Those keen on longer tours can sample the Pinellas Trail, which stretches from Tarpon Springs to St. Petersburg, passing through pretty towns and scenic coastal areas for 43 miles (69 km). The Florida Keys Overseas Heritage Trail runs for 61 miles (98 km) between the villages of the Keys, with peerless views of ocean and Gulf waters on either side. Check out **Bike Florida** for more information and ideas.

By boat

The Intracoastal Waterway parallels the Atlantic coastline of Florida for 380 miles (611 km), and offers calm water for sailing or motorboats. Boat rentals are available in many towns, particularly in Fort Lauderdale and Miami. Boats with a crew can also be chartered. **Fort Lauderdale Water Taxi** (see p80) and **Delray Beach Cruises** offer sightseeing cruises.

Great Rivers of Florida, a 7-day cruise offered by the **American Cruise Lines** on the American Glory riverboat from Jacksonville, takes passengers along the St. Johns and Tolomato rivers, passing through Ocala National Forest and with stops at St. Augustine and Amelia Island. Houseboating offers the chance to explore the islands of southwestern Florida around Sanibel, cruise the Keys, or discover the beauty of the St. Johns or Suwannee rivers. Operators such as **Suwannee Houseboats** offer rentals by the day, the weekend, or the week.

The Lowdown

By car or RV
Avis www.avis.com
Budget www.budget.com
Cruise America www.cruiseamerica.com
Expedia www.expedia.com
Florida Highway Safety and Motor Vehicles 840 617 2000; flhsmv.gov
Florida RV World floridarvworld.com
Thrifty www.thrifty.com

By bike
Bike Florida www.bikeflorida.com

Public transportation
South Beach Local www.miamidade.gov/transit
Suncoast Beach Trolley www.psta.net/beachtrolley.php

By boat
American Cruise Lines www.americancruiselines.com
Delray Beach Cruises www.delraybeachcruises.com
Fort Lauderdale Water Taxi www.watertaxi.com
Suwannee Houseboats www.suwanneehouseboats.com

Below left A bike route signboard in Sanibel Island
Below right A trolley driving up Fifth Avenue in Naples

Practical Information

Florida is well prepared with all the practical facilities and services visitors might need, from health care to Wi-Fi connections and ATMs. Advance planning will help to keep things running smoothly and avoid any travel hassles, which can be magnified when holidaying with kids. Travel insurance is always a wise investment for visitors arriving from other countries.

Insurance

The high cost of medical care for non-US residents in America, and the difficulties of lost luggage or flight delays, mean that travel insurance is essential. Policies should cover emergency medical and dental care, trip cancellation, and baggage, as well as travel document loss. Transportation back home in case of emergency is another option to consider. Your travel agent or insurance company can recommend a suitable policy.

Health

Prescription medications should always be carried in hand baggage, along with general medications for headache, allergies, or stomach upset. Keep prescriptions in their original containers with pharmacy labels so they will pass easily through airport security. Notify security officials if carrying any special items, such as supplies for diabetics. Bring sunscreen for protection from the strong Florida sun, and carry bottled water to avoid dehydration.

MEDICAL EMERGENCIES

Your hotel can recommend a nearby doctor or walk-in facility. While physicians and dentists usually accept credit cards, some may want payment in cash. The locations of hospital emergency rooms can be found in the yellow pages of the local telephone book. Pharmacies are listed on the map pages in this book. Dial 911 for an **ambulance**.

Personal safety

It pays to be alert, especially to pickpockets, in cities or crowded amusement parks. Keep wallets safe in an inside pocket and carry bags in the crook of the elbow, close to the body. Bags with shoulder straps should go over the head and across the body, and all bags should be kept in the lap in restaurants. Do not flash smartphones or tablets about, and avoid bringing expensive jewelry. Cash must not be left unattended at the beach; waterproof containers that hang around the neck can be purchased from travel stores.

Use the hotel safe to hold passports, a credit card, and some cash; laptops or tablets can fit into many safes. Bringing a photocopy of your passport and credit cards will help with quick replacements in case they are lost. At night, ask the hotel concierge if a neighborhood is safe before venturing out.

Keep your hotel room locked when inside, and don't put out the "make up the room" sign when you go out for the day. Make sure that luggage is only given to a member of the hotel staff, and that a receipt

Below left *A crowded amusement park, where visitors should be careful of pickpockets*
Below right *A City National Bank of Florida ATM, which can be used by most major card holders*

is issued for stored luggage. Never leave luggage unattended at airports, at taxi stands, or in hotel lobbies.

Calling 911 is the quickest way to reach the **police** to report a crime, in case of a **fire**, or to summon help if you are hurt. If valuables are lost or stolen, make sure you get a copy of the police report for your insurance claim at home. Contact the embassy of your home country if your passport is lost. The **US Department of State** website has contact information for all foreign embassies in the US.

When visiting crowded theme parks or beaches, decide in advance on a meeting place in case you are separated. Advise kids to look for someone in an official uniform for help if they are lost.

DRIVING SAFETY

Most visitors to Florida get around by car, and while crime is rare, car safety is prudent. Have keys out and ready in order to get into your car quickly, and keep the tank filled to avoid having to search for a service station in an unfamiliar area. It is safer to keep the doors locked and the windows up, using the air-conditioning if necessary. Program an emergency breakdown number into your cell phone and, if an accident occurs, dial 911 to call for police and medical help.

If arriving at an airport late at night, it may be best to stay at an airport hotel and pick up a car in the morning, rather than try to reach an unfamiliar destination on dark roads.

Money

BANKS & BUREAUX DE CHANGE

Foreign currency can be changed into dollars at banks and bureaux de change such as **Travelex**, which are found at major airports. However, ATMs offer the best exchange rates and the fee is usually lower than at a bureau. Most bank ATMs are part of the worldwide Plus or Cirrus network. ATMs, and almost all businesses and restaurants, accept popular debit and credit cards, though cash advances with credit cards carry interest fees. Check the fees with your own bank or credit card provider before traveling. To guard against crime in towns, use an ATM inside the bank rather than those accessed from the street.

CURRENCY

The basic unit is the dollar, which equals 100 cents. Coins come in one cent (penny), five cent (nickel), ten cent (dime), and 25 cent (quarter) denominations. Each is of a different size, so it is easy to tell

them apart. There is a $1 coin but it is rarely used. The most common bills are $1, $5, $10, and $20, though $50, $100, and larger denominations are available. ATMs give out mostly $20 bills.

CREDIT CARDS, TRAVELER'S CHECKS, AND CASH CARDS

Major credit cards, such as Visa, MasterCard, and American Express, and debit cards are widely accepted throughout the US. Large purchases are best paid for with credit cards.

Traveler's checks are still accepted, but have become less common due to ATMs, and are slowly being replaced by travel cards. As with traveler's checks, these cards are paid for in advance, and funds are drawn on as the card is used. Travel cards are issued by card companies such as Visa or MasterCard, and are as easy to use as a credit card, but exchange rates are fixed in advance and security is greater as they have a limited value. These are protected by use of a PIN and/or signature. Fees apply to some services, including reloading the cards.

Visitor information

Visit Florida is the state's official tourism bureau and it can provide contact details for local tourist offices.

Below left Sunbathing near a lifeguard tower at South Beach, Miami
Below right Motorbike policeman patrolling a busy street in Daytona Beach during Bike Week

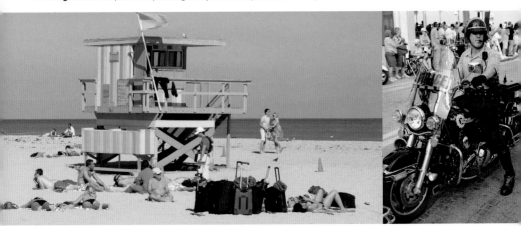

Communications

Florida has a number of area codes. Toll-free calls are prefixed by 800, 866, 877, or 888. To call outside the area, dial 1 before the area code, even on toll-free calls. To call overseas directly, dial 011, plus the country code, city area code, and number. For operator-assisted calls, dial 01, country code, city code, and number.

CELL PHONES

The prevalence of cell phones has limited public telephones to airports and rail terminals. Hotels add a hefty charge for phone calls, making cell phones a convenient and economical option. Most modern phones will be compatible with US services, though they may run up high roaming charges; check with your service provider at home. If your phone is not compatible, you can easily rent one. **Online rental sites** offer an overview of typical rental options. Prepaid phone cards are available at most newsstands and offer lower per-minute rates than most phones.

INTERNET AND EMAIL

Most hotels offer Internet access and/or Wi-Fi, some for free. Free Wi-Fi is also available at many city libraries, and at many Barnes & Noble bookstores and branches of Starbucks and McDonald's.

POSTAL SERVICE

Many hotels sell stamps and will mail postcards for guests, or they can direct you to the nearest post office. Delivery of mail abroad usually takes 5 to 10 working days.

Media

NEWSPAPERS AND MAGAZINES

Every large Florida city has its own daily newspaper. Among the most widely read are the *Miami Herald* and *St. Petersburg Times*. National publications such as *USA Today* and *The New York Times* can often be found in street dispensers, along with local papers. For foreign newspapers and other publications, a bookstore is the best bet.

TELEVISION AND RADIO

The major national TV networks are CBS, NBC, ABC, and PBS. Several channels, including CNN, Fox, and ESPN, are available on cable. Kids will enjoy Nickelodeon, Disney, and Cartoon Network, while MTV will appeal to teens. Hotels may also offer pay-per-view movie channels.

Every area has its own radio stations. AM consists mostly of pop music, rock, and talk shows, and some religious stations. In southern Florida, Spanish talk shows and music are popular. Classical music

stations are found on the FM band. National Public Radio is popular, with news, talk, and classical music.

Disabled access

Most public transportation, public buildings, hotels, theme parks, restaurants, and attractions are accessible to people with disabilities. **State parks** offer many accessible trails, and many beaches provide wheelchairs that can navigate over sand. Check **Visit Florida**, or the sites you plan to visit, for specific local information.

Restrooms

Most attractions, museums, department stores, and shopping malls have restrooms, complete with baby-changing facilities.

What to pack

Florida life is informal, and dressy clothing is rarely needed, even at upscale restaurants. The air-conditioning in restaurants and theaters can be frigid, so taking a sweater along is advisable.

Hats, insect repellent, sunglasses, and sunscreen are a must for everyone. Bathing suits need time to dry, so a few changes are useful.

Below left *Street dispensers for newspapers and magazines on Sanibel Island*
Below right *Free Internet access for guests advertised at The Radisson Hotel in Buena Vista, Orlando*

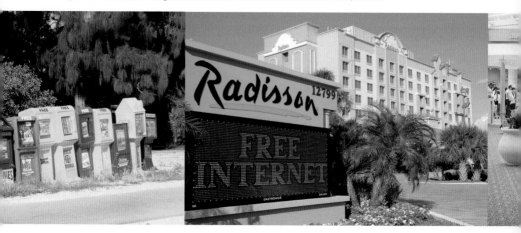

Florida does have cool spells in winter, so if you are visiting then, pack a jacket. Do bring rain gear too, as there can be showers year-round.

Stores carrying diapers and formula for infants are plentiful, but carry an emergency supply. Pack a favorite game or book, pajamas, a sweater, water, and a snack in a separate small wheeled suitcase or backpack for each child to carry for quick access en route.

Involving the kids

Children are more excited about travel when they share in the planning. Look at this book with them in advance, and let them choose and look forward to some of the activities ahead. The Internet also has many resources for planning. An inexpensive camera for each child keeps kids interested and provides wonderful souvenirs of the trip.

Opening hours

Business hours are usually 9am to 5pm. Stores open at around 9 or 10am and close at 5 or 6pm, Monday through Saturday, though some may stay open later. Sunday hours vary: some stores open at noon, others do not open at all. Banking hours are traditionally 9am to 3pm Monday to Thursday, and to 6pm on Friday, though several larger banks now remain open until 5 or 6pm during the week. Banks with Saturday hours usually open from 9am to noon. Most museums are open daily, 10am to 5:30pm, but check individual listings.

Electricity

The standard US electric current is 110 volts. An adapter is necessary for European appliances, which run on 220–240 volts.

Florida time

Most of Florida is on Eastern Standard Time, 5 hours behind Greenwich Mean Time (GMT). The exception is the western Panhandle, which is in the Central Standard Time zone, 1 hour behind EST.

Etiquette and tipping

Florida is a favorite family destination and everyone from hotel clerks to bus drivers usually has a friendly smile for young visitors. However, parents should encourage children to be polite and respectful, and if noisy squabbles or loud crying occur in public places, it is best to take kids outside until they calm down.

Visitors should remember that tips are expected for service personnel in the US. The usual amounts are 15–20 percent for waiters or taxi drivers, as well as barbers or hair stylists. Room service tips are often added to the bill. Hotel bellhops should receive around $1 per bag, hotel maids $1–2 per day, and coat checks $1 per garment. While not mandatory, when waiters or others are especially helpful with children, a small extra tip is always appreciated.

The Lowdown

Health and safety
Police, ambulance, fire 911
US Department of State
www.usembassy.gov

Money
Currency exchange locations
www.us.travelex.com

Visitor information
Visit Florida 2540 West Executive Center Circle, Suite 200, Tallahassee, 32301; 866 972 5280; www.visitflorida.com

Communications
Online cell phone rental
www.rentcell.com

Disabled access
State parks floridastateparks.org
Visit Florida www.visitflorida.com/articles/florid-able

Below left Travelers by the arrival and departure schedule at Orlando International Airport
Below right Disability access on the Miami-Dade transit Metrobus

Where to Stay

With hundreds of lavish resorts, thousands of condos for rent, and campgrounds that attract millions of visitors every year, Florida truly can accommodate every taste and budget. Families are catered to across the spectrum of accommodations – from Florida's most exclusive resorts to its most basic motels, which usually have a pool where kids can splash around. Listings of suggested lodgings appear at the end of each chapter in this book.

Getting the best deals

The winter months, especially holiday periods, are the most popular and the most expensive. Generally, the closer to the beach, the higher the price, so staying in a basic highway motel and driving to the beach means saving, with rooms lodging four for as little as $150 per night, even in high season. Most places let kids stay free in their parents' room; but some specify that sharers must be under age 12. Bargains can be found in the off-seasons, spring and fall. **Hotels.com**, **Travelocity**, and **Expedia** are good sources to find the lowest rates, while **Kayak** compares many discount hotel sites.

Hidden extras

The state's 6 percent sales tax, plus tourism taxes, can bring the total up a hefty 12 percent.

Remember that tipping (*see p29*) is not discretionary in the US. Hotels that include free breakfast, Wi-Fi or Internet access, and an in-room refrigerator will help the budget considerably.

Resorts

Florida boasts resorts with golf, spas, tennis, beaches, and a variety of dining options. **Sandestin Golf and Beach Resort** (*see p204*) is one that offers a range of accommodations, kids' programs, and its own shops and restaurants. If budget allows, **Ritz-Carlton** resorts and hotels are among the top facilities in the state.

Hotels and motels

Space and cooking facilities are two important pluses for families choosing a hotel or motel. All-suite properties offer extra space, kitchens, and sometimes two TVs. Many modest hotels and motels provide microwaves and small refrigerators. Check whether cots or cribs are available and if they are free, if kids' menus are offered in hotel restaurants, and if the hotel will help with recommended babysitters.

Condos and apartments

Florida is filled with condominiums and efficiency or studio apartments whose owners rent out their quarters when not in residence. Condo units provide comfortable space plus kitchens. Many condo buildings are conveniently located, some right on the beach, and usually have a pool. One-, two-, and three-bedroom units are available, and prices are competitive with hotels. However, there is usually no maid service.

Below left *Tents pitched in Little Talbot Island State Park*
Below right *Kitchen, dining, and living area in Hawks Cay Resort, Duck Key*

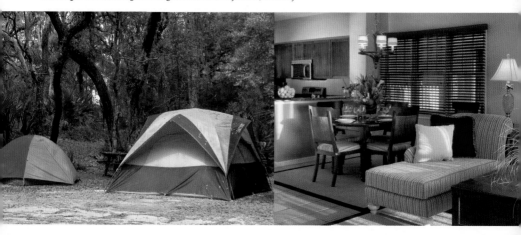

Condo listings are found in the accommodations guides published by local tourist offices, and also on websites such as **HomeAway**.

House-swapping

Many families report success with house swaps. If you live in Europe, for example, a Florida family might be happy to swap their home for yours, saving each of you a considerable amount of money. Swaps are arranged through specialized agencies such as **Home Exchange** and **Home Link**. For a small monthly fee, prospective swappers sign up and list their homes. Members can scan listings for the places they want to go, select properties, and send privacy-protected emails directly to the owners. It is always a good idea to exchange emails, talk on the phone, and trade recent home photos before signing an agreement.

Campgrounds

Many of the campgrounds for RVs across the state offer playgrounds and pools, as well as table tennis, volleyball, and basketball courts. All offer picnic grounds and convenient laundry facilities. **Camp Florida** offers a complete RV Park directory,

with hundreds of listings across the state. There are several RV rental agencies *(see p25)*. Some campgrounds also provide rustic cabins for those without RVs. Guests staying in the cabins at **Disney's Fort Wilderness Resort & Campgrounds** *(see p136)* are offered complimentary coach transfers from the airport, and transportation to all of Walt Disney World® attractions is available from the resort's campground.

State parks

Most of Florida's state parks have campgrounds for tents, and 19 of them also have cabins for rent at rates below most motels, with access to all park facilities. Lodgings range from well-equipped modern cottages such as those at **Grayton Beach State Park** *(see p205)* to simple log cabins at **Myakka River State Park** *(see p229)*. Bookings are essential and can be made 11 months in advance; check the **Florida State Parks** website for more information.

Bed & breakfast

B&B inns are listed in local tourism directories and can be found through several booking services. These lodgings may be

private homes or small inns. While often charming, not all offer the privacy or noise tolerance that families appreciate. Be sure to ask about specifics and family policies before booking.

The Lowdown

Getting the best deals
Expedia www.expedia.com
Hotels.com www.hotels.com
Kayak www.kayak.com
Travelocity www.travelocity.com

Resorts
Ritz-Carlton www.ritzcarlton.com

Condos and apartments
HomeAway www.homeaway.com

House-swapping
Home Exchange www.homeexchange.com
Home Link www.homelink.com

Campgrounds
Camp Florida www.campflorida.com

State parks
Florida State Parks www.floridastateparks.org

Bed & breakfast
B&B agencies www.bedandbreakfast.com www.florida-bed-and-breakfasts.net www.floridainns.com

Below left Loungers near the swimming pool at The Biltmore Hotel, Miami
Below right Lavishly decorated lounge at the Hilton Hotel, St Augustine

Where to Eat

Florida dining offers something to please every palate. Bountiful waters and a benign climate produce superb seafood and tropical fruits. A wide variety of cuisines is available, including simple food for those who prefer it. Because families make up such a large share of the state's visitors, there are plenty of kid-friendly informal restaurants. The price categories in this guide allow for a two-course lunch with a family of four, excluding wine but including soft drinks.

Eating out

Formal restaurants usually open from 7 to 10am for breakfast, from 11:30am to 2pm for lunch, and from 5:30 to 10pm for dinner, but many places serve food all day. "Earlybird specials," for dinner served before 6pm, are economical for families with kids.

A reservation is usually not needed for lunch or at budget restaurants, but dinner at a popular spot usually requires one, especially during the busy winter season. Most restaurants can accommodate strollers and will offer booster seats, but ask in advance at upscale places. A smoking ban is enforced in all restaurants, cafés, and even bars. Tipping is considered mandatory at any non self-service eatery. The minimum acceptable tip is 15 percent, and the standard tip for good service is 20 percent.

Catch of the day

Firm and tender fish such as grouper, mahi mahi, amberjack, pompano, snapper, tuna, and wahoo are staples on the menu, both as entrées and in tasty sandwiches. Large, sweet Gulf shrimp are legendary, and may be served cold with cocktail sauce or used as an ingredient in many dishes. Stone-crab claws are another Florida delicacy, especially prized as they are only available from mid-October to mid-May. Head to Miami's **Joe's Stone Crab** (see p69), where these sweet, meaty claws are served chilled, with a melted butter and mustard sauce.

Tropical treats

Florida is blessed with a bounty of tropical fruits such as oranges, mangoes, melons, and papayas. Weekly farmers' markets are good places for sampling them. Stands in the markets offering fresh-squeezed orange-strawberry juice should not be missed.

Southern comfort

Northern Florida shows its Southern heritage at stops such as **Fish House** (see p195) in Pensacola, which serves a delicious Southern specialty made with grits, a savory porridge made of fine-ground corn, similar to polenta. Farther south, the Latin American influence can be seen on menus featuring ceviche (a first course of raw seafood usually with a citrus sauce), beans and rice, and plantains.

Choice Cuban

Tampa and Miami, with their large Cuban populations, have restaurants serving Spanish dishes

Below left Elegantly decorated Patio Dining Room of the Columbia Restaurant, Ybor City
Below centre Fresh tropical fruit at the Lincoln Road Farmers' Market, South Beach

such as roast pork, *arroz con pollo* (chicken with spiced rice), and paella. Cuban sandwiches of ham, roast pork, cheese, and pickles served on crunchy bread are a mainstay. **Versailles Restaurant** *(see p62)* is the best-known Little Havana stop on Miami's Calle Ocho, and Tampa's **Columbia Restaurant** *(see p218)* in Ybor City, founded in 1905 and the oldest restaurant in the state, is a must for its flamenco dancers, traditional decor, and great food. It has branches in St. Petersburg, Sarasota, and St. Augustine.

Family favorites

Well-behaved kids will be welcome anywhere, but Florida's many informal outdoor dining choices, especially those on the water, are good for families with young children. Watching the boats at **The Old Salty Dog** *(see p226)* in Sarasota will help to keep youngsters happily occupied. The **Five Guys Burgers and Fries** *(see p218)* and **Johnny Rockets** *(see p84)* chains found in many cities offer burgers that are sure to please. For more formal restaurants, dining early, before things get crowded, is a good idea with kids. To be certain whether better restaurants encourage families,

ask if they offer a kids' menu. If children want more than the usual burgers, chicken fingers, or hot dogs, consider having them split an adult portion.

Sweet treats

The most typical dessert found on menus is Key lime pie, truly authentic only when the tangy filling is made with the small, round, yellow-green limes grown in southern Florida. Flan, a typical Spanish custard, will appeal to youngsters. Many towns have locally owned ice cream parlors that offer specialties such as home-made cones or real Italian-style ices. Miami's **Dolce Vita Gelato Cafe** *(see p55)* is famous for its gelato, while St. Augustine's **Hyppo** *(see p168)* serves gourmet popsicles in unusual flavors.

Allergies and diets

Wheat, milk, and shellfish are mainstays of Florida cooking, so tell your waiter about any special food needs. Most restaurants are good about substitutions, including vegetarian dishes and gluten-free foods. Be sure to mention any nut allergies and carry emergency medications for the whole family.

Below left The Old Salty Dog, a waterfront restaurant that serves hearty food, Sarasota
Below right Diners enjoying a meal at Johnny Rockets, Fort Lauderdale

KIDS' CORNER

Florida food facts
1 Florida is known for its Key limes, which ripen from green to yellow and have greenish-yellow flesh. What is the famous dessert made from them?
2 Florida grows over a dozen kinds of tropical fruit. Oranges, grapefruit, lemons, and limes are the most common. How many others can you name?
3 Cuban sandwiches are popular in Florida. They are made with ham, pork, cheese, and a suprise ingredient. Do you know what it is?

Answers at the bottom of the page.

A CITRUSY HISTORY

The first orange trees in Florida were planted in the mid-1500s by the early Spanish explorers near St. Augustine. There are now more than 74 million orange trees in the state.

Armed to the claws

Stone crabs are found all along the Atlantic and Gulf coasts but are commercially harvested almost exclusively in Florida. The only part of the crab served is the big, meaty claw. Fishermen are allowed to take only one claw, at least 2 ¾ inches (7 cm) long, and are required to return the crab safely to the water. Claws detach easily and the stone crab can grow them three to four times.

Answers: 1 Key lime pie. **2** Mango, papaya, kiwi fruit, star fruit or carambola, passion fruit, avocado, lychee, guava, jackfruit, banana, and tangerine, among others. **3** Pickles.

Shopping

Whether bargain buys, high fashion, toys, books, arts, or handicrafts are on the most-wanted list, Florida does not disappoint shoppers. Children will find irresistible souvenirs across the state, from spacemen and rockets to clown noses and Mickey Mouse ears.

Opening hours

All shops are open from at least 10am to 5pm Monday to Saturday. Sunday hours are generally noon to 5 or 6pm. Call ahead to check if you want to visit a specific shop or mall.

Bargain bonanzas

The state's big outlet malls, with stores from major manufacturers, sometimes called factory stores, promise savings. The biggest outlet is **Sawgrass Mills** in Sunrise, with more than 350 shops including Polo Ralph Lauren for Children, Tommy Hilfiger Kids, and the Children's Place Factory Store. Patient kids can be rewarded with stops at the Build-a-Bear Workshop, LEGO® store, and the Game Works arcade.

The **Dolphin Mall** in Miami offers well-known brands and factory outlets for popular stores such as Coach Leather and Banana Republic. Toy World and Toy Zam will please kids, Gymboree has clothes for newborns to age 12, and Justice and Journeys are stores aimed at tweens and teens.

Premium is a major outlet operator with malls around the state, including in Orlando and St. Augustine. **Silver Sands Factory Stores** in Sandestin (*see p191*) offers GapKids, Socks Galore, and Strasburg Children outlets. The customer service offices at the malls usually have a free coupon book with extra savings at selected stores.

Markets

Most communities have weekly markets where local farmers display fresh produce and stalls sell cooked cooked savories and desserts. The **Saturday Morning Market** on St. Petersburg's waterfront (*see p210*) is one of the biggest and best of these events, as is the colorful **Daytona Flea and Farmers' Market**, where flea market finds add to the fun every Friday, Saturday, and Sunday.

Arty adventures

Artists and artisans seem to thrive in the Florida sun, and galleries abound in every town. The **Quayside Art Gallery** (*see p195*) in Pensacola is owned and run by local artists, and the **Florida Craftsmen Gallery** in St. Petersburg shows the best of jewelry and other creative crafts.

The many colorful outdoor fairs that take place around the state are fun for the family, and often offer a chance to talk to the artists. The **Florida Folk Festival** (*see p14*), on the Panhandle, is one where artisans show and sell traditional folk crafts.

Disney delights

The World of Disney® store in the **Downtown Disney® Marketplace** (*see p117*) has everything any kid

Below left Fresh produce for sale at one of the many farmers' markets across Florida
Below right Prints and gifts inspired by Salvador Dalí at the store in The Dalí Museum, St. Petersburg

could want, from a Mickey Mouse watch to a princess tiara. Even better, at Mickey's Mart everything is $10 and under. Once Upon a Toy, a delightful toy store with a miniature train running on suspended tracks overhead, stocks some classic games redesigned with Disney themes. The LEGO® Imagination Store here is sure to inspire young builders with its fun LEGO® display sculptures. Little girls love LittleMissMatched, where socks come in packs of three to be mixed not matched, and the age-old problem of the missing sock is resolved.

Museum shops

Museum shops stock items to interest all ages, especially the one in the **Ringling Museum** (see p225), which has all kinds of circus paraphernalia, including juggling balls and puzzles, and **The Dalí Museum** (see p221) with its melted watches and other souvenirs.

Pocket-money toys

Learning Express stores, located across Florida, will please parents and kids alike with their stock of toys that are educational as well as fun. Stores such as **Dollar General** and **Family Dollar**,

where many things, including toys and snacks, cost just $1, are a shopper's delight. Almost every town has a dollar store and the variety of offerings is surprising.

Books

The big stores, such as **Barnes & Noble**, are almost everywhere, and have extensive kids' departments, but book-loving Florida still has many independent stores. The enormous **Vero Beach Book Center** includes a separate store dedicated to kids. In St. Petersburg is Florida's largest book store, **Haslam's Book Store**, packed with some 350,000 new and used books.

Many Florida communities hold outdoor book fairs that are fun for the entire family. Author signings and children's events are part of the festivities. The biggest, the **Miami Book Fair International**, held in November, draws as many as 350 authors and includes a Children's Alley with storytelling, puppets, and games. The March **Festival of Reading** in St. Petersburg features a Children's Storyland with costumed characters, games, and activities.

The Lowdown

Bargain bonanzas
Dolphin Mall www.shopdolphin mall.com
Premium www.premiumoutlets.com
Sawgrass Mills www.simon.com/mall/?id=1262

Markets
Daytona Flea and Farmers' Market 2987 Bellevue Ave, 32124; 386 253 3330; www.daytonafleamarket.com

Arty adventures
Crafts Fairs www.artfestival.com
Florida Craftsmen Gallery 501 Central Ave, St. Petersburg, 33701; 727 821 7391; floridacraftsmen.net

Pocket-money toys
Dollar General www.dollargeneral.com

Family Dollar www.familydollar.com
Learning Express www.learning express.com

Books
Barnes & Noble www.barnesand noble.com
Festival of Reading University of South Florida, St. Petersburg; 727 445 4142; www.festivalofreading.com
Haslam's Book Store, 2025 Central Ave, St. Petersburg, 33713; 727 822 8616; www.haslams.com
Miami Book Fair International, Miami-Dade College, 33132; 305 237 3258; www.miamibookfair.com
Vero Beach Book Center, 2145 Indian River Rd, Vero Beach; 772 569 2050

Below left Part of the Crochet Coral Reef project at the Florida Craftsmen Gallery, St. Petersburg
Below right A plethora of Disney plush toys and memorabilia at the Downtown Disney® Marketplace

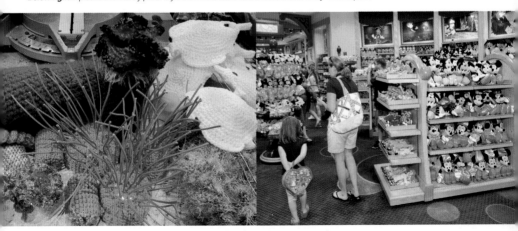

Entertainment

Florida's rich menu of entertainment runs the gamut from Broadway musicals and symphony and rock concerts to the circus, ballet, and theater, with many performances designed for kids. The greatest range of events is found in southern Florida, especially in Miami and along the Gold Coast. Tampa and Sarasota are major cultural centers on the Gulf Coast, and university cities such as Gainesville and Tallahassee often host exciting events as well.

Sources of information

In most Florida cities the Friday newspapers usually include a weekend section listing regional events. Convention and Visitors' Bureaus and Chambers of Commerce are good sources for brochures and local information.

Making reservations

It is best to check online for advance sales information and pay by credit card. Buying by phone or online usually involves a service charge anywhere from $2–8 above the ticket price. Some venues handle sales through **Ticketmaster**.

Major venues

The largest venues feature a range of offerings that may include appearances by touring Broadway companies and well-known national performers, and local companies. The largest centers on the east coast are the **Adrienne Arsht Center for the Performing Arts** in Miami, **Broward Center for the Performing Arts** in Fort Lauderdale, and the **Raymond F. Kravis Center for the Performing Arts** in West Palm Beach. West coast centers include the **David A. Straz Center for the Performing Arts** in Tampa, the **Barbara B. Mann Performing Arts Hall** in Fort Myers. Rock stars usually play in sports stadiums such as the **Sun Life Stadium** in Miami Gardens, **Florida Citrus Bowl** in Orlando, and **EverBank Field** in Jacksonville.

Theater

The **Asolo Repertory Theatre** in Sarasota and the **Florida Repertory Company** in Fort Myers present a range of plays, including many musicals that enthrall families. The **Orlando Shakespeare Theater** (see p130) offers modern plays and the Bard's works, along with plays for kids. The **Riverside Children's Theater** (see p94) in Vero Beach and **Actors' Playhouse** (see p52) in Miami also include kids' theater, while the **Miami Children's Theater**, **Fort Lauderdale Children's Theater**, and Jacksonville's **Theatreworks** are devoted to young audiences. In Delray Beach, the **Puppetry Arts Center** delights with its puppet productions and museum.

Dinner theater

Serving entertainment along with dinner, theaters such as the **Golden Apple Dinner Theater** in Sarasota generally offer family-friendly works,

Below left The Orlando Shakespeare Theater staging the classic fairy tale Snow White and the Seven Dwarfs
Below centre Graceful aerialists performing at the Flying High Circus in Tallahassee

including Broadway musicals. Theme theaters such as **Medieval Times** in Kissimmee have special lures, in this case knights in armor jousting on horseback. The **Murder Mystery Dinner Train** in Fort Myers combines dinner with a train ride and the chance to solve a mystery.

Music, dance, and film

The **Miami Symphony Orchestra** plays in several venues around the region, while a stunning Miami Beach building by architect Frank Gehry, the New World Center, is home to the **New World Symphony**. **Sunday Musicals** has presented concerts for adults and children for over 25 years at the University of Miami campus. The **Miami City Ballet** dances in Miami, Palm Beach, Fort Lauderdale, and Naples, and presents free programs for young people in winter. The **Sarasota Orchestra**, founded in 1960, plays both classical and pop music. The **Sarasota Film Festival** devotes a day to "Short Stacks," with pancakes to eat and short films for family viewing.

Circuses

Florida's circus heritage can be seen in several shows that delight all ages. **Circus Sarasota**, a one-ring

circus with many international stars, pitches its tent for the month of February. The **PAL Sailor Circus**, featuring young performers, takes place in Sarasota during the last week in December and January and the first week in April. The **Flying High Circus** shows off

awe-inspiring routines in the air and on the ground in Tallahassee each April. **Ringling Brothers and Barnum & Bailey** brings its big traveling shows to Miami, Fort Myers, Jacksonville, Tampa, Tallahassee, Orlando, and Pensacola each year, usually in January.

The Lowdown

Making reservations
Ticketmaster www.ticketmaster.com

Major venues
Adrienne Arsht Center for the Performing Arts www.arshtcenter.org
Barbara B. Mann Performing Arts Hall bbmannpah.com
Broward Center for the Performing Arts browardcenter.org
David A. Straz Center for the Performing Arts www.strazcenter.org
EverBank Field 1 Stadium Blvd, Jacksonville; 954 522 5334
Florida Citrus Bowl www.fcsports.com
Raymond F. Kravis Center for the Performing Arts www.kravis.org
Sun Life Stadium sunlifestadium.com

Theater
Asolo Repertory Theatre www.asolorep.org
Florida Repertory Company floridarep.org
Fort Lauderdale Children's Theater flct.org
Miami Children's Theater www.miamichildrentheater.com

Puppetry Arts Center
puppetcenter.org
Theatreworks theatreworksjax.com

Dinner theater
Golden Apple Dinner Theater 25 N Pineapple Ave, Sarasota; 800 652 0920
Medieval Times medievaltimes.com
Murder Mystery Dinner Train semgulf.com

Music, dance, and film
Miami City Ballet miamicityballet.org
Miami Symphony Orchestra themiso.org
New World Symphony www.nws.edu
Sarasota Film Festival www.sarasotafilmfestival.com
Sarasota Orchestra sarasotaorchestra.org
Sunday Musicals sundaymusicals.org

Circuses
Circus Sarasota circussarasota.com
Flying High Circus circus.fsu.edu
PAL Sailor Circus sailorcircus.org
Ringling Brothers and Barnum & Bailey Circus www.ringling.com

Below left An actor mingling with guests aboard the Murder Mystery Dinner Train, Fort Myers
Below right Dance performance at Sunday Musicals, a popular concert series in Miami

The History of Florida

Beyond its sunny beaches and theme parks, Florida has a rich history to share – from prehistoric times and Native American settlements to Spanish discovery and an eventful couple of hundred years when the area constantly changed hands, before relaxing into a Golden Age. The grand buildings of yesteryear that sit alongside modern architecture are just one example of the fascinating remnants of Florida's past waiting to be discovered.

Early settlers

Florida's history began with the Paleo-Indians – big-game hunters who probably crossed the Bering Strait from Asia (Eurasia) into North America over a land and ice bridge as long as 12,000 years ago. They settled where fresh water was available, sharing the land with massive animals such as mastodon, giant sloths, and mammoths.

Over the centuries, tribes settled down into villages, grew crops, and began customs such as creating burial mounds, which can still be seen today. By the time Europeans arrived in this part of the New World, Florida was inhabited by an estimated 350,000 people from a number of tribes. The Spanish and British recorded the names of nearly 100 groups they came across; the largest among these were the Apalachee and the Timucua.

Timucua Indians killing alligators in northeast Florida, around the mid-16th century

Spanish Florida

Florida's written history began when the Spanish explorer Ponce de León "discovered" the region in 1513, probably landing near St. Augustine. He named his discovery "La Florida" after the Spanish Easter feast known as Pascua Florida. More explorations followed, some led by the ruthless conquistador Hernando de Soto (around 1497–1542). The Spanish introduced Christianity, horses, and cattle to Florida, but they also brought new diseases such as smallpox and typhoid fever, and massacred many of the local people in their quest to find gold and treasure. In the 1770s, Florida's Native American tribes became known collectively as Seminoles, a name meaning "wild people" or "untamed."

Hot on the heels of the Spanish came the British, who wanted another kind of treasure – valuable hides and furs. They took control of Florida in 1763 by swapping Cuba for it. After the British lost the Revolutionary War to the US, the Spanish regained Florida with the Second Treaty of Paris of 1783. They remained in charge until 1819, when the region was handed over to the US to settle Spain's debts and

Timeline

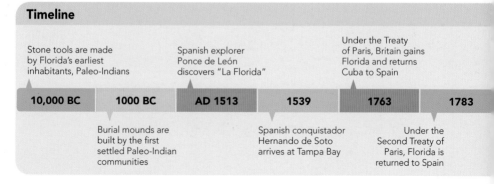

| 10,000 BC | 1000 BC | AD 1513 | 1539 | 1763 | 1783 |

Stone tools are made by Florida's earliest inhabitants, Paleo-Indians

Spanish explorer Ponce de León discovers "La Florida"

Under the Treaty of Paris, Britain gains Florida and returns Cuba to Spain

Burial mounds are built by the first settled Paleo-Indian communities

Spanish conquistador Hernando de Soto arrives at Tampa Bay

Under the Second Treaty of Paris, Florida is returned to Spain became a US territory. Spain's lasting influence can be seen in the state's churches, architecture, and food.

The Seminole Wars

In the period before the Civil War, known as the antebellum, runaway slaves taking refuge in Florida found sympathy from the Indian tribes, creating growing conflicts with the US. By 1817, antagonism had escalated into the first of three Seminole wars. Future US president Andrew Jackson invaded the then-Spanish Florida and defeated the Seminoles. Under the US flag, a plantation economy based on slavery, as in other Southern states, began to develop here. Land was at a premium and pressure grew on the US government to remove the Indians from their lands. In 1832, the US signed the Treaty of Payne's Landing with some of the Seminole chiefs, promising them lands west

Seminole Indians preparing to ambush American troops in the First Seminole War

of the Mississippi River if the tribes would leave Florida peacefully. Many agreed, but those who remained were prepared to defend their land. From 1835 to 1842, and again from 1855 to 1858, Seminole warriors defied the far more powerful US Army. In the end, though, it was a lost cause and almost all the Seminoles were forcibly exiled. But a band of some 300 stubbornly remained, hiding in the Everglades wilderness. Their descendants are the Seminole tribes of today.

The State of Florida

Florida became the 27th US state in 1845. Most of the state's population was in the northern area, where the plantation culture flourished. By 1850, the population had grown to 87,445; almost half were African-American slaves. In 1861, to preserve its plantation way of life, the state broke away from the Union and joined the Confederate States of America. Located well south of the fighting, Florida was spared the destruction experienced in other Southern states during the Civil War (1861–5). Its main role was to provide an estimated 15,000 troops, plus cotton, and food supplies including salt, beef, and pork to the Confederacy. When the Confederates lost the war and slavery was outlawed, the plantation economy waned. But soon canny developers had their eyes on a new source of wealth – tourism.

HISTORICAL SITES

Cathedral Basilica of St. Augustine
Admire the fine example of Spanish architecture that has influenced much of Florida's buildings *(see p171)*.

Museum of Arts and Sciences (MOAS)

Gaze at the prehistoric giant sloth here, which stands 12 ft (4 m) high *(see pp176–7)*.

Indian Temple Mound Museum
Discover the huge collection of ceramic artifacts at this museum adjacent to one of Florida's largest Indian ceremonial mounds *(see p191)*.

Mission San Luis
Witness a rare example of racial harmony, as costumed interpreters bring to life the site shared by the Spanish and Apalachee Indians *(see p200)*.

Kingsley Plantation
Visit the oldest plantation house in Florida and explore its restored main house, kitchen and barn, plus the ruins of 25 of the original slave cabins *(see p165)*.

Ybor City Museum State Park

Trace the story of the city's cigar industry and look at a restored cigar worker's home *(see p218)*.

Andrew Jackson's army enters Florida in First Seminole War

Florida becomes the 27th US state

1818 | **1825** | **1845** | **1861**

The village of Talasi is chosen as the state capital and renamed Tallahassee

Florida joins the Confederate States of America

Florida's Golden Age

While most of Florida's early development had been in the northern part of the state, the agreeable climate of the land further south made it attractive for development. Railroad barons such as Henry Flagler on the east coast and Henry Plant on the west expanded their railroads in the late 1880s and 1890s, and began building the first grand hotels to attract passengers. Tourism boomed, fortunes were made, and fine mansions were built.

The railroads also meant that the Sunshine State's juicy crops of oranges and lemons could reach eager buyers all over the country, and soon Florida was the nation's biggest citrus fruit producer. Immigrants from the nearby Caribbean island of Cuba brought with them the skill of making highly

Portrait of Henry Flagler, founder of the Florida East Coast Railway

prized cigars. Tampa's warm, humid climate suited the rolling of tobacco leaves perfectly, and Ybor City (see p218) was founded there in 1885 by Cuban manufacturer Vicente Martinez Ybor as a home for his factory and workers.

Boom and bust

Henry Ford's Model T began rolling off the assembly lines in 1908, making automobiles affordable for the first time, and nowhere was the effect felt more strongly than in Florida, where "tin can tourists" came streaming in. In 1914, entrepreneur Carl Fisher came up with the idea of building the north–south Dixie Highway, which eventually ran all the way from the Canadian border to southern Florida. At the southern end of the highway, Fisher dreamed of a new resort city, Miami Beach (see pp66–7). During the 1920s, investors of all kinds raced to buy and sell land in South Florida communities such as Miami and Palm Beach (see pp88–9). Prices soared, and con men entered the picture. Some foolish buyers purchased land sight unseen, only to find themselves the owners of worthless swampland. By 1925, prices were astronomical, buyers became scarce, and the real estate boom turned to bust. A devastating hurricane in Miami in 1926 depressed the market even further. By the time the Great Depression began in the rest of the nation in 1929, residents of Florida had already experienced economic hardship.

Children riding on a flivver car in Coral Gables, a "tin can tourist" tent city

A second boom

Government work programs and the flourishing citrus industry helped Florida ride out the Depression, and many unemployed people arrived from all over the US, looking for work, and helping the state's economy grow. World War II brought another boom as Florida's year-round mild climate made it ideal as a major training center for the US army and navy. Highway and airport construction followed, and by the war's end an up-to-date transportation system was ready and waiting for visitors.

Newcomers arrived from other countries too, especially in Miami. Fidel Castro's rise to power in Cuba in 1959 brought an influx of Cubans, and unrest in Haiti in the 1970s led to the founding of the community known as Little Haiti.

The first Daytona 500 roared into action in 1959, making the Daytona International Speedway (see p174) a mecca for auto-racing fans the world over. Space exploration and the arrival of NASA

Timeline

Vicente Ybor transfers his cigar industry to Tampa

The Great Depression hits Florida

Walt Disney World® opens in Orlando at a cost of $700 million

| 1885 | 1915–27 | 1929–34 | 1958 | 1971 | 1980 |

Dixie Highway is constructed, connecting the Midwest to southern Florida

The first Earth satellite, Explorer I, is launched from Florida

125,000 Cubans arrive in Florida in the five-month Mariel boatlift and the Kennedy Space Center *(see pp144–7)* in 1962 also brought jobs and more visitors. The theme park era began in 1959 when Busch Gardens *(see pp214–5)* opened in Tampa, and 10,000 people were waiting impatiently at the gates when Walt Disney World® *(see pp106–17)* made its debut in 1971.

Florida today

Modern-day Florida is the fourth most populous state in the US, and one of the most popular vacation destinations in the world. Twenty percent of this flourishing state's diverse population consists of retirees aged over 65, who are drawn by its mild climate. Well over 300,000 of the Cubans who fled to South Florida in the 1960s have settled here, raised families, and become influential in business and state politics. Walt Disney World® grows bigger every year and has been joined by Universal Studios Florida®

(see pp118–19), SeaWorld® *(see pp122–3)* and LEGOLAND® *(see pp132–5)* to make Orlando the theme park capital of the world.

The 1930s Art Deco architecture of Miami Beach has been rediscovered by the young and hip, who flock to the hotels and nightclubs in town. The state has also become the major US center for the growing cruise industry, with busy ports in Miami, Fort Lauderdale *(see pp80–81)*, Tampa, and other coastal cities serving thousands of cruisers each year. All of this means jobs, and with the citrus industry and tourism joined by more recent industries including electronics, plastics, construction, and international banking, younger job aspirants have added to the rush to Florida. Like most of the world, Florida has felt the cloud of the global economic slowdown that began in 2008, but whatever lies ahead, the sun will continue to shine in Florida.

The Art Deco facade of the Jackie Gleason Theater of the Performing Arts, Miami

George Bush wins presidential election, with Florida as the decisive state

A major oil spill by a BP tanker slows down tourism. A successful clean-up effort follows

2000 **2004** **2010** **2014**

One of the deadliest hurricanes in history, Hurricane Frances, inflicts $40 billion of damage

NASA plans to test launch the Orion manned spacecraft

FACTS & FIGURES

What's in a name?
Many of the names in today's Florida – Hialeah (pretty meadow) in Miami, Appalachee (people on the other side) Parkway in Tallahassee, and the town of Apalachicola (land of friendly people) – come from the original Native American settlers. The Spanish also left a legacy of names, such as Fernandina (a popular name for girls in Spain).

Florida's flying firsts
Florida aviator Tony Jannus flew the first airplane from which a parachute jump was made in 1912, and on January 1, 1914, piloted the world's first scheduled passenger service flight – from St. Petersburg to Tampa (about 20 miles/32 km).

Cooking up a tan
In 1944, Miami Beach pharmacist Benjamin Green invented the first suntan cream, by cooking cocoa butter in a coffee pot on his wife's stove.

Drink to win
The sports drink Gatorade® was developed in 1965 at the University of Florida to help its sports teams withstand the heat, and was named for the "Gators," the teams' nickname.

State symbols
Florida's state bird is the mockingbird and the state flower is the orange blossom. The seal on Florida's flag represents the state with a brilliant sun, a cabbage palmetto tree, a steamboat, and a Seminole woman scattering flowers.

The beautiful white-sand beach at Fort Zachary Taylor Historic State Park, Key West, with coral rocks and a backdrop of Australian pines

Exploring

FLORIDA

Miami

Exotic, glamorous, colorful, and cosmopolitan: Miami is everything the movies make it out to be. The city took on its multicultural character with the early migrations of New York Jews and Bahamians. Since then, an influx of people of other nationalities, including Cubans, Haitians, Brazilians, and Jamaicans, has influenced Miami's food, arts, and culture. Families will enjoy the city's carnival-like atmosphere.

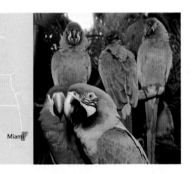

Miami

Highlights

Vizcaya Museum and Gardens
Miami's best-known and most-eccentric landmark, this fantasy palace and its gardens offer a fun, imaginative day out (see pp60–61).

South Beach
Admire this neighborhood, Miami's most-filmed district, with its dazzling Art Deco buildings. Kids love it for its great beach (see pp68–9).

Coral Gables
Built out of locally quarried rock in the 1920s, the "City Beautiful" boasts elegant architecture, and offers family-friendly museums and parks (see pp52–3).

Coconut Grove
Shop, dine, and enjoy the festive atmosphere in this fashionable destination, once a Bahamian settlement and then a hippie hangout (see p54).

Downtown Miami
Head to this bustling area that is home to the lively Bayfront Park and Marketplace, as well as the Little Havana Cuban community (see pp58–9).

North Miami Beach
Enjoy the world-class shopping and high-rise resorts in Miami's latest hot spots: Surfside, Sunny Isles, and Bal Harbour (see p70).

Left Classic vintage Thunderbird parked outside a hotel in the historic Art Deco District, South Beach
Above right Brightly plumaged macaws in Jungle Island

The Best of
Miami

Though Miami is famous for its nightlife, the city also ranks high as an artsy destination, with annual festivals, museums, theaters, and galleries that reflect its rich and varied cultural heritage. The city's coastal location makes it attractive to families interested in watersports and other seaside activities. In addition, there are a variety of parks, zoos, and hands-on attractions that are of great interest and appeal to visitors of all ages.

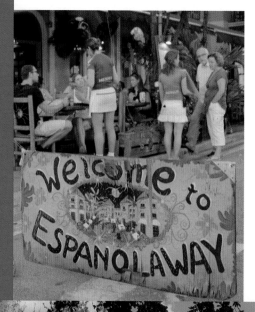

A weekend at the beach

The best family beaches lie across the causeway from downtown on Virginia Key and Key Biscayne. Get to **Bill Baggs Cape Florida State Park** (see p65) in time for a lighthouse tour, and climb the lighthouse for an overview of Key Biscayne's beaches and beyond. Have lunch at the park's beach restaurant before renting a kayak or hydro-bike to play in the waves. Visit **Crandon Park** (see pp64–5) in the afternoon to relax on the beach, then explore the park's **Marjory Stoneman Douglas Biscayne Nature Center** (see p65) for a break from the sun. Next, go to **Virginia Key Beach Park** (see p64) for some fun in the playground. Visit **South Beach** (see pp68–9) to round off a weekend on the beaches of Miami. Head for **South Pointe Park** (see p68) to get away from the crowds and watch cruise ships chugging in and out of port.

Left Signboard at the entrance to Española Way, South Beach
Below The Stone House in the Deering Estate at Cutler

Above One of the numerous brightly colored lifeguard stations in South Beach

Retro ride through the city

For a relatively new city, Miami has lots of history, most of which centers around the 1910s and 1920s. Start with a guided Art Deco District walking tour in **South Beach**, then visit the **Jewish Museum of Florida** *(see p68)*, which explores another aspect of the state's past. South of downtown, the **Vizcaya Museum and Gardens** *(see pp60–61)* was built in 1916 to look old and European. In **Coral Gables** *(see pp52–3)*, homes dating back to the 1920s populate one of the country's most successful planned developments; learn more at the **Coral Gables Museum** *(see p53)*. Built around 1891 in a virgin hardwood forest, **The Barnacle Historic State Park** *(see p54)* in **Coconut Grove** *(see p54)* offers a chance to glimpse old Florida. Visit the **Deering Estate at Cutler** *(see p56)*, which belonged to Charles Deering, brother of James Deering, who built **Vizcaya**. See another historic structure that reveals a man's bizarre dream in the **Coral Castle** *(see p57)* in Homestead.

Animal safari

Families that love animals can see them in the wild and at attractions throughout Miami. Take a boat excursion from **Bayside Marketplace** *(see p61)* to look for dolphins in the sea, then head to **Miami Seaquarium®** *(see p64)* on Key Biscayne to watch them perform, along with whales and sea lions. Sign up for a dolphin encounter, and check out the crocodiles, sharks, manatees, and other sea creatures. Heading south, the **Miami Science Museum** *(see p55)* and

Zoo Miami *(see pp56–7)* both provide opportunities to get up-close with animals. En route to **South Beach**, **Jungle Island** *(see p63)* is filled with exotic birds, kangaroos, and big cats.

Culture quest

The clacking of dominoes, the whiff of strong coffee, the strains of Latin salsa, and the thick, heady aroma of cigar smoke are as much a part of Miami as its beaches. Little Havana is the place to start cultural explorations. Walk **Calle Ocho** *(see p62)* and take in Domino Park, the shops, and the food. While in downtown, check out **Miami Art Museum** *(see p62)*. In **Coconut Grove**, get a taste of Bahamian architecture in Charles Avenue Historic District. In **South Beach**, the **Tap Tap Haitian Restaurant** *(see p63)* offers a true taste of Haiti. Along **Española Way** *(see p68)*, Latin is the flavor *du jour*.

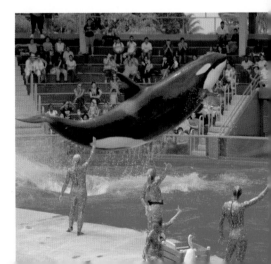

Right Lolita, an orca, performing for visitors at the Miami Seaquarium®, Key Biscayne

Miami

The southernmost point in Florida, before the mainland tapers off into the string of islands known as the Florida Keys, Miami consists of a massive metropolitan and suburban area fronted by bustling Miami Beach and quieter Key Biscayne. Biscayne Bay separates the mainland from the islands; the toll causeway leads to Key Biscayne, and five bridges cross over to Miami Beach. Interstate 95 and Florida's Turnpike (Route 821) dissect the city north to south. Highway 1, also known as Dixie Highway, runs parallel near the bay. The Miami-Dade Transit buses and trains provide public transportation.

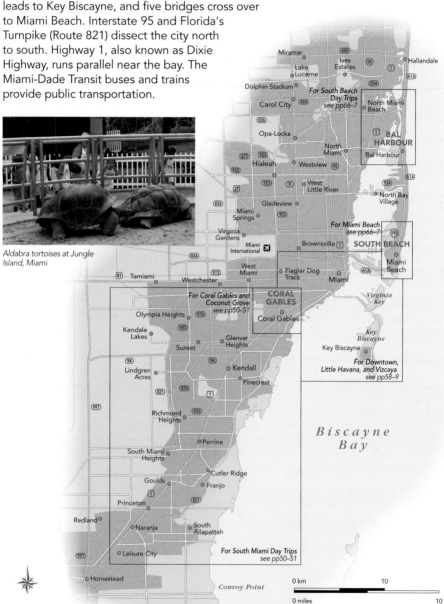

Aldabra tortoises at Jungle Island, Miami

Miramar · 858 · Ives Estates · 95 · 1 · Hallandale
Lake Lucerne · 854 · A1A
Dolphin Stadium · For South Beach Day Trips see pp66–7
Carol City · 860 · North Miami Beach
826
Opa-Locka · 1 · BAL HARBOUR
North Miami · Bal Harbour
825 · 924
932 · Hialeah · Westview · 95
27 · 953 · 9 · West Little River · 934 · A1A
826 · North Bay Village
Miami Springs · 953 · Gladeview
For Miami Beach see pp66–7 · 195
Virginia Gardens · Brownsville · 1 · SOUTH BEACH
Miami International ✈ · 836
West Miami · Flagler Dog Track · A1A · Miami Beach
41 · Tamiami · 973 · Westchester · Miami
For Coral Gables and Coconut Grove see pp50–51 · CORAL GABLES · Virginia Key
Olympia Heights · 976 · Coral Gables
Kendale Lakes · 985 · Key Biscayne
Glenvar Heights · Key Biscayne
Sunset
94 · 94 · Kendall · For Downtown, Little Havana, and Vizcaya see pp58–9
Lindgren Acres · Pinecrest
821 · 874 · 1
997
Richmond Heights · 992
Perrine · *Biscayne Bay*
South Miami Heights
Cutler Ridge
Goulds · Franjo
1 · 821
Princeton
Redland · South Allapattah
997 · Naranja · Leisure City
For South Miami Day Trips see pp50–51
Homestead
Convoy Point

0 km   10
0 miles   10

The famous Big Pink restaurant on Collins Avenue, Miami Beach

Bronze statue of founder George Merrick outside the Coral Gables City Hall

Kids learning about the Cruise Ship exhibit at Miami Children's Museum

View from the lighthouse at Bill Baggs Cape Florida State Park, Key Biscayne

The Lowdown

🚗 **Getting there and around**
Air Fly into Miami International Airport (www.miami-airport.com). Taxis are readily available at the airport, but not on the streets; call ahead on 305 876 7024 to reserve. **Bus** and **Train** Miami-Dade Transit (www.miamidade.gov/transit) operates Metrobus, Metromover (in Downtown), and Metrorail, with airport connections. **Car** Rental services such as Avis (www.avis.com) and Hertz (www.hertz.com) are available at the airport; note that all cars, including rentals, need a transponder device to use Florida's Turnpike.

ℹ️ **Visitor information** Greater Miami Convention and Visitors Bureau, 701 Brickell Ave, St 2700, Miami, 33131; 305 539 3094 & 800 933 8448; www.miamiandbeaches.com

🏪 **Supermarkets** Publix (www.publix.com) and Winn-Dixie (www.winndixie.com) have outlets throughout the city. **Markets** Families will find small ethnic food shops in Little Havana, Little Haiti, South Beach, and other cultural enclaves.

🎪 **Festivals** See Coral Gables and Coconut Grove (see pp50–51), Downtown, Little Havana, and Vizcaya (see pp58–9), and Miami Beach (see pp66–7).

➕ **Pharmacies** Publix, Walgreens (www.walgreens.com), and CVS (www.cvs.com/pharmacy) pharmacies can be found around the city; some CVS and Walgreens branches are open 24 hours.

🚻 **Restrooms** Almost all major attractions, restaurants, malls, and most gas stations have public restrooms.

Coral Gables, Coconut Grove, and around

South Miami has some of the metropolitan area's oldest, most interesting, and most family-friendly neighborhoods. Towering trees, tangled with Spanish moss, shade winding streets where beautiful mansions and well-manicured parks can be found. Coral Gables and Coconut Grove are the two most popular districts in this part of the city, but visitors should not miss historic Cutler Bay, nor Homestead, an agricultural town at the edge of the Everglades National Park and the Florida Keys. Further afield, families will find plenty to see and do at the Fruit & Spice Park (see p57), Coral Castle, and Zoo Miami.

Elegantly decorated interior of the house in Barnacle Historic State Park, Coconut Grove

Places of interest

SIGHTS

1. Coral Gables
2. Coconut Grove
3. The Barnacle Historic State Park
4. Peacock Park
5. Fairchild Tropical Garden
6. Deering Estate at Cutler
7. Zoo Miami
8. Coral Castle

EAT AND DRINK

1. Publix Supermarket and Deli
2. Al's Coffee Shop
3. The Cascade
4. Ortanique on the Mile
5. The Cheesecake Factory
6. Le Bouchon du Grove
7. Rincón Argentino
8. LuLu
9. Dolce Vita Gelato Cafe
10. Peacock Garden Cafe

SHOPPING

1. Miracle Mile

WHERE TO STAY

1. The Biltmore Hotel
2. Sonesta Bayfront Hotel

The Lowdown

🚗 **Getting around** Hiring a car is the best way to get around Coral Gables and Coconut Grove, though traffic gets quite heavy. The Florida's Turnpike (see inset map) is quickest when traveling to the southwest quadrant. Metrorail from downtown travels to both neighborhoods and beyond, but not as far as Homestead. However, bus 34 connects the Metrorail terminus with Homestead.

ℹ️ **Visitor information** Coral Gables Chamber of Commerce, 224 Catalonia Ave, Coral Gables 33134; 305 446 1657; *coralgables chamber.org*. Coconut Grove Chamber of Commerce, 2820

McFarlane Rd, 33133; 305 444 7270; *www.coconutgrove chamber.com*. Tropical Everglades Visitor Center, 160 US 1, Florida City, 33034; 305 245 9180; *www.tropicaleverglades.com*

🚢 **Supermarkets** Publix,14601, S Dixie Hwy, 33176; 305 255 8005 & 2270 SW 27th Ave, 33145; 305 445 9661; *www.publix.com*
Markets Saturday Farmers' Market, 405 Biltmore Way, Coral Gables, 33134 & Grand Ave at the intersection of Margaret St, Coconut Grove, 33133; every Sat

🎌 **Festivals** Redland Heritage Festival (Jan). Coconut Grove Arts Festival, *new.cgaf.com*

(Feb). Washington Day Regatta (Feb). Deering Seafood Festival (Mar). Youth Arts Day & Music Fest (May–Jun). The Goombay Festival, *www.goombayfestival coconutgrove.com* (Jun). International Mango Festival (Jul). Spooktober at Zoo Miami (Oct)

➕ **Pharmacy** Walgreens, 3595 Coral Way, Coral Gables, 33145; 305 444 8427; *www.walgreens.com*; open 24 hours

🛝 **Nearest playgrounds** Douglas Park, 2765 SW 37th Ave, 33134; daily (see p53). Peacock Park, 2820 McFarlane Rd, 33133; daily (see p55).

Children playing in a tidal pool in Matheson Hammock County Park, Coral Gables

① Coral Gables
City of fantasy

A city out of a storybook, Coral Gables was built by real estate developer George Merrick, who envisioned one of the first and most successfully planned suburbs in the US. Known as the "City Beautiful," it earns its moniker from oak-shaded streets lined with homes of international lineage. The city boasts one of the most beautiful public swimming pools in the world – the Venetian Pool, formerly a limestone quarry. Families will enjoy the area's green spaces and its splendid architecture.

Exterior of The Biltmore Hotel

Key Sights

① **Miracle Mile** Graceful stone fountains bookend this 1950s strip of shops and restaurants decorated down the middle with pretty pineapple-shaped date palms.

② **Actors' Playhouse** Housed within the vintage Miracle Theatre, with an old-fashioned marquee, it stages plays by and for kids, as well as adult programs.

③ **City Hall** Built in Mediterranean Revival style, to match the homes and commercial buildings of the Coral Gables community, this circa-1927 beauty sits at the end of Miracle Mile.

④ **Venetian Pool** Stone bridges, caves, waterfalls, and lush vegetation surround this fantasy swimming pool carved from a former coral limestone quarry – the source of building materials in Coral Gables.

⑤ **The Biltmore Hotel** Favored by the rich and famous since its opening in 1926, this historic hotel looks like a castle out of a fairy tale.

⑥ **Lowe Art Museum** This museum at the University of Miami has American, Native American, Renaissance, European, and Asian art in its permanent collection, and also hosts traveling exhibitions.

Prices given are for a family of four

⑦ **French Country Village** One of Coral Gables' international villages, this residential village still has several examples of its original architecture. Ivy, wood-slat accents, and cottage styling give the homes a French provincial feel.

⑧ **Matheson Hammock County Park** A major draw for families, the Atoll Pool Beach here is entirely enclosed and ringed by palm trees, and is safe for small kids. Playgrounds, shaded picnic areas, bike paths, nature trails, and a sailing school make the park fun for all ages.

The Lowdown

🌐 **Map reference** 11 C4
Address Actors' Playhouse: 280 Miracle Mile, 33134; *www.actors playhouse.org*. City Hall: 405 Biltmore Way, 33134; *www.coral gables.com*. Venetian Pool: 2701 DeSoto Blvd, 33134; *www.coral gables.com*. The Biltmore Hotel: 1200 Anastasia Ave, 33134; *www.biltmorehotel.com*. Lowe Art Museum: 1301 Stanford Ave, 33134; *www.lowemuseum.org*. Matheson Hammock County Park: 9610 Old Cutler Rd, 33156; *www.miamidade.gov*

🚇 **Metro** Metrorail to Douglas Road station, then bus 42

ℹ️ **Visitor information** Coral Gables Chamber of Commerce,

224 Catalonia Ave, 33134; *coralgableschamber.org*

🕐 **Open** Actors' Playhouse: box office 10am–6pm Mon–Fri & noon–6pm Sat–Sun. City Hall: 8am–5pm Mon–Fri. Venetian Pool: 11am–5:30pm Tue–Fri & 10am–4:30pm Sat–Sun, closed Dec–Jan. Lowe Art Museum: 10am–4pm Tue–Sat & noon–4pm Sun. Matheson Hammock County Park: sunrise–sunset daily

💲 **Price** Actors' Playhouse: ticket prices vary. City Hall & The Biltmore Hotel: free. Venetian Pool: $35–44. Lowe Art Museum: $30–40; under 12s free. Matheson Hammock County Park: $5–6 per vehicle

Map labels

ARAGON AVE
CORAL WAY
BILTMORE WAY
Miracle Mile ①
City Hall ③
Actors' Playhouse ②
Venetian Pool ④
GRANADA BLVD
DE SOTO BLVD
SEGOVIA STREET
SEVILLA AVE
ANDERSON RD
ANASTASIA AVE
LE JEUNE RD
PONCE DE LEON BLVD
UNIVERSITY DR
DOUGLAS RD
The Biltmore Hotel ⑤
Lowe Art Museum 2 miles (3 km) ⑥
French Country Village 3 miles (5 km) ⑦
Matheson Hammock County Park 5 miles (8 km) ⑧

0 meters 500
0 yards 500

Letting off steam
Head to **Douglas Park** (2755 SW 37th Ave, 33134) for open green spaces shaded by gargantuan trees, plus playgrounds and picnic shelters. **Todo Frio Ice Cream N More** (www. todofrio.net), next door, scoops up cones at reasonable prices.

Snacks and coffee at the popular Al's Coffee Shop, Coral Gables

Eat and drink
Picnic: under $25; Snacks: $25–50; Real meal: $50–80; Family treat: over $80 (based on a family of four)

PICNIC Publix Supermarket and Deli (2270 SW 27th Ave, 33145; 305 445 9661; www.publix.com) sells take-out subs, salads, chicken wings, beverages, and other snacks. Zip to Douglas Park for a picnic.
SNACKS Al's Coffee Shop (2121 Ponce de Leon Blvd, 33134; 305 461 5919; www.alscoffeeshop.com) is the place to find sandwiches, salads, burgers, and good coffee.
REAL MEAL The Cascade (in The Biltmore Hotel; 855 445 8066; www. biltmorehotel.com), overlooking the

hotel's famed swimming pool, serves contemporary French and Caribbean cuisine. It also offers a kids' menu.
FAMILY TREAT Ortanique on the Mile (278 Miracle Mile, 33134; 305 446 7710 or 877 446 7710; www. cindyhutsoncuisine.com) has a Caribbean-style decor and cuisine. Adults can enjoy dishes such as curry crab cake melt, or corn fritters, while kids can ask for chicken fingers.

Shopping
Shop for electronics, books, antiques, and more in **Miracle Mile** (shop coralgables.com). Most shops and restaurants here are independently owned and known for their quality and variety. Many shops are devoted to weddings, and children's apparel.

Take cover
The **Coral Gables Museum** (285 Aragon Ave, 33134; 305 603 8067; www.coralgablesmuseum.org) reveals the heritage of the Coral Gables community through permanent and traveling exhibits devoted to the city's history and Spanish roots, architecture, and art.

Miracle Mile, the shopping strip in Coral Gables

Next stop...
CAULEY SQUARE SHOPS Head 14 miles (22 km) southwest of Coral Gables to shop at Cauley Square Shops (www.cauleysquareshops.net). This is where the old railroad made its last stop in Miami before heading down to the Florida Keys. Check out the Aviary Birdshop with live birds, dine in restaurants housed in vintage cottages, and admire Spanish-style buildings along cobbled streets.

KIDS' CORNER

Coral Gables mix-up
Unscramble these jumbled up words and names that are part of the Coral Gables story:
1 EETIMLONS
2 CRMRKEI
3 HSSAINP
4 TROEMIBL
5 RCCHERATIUET

Answers at the bottom of the page.

BED OF LIMESTONE
Miami sits on a foundation of bedrock known as Miami oolite or Miami limestone. It was formed from ancient coral beds when the sea covered southern Florida as a result of drastic climate changes. If you look closely, you can often spot fossilized sea creatures embedded within the rock's surface.

Très français
Many of the homes that were part of the French Country Village can still be seen along Hardee Road. Walk or drive along the road to spot house numbers 500, 501, 508, 524, 535, and 536. What makes them look as if they belong in the French countryside? (Hint: Note the red-brick houses, walled gardens, and decorative balconies.)

Answers: 1 Limestone. **2** Merrick. **3** Spanish. **4** Biltmore. **5** Architecture.

Cutting the line Miracle Mile and the areas in its vicinity are quietest in the morning.

Age range 3 plus for Venetian Pool; 5 plus for other sights; all ages for Matheson Hammock Park

Activities Lowe Art Museum hosts Family Days twice a year.

Allow A day

Café Matheson Hammock County Park has a snack bar.

Restrooms In all commercial establishments

Good family value?
Driving around Coral Gables' streets is entertainment enough, besides visiting its superb attractions.

The shaded patio of CocoWalk, an upscale shopping mall in Coconut Grove

② Coconut Grove
Groovy in "the Grove"

Luxurious mansions, and the sight of sailboats racing in the wind or anchored in Biscayne Bay, define Coconut Grove as an affluent community where dining at a sidewalk café is a quintessential experience. The area has come a long way since its countercultural hippie days of the 1960s. Today it

The Lowdown

🌐 **Map reference** 12 G5

🚌 **Bus** 42 from Coral Gables. **Metro** Metrorail from Coral Gables

ℹ️ **Visitor information** Coconut Grove Chamber of Commerce, 2820 MacFarlane Rd, 33133; 305 444 7270; www.coconut grovechamber.com

👫 **Cutting the line** Visit on a weekday if possible, as the town gets crowded on weekends.

🚩 **Guided tours** Ghost Tours Miami (786 236 9979; www.ghostgrove. com) offers family-friendly historic tours of Coconut Grove. Reserve a month in advance.

🚶 **Age range** 5 plus

⏱️ **Allow** Half a day to a full day

☕ **Eat and drink** SNACKS The Cheesecake Factory (CocoWalk, 3015 Grand Ave, 33133; 305 447 9898; www.thecheesecakefactory. com) offers small plates such as mini-corndogs and Dynamite Shrimp. FAMILY TREAT Le Bouchon du Grove (3430 Main Hwy, 33133; 305 448 6060; lebouchon dugrove.com) serves sandwiches, salads, soups, and entrées with a French influence.

🎪 **Festival** The Goombay Festival celebrates Coconut Grove's Bahamian heritage, featuring Junkanoo groups (Jun or Aug)

Yachts and small boats moored at the marina, Dinner Key

appeals to families with its Peacock Park (see p55), a lively street scene, art galleries, and CocoWalk, an outdoor mall. Surrounding the area's main hub, at the intersections of Grand Avenue, McFarlane Avenue, and Miami Highway, are neighborhoods of Mediterranean-style mansions that stand in contrast to the simple Bahamian clapboard "conch" homes.

Letting off steam

Head 2 miles (3 km) northeast of Coconut Grove's outskirts to **Dinner Key** (www.miamigov.com), a mega yacht basin. This was a seaplane base for Pan American Airways in the 1930s. Take a walk around the marina to look at the historic "PanAm" buildings – one of which now houses Miami's City Hall – and the shiny modern yachts.

③ The Barnacle Historic State Park
A slice of old Miami

Like many Florida pioneers and modern-day residents, Commodore Ralph Munroe moved to Coconut

The Lowdown

🌐 **Map reference** 12 G5
 Address 3485 Main Hwy, Coconut Grove, 33133; 305 442 6866; www.floridastateparks.org/ thebarnacle

🚌 **Bus** 42 from Coral Gables. **Metro** Metrorail from Coral Gables

ℹ️ **Visitor information** Coconut Grove Chamber of Commerce, 2820 MacFarlane Rd, 33133; 305 444 7270; www.coconutgrove chamber.com

🕐 **Open** 9am–5pm Fri–Mon

💲 **Price** $8–18

🚩 **Guided tours** There are guided tours ($5–12; under 5s free) of The Barnacle house at 10am, 11:30am, 1pm & 2:30pm Fri–Mon.

🚶 **Age range** 5 plus

⏱️ **Allow** 1 hour

☕ **Eat and drink** REAL MEAL Rincón Argentino (2345 S Douglas Rd, 33145; 305 444 2494; www. rinconargentino.com) serves soups, salads, steaks, seafood, and scrumptious home-made pasta. FAMILY TREAT Lulu (3105 Commodore Plaza, Coconut Grove, 33133; 305 447 5858; www.luluinthegrove.com) has al fresco seating with views of Coconut Grove's festive street scene. Try their green tomato BLT.

Grove from the north of the state. In the late 1800s, he established this extensive homesite and built a house called The Barnacle, named for its octagonal central room. Families can visit this narrow strip of land, which runs from Main Highway to Biscayne Bay, and see how Coconut Grove looked more than 100 years ago. Part of the once-vast Miami Hammock, the old-growth forest here harbors secret spots, such as a cemetery with unmarked graves and benches shaded by trees.

The red-roofed Barnacle house in The Barnacle Historic State Park

Letting off steam

The Barnacle has lots of wide-open spaces, but if kids still need some outdoor action, head to **Kampong Botanical Garden** *(4013 Douglas Rd, 33133; 305 442 7169; ntbg.org)*, which runs guided tours of its lush grounds every Wednesday and Saturday. Check out the massive 80-year-old baobab tree, and see the home and collection of Dr. David Fairchild, who is renowned for **Fairchild Tropical Garden** *(see p56)*.

Banyan trees lining a path in Kampong Botanical Garden

④ Peacock Park

Hoops, ramps, and gumbo limbos

Named not for the bird, but for a Coconut Grove pioneer family, the Peacocks, whose daughter married Coral Gables founder George Merrick, this park spreads like a green blanket down to Biscayne Bay. Kids can play baseball, basketball, and soccer, or skate down the ramps in **Grove Skate Park**, which is geared toward beginners. Gracious old oaks and

gumbo limbo trees shade a playground and outdoor tables, where families can stop for great views or a picnic.

Take cover

Head 2 miles (4 km) northeast to the **Miami Science Museum** *(3280 S Miami Ave, Miami, 33129; 305 646 4200; miamisci.org)*, which has three separate facilities – a Wildlife Center, Planetarium, and Museum – that appeal to kids' curiosity about animals, the heavens, and scientific phenomena. The museum offers a daily schedule of demonstrations and shows.

View of Biscayne Bay from the boardwalk in Peacock Park

⑤ Fairchild Tropical Garden

Butterflies, cactuses, and mango mania

At the start of the 20th century, Dr. David Fairchild began a 37-year quest to collect plant specimens from all over the world. The collection continues to grow, and is now one of the most respected of its kind in the world. Brilliant blossoms scent the lakeside botanical gardens, known for their orchids, mangoes, palm trees, and other tropical flora. The gardens include the only outdoor tropical rain forest plantings in the US. Children will enjoy the colorful butterfly garden, the cactus collection, and the edible garden. The gardens also showcase exhibits by noted artists, offer birding opportunities, and organize family programs such as afternoon teas.

The Lowdown

🌐 **Address** 10901 Old Cutler Rd, Miami, 33156; 305 667 1651; www.fairchildgarden.org

🚌 **Bus** Route 136 (weekdays only).
🚗 **Car** From Coral Gables follow LeJeune Rd to Old Cutler Rd

🕐 **Open** 9:30am–4:30pm daily

💲 **Price** $74–84; under 6s free

👪 **Cutting the line** Check the events calendar online to avoid parking and admission lines when the gardens host art events and family programs.

🚩 **Guided tours** Narrated open-air tram tours depart on the hour 10am–3pm Mon–Fri, 10am–4pm Sat–Sun

👫 **Age range** 3 plus

👫 **Activities** For identifying plants and wildlife, ask about activity sheets at the information desk.

⏱ **Allow** 2 hours

🍴 **Eat and drink** SNACKS Lakeside Café (on site) serves kids' meals, made-to-order sandwiches and salads, desserts and ice cream. FAMILY TREAT Red Fish Grill (9610 Old Cutler Rd, Miami, 33156; 305 668 8788; redfishgrill.net; dinner only), in Matheson Hammock County Park (see p52), next door to Fairchild Tropical Garden, offers a fine-dining experience by the waterside.

🎪 **Festival** The International Mango Festival features mango treats, a fruit market, mango experts, and kids' activities (mid-Jul).

Take cover
The air-conditioned **Dadeland Mall** (7535 SW 88th St, Miami, 33156; 305 665 6226; www.simon.com/mall), 3 miles (5 km) west of the garden, has toy and kids' clothing stores, and is a perfect place to chill on a hot day, or stay dry on a wet one.

⑥ Deering Estate at Cutler

Can you keep a secret?

Once hunting grounds for the Seminole Indians, and then the settlement of Cutler in the late 19th century, this site has a rich history. Today, the property holds two houses. Richmond Cottage, the older one, built in Cutler's early days, was bought in 1915 by Charles Deering, a businessman and art collector. He built a sturdy Stone House here to contain his vast art collection, which resulted from years of travel abroad. His secret Prohibition-era wine vault adds a dimension of mystery to the house. Richmond Cottage holds historic exhibits, including pictures of the devastating damage from Hurricane Andrew in 1992, from which it took the estate seven years to recover. The estate also offers guided canoeing and biking tours, storytelling, and a tour of its Artist Village; check website for timings.

Letting off steam
The estate's extensive grounds provide plenty of space to run around and explore nature.

A white tiger in front of a mock Khmer temple, Zoo Miami

Elegant Richmond Cottage on the Deering Estate at Cutler

The Lowdown

🌐 **Address** 16701 SW 72nd Ave, Miami, 33157; 305 235 1668 (ext. 233); www.deeringestate.org

🚗 **Car** Rent a car from Coral Gables.

🕐 **Open** 10am–5pm daily

💲 **Price** $38–48; under 4s free

👪 **Cutting the line** Avoid visiting when school or other groups might be touring.

🚩 **Guided tours** Guides tour the homes 10:30am & 3:30pm daily.

👫 **Age range** 6 plus

👫 **Activities** Special canoe tours for kids 9 plus and other kids' events.

⏱ **Allow** 1–2 hours

🍴 **Eat and drink** PICNIC Panera Bread (13617 S Dixie Hwy, Miami, 33176; www.panerabread.com) stocks baked goodies for a picnic in the estate's grounds. SNACKS Offerdahl's Café Grill (14685 S Dixie Hwy, Miami, 33176; www. offerdahls.com) offers family meals, and half-portions for kids.

⑦ Zoo Miami

Into the ToadStool

Formerly known as Miami MetroZoo, Zoo Miami has lots of open space and natural barriers instead of cages and fences. Beside the joy of seeing and even petting animals from around the world, kids can enjoy special attractions designed specifically for them. In the Children's Zoo, they can ride a camel, feed giraffes and parrots, wonder at the Butterfly Garden, ride a carousel depicting 30 endangered animals, or chill out in the air-conditioned ToadStool, where small animals live. The zoo also has a state-of-the-art playground with water features.

The Lowdown

🌐 **Address** 12400 SW 152nd St, Miami, 33177; 305 251 0400; www.miamimetrozoo.com

🚆 **Train** Metrorail to Dadeland South, then bus 252

🕙 **Open** 9:30am–5:30pm daily

💲 **Price** $56–66; under 2s free

👥 **Cutting the line** The zoo is busiest on weekends.

🚩 **Guided tours** Various tours and programs including guided tram or walking tours and an elevated air-conditioned monorail tour

👫 **Age range** 2 plus

🦒 **Activities** Family-friendly activities include a giraffe feeding station and wild animal encounters.

⏱ **Allow** 2–3 hours

🍴 **Eat and drink** PICNIC The Pink Flamingo (on site) serves nachos, hot dogs, and ice cream. The zoo has picnic tables. SNACKS Carousel Café (on site) has burgers, pizza, sandwiches, and chicken tenders.

Take cover

A short walk southwest of the zoo is the **Gold Coast Railroad Museum** (www.gcrm.org), which entertains families with train rides on weekends, a Thomas play table, and a collection of vintage railroad cars including the presidential *Ferdinand Magellan*.

⑧ Coral Castle

Thousands of pounds of stone and a 100-pound weakling

Latvian immigrant Edward Leedskalnin may have suffered a broken heart, but that did not stop him from creating an engineering feat. In fact, unrequited love is what motivated him. This 100-lb (45-kg) man built a castle out of local coral

rock as a monument to his lost love, and the three children he fantasized. A National Register of Historic Places site, its highlights include a Polaris telescope for spotting the North Star, a 5,000-lb (2,268-kg) heart-shaped table featured in *Ripley's Believe It or Not!*, the "Grotto of the Three Bears" playground, and a working sundial.

Letting off steam

In Homestead's historic agricultural district, known as Redland, **Fruit & Spice Park** (www.fruitandspicepark. org) offers a see-hear-taste tour that takes in the park's 70-plus varieties of banana and avocado, and 160 types of mango, plus gardens representing Asia and other warm climes.

The Lowdown

🌐 **Address** 28655 S Dixie Hwy, Homestead, 33031; 305 248 6345; www.coralcastle.com

🚆 **Train** Metrorail to Dadeland South, then bus 34 or 35

ℹ️ **Visitor information** Tropical Everglades Visitor Center, 160 US 1, Florida City, 33034; 305 245 9180; www.tropical everglades.com

🕙 **Open** 8am–6pm Sun–Thu (till 8pm Fri–Sat)

💲 **Price** $44–60; under 6s free

👫 **Age range** 4 plus

⏱ **Allow** 1 hour

🍴 **Eat and drink** PICNIC Rosita's Restaurante (199 W Palm Dr, Florida City, 33034; 305 245 8652) offers authentic Mexican food to pack and take to the Homestead Bayfront Park nearby. SNACKS Mango Café (24801 SW 187th Ave, 33031; 305 247 5727), in Fruit & Spice Park, uses the park's produce to complement its sandwiches, pizzas, and salads.

Outer walls of the unique Coral Castle, Homestead

Downtown, Little Havana, Vizcaya, and around

Although prettiest at night, when its city lights reflect on the bay, downtown Miami exudes aesthetic appeal in the daytime too. Dotted with skyscrapers, the district is also home to numerous charming old-fashioned buildings. Families will enjoy exploring the beautiful gardens at Vizcaya to the south of downtown. Across the bay, Key Biscayne offers beachy bliss to visitors who want to escape the bustle of the Cuban neighborhood of Little Havana.

Ligers – a lion/tiger cross – lounging in Jungle Island, an interactive zoo

Places of interest

SIGHTS
1. Vizcaya Museum and Gardens
2. Calle Ocho – Little Havana
3. Miami Art Museum
4. Miami Children's Museum
5. Jungle Island
6. Miami Seaquarium®
7. Virginia Key Beach Park
8. Crandon Park
9. Bill Baggs Cape Florida State Park

● **EAT AND DRINK**
1. Cacique's Corner Restaurant
2. Vizcaya Café
3. Seasons 52
4. Tradewinds Waterfront Bar & Grill
5. Tinta y Café
6. Versailles Restaurant & Bakery
7. La Sandwicherie Brickell
8. Rigatti's Café
9. The Food Court
10. Jerry's Famous Deli
11. Lakeside Café
12. Tap Tap Haitian Restaurant
13. Dolphin Lobby
14. Donut Gallery Diner
15. Winn-Dixie
16. The Rusty Pelican
17. La Nouvelle Boulangerie
18. Cantina Beach
19. Lighthouse Café
20. Boater's Grill

● **SHOPPING**
1. Miracle Mile
2. CocoWalk
3. Bayside Marketplace

● **WHERE TO STAY**
1. Mandarin Oriental
2. The Ritz-Carlton Key Biscayne
3. Silver Sands Beach Resort
4. Doral Golf Resort and Spa Marriott

Sculpture on the facade of an ice cream shop across Domino Park, Calle Ocho

Miami

Miami Beach *p66*

Coral Gables and Coconut Grove *p50*

Downtown, Little Havana and Vizcaya

VENETIAN ISLAND

VENETIAN CAUSEWAY

DADE BLVD

COLLINS PARK

5 Jungle Island
4
11

Miami Children's Museum

MACARTHUR

PALM ISLAND

STAR ISLAND

FLAMINGO PARK

LUMMUS PARK

History Miami
3 Miami Art Museum
9
8

PORT BOULEVARD

CAUSEWAY

12
MIAMI BEACH
5TH ST

BAYFRONT PARK

DODGE ISLAND

Miami Beach Marina

PIER PARK

CLAUGHTON ISLAND

SOUTH POINTE PARK

7
Brickell
1

SIMPSON PARK

FISHER ISLAND

RICKEL

RICKENBACKER

16

CAUSEWAY (TOLL)

ARTHUR LAMB JR RD

Hobie Beach

Miami Seaquarium® **6**
13

7 Virginia Key Beach Park

Biscayne Bay

Atlantic Ocean

0 km 1
0 mile 1

CRANDON PARK GOLF COURSE

CRANDON BOULEVARD

Marjory Stoneman Douglas Biscayne Nature Center

Crandon Park Tennis Center

8 Crandon Park

CRANDON DRIVE

HARBOR DRIVE

14 Toy Town
17
3

i
15
18
2

KEY BISCAYNE

CRANDON BLVD

20

Bill Baggs Cape Florida State Park **9**
19

Lighthouse Keeper's Cottage

The Lowdown

🚗 **Getting around** Traffic in the downtown area is not only confusing but also frustrating during rush hour. The elevated Metromover and Metrobus (*www.miamidade.gov/transit*) vehicles make it easier to get around these parts of town.

ℹ️ **Visitor information** Greater Miami Chamber of Commerce, 1601 Biscayne Blvd, 33132; *www.miamichamber.com*. Greater Miami Convention and Visitors Bureau, 701 Brickell Ave, Ste 2700, Key Biscayne, 33131; 305 539 3094, 800 933 8448

🛒 **Supermarkets** Publix at Miami River, 311 SW 7th St, 33130; 305 860 9477. Publix at Mary Brickell village, 911 SW 1st Ave, 33130; 305 358 1575. Publix at Brickell Village, 1345 SW 13th St, 33130; 305 860 2280. Check *www.publix.com*. **Markets** El Palacio De Los Jugos, 5721 W Flagler St, 33144; 305 264 4557

🎪 **Festivals** Miami International Regatta, *www.miami internationalregatta.com* (Mar). International Hispanic Theatre Festival, *www. teatroavante.com* (Jul)

➕ **Pharmacy** Walgreens, 1 SE Third Ave, 33131; 305 373 4320; *www.walgreens.com*; open 24 hours daily

👟 **Nearest playgrounds** Bayfront Park, 301 N Biscayne Blvd, 33132; open 24 hours (see p62). Bill Baggs Cape Florida State Park, 1200 S Crandon Blvd, 33149; 8am–sunset daily (see p65). Crandon Park, 4000 Crandon Blvd, 33149; sunrise–sunset daily (see p64). Virginia Key Beach Park, 4020 Virginia Beach Dr, 33149; sunrise–sunset daily (see p64)

① Vizcaya Museum and Gardens
Sea horses and frogs in an architectural gem

Miami's iconic sight on Biscayne Bay, the palatial Vizcaya is a monument to early 20th-century opulence and one man's admiration for all things European. Millionaire industrialist James Deering commissioned the 30-plus-room mansion to be built in the style of an Italian palazzo, and filled it with fine furnishings and art. For families, the greatest interest lies outdoors, on the waterfront and in the gardens, where carved dragons, mermaids, and frogs spitting water into basins await.

Carved light fixture

Key Features

Courtyard A glass dome was added in the 1980s to protect the museum's art collection. The leaded glass doors offer views of the bay and gardens.

Entrance

Dining Room This sumptuous room was used mainly for entertaining. Its ornate ceiling is decorated with carved motifs of snakes and sea horses.

East Terrace An outdoor paved space overlooking the bay and a barge built to buffer the shoreline from waves. The barge is decorated with mermaids and dolphins.

Deering Suite The master bedroom overlooks the bay. In the bathroom, the gold-plated swan-shaped faucets dispensed both fresh and salt water.

Swimming Pool The pool, complete with a diving platform, is partially covered. The doors at the back of the pool lead to a bowling alley and billiard room.

Maze Garden South of the East Terrace are the Secret Garden, the Theater Garden, and the Maze Garden, a favourite with families because of its circular maze.

Garden Mound and Casino Steps lead to the elevated mound, with its gazebo-like house or "Casino." The ceiling has paintings of angels and minstrels that seem to look down on visitors.

The Lowdown

🌐 **Map reference** 13 D6
Address 3251 S Miami Ave, 33129; 305 250 9133; www.vizcayamuseum.org

🚗 **Metro** Metrorail to Vizcaya station. **Bus** Metrobus 48

🕐 **Open** 9:30am–4:30pm daily, closed Tue, Thanksgiving Day & Dec 25. Gardens: till 5:30pm

💲 **Price** $42–52; under 6s free

👥 **Cutting the line** Arrive early to explore the site by audio tour or to join a guided tour.

👆 **Guided tours** Vizcaya runs guided tours in English at 11:30am, 12:30pm, 1:30pm & 2:30pm Wed–Mon and in Spanish at 2pm Fri, 2 & 3pm Sat–Sun. Self-guided audio tours are available in five languages, but sell out quickly when the museum is crowded.

👫 **Age range** 6 plus; not suitable for younger kids as the interior of the house is strictly hands-off.

👫 **Activities** Special maps and guide sheets are available for young visitors.

⏱ **Allow** 1–2 hours

♿ **Wheelchair access** Yes

☕ **Café** Vizcaya Café (see p61)

🛍 **Shop** Vizcaya Shop (see p61)

🚻 **Restrooms** Near Vizcaya Café and Vizcaya Shop, south of the house entrance, and southwest of the gardens

Good family value?
Reasonable prices and impressive gardens and mansion interiors make this great value for money.

Prices given are for a family of four

CocoWalk, an open-air shopping mall in nearby Coconut Grove

Letting off steam

Hit **Bayside Marketplace** *(401 Biscayne Blvd, 33132; 305 577 3344; www.baysidemarketplace.com)* for a half-day or so of shopping and dining, catch a boat excursion, or rent jet skis. Some of the shops here specialize in kids' toys and clothing.

Eat and drink

Picnic: under $25; Snacks: $25–50; Real meal: $50–80; Family treat: over $80 (based on a family of four)

PICNIC Cacique's Corner Restaurant *(100 W Flagler St, 33130; 305 371 8317)* is one of a number of downtown eateries selling quick Cuban take-out items that can be enjoyed on the waterfront at Bayside Park.

SNACKS Vizcaya Café *(ground floor, north wing of Vizcaya; 305 856 8189)* serves sandwiches, burgers, and snacks. Seating is indoors in a library setting and outdoors near the pool. Kids' meals come with French fries and applesauce. Top them off with a dark-chocolate-dipped Key lime popsicle.

REAL MEAL Seasons 52 *(321 Miracle Mile, Coral Gables, 33134; 305 442 8552; www.seasons 52.com)* is part of a small, Florida-born chain, with a healthy menu that is great for families concerned about their eating habits. Everything is fresh, seasonal, and under 475 calories.

FAMILY TREAT Tradewinds Waterfront Bar & Grill *(401 Biscayne Blvd; 305 416 6944; www.tradewindsbarandgrill.com; open 9am until late)* offers pierside dining. There are inexpensive lunch specials, plus seafood, ribs, steaks, and hot fudge sundaes.

Shopping

The **Vizcaya Shop**, in the museum's north wing, has a vast range of gifts, including postcards, books, and jewelry. The museum is also close to the shopping districts of **Miracle Mile** *(see p53)*, **CocoWalk** *(see p54)*, and **Bayside Marketplace**.

Footwear and other merchandise in the plush Vizcaya Shop

Find out more

DIGITAL For more information about the Vizcaya Museum and Gardens, download worksheets from the Vizcaya website, *www. vizcayamuseum.com.*

Next stop...

CHARLES DEERING ESTATE
James Deering decided to build a winter home in Miami because his father had moved there, and his half-brother, Charles, had also built a splendid home. The Charles Deering Estate *(see p56)*, 14 miles (23 km) to the south of Vizcaya, makes for a fitting family reunion of historic sites.

A game of dominoes in Domino Park, Calle Ocho

② Calle Ocho – Little Havana

Cubanos, café leche, and dominoes

Cuban refugees settled around Calle Ocho, meaning Eighth Street in Spanish, in the mid-20th century; another major influx occurred during the infamous Mariel boatlift of 1980. Today, the Cuban population constitutes a majority on the streets of Miami. Stroll along Calle Ocho to experience Cuban culture and food. Stars inset along the sidewalk

The Lowdown

🌐 **Map reference** 13 D3

🚇 **Metro** Metromover from downtown. **Bus** Metrobus 6 from downtown.

ℹ️ **Visitor information** Greater Miami Chamber of Commerce, 1601 Biscayne Blvd, 33132; 305 350 7700; www.miamichamber.com

🚩 **Guided tours** LittleHavanaGuide (littlehavanaguide.com) offers themed guided tours on the arts, music, and local secrets.

🚻 **Age range** 6 plus

⏱️ **Allow** A day

🍽️ **Eat and drink** SNACKS Tinta y Café (268 SW 8th St, 33130; 305 285 0101), a typical Cuban café, offers sandwiches in full and half portions. Do try the guanabana or mango juice. REAL MEAL Versailles Restaurant & Bakery (3555 SW 8th St, 33135; www.versaillesrestaurant.com) serves soups, salads, and omelets.

🎭 **Festival** Carnaval Miami celebrates Latino culture (Feb or Mar)

remember Latino celebrities such as baseball player Sammy Sosa and singer Celia Cruz. Windows open onto restaurants and bakeries where locals order Cuban sandwiches and papaya shakes. Cigar-makers roll fragrant leaves and stores sell pleated guayabera shirts and tables made for slapping dominoes. In Domino Park, the games go on all day and well into the night.

Take cover

To get an overview of downtown Miami, board the **Metromover** (www.miamidade.gov/transit), an automated, elevated transportation system that goes round in a 2-mile (4-km) loop. The ride is fun and free, and the closest boarding station is at 59 SE 8th Street.

③ Miami Art Museum

A palette of cultures

Located next door to HistoryMiami (see p63) in Cultural Plaza, the Miami Art Museum (MAM) has permanent collections that display the art of the Americas, Europe, and Africa in the 20th and 21st centuries. Both kids and adults will find interaction and learning opportunities upstairs in the Visitors' Gallery. MAM is scheduled to move to the new bayside Museum Park, now known as Bicentennial Park, in fall 2013.

Letting off steam

The lush and lovely **Bayfront Park** (301 N Biscayne Blvd, 33132; 305 358 7550; www.bayfrontpark miami.com) may have one of the coolest playgrounds ever. It features a pirate ship, trampolines, and a play sculpture depicting a life-size wave with a dolphin, a sea turtle, and a manatee surfing it.

The Lowdown

🌐 **Map reference** 14 F1
Address 101 W Flagler St, 33130; 305 375 3000; www.miamiartmuseum.org

🚌 **Bus** Metromover and Metrobus route 103/C are best for getting around downtown.

ℹ️ **Visitor information** Greater Miami Chamber of Commerce, 1601 Biscayne Blvd, 33132; 305 350 7700; www.miamichamber.com

🕐 **Open** 10am–5pm Tue–Fri & noon–5pm Sat–Sun

💲 **Price** $24–34; under 11s free (free on second Sat each month)

🚩 **Guided tours** Private tours by appointment on second Sat each month; check website for details.

🚻 **Age range** 5 plus

🎨 **Activities** Special hands-on art activities and guided tours on second Sat each month

⏱️ **Allow** 1–2 hours

♿ **Wheelchair access** Yes

🍽️ **Eat and drink** SNACKS La Sandwicherie Brickell (34 W 8th St, 33130; www.lasandwicherie. com) offers French-style sandwiches, juices, and tasty smoothies. REAL MEAL Rigatti's Café (100 S Miami Ave, 33130; 305 377 1672) is an Italian restaurant that serves pasta, soups, salads, and sandwiches.

🎭 **Festival** MAM Family Festival, art activities and themed games (Apr)

④ Miami Children's Museum

Kids playing grown-up

This museum immerses families in the worlds of finance, business, health, art, and Miami's tropical beat. Become a rock star in the music recording studio, dress up as a policeman and hop on a motorcycle, operate an ATM machine, and cook in a Miccosukee Indian chickee (hut). Try to limbo

Kids playing with the giant Pink Snail outside Miami Children's Museum

dance aboard a cruise ship, then head to the Everglades Park to see where alligators live. Do not miss the Castle of Dreams exhibit – possibly the biggest and most enchanting sand castle ever built. Children can climb into it, slide out of it, and feel the texture of sand from around the world.

Letting off steam

Kids can play in the **Kaboom! Peace Playground** (on site) and enjoy a picnic at the tables on the plaza.

The Dr. Wasabi's Wild Adventures show featuring an alpaca, Jungle Island

⑤ Jungle Island

Parrots and monkeys and a liger? Oh, my!

Begun as a parrot attraction in Coral Gables in 1936, Jungle Island has grown over the years, and now houses animals native to Florida and from around the world. Parrots and macaws remain a major focus, and families can feed and have their pictures taken with the brightly plumaged birds. There is also a lorikeet house, a petting farm, wallabies, penguins, kangaroos, and a liger – a cross between a lion and a tiger. The park hosts shows and keeper talks throughout the day.

Take cover

At **HistoryMiami** (101 W Flagler St, 33130; 305 375 1492; www.history miami.org), engaging vignettes and exhibits tell the story of south Florida – from the arrival of mammoths and bison to the immigration of people from the Bahamas, Cuba, and other countries. The museum also offers walking, boat, and coach tours of downtown and other area sights.

The Lowdown

- 🌐 **Map reference** 15 A3
- **Address** 980 MacArthur Causeway, 33132; 305 373 5437; www.miamichildrensmuseum.org
- 🚌 **Bus** Metrobus 113/M or 119/S from downtown
- ℹ️ **Visitor information** Greater Miami Convention and Visitors Bureau, 701 Brickell Ave, Ste 2700, 33131; 305 539 3094
- 🕐 **Open** 10am–6pm daily
- 💲 **Price** $60–70 (free 3–9pm third Fri each month); under 1s free
- 👪 **Cutting the line** Call ahead to check if schools or groups will be visiting.
- 👫 **Age range** 2 plus
- ✏️ **Activities** Download kids' activity sheets from the website.
- ⏱️ **Allow** 2 hours
- ☕ **Eat and drink** PICNIC The Food Court (401 Biscayne Blvd, 33132; 305 577 3344; www.bayside marketplace.com) has lots of take-out food counters. Take the picnic to the adjacent Bayfront Park. REAL MEAL Jerry's Famous Deli (1450 Collins Ave, 33139; 305 532 8030; www.jerrysdeli. com) offers pizza, Jewish specialties, and a kids' menu.

The Lowdown

- 🌐 **Map reference** 15 A3
- **Address** 111 Parrot Jungle Trail, 33132; 305 400 7000; www.jungleisland.com
- 🚌 **Bus** Metrobus 113/M or 119/S from downtown
- ℹ️ **Visitor information** Greater Miami Convention and Visitors Bureau, 701 Brickell Ave, Ste 2700, 33131; 305 539 3094; www.miamiand beaches.com
- 🕐 **Open** 10am–5pm Mon–Fri & 10am–6pm Sat–Sun
- 💲 **Price** $112–132; under 3s free
- 👪 **Cutting the line** Book tickets online and save $2 per ticket.

- 🎏 **Guided tours** The park offers special tours, including Jungle Encounter, Lemur Experience, VIP Safari tours, and guided audio tours in English and Spanish.
- 👫 **Age range** 2 plus
- ⏱️ **Allow** 2 hours
- ☕ **Eat and drink** SNACKS Lakeside Café (on site) offers pizza, wraps, and burgers. REAL MEAL Tap Tap Haitian Restaurant (819 Fifth St, 33139; 305 672 2898; www. taptaprestaurant.com) serves West Indian-inspired cuisine.

Picnic under $25; **Snacks** $25–50; **Real meal** $50–80; **Family treat** over $80 (based on a family of four)

⑥ Miami Seaquarium®

Huge water-critters for little squirts

The world's longest-operating aquarium, the Miami Seaquarium® is the place where episodes of the

Killer whales performing at the Miami Seaquarium®

1960s TV show *Flipper* were filmed. Dolphins – along with killer whales, sea lions, and manatees – are still the star attractions here. The aquarium also houses sea turtles, crocodiles, stingrays, and sharks. See them in the exhibits that re-create their habitats and during the 10–20-minute shows and feedings. Special programs such as Dolphin Encounter and feeding sea lions bring kids up close to the animals. An elevated ropes course, a playground, fish aquariums, and remote-controlled boats, and trucks provide further entertainment.

Letting off steam

Kick up sand on **Hobie Beach** *(Rickenbacker Causeway, 33149; 305 361 2833)* – also known as Windsurfer Beach because of its relatively dependable winds. The beach is good for fishing, taking in the views, running off excess energy, or simply relaxing on the sand. There is also free beachside parking.

⑦ Virginia Key Beach Park

A park with a history

This beach park was developed in the 1940s, before desegregation and before it was accessible by car, as a "Blacks-Only" beach. Some of the old structures, such as the covered Dance Floor, can still be seen at the main entrance, where there are also picnic areas, a playground, and a soccer field. The western entrance has more of a family feel, with thatch *chickee* umbrellas and another playground.

Like all of the Virginia Key–Key Biscayne area, the park is extremely popular with cyclists.

Take cover

Drop in at **Toy Town** *(260 Crandon Blvd 43, 33149; 305 361 5501; www. toytownonline.com)* for a shopping break. The store stocks educational and other toys and baby equipment. It also has a teen fashion section.

⑧ Crandon Park

Fun for all the family

Most tennis fans will probably recognize Crandon Park as the host of the Sony Ericsson Open, an annual tennis tournament. This expansive park takes up a third of Key Biscayne and offers an 18-hole golf course, a marina, cycle paths, a carousel and amusement area, a playground, 3 miles (5 km) of gorgeous beach, a garden, nature trails, a nature preserve, and a nature center. It also hosts a number of recreational and environmental programs.

Touch tank at the Marjory Stoneman Douglas Biscayne Nature Center

The Lowdown

- 🌐 **Address** 4400 Rickenbacker Causeway, 33149; 305 361 5705; www.miamiseaquarium.com
- 🚗 **Car** Route 102/B from downtown. Bridge toll $1.50 round-trip
- ℹ️ **Visitor information** Key Biscayne Chamber of Commerce and Visitor Center, 88 W. McIntyre St Ste. 100, 33149; 305 361 5207; www.keybiscaynechamber.org
- 🕐 **Open** 9:30am–6pm daily
- 💲 **Price** $140–160; under 2s free ($8 parking)
- 👫 **Cutting the line** Order tickets online and save $2 per ticket.
- 🚩 **Guided tours** Sea Trek Reef Encounter lets visitors walk through an underwater tropical reef, wearing a special breathing helmet, while the staff feeds the fish.
- 👫 **Age range** 2 plus
- ⏱️ **Allow** 4 hours
- 🍴 **Eat and drink** SNACKS Dolphin Lobby *(on site)* sells hot dogs, soft pretzels, nachos, and ice cream. REAL MEAL Donut Gallery Diner *(83 Harbor Dr, 33149; 305 361 9985; www.donutgallery diner.com)* serves breakfast, and sandwiches and entrées for lunch, as well as a good selection of salads, but no donuts.
- 🎡 **Festival** Bunny Palooza has Easter egg hunts and rides (Mar–Apr)

The Lowdown

- 🌐 **Address** 4020 Virginia Beach Dr, 33149; 305 960 4600; www.virginia keybeachpark.net
- 🚗 **Car** Route 102/B from downtown Miami. Bridge toll $1.50 round-trip
- ℹ️ **Visitor information** Key Biscayne Chamber of Commerce and Visitor Center, 88 W. McIntyre St Ste. 100, 33149; 305 361 5207; www.keybiscaynechamber.org
- 🕐 **Open** Sunrise–sunset daily
- 💲 **Price** $5 per vehicle
- 👫 **Age range** All ages
- ⏱️ **Allow** Half a day

- 🍴 **Eat and drink** PICNIC Winn-Dixie *(604 Crandon Blvd, Key Biscayne, 33149; 305 361 8261; www.winn dixie.com)* has a deli and bakery. Pick up readymade sandwiches and dessert for a beach picnic. FAMILY TREAT The Rusty Pelican *(3201 Rickenbacker Causeway, 33149; 305 361 3818; www.the rustypelican.com)* gives diners a choice of sushi, small plates, sandwiches, and grilled seafood and steaks, along with views of Biscayne Bay.

The Lowdown

- 🌐 **Address** 6747 Crandon Blvd, 33149; 305 361 5421; *www.miami-dade.gov/parks*
- 🚗 **Car** Route 102/B from downtown Miami. Bridge toll $1.50 round-trip
- ℹ️ **Visitor information** Key Biscayne Chamber of Commerce and Visitor Center, 88 W. McIntyre St Ste. 100, 33149; 305 361 5207; *www.keybiscaynechamber.org*
- 🕐 **Open** 8am–5pm daily
- 💲 **Price** $5–6 per vehicle; no parking fees at nature center
- 👫 **Cutting the line** Arrive early, especially on weekends. Avoid visiting during the Sony Ericsson Open in March.
- 🌿 **Guided tours** Eco Adventures (*www.miamiecoadventures.org*) leads biking, canoeing, and kayak-snorkeling tours.
- 👫 **Age range** All ages
- 🧍 **Activities** The nature center hosts various programs. Check website for details & its "Kids Only" page.
- ⏱️ **Allow** Half a day to a full day
- 🍽️ **Eat and drink** PICNIC La Nouvelle Boulangerie (*328 Crandon Blvd, 33149; 305 365 5260*) offers fresh pastries and sandwiches for a picnic in Crandon Park. FAMILY TREAT Cantina Beach (*455 Grand Bay Dr, 33149; 305 365 4500; www.ritzcarlton.com/keybiscayne*), in The Ritz-Carlton Key Biscayne, has Mexican and American choices, plus fruit smoothies, on its kids' menu.

Take cover

Named for the hero who helped save the Everglades, the **Marjory Stoneman Douglas Biscayne Nature Center** (*www.biscaynenaturecenter.org*) occupies Crandon Park's north end. It displays exhibits that introduce the park's ecology along its trails. Kids will enjoy the touch tank and shell exhibit.

⑨ Bill Baggs Cape Florida State Park

Come one, come all

Often listed among America's top beaches, the park's beach remains relatively uncrowded because of the causeway toll and park entrance fee. There is plenty to do here: renting bikes and kayaks, eating at the two restaurants, hiking the nature trail, running around in the playground, and climbing the 109 steps to the

top of its Cape Florida Lighthouse, which was built in 1825. The park has been designated part of the National Underground Railway Network to Freedom due to its role in helping slaves escape to the Bahamas.

Take cover

Explore the little brick **Lighthouse Keeper's Cottage** nearby. There are exhibits on the life of the keeper's family, period-furnished rooms, and kids' toys from the past. An orientation video is screened in the old cookhouse.

Inside the Cape Florida Lighthouse, Bill Baggs Cape Florida State Park

The Lowdown

- 🌐 **Address** 1200 S Crandon Blvd, 33149; 305 361 5811; *www.floridastateparks.org/capeflorida*
- 🚗 **Car** Route 102/B from downtown. Bridge toll $1.50 round-trip.
- ℹ️ **Visitor information** Key Biscayne Chamber of Commerce and Visitor Center, 88 W. McIntyre St Ste. 100, 33149; 305 361 5207; *www.keybiscaynechamber.org*
- 🕐 **Open** Park: 8am–sunset daily. Lighthouse grounds: 9am–5pm Thu–Mon.
- 💲 **Price** $8 per vehicle
- 👫 **Cutting the line** Arrive early on weekends and during the winter and spring seasons.
- 🌿 **Guided tours** There are guided tours of the lighthouse Thu–Mon.
- 👫 **Age range** All ages
- ⏱️ **Allow** Half a day
- 🍽️ **Eat and drink** REAL MEAL Lighthouse Café (*on site; www.lighthouserestaurants.com*) offers breakfast dishes, sandwiches, and Cuban entrées. FAMILY TREAT Boater's Grill (*on site; 305 361 0080*) serves burgers, pasta, and fancy seafood dinners.

Miami Beach and around

A long barrier island, Miami Beach stretches from hip South Beach to high-rise communities at the north end. Locals refer to the central part of the island as Middle Beach. Visitors will find a contrast to the mainland's big-city vibe in the wide white sands that carpet Miami Beach's waterfront. Still, the various island communities offer plenty of shopping and dining options that have all the sophistication of the mainland. Haulover Park in North Miami Beach offers a wide variety of watersports. Lummus Park, located in bustling South Beach, is also a popular destination, while to its south, South Pointe Park, with an ocean-themed playground, is quieter.

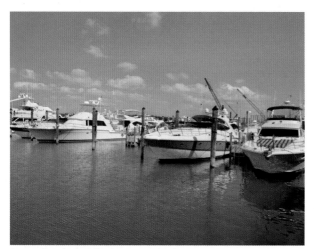

Boats anchored at the Bill Bird Marina in Bal Harbour

Places of interest

SIGHTS
1. South Beach
2. Middle Beach, Bal Harbour, North Miami Beach
3. Enchanted Forest Elaine Gordon Park
4. Oleta River State Park
5. Ancient Spanish Monastery

EAT AND DRINK
1. T-Mex Tacos
2. La Sandwicherie
3. Big Pink
4. Joe's Stone Crab
5. Café Vert

6. Timó Restaurant & Bar
7. Bulldog Barbecue
8. Flanigan's Seafood Bar and Grill
9. Blue Marlin Fish House
10. Carpaccio at Bal Harbour Shops
11. Aventura Latin Café Express
12. Kitchen 305

SHOPPING
1. Alvin's Island

WHERE TO STAY
1. Acqualina Resort & Spa on the Beach
2. Beacon Hotel

3. Century Hotel
4. Eden Roc Renaissance Miami Beach
5. Fontainebleau Miami Beach
6. Miami Beach Resort & Spa
7. Nassau Suite Hotel
8. Newport Beachside Hotel & Resort
9. Oleta River State Park
10. Sea View Hotel
11. Trump International Beach Resort
12. Shula's Hotel and Golf Course

Daniyyel by Boaz Vaadia in the Bass Museum, South Beach

Pelican Harbor Marina
5 miles (8 km)
LAKEVIEW DRIVE
COLLINS AVENUE
INDIAN BEACH PARK
W 47TH ST
W 48TH ST
N BAY ROAD
ALTON ROAD
PINE TREE DRIVE
ALTON ROAD
NAUTILUS DRIVE
JEFFERSON AVENUE
MICHIGAN AVENUE
ADAMS AVE
MERIDIAN
N CHASE AVE
W 45TH ST
W 44TH ST
MIDDLE BEACH 2
W 42ND ST
ARTHUR GODFREY ROAD
W 40TH ST
CHASE AVENUE
PINE TREE DRIVE
COLLINS AVENUE
W 37TH ST
W 34TH ST
INDIAN CREEK
COLLINS
PINE TREE DRIVE
W 31ST STREET
W 30TH ST
W 29TH ST
W 28TH ST
PINE TREE DRIVE
BAYSHORE MUNICIPAL GOLF COURSE
Lake Pancoast
MIAMI BEACH GOLF CLUB
MERIDIAN AVE
PRAIRIE AVE
NORTH
BOULEVARD
DADE
Bass Museum of Art
21ST ST
20TH ST
19TH ST
COLLINS
AVENUE
COLLINS PARK
WASHINGTON
JAMES AVENUE
HANK MEYER BLVD
LINCOLN ROAD MALL
16TH STREET
15TH STREET
ESPANOLA WAY
MERIDIAN AVENUE
EUCLID
14TH ST
13TH ST
FLAMINGO PARK
12TH ST
COLLINS
OCEAN DRIVE
DRIVE
Atlantic Ocean
STREET
EUCLID
PENNSYLVANIA
Wolfsonian Museum
LUMMUS PARK
STREET
AVENUE
STREET
SOUTH BEACH 1
OCEAN
DRIVE
STREET
TH ST
H ST
ST
D ST
T ST
BISCAYNE ST
WASHINGTON AVE
COLLINS AVE
Jewish Museum of Florida
MARJORY STONEMAN DOUGLAS PARK
PIER PARK
JTH POINTE PARK
0 meters   800
0 yards   800

Miami Beach Day Trips
INDIAN BEACH PARK
NORTH MIAMI BEACH 2
NE 19TH AVENUE
NE 18TH AVENUE
NE 20TH AVE
W DIXIE HWY
BISCAYNE BLVD
Maule Lake
EASTERN SHORES
NE 174TH ST
SUNNY ISLES
5 Ancient Spanish Monastery
NE 163RD STREET
NE 163RD ST
COLLINS
AVENUE
Shula's Hotel and Golf Club
10 mile (16km)
SOUTHERN MEMORIAL PARK
W DIXIE HWY
BISCAYNE BLVD
NE 151ST ST
4 Oleta River State Park
HAULOVER BEACH PARK
Atlantic Ocean
16TH AVENUE
BISCAYNE
BISCAYNE NATIONAL PARK
3 Enchanted Forest Elaine Gordon Park
NE 135TH ST
KEYSTONE ISLANDS
BISCAYNE BLVD
NE 123RD ST
Museum of Contemporary Art
1 mile (1.5 km)
BROAD CAUSEWAY
96TH STREET
COLLINS AVENUE
BAL HARBOUR 2
Bal Harbour Shops
Bal Harbour Beach
HARDING AVE
COLLINS AVE
0 km   1
0 mile   1

The Lowdown

🚗 **Getting around** Traffic can get heavy along Collins Avenue and South Beach's Ocean Drive, especially at night. Miami-Dade buses (www.miamidade.gov) run the length of the beach regularly. Note that most meter stations do not accept credit cards.

ℹ️ **Visitor information** Miami Beach Chamber of Commerce, 1920 Meridian Ave, Miami Beach, 33139; 305 674 1300; www.miamibeachchamber.com

🛒 **Supermarkets** Publix on the Bay, 1920 West Ave, 33139; 305 535 4268 & Publix Super Market, 1045 Dade Blvd, 33139; 305 534 4621; www.publix.com.
Markets Lincoln Road Farmers' Market, South Beach, 33139; Sun

🎪 **Festivals** Art Deco Weekend, www.mdpl.org/events (Jan).

South Beach Wine & Food Festival, 2012.sobefest.com (Feb). Miami Beach Festival of Arts, web.miamibeachfl.gov (Apr). Art Basel, www.artbasel.com (Jun & Dec)

➕ **Pharmacy** Walgreens, 100 Lincoln Rd, 33139; 305 532 7909; open 24 hours daily

🛝 **Nearest playgrounds** Enchanted Forest Elaine Gordon Park, 1725 NE 135th St, 33167; sunrise–sunset (see p70). Indian Beach Park Tot Lot, Collins Ave and 46th St, 33140. Lummus Park, Ocean Dr at 13th St, 33139; 24 hours daily. Marjory Stoneman Douglas Park, 2901 SW 22nd Ave, 33133. South Pointe Park, 1 Washington Ave, 33109; 24 hours daily (see p68)

① South Beach
SoBe it

Boom and bust best describe the history of South Beach, nicknamed SoBe. A well-developed neighborhood before the Great Depression of the 1930s, it was later resurrected as a showcase of Art Deco architecture. In the 1980s, when developers wanted to raze decrepit buildings, activists began a campaign that turned South Beach into America's Riviera. Besides admiring its preserved Art Deco buildings, families can enjoy relaxing on sandy beaches, and great shopping.

Detail of an Art Deco building, South Beach

Key Sights

① Bass Museum of Art
② Lincoln Road
③ Española Way
④ Ocean Drive
⑤ Wolfsonian Museum
⑥ Jewish Museum of Florida
⑦ South Pointe Park

Flamingo Park
MIAMI BEACH
Lummus Park
Pier Park
Miami Beach Marina

0 meters 800
0 yards 800

② **Lincoln Road** South Beach's main shopping stretch is a pedestrian mall that contains elements of its past and present, including galleries and historic theaters.

③ **Española Way** This pretty little tree-shaded lane is lively, and lined with Spanish-style buildings housing restaurants, shops, and bars, several of them Latino.

④ **Ocean Drive** South Beach's fabled runway for aspiring models, this street extends over 15 blocks of Art Deco hotels, with cafés and bars spilling onto sidewalks.

⑤ **Wolfsonian Museum** Devoted to the decorative arts from 1885 to 1945, this museum's retro vibe fits in well with South Beach's Art Deco orientation. Displays range from sculptures to household items.

⑥ **Jewish Museum of Florida** While some museums of this nature can be overwhelming, this one focuses on the upbeat history of Jews in Florida.

⑦ **South Pointe Park** Families looking for a break from the bustle of South Beach can relax at this park while watching cruise ships sail by. There is a playground for kids.

① **Bass Museum of Art** Although it mainly hosts temporary exhibitions of modern art, the museum also has a permanent collection of ancient Egyptian artifacts – including mummies and sarcophagi – that will fascinate kids.

The Lowdown

🌐 **Map reference** 16 G4
Address Bass Museum of Art: 2100 Collins Ave, 33139; 305 673 7530; www.bassmuseum. org. Wolfsonian Museum: 1001 Washington Ave, 33139; 305 531 1001; www.wolfsonian.org. Jewish Museum of Florida: 301 Washington Ave, 33139; 305 672 5044; www.jewishmuseum.com. South Pointe Park: 1 Washington Ave, 33139; 305 673 7006; www.miamibeachfl.gov

🚌 **Bus** Miami-Dade buses to South Beach and bus 123 within the city

🕐 **Open** Bass Museum of Art: noon–5pm Wed–Sun. Wolfsonian Museum noon–6pm daily (till 9pm Fri), closed Wed. Jewish Museum of Florida: 10am–5pm Tue–Sun. South Pointe Park: sunrise–10pm

💲 **Prices** Bass Museum of Art: $28–38; under 6s free. Wolfsonian Museum: $24–34; under 6s free. Jewish Museum of Florida: $12–22; under 6s free (free on Sat)

👪 **Cutting the line** Avoid traffic around South Beach's eastern side anytime after noon.

🚩 **Guided tours** Daily Art Deco District guided walking tours (1001 Ocean Dr, 33139; 305 531 3484; www.mdpl.org) take in more than 100 historic structures in 90 mins and 20 stops. Cell phone and iPod self-guided tours are also available. Call ahead to make reservations.

👫 **Age range** 7 plus

👫 **Activities** The Bass Museum of Art hosts kids' activities on the last Sun of the month. The Jewish Museum of Florida has a scavenger hunt, and kids who

Prices given are for a family of four

Letting off steam

Head to **Lummus Park** *(5th–15th St and Ocean Dr, 33139)*, which has paved pathways for biking and walking, as well as playgrounds that will engage the little ones.

Eat and drink

Picnic: under $25; Snacks: $25–50; Real meal: $50–80; Family treat: over $80 (based on a family of four)

PICNIC T-Mex Tacos *(235 14th St, 33139; 305 538 3009; www.t-mex. net)* has the makings of a beach picnic, including tacos, nachos, and burritos. Enjoy the picnic in Lummus Park.

SNACKS La Sandwicherie *(229 14th St, 33139; 305 532 8934; www.lasandwicherie.com)* offers salads, juices, and smoothies, as well as sandwiches.

REAL MEAL Big Pink *(157 Collins Ave, 33139; 305 531 0888; www. mylesrestaurantgroup.com)* is like an old-fashioned diner, but huge,

Lunchtime at Big Pink, a family-friendly diner in South Beach

and with TVs everywhere. Families can order the day's TV dinner or food from the regular or kids' menu.

FAMILY TREAT Joe's Stone Crab *(11 Washington Ave, 33139; 305 673 0365; www.joesstonecrab.com; closed for lunch in summer)*, in business since 1913, claims to have discovered stone crab as a food source in the 1920s. The crabs, and most other seafood items, are high-priced, but the menu does contain some more affordable meals.

Moss-covered fountain in the courtyard of Joe's Stone Crab

Shopping

South Beach is all about shopping, particularly along Lincoln Road and Collins Avenue. Families can find souvenirs and beach buys at **Alvin's Island** *(200 Lincoln Rd, 33139; 305 531 9766; www.alvinsisland.com)*.

Find out more

FILM Miami appears in dozens of major movies, and South Beach stars in most of them. Disney® movies *Old Dogs* (2009) and *Snow Dogs* (2002) were filmed in this area, as was *Marley and Me* (2008).

Next stop…

AMELIA EARHART PARK Families that prefer greenery to city streets might like the Amelia Earhart Park *(401 E 65th St, 33014; 305 685 8389; www.miamidade.gov/parks/parks/amelia_earhart)*, located 14 miles (23 km) northwest of South Beach. The park's farm has cows, goats, sheep, and geese that younger children adore. Kids will also love the rope bridge that takes them to Tom Sawyer Island's playground. The park's five lakes are stocked with fish, and one is set up with a water-skiing and wakeboarding tow cable. Also on offer are lessons in wakeboarding, and wake surfing, as well as barefoot skiing.

KIDS' CORNER

Deco details

Look for typical features of Art Deco design:
1 Tropical doodads. Look for carved, painted, and plasterwork palm trees, dolphins, waves, flamingos, and sunbursts. Can you try to draw some of these on your own?
2 Neon signs. How many can you count?
3 Back to the future. Some elements of Art Deco looked futuristic at the time they were built. Can you find Space Age details? Do they look futuristic to you?

BRIGHT BRITTO

Romero Britto is one of Miami's most popular and recognizable artists. He uses a lot of vibrant colors and patterns – especially stripes and spots. Many of his colorful sculptures and paintings can be found around town, and at his gallery on Lincoln Road.

Family stories

In the Jewish Museum of Florida, 40 local Jewish families tell their stories with words, pictures, and objects. Ask your parents and grandparents questions about how your family came to live where you do. Did your family always live there? From which country did they originate? Tell your family's story with words and drawings. You may even want to design an exhibit like those at the Jewish Museum. What artifacts would you include?

complete it get a booklet with puzzles, games, and recipes.

⏱ **Allow** 1–2 days

☕ **Café** In Jewish Museum of Florida (closed for Sabbath Sat)

🚻 **Restrooms** At most attractions and restaurants, and at South Pointe Park

Good family value?
The bustle along Ocean Drive and the parks and museums in this area make boredom impossible.

② Middle Beach, Bal Harbour, North Miami Beach

Beachfront communities

North of SoBe, the pace changes a bit, as Collins Avenue passes through quieter neighborhoods. Beginning at around 23rd Street is Middle Beach, with its quaint restaurants and shops. North of Middle Beach, the cozy community of Surfside, with a charming shop-and-dine strip, starts at 87th Street. Bal Harbour, a fashionable enclave dotted with soaring hotels and a plush mall, neighbors Surfside. Further north is Sunny Isles, the last of the beachfront communities. A bridge from here crosses over to North Miami Beach, an older mainland neighborhood with a family feel and some worthwhile stops. Beaches and parks are the biggest draw to the area.

Letting off steam

Located north of Bal Harbour, **Haulover Beach Park** (10800 Collins Ave, 33128; www.miamidade.gov) contains a 1-mile (2-km) long beach with picnic tables. On the bay side, a marina complex houses boat rentals, a kite shop, and a restaurant. Part of the beach is a clothing-optional zone.

The Lowdown

🚌 **Bus** Metrobus 119/S and 120 from South Beach

ℹ **Visitor information** Miami Beach Visitor Center, 9700 Collins Ave, 33154; 305 866 0311; www.miami beachvisitorscenter.com. Sunny Isles Beach Visitor Center, 18070 Collins Ave, 33160; 305 792 1952; www.sunnyislesbeachmiami.com

👫 **Cutting the line** This area is busiest in winter and early spring, when crowds and prices increase.

👫 **Age range** All ages

⏱ **Allow** 1–2 days

☕ **Eat and drink** SNACKS Café Vert (9490 Harding Ave, Surfside, 33154; 305 867 3151; 7:30am–5pm daily, till 3pm Fri), a Jewish-French café, has salads, quiches, crêpes, and kosher dishes. FAMILY TREAT Timó Restaurant & Bar (17624 Collins Ave, Sunny Isles Beach, 33160; 305 936 1008; www.timorestaurant.com) serves pizza and seafood.

🎪 **Festival** Kite Festival (Feb)

High-end shops lining a street in Bal Harbour

③ Enchanted Forest Elaine Gordon Park

Trees with beards

This old-fashioned park is overgrown with tall, gnarled trees wearing Spanish moss beards. The trees shade lovely, spacious picnic grounds and trails that follow and cross over a gurgling creek in the middle of the city. Two playgrounds and pony-riding cinch the deal for kids.

Take cover

The nearby **Museum of Contemporary Art** (770 NE 125th St, 33161; 305 893 6211; www. mocanomi.org) houses a collection of works by emerging and well-known artists. Preschooler art and reading programs are held on the second Thursday of the month, and school-aged kids' art classes on the first Saturday of the month.

Ponies in the lush Enchanted Forest Elaine Gordon Park

The Lowdown

🌐 **Address** 1725 NE 135th St, North Miami, 33181; 305 895 1119

🚌 **Bus** Metrobus 107/G from Miami Beach

ℹ **Visitor information** The Greater North Miami Beach Chamber of Commerce, 1870 NE 171st St, 33162; 305 994 8500; www.nmbchamber.com

🕐 **Open** Sunrise–sunset daily

👫 **Age range** All ages

⏱ **Allow** 2–3 hours

☕ **Eat and drink** SNACKS Bulldog Barbecue (15400 Biscayne Blvd, 33160; 305 940 9655; www.bulldog-bbq.com) serves delicious chili cheese fries, BBQ sandwiches, and shrimp and grits. REAL MEAL Flanigan's Seafood Bar and Grill (72721 Bird Ave 33133; 305 446 1114; www.flanigans.net) is known for its fresh, home-made dishes. There is also a kids' menu.

④ Oleta River State Park

A little country in the big city

Florida's largest urban park has it all – from a cross-country bike course and a sandy beach to a fishing pier and cabins. The river and the bay afford budding fishermen the opportunity to hook both saltwater and freshwater fish. Rent a kayak, a paddleboard, or a bicycle to explore the park's trails, the river, and the bay front. Bicycling on the park's 10 miles (16 km) of challenging mountain bike trails is one of the most popular activities, but families can also ride the paved trail.

Prices given are for a family of four

The Lowdown

🌐 **Address** 3400 NE 163rd St, North Miami Beach, 33160; 305 919 1846; www.floridastateparks.org/oletariver

🚌 **Bus** Metrobus105/E and 108/H from Miami Beach

ℹ️ **Visitor information** The Greater North Miami Beach Chamber of Commerce, 1870 NE 171st St, 33162; www.nmbchamber.com

🕐 **Open** 8am–sunset daily

💲 **Price** $6 per vehicle

👥 **Cutting the line** Avoid weekends as they are the busiest days.

⏱️ **Allow** Half a day to a full day

🍽️ **Eat and drink** PICNIC Blue Marlin Fish House (2500 NE 163rd St, 33160; 305 957 8822) offers kids' entrées, pizza, and Oleta burgers. Picnic by the bay. REAL MEAL Carpaccio at Bal Harbour Shops (9700 Collins Ave 139, 33154; 305 867 7777; www.carpaccioatbalharbour.com) serves pizza, pasta, and other Italian specialties.

Take cover

Bal Harbour Shops (9700 Collins Ave, 33154; 305 866 0311; www.balharbourshops.com), an upscale shopping mall, also has shops for kids. Check out Young Versace, which even has a merry-go-round. Books & Books features weekly story times for children.

5 Ancient Spanish Monastery

A saintly puzzle

Newspaper publisher William Randolph Hearst purchased the cloisters and outbuildings of a 12th-century Spanish monastery and had them dismantled and shipped to North Miami in 1925. A few years later, the pieces were reassembled like a puzzle, a process that lasted 19 months and cost $1.5 million. The monastery is famed as the oldest building in the western hemisphere. Set amid gardens, the chapel, which serves as a parish church, has arched arcades surrounding a courtyard. Carvings, paintings, and shrines lie along the square walkway. The museum and gift shop hold an old Spanish hearse and other artifacts, and tell the story of the structure's travels from Sacramenia in Spain to Florida.

Letting off steam

Catch a water taxi from **Pelican Harbor Marina** (1275 NE 79th St, 33138; 305 754 9330; www.miamidade.gov/parks) to Pelican Island nature preserve and bird sanctuary. Only 400 yards (365 m) off-shore, the island is equipped with picnic tables, chickee, barbecue grills, and has room to roam.

Classic dining bell at the entrance to the chapel of Ancient Spanish Monastery

The Lowdown

🌐 **Address** 16711 W. Dixie Hwy, North Miami Beach, 33160; 305 945 1461; www.spanishmonastery.com

🚌 **Bus** Metrobus 108/H from Miami Beach

ℹ️ **Visitor information** The Greater North Miami Beach Chamber of Commerce, 1870 NE 171st St, 33162; www.nmbchamber.com

🕐 **Open** 10am–4pm Mon–Sat, 11am–4pm Sun

💲 **Price** $24–34; under 6s free

👥 **Cutting the line** Call ahead to avoid visiting during church services (the chapel will be closed) or when special events are taking place (the monastery may be closed).

🚩 **Guided tours** The monastery offers tours in English, Spanish, French, Italian, and German; call ahead to book.

👫 **Age range** 5 plus

⏱️ **Allow** 1 hour

🍽️ **Eat and drink** SNACKS Aventura Latin Café Express (17070 W Dixie Hwy, 33160; 305 705 2434; www.aventuralatincafeexpress.com; closed Sun) has kids' meals, as well as Cuban sandwiches and other specialties. FAMILY TREAT Kitchen 305 (16701 Collins Ave, 33160; 305 949 1300, ext. 1593; www.newportbeachside.com) serves flatbreads, seafood, and meat; it also has a kids' menu.

Where to Stay in Miami

Accommodations in Miami come in all shapes and sizes. The most iconic are the small hotels and larger resorts that occupy Miami Beach's historic Art Deco buildings, but the city is also known for its family-friendly luxury resorts, which offer kids' programs. Families will find many modest rental condos and homes.

AGENCIES
HomeAway
www.homeaway.com
This website lists nearly 1,000 short-term condo and home rentals in Greater Miami. Some can be rented only by the week.

Vacation Rentals
www.vacationrentals.com
Find apartments, penthouses, and homes in all sizes, locations, and price ranges on this website.

Airport
Map 10 H2
HOTELS
Doral Golf Resort and Spa Marriott
4400 NW 87th Ave, 33178; 305 592 2000; www.doralresort.com
This resort does not have a beach, but the Blue Monster water park on site makes up for it. Doral is most famous for its golf courses and spa. Golf and tennis lessons, as well as a daily kids' program, engage youngsters of all ages. Check out family packages on the website.
🐿 🍴 P 🅿 $$

Shula's Hotel and Golf Club
6842 Main St, Miami Lakes, 33014; 305 821 1150 or 800 24 SHULA; www.donshulahotel.com
Named for former Miami Dolphins coach Don Shula, this hotel appeals to golfers and spa-lovers, but its location – close to Sun Life Stadium, home of the Dolphins – makes it great for families. Daycare facility available.
🐿 🍴 ⛵ 🅿 $$

Bal Harbour
Map 10 H2
HOTEL
Sea View Hotel
9909 Collins Ave, 33154; 305 866 4441; seaview-hotel.com
Located in a forest of high-rises, this hotel's reasonable rates and friendly waterfront location make it popular with families. In summer,

it partners with Miami Children's Museum *(see pp62–3)* to organize beach camp programs for ages 3 to 10.
🐿 🍴 💲 🌀 $$$

Coconut Grove
HOTEL
Sonesta Bayfront Hotel Coconut Grove
Map 12 G4
2889 McFarlane Rd, 33133; 305 529 2828; www.sonesta.com
Right across the street from Peacock Park *(see p55)*, and within easy walking distance of the area's shops and restaurants, the Sonesta offers gorgeous views of the bay from its 22 floors. Among the 210 units are double rooms and one- or two-bedroom suites with full kitchens.
🐿 🍴 ⛵ 🍴 🅿 $$$

Coral Gables
HOTEL
The Biltmore Hotel
Map 11 B2
1200 Anastasia Ave, 33134; 855 311 6903; www.biltmorehotel.com
A stay at The Biltmore Hotel will make kids and grown-ups feel as if they are guests in a castle straight out of a storybook. Kids can sign up for cooking and golf, as well

as tennis classes, and also spa treatments designed especially for them or swim in the famous pool.
💲 🐿 🍴 🅿 $$$

Downtown
HOTEL
Mandarin Oriental, Miami
Map 14 G3
500 Brickell Key Dr, 33131; 305 913 8288; www.mandarinoriental.com
Though expensive, the family suites in this hotel are an excellent option; guests receive welcome cocktails and free domestic phone calls. Double-bedded rooms are less expensive. Babysitting, kids' yoga, teen spa treatments, and a private beach club are available.
🐿 🍴 ⛵ 🅿 $$$

Key Biscayne
Map 10 H3
RESORT
Silver Sands Beach Resort
301 Ocean Dr, 33149; 305 361 5441; www.silversandsbeachresort.net
With its homey charm and relatively affordable rates, this resort is great for families. Set on the beach, it has a playground, and complimentary cribs are available in its brightly

The magnificent ballroom in The Biltmore Hotel, Coral Gables

decorated rooms and cottages. While the rooms have kitchenettes, the cottages come with full kitchens.

🌊 🍴 🅿 ❷ ⚓ **$$**

HOTEL
The Ritz-Carlton Key Biscayne
455 Grand Bay Dr, 33149; 305 365 4500; www.ritzcarlton.com
The beachfront Ritz-Carlton provides a number of family-friendly amenities, such as swim diapers, toys, and bed rails. It also offers a supervised kids' program. Consider a room on the club floor to save money on snacks, meals, and beverages.

🌊 🍴 ❷ **$$$**

Middle Beach   Map 10 H2

RESORTS
Miami Beach Resort
4833 Collins Ave, 33140; 866 765 9090; www.miamibeachresortand spa.com
A good option for active families, the resort offers extensive watersports opportunities, including jet-skiing and parasailing. Rooms and suites are well equipped and family packages are available.

🌊 🍴 P ❷ ❷ **$$**

Eden Roc Renaissance Miami Beach
4525 Collins Ave, 33140; 305 531 0000 or 800 319 5354; www.edenrocmiami.com
The Camp Roc! day camp keeps kids aged 5 to 12 supervised while grown-ups take advantage of the spa, adult pool, and fine dining. Also on offer are a family infinity pool, a beach, jet-skiing, sailing, and water-skiing.

🌊 🍴 ❷ **$$$**

Fontainebleau Miami Beach
4441 Collins Ave, 33140; 305 538 2000; www.fontainebleau.com
Perhaps Miami Beach's most famous resort, the Fontainebleau is also its most family-friendly. This Art Deco gem and its two newer towers hold more than 1,500 rooms and suites, eight dining venues, a spa, several bars, and water features – all on the beachfront. The FB Kids program has day sessions and nighttime ones over the weekend.

🌊 🍴 ❷ ❷ **$$$**

North Miami Beach

CAMPING
Oleta River State Park   Map 10 H2
3400 NE 163rd St, 33160; 305 919 1846; www.floridastateparks.org
The 14 new barn-like cabins here make camping comfortable for families; most have a double bed and bunk beds. The cabins have no TV, kitchen, bathroom, or phone and guests must bring their own linen. Families will like the park's beach, trails, and watersports.

🍴 🏕 **$**

A rustic log cabin at Oleta River State Park campground

South Beach

HOTELS
Century Hotel   Map 16 G5
140 Ocean Dr, Miami Beach, 33139; 305 674 8855
This Art Deco-style hotel is tucked away from the crowds at the south end of South Beach. Some of its rooms have two double beds to lodge families. Continental breakfast is included, and the beach is nearby.

🌊 **$**

Nassau Suite Hotel   Map 16 G3
1414 Collins Ave, Miami Beach, 33139; 866 859 4177; www.nassau suite.com
Classic Art Deco, this hotel's studio and one-bedroom suites are modern and convenient for families. The movie theater on site has a collection of films for families. Continental breakfast is included in the rates. The beach is a short walk away.

🌊 🏖 🍴 **$$**

Beacon Hotel   Map 16 G4
720 Ocean Dr, Miami Beach, 33139; 305 674 8200 or 877 674 8200; www.mybeaconhotel.com
Across the street from the beach, and in the heart of the Art Deco district, this casual 1930s-built hotel

offers complimentary Continental breakfast and beach chairs. The hotel has a restaurant and room service, but is also close to the sidewalk cafés along Ocean Drive.

🌊 🍴 ❷ **$$$**

Sunny Isles   Map 10 H2

RESORTS
Newport Beachside Hotel & Resort
16701 Collins Ave, 33160; 305 949 1300 or 800 327 5476; www.new portbeachside.com
A playground on the beach, a children's pool, and chirpy caged birds in the lobby ensure families with kids of all ages are happy here. There are fold-down wall beds in half of the rooms and doors to separate sleeping spaces. Kitchen 305 serves dinner only.

🌊 🍴 ❷ ❷ **$$**

Acqualina Resort & Spa
17875 Collins Ave, 33160; 305 918 8000 or 877 312 9742; www.acqualina resort.com
Though pricey, the suites are the best option for families here, as the resort does not offer two-bed rooms. A Children's Center, movie nights, arts and crafts, and private swimming and sports lessons also make it a hit with families. Its award-winning marine biology-focused children's program is free for guests.

🌊 🍴 🏖 ❷ ❷ **$$$**

Trump International Beach Resort
18001 Collins Ave, 33160; 305 692 5612 or 866 628 1197; www.trump miami.com
This luxurious resort towers over the beach, where a grotto-style pool, watersports rentals, and cabana rentals make it even more fun. The resort's Planet Kids children's club offers exciting half- and full-day programs, featuring an "Enviro-Adventures" themed curriculum.

🌊 🍴 ❷ ❷ **$$$**

Key to symbols *see back cover flap*

The Gold and
Treasure Coasts

North of Miami, Florida's sun-drenched Atlantic shoreline is blessed with miles of fine beaches as well as parks and family-friendly attractions. The Gold Coast has a huge variety of theme parks, zoos, and museums. By contrast, the Treasure Coast, north of Palm Beach, is all about nature, with wild, unspoiled beaches and pine-covered barrier islands set in pristine waters that attract sea turtles, dolphins, and manatees.

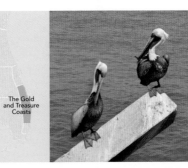

The Gold
and Treasure
Coasts

Highlights

Museum of Discovery and Science
See dinosaur fossils, visit a storm center, feel space simulations, and watch IMAX® movies at this absorbing museum *(see p80)*.

John U. Lloyd Beach State Park
Discover one of the best stretches of unspoiled sand on the Gold Coast, follow a hiking trail, or rent a kayak to explore a creek favored by manatees *(see p82)*.

Butterfly World
Admire tropical greenhouses brimming with butterflies, and then go see the colorful parrots and scary spiders *(see p86)*.

Flagler Museum
Check out the "palace on wheels," tycoon Henry Flagler's private railcar, at this fascinating museum *(see pp90–91)*.

Juno Beach: Loggerhead Marinelife Center
Watch turtle shows, take part in a turtle walk, or see how these injured amphibians are treated in the Sea Turtle Hospital *(see p93)*.

Florida Oceanographic Coastal Center
Learn all about Florida's marine life, stroke a stingray, and take a walk through the mangroves of the Indian River Lagoon *(see p97)*.

Left *Spectacular drawing room at the Flagler Museum, Palm Beach*
Above right *Migratory pelicans on a perch near the beach in Fort Pierce, Hutchinson Island*

The Best of
The Gold and Treasure Coasts

This part of Florida has something to suit every taste. Fort Lauderdale is a fun, full-scale resort, while the state parks provide opportunities for hiking and kayaking, and reserves such as Hobe Sound National Wildlife Refuge offer pristine strips of sand. Inland, there is plenty to do – wildlife parks, zoos, and marine life centers provide a window into Florida's rich natural habitats, and historic sites and art galleries dish up a slice of culture.

In a week

Start with **Fort Lauderdale** (see pp80–81), taking in a museum or two before sunbathing on the beach or enjoying a cruise on the Jungle Queen. Spend day two on the **Big Cypress Seminole Indian Reservation** (see p81), then return to **Fort Lauderdale beach** for an evening dip. Hit the road on day three, stopping at **Butterfly World** (see p86) before sampling the varied delights of **Boca Raton** (see p86). Take a trip to Japan on day four, courtesy of the **Morikami Museum and Japanese Gardens** (see p87), and end the day with a swim at **Palm Beach** (see pp88–9). Stay in town for another day to explore the **Flagler Museum** (see pp90–91), **Palm Beach Zoo** (see p92), and **Lion Country Safari** (see p92). Spend the last two days trawling the Treasure Coast, traveling via **Juno Beach** (see p93) and **Hutchinson Island** (see pp96–7) to an overnight at **Fort Pierce** (see p96), then finishing off at the seaside town of **Vero Beach** (see pp94–5).

Left Great Gravity Clock in the grand atrium of the Museum of Discovery and Science, Fort Lauderdale *Below* Galleries at the Vero Beach Museum of Art, Vero Beach *Below right* A green sea turtle on the shore at Juno Beach

Above *Families enjoying a sunny day out on the beach in J. D. MacArthur State Park, Palm Beach*

On the manatee and turtle trail

On Florida's Atlantic coast summer is turtle nesting time, and hundreds of them crawl up to the beach to lay their eggs. The best place to see them is the **Hobe Sound National Wildlife Refuge** *(see p97)*, where there are guided turtle walks through June and July. The **Florida Oceanographic Coastal Center** *(see p97)* on **Hutchinson Island** runs a sea turtle program, while the **Loggerhead Marinelife Center** *(see p93)* is a hospital for sick or injured sea turtles.

Winter is the best time to see manatees in these parts: try the **John U. Lloyd Beach State Park** *(see p82)*, or the **Manatee Observation & Education Center** in **Fort Pierce** *(see p96)*.

Art versus science

Florida's east coast is best known for its beaches, but the region also offers plenty to stimulate young minds. Bright avant-garde works and

US Impressionism reign at the **Museum of Art** *(see p80)* in **Fort Lauderdale**, while kids with an inclination for science will find heaps to explore at the nearby **Museum of Discovery and Science** *(see p80)*. Get a dose of Native American culture at the **Seminole Okalee Indian Village** in the **Seminole Indian Hard Rock Hotel and Casino** *(see p84)*. Younger ones will enjoy the **Young at Art Children's Museum** *(see p84)* in **Davie** *(see pp84–5)*, and aspiring astronomers can gaze at the stars at the nearby **Buehler Planetarium & Observatory** *(see pp84–5)*. **Boca Raton Children's Museum** *(see p86)* provides a hands-on, absorbing introduction to Florida's history. Older kids will appreciate the colorful works of US glass sculptor Dale Chihuly on display at the **Norton Museum of Art** *(see p88)* in **Palm Beach**.

The great outdoors

Nothing quite beats a day lounging or playing on the beach, but active families will find plenty to do off the sands. Tranquil **Hugh Taylor Birch State Park** *(see p82)*, just minutes from downtown **Fort Lauderdale**, offers canoeing, hiking, and biking, while the **John U. Lloyd Beach State Park** features a hammock forest hiking trail and a creek perfect for kayaking. Marvel at the exotic wildlife on show at the **Lion Country Safari**, **Palm Beach Zoo**, **Butterfly World**, or **Flamingo Gardens** *(see p85)*. Rent bikes and circle **Palm Beach** on the 3-mile (5-km) **Lake Trail** *(see p88)*, or head inland to **Jonathan Dickinson State Park** *(see p97)* near Stuart, where intrepid families can explore the pine flatwoods, mangroves, and river swamps along the Loxahatchee River.

The Gold and Treasure Coasts

Running along Florida's Atlantic seaboard, the Gold and Treasure Coasts extend for some 200 miles (322 km) from Miami to the Space Coast and the Northeast. The area is battered by tropical storms in summer, but the weather is sub-tropical, balmy, and hot most of the year. The beaches are superb. The coastline is heavily built up as far as Palm Beach, trailing off into sparsely populated barrier islands, swamp, and pine forest further north. Separated from the barrier islands and beaches by the Intracoastal Waterway, the mainland is dotted with mansions and is rich in marine and bird life. Roads are great in this region, but public transportation is limited north of West Palm Beach.

Birds in the Flamingo Gardens, Davie

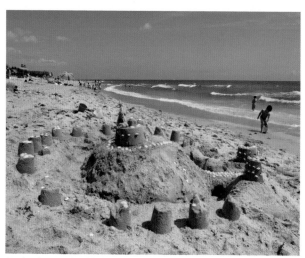
Sand castle at a wide public beach, Palm Beach

Spanish moss and lily pond in the lush McKee Botanical Gardens, Vero Beach

The Lowdown

Getting there and around
Air Flights connect almost every major city in the US with Fort Lauderdale (www.broward.org/airport). Taxis ($15–20), and the Go Airport Shuttle (www.floridalimo.com) provide shared shuttle van rides from the airport to Fort Lauderdale. Flights connect Palm Beach Airport (www.pbia.org) with all the major east coast hubs. Southeastern Florida Transportation Group (www.yellowcabflorida.com) provides taxis and shared rides. **Train** Amtrak (www.amtrak.com) connects West Palm Beach and Fort Lauderdale with Miami, Tampa, Jacksonville, Orlando, and places north along the east coast to New York. Tri-Rail (www.tri-rail.com) makes local stops between West Palm Beach and Miami. **Bus** Greyhound (www.greyhound.com) connects Fort Pierce, Fort Lauderdale, and West Palm Beach with Miami and points north. Local buses are limited. **Car** Much of the region is best explored by car. Avis (www.avis.com) and Hertz (www.hertz.com) have rental offices at airports.

Visitor information See individual entries.

Supermarkets Publix (www.publix.com) is the major supermarket chain with outlets throughout this region.

Festivals Easter Egg Hunt, Flagler Museum: kids are invited to hunt for 7,000 eggs on the museum's lawns; www.flaglermuseum.us (Mar). Mardi Gras Parade & Party, Fort Pierce: 772 460 5299; www.jazzsociety.org/mardi-gras (Mar). SunFest, West Palm Beach: live music, a Youth Park area with activities for kids, and a huge fireworks show; sunfest.com (May). Pineapple Festival, Jensen Beach: 772 334 3444; www.pineapplefestival.info (Nov)

Pharmacies Check the Publix chain of supermarkets (www.publix.com), CVS (www.cvs.com), or Walgreens (www.walgreens.com) to find an all-night pharmacy.

Restrooms All major shopping malls, attractions, and most gas stations have public restrooms.

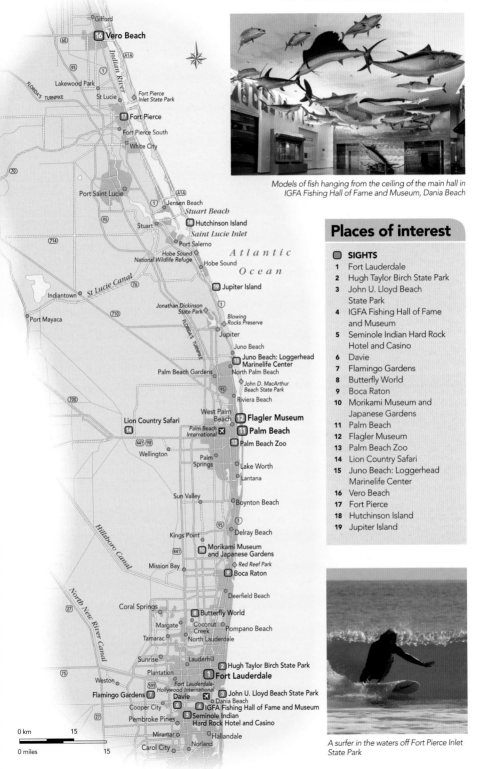

Models of fish hanging from the ceiling of the main hall in IGFA Fishing Hall of Fame and Museum, Dania Beach

Places of interest

☐ **SIGHTS**

1   Fort Lauderdale
2   Hugh Taylor Birch State Park
3   John U. Lloyd Beach
    State Park
4   IGFA Fishing Hall of Fame
    and Museum
5   Seminole Indian Hard Rock
    Hotel and Casino
6   Davie
7   Flamingo Gardens
8   Butterfly World
9   Boca Raton
10 Morikami Museum and
    Japanese Gardens
11 Palm Beach
12 Flagler Museum
13 Palm Beach Zoo
14 Lion Country Safari
15 Juno Beach: Loggerhead
    Marinelife Center
16 Vero Beach
17 Fort Pierce
18 Hutchinson Island
19 Jupiter Island

A surfer in the waters off Fort Pierce Inlet State Park

① Fort Lauderdale

Beaches, vintage cars, and a rocket into space

Little more than a riverside trading camp in 1900, Fort Lauderdale became known as "the Venice of America" when its mangrove swamps were transformed into canals during the 1920s. Today, water taxis and an old-fashioned riverboat, the *Jungle Queen*, glide along these mansion-lined waterways, connecting downtown with a stunning beach. The city is crammed with creaky old houses to explore, hands-on art galleries, and an excellent science museum.

Intricately carved door at Bonnet House

Key Sights

③ Museum of Art Core exhibits here include the vivid Impressionism of American artist William Glackens, contemporary Cuban art, and the amazing Indigo Room installation by Haitian artist Edouard Duval-Carrié, with its themes of voodoo and migration.

① Museum of Discovery and Science Become an astronaut and travel to Mars, dig for fossils alongside a megalodon shark, or watch a 3-D IMAX® movie at this entertaining museum.

② Riverwalk Park Running along the banks of the New River, this shaded waterside park has winding walkways that take in all sorts of shops and cafés.

④ Stranahan House Built in 1901, this creaky pinewood home served as a trading post where pioneer Frank Stranahan would buy goods such as egret plumes and alligator hides from the local Seminole Indians.

⑤ Fort Lauderdale Antique Car Museum The 22 vintage cars at this museum, which date from 1909 to the 1940s, keep alive the spirit of the Packard automobiles that were once made in Detroit, Michigan.

⑥ Bonnet House Museum and Gardens Explore the lush gardens of this Caribbean-style plantation house, designed by painter Frederic Clay Bartlett in 1920.

⑦ International Swimming Hall of Fame This museum is packed with swimming memorabilia, including exhibits relating to Olympic legend Mark Spitz, and the history of water polo.

The Lowdown

Map reference 10 H1
Address Museum of Discovery and Science: 401 SW 2nd St, 33312; www.mods.org. Riverwalk Park: 20 N New River Dr, 33312; www.goriverwalk.com. Museum of Art: 1 E Las Olas Blvd, 33301; www.moafl.org. Stranahan House: 335 SE 6th Ave, 33301; stranahanhouse.org. Fort Lauderdale Antique Car Museum: 1527 SW 1st Ave, 33315; antiquecarmuseum.org. Bonnet House Museum and Gardens: 900 N Birch Rd, 33304; www.bonnethouse.org. International Swimming Hall of

Fame: 1 Hall of Fame Dr, 33316; www.ishof.org

Train Tri-Rail (www.tri-rail.com) from Miami and West Palm Beach, or Amtrak (www.amtrak.com) from Orlando or Miami. **Bus** 22 links the railroad station to the city center.

Visitor information 100 E Broward Blvd, Suite 200, 33301; 954 765 4466; www.sunny.org

Open Museum of Discovery and Science: 10am–5pm Mon–Sat & noon–6pm Sun. Riverwalk Park: 24 hours. Museum of Art: 10am–5pm Tue, Wed & Sat, noon–5pm Sun (till 7pm Thu). Stranahan House:

tours at 1pm, 2pm and 3pm daily. Fort Lauderdale Antique Car Museum: 9am–3pm Mon–Fri (call Sat & Sun). Bonnet House Museum and Gardens: 10am–4pm Tue–Sat, 11am–4pm Sun. International Swimming Hall of Fame: 9am–5pm Mon–Fri (till 2pm Sat–Sun)

Prices Museum of Discovery and Science: $64–75. Museum of Art: $30–40. Stranahan House: $38–48. Fort Lauderdale Antique Car Museum: $16–32; under 12s free. Bonnet House Museum: $72–80; under 6s free. International Swimming Hall of Fame: $24–32

Prices given are for a family of four

Fort Lauderdale beach, fringed with coconut palm trees

Letting off steam
Just 3 miles (5 km) east of downtown is a sandy beach 7 miles (11 km) long. Backed by an attractive promenade and fringed with palms, it is perfect for swimming.

Eat and drink
Picnic: under $25; Snacks: $25–50; Real meal: $50–80; Family treat: over $80 (based on a family of four)

PICNIC Publix at Las Olas *(601 S Andrews Ave, 33301; 954 728 8330; www.publix.com)*, the closest major supermarket to downtown Fort Lauderdale, is a 2-minute drive along the beach. It offers sandwiches, breads, and deli products that can be enjoyed on the beach.

SNACKS Hot Dog Heaven *(101 E Sunrise Blvd, 33304; 954 523 7100; hotdogheaven.infinology.net; till 4:30pm Mon–Sat)*, a 10-minute drive up Federal Highway, is a small place with bar stools inside and two tables outside. A local favorite, it serves superb beef Chicago hotdogs with the works.

Guided tours M. Cruz Rentals *(www.mcruzrentals.com)* runs Segway tours of Fort Lauderdale beach district.

Age range All ages

Activities Explore the waterways aboard the *Jungle Queen* riverboat *(www.junglequeen.com)* or a water taxi shuttle *(www.water taxi.com)*.

Allow At least 2 days

Good family value?
Educative and entertaining sights, as well as a delightful beach, make the city a superb family destination.

REAL MEAL Coconuts *(429 Seabreeze Blvd, 33316; 954 525 2421; www.coconutsfort lauderdale.com)* offers outdoor seating on the water's edge next to the International Swimming Hall of Fame, with views of the local pelicans and a daily fish feeding. Feast on stone crab, fish tacos, and fresh local seafood.

FAMILY TREAT 3030 Ocean *(Harbor Beach Resort Marriott, 3030 Holiday Dr, 33316; 954 765 3030; www.3030ocean. com; dinner only)* serves innovative, contemporary American seafood such as salt-block seared spearfish with almonds, and apricot-glazed local mahi.

Shopping
Las Olas Boulevard is the city's upscale shopping strip, with plenty of fashion stores and boutiques that will appeal to teenagers. **Galleria** *(2414 E Sunrise Blvd, 33304; 954 564 1015; www.galleriamall-fl.com)* is one of the best malls.

Find out more
FILM The dog-friendly tear-jerker *Marley & Me* (2008) was set in Fort Lauderdale.

Guided airboat ride in Big Cypress Seminole Indian Reservation, Clewiston

Next stop...
BIG CYPRESS SEMINOLE INDIAN RESERVATION Visit Big Cypress Seminole Indian Reservation, a Native American outpost 78 miles (125 km) northwest of the city, for its fun "swamp safaris" *(www.billieswamp. com)* and the enlightening Ah-Tah-Thi-Ki Museum *(www.ahtahthiki.com)*.

KIDS' CORNER

Creature quest
There are many animals hiding among the ponds, palms, and gardens of Bonnet House. See if you can spot any of these creatures:
1 Amazon parrot
2 Cockatiel
3 Swan
4 Squirrel monkey
5 Gopher tortoise
6 Manatee

Venice in America?
Venice is a famous city in Italy. Why do you think Fort Lauderdale is called "the Venice of America"?

THE OLD NEW RIVER
Is Fort Lauderdale's New River really "new"? Not really – the river was given its name by the Spanish in the 1600s, possibly as the result of a legend that claimed the river had miraculously sprung into existence overnight. The river has actually been here for thousands of years.

"Count" time on the great gravity clock
The giant clock in the Museum of Discovery and Science is 52 ft (16 m) tall. Unlike a regular clock, it has no hands: you tell the time by counting how many balls are on the lower rails:
1 Each ball on the bottom rail counts as 1 hour.
2 Each ball on the middle rail counts as 10 minutes.
3 Each ball on the top rail counts as 1 minute. What time is it now?

② Hugh Taylor Birch State Park

Canoes, hikes, and bikes

This rustic park, just minutes away from downtown Fort Lauderdale, preserves a pristine slice of Florida's wilderness, thanks to Chicago attorney Hugh Taylor Birch, who donated his estate as a public park in 1941. The park provides access to an especially inviting section of Fort Lauderdale Beach, but to paddle up and down the park's mile-long (1.6-km) freshwater lagoon Lake Helen with younger children, it's best to rent canoes that hold 3–4 people. Older kids might prefer their own kayak. Look out for turtles, ducks, herons, gray squirrels, wading birds, raccoons, and the occasional marsh rabbit.

Back on dry land, the Coastal Hammock Trail is an easy 20–30-minute walk through a tropical hardwood hammock (forest). There are interpretive signs along the way

Canoes for hire at Lake Helen in Hugh Taylor Birch State Park

that provide information about native fauna – try spotting one of the park's rare gopher tortoises or gray foxes.

Another fun thing to do is to rent bikes and cycle through the park on the 2-mile (3-km) park road.

Letting off steam

If kids don't get wet enough kayaking, then go 2 miles (3 km) south to splash in the outdoor pools at the **Fort Lauderdale Aquatic Complex** (ci.ftlaud.fl.us/flac).

③ John U. Lloyd Beach State Park

A day at the beach

The main attraction at this park is the beach – a wonderful 2-mile (4-km) stretch of unspoiled sand that is evocative of old Florida and perfect for swimming. Just inland is the 45-minute Barrier Island Nature Trail through hammock forest, where squirrels and raccoons sometimes scamper into the brush. Whiskey Creek, which divides the park along its length, has lots of

The Lowdown

📍 **Map reference** 10 H1
Address 3109 E Sunrise Blvd (off Hwy-A1A), 33304; 954 564 4521; www.floridastateparks.org/hughtaylorbirch

🚌 **Bus** Broward County Transit bus 11 from downtown Fort Lauderdale to the park entrance

🕐 **Open** 8am–sunset daily

💲 **Price** $6 per vehicle & $2 per pedestrian or cyclist

🚩 **Guided tours** Ranger-guided walks on the Coastal Hammock Trail at 10:30am Fri

👫 **Age range** All ages

🏃 **Activities** The park offers canoe rentals ($5.30 per boat), kayak rentals ($10 per hour in the lagoon; $20 per hour in the ocean, and $35 for 3 hours in the ocean), and bike rentals ($12.50 for 1 hour, $25 for 4 hours, and $35 for 24 hours).

⏱ **Allow** Half a day to a full day

🍴 **Eat and drink** SNACKS M. Cruz Rentals (on site) has a stall offering cold drinks and snacks such as hot dogs. REAL MEAL Franco & Vinny's Pizza Shack (2884 E Sunrise Blvd, 33304; 954 564 9522; francoandvinnys.com; 4–11pm daily) serves excellent pizza and pasta dishes, as well as children's specials including spaghetti with meatballs.

The Lowdown

📍 **Map reference** 10 H2
Address 6503 N Ocean Dr, Dania Beach, 33004; 954 923 2833; www.floridastateparks.org/lloydbeach

🚗 **Car** Rent a car from Fort Lauderdale Airport.

ℹ️ **Visitor information** Dania Beach Chamber of Commerce, 102 W Dania Beach Blvd, Dania Beach, 33004; 954 926 2323; www.daniabeachchamber.org

🕐 **Open** 8am–sunset daily

💲 **Price** $6 per vehicle; $2 per pedestrian or cyclist

👫 **Age range** All ages

🏃 **Activities** There are 45-min self-guided nature walks at the south end of the park.

⏱ **Allow** Half a day to a full day

🍴 **Eat and drink** SNACKS Publix Beachway Plaza (402 E Dania Beach Blvd, 33004; 954 90 4289; www.publix.com) is a short drive from the park and has a range of cold cuts and sandwiches. REAL MEAL Dania Beach Bar & Grill (65 N Beach Rd, 33004; 954 923 4148; www.daniabeachgrill.com; 11am–6pm daily), just outside the park, has a full range of salads, sandwiches, and burgers.

manatees, especially in winter, and there is plenty of bird life to see in the mangroves. Younger children might enjoy watching the boats coming and going at the northern end of the park.

Take cover

Head 2 miles (3 km) southwest to watch a game of jai-alai at the **Dania Jai-Alai Stadium** (301 E Dania Beach Blvd, 33004; 954 920 1511; www.betdania.com). Jai-alai is an ancient game from northern Spain – a bit like squash, but much faster.

Sunbathing at the beach in John U. Lloyd Beach State Park

Above *In the Catch Gallery, IGFA Fishing Hall of Fame and Museum* Below *Sword Dance by Kent Ullberg outside IGFA*

④ IGFA Fishing Hall of Fame and Museum

All about fishing – and an alligator lake

Fishing is a major activity in southern Florida. The International Game Fish Association's museum offers a detailed introduction to the sport. Galleries highlight the history of fishing, and fisheries conservation through interactive exhibits. There is also a Hall of Fame here, where the world's greatest sports fishermen are inducted every year. Models of the largest fish ever caught are also on display.

The virtual-reality fishing games are heaps of fun: grab a fishing rod and haul in huge fish on video screens. Younger kids will enjoy the Wetlands Walk, a short boardwalk that winds through cypress swamp, mangrove, and marsh, home to wading birds, turtles, exotic fish, and best of all, alligators. Be sure to visit the museum's Discovery Room, where displays and fish-related activities await kids, then wander over

to the vast **Bass Pro Shops Outdoor World**, next door, where fish glide around a massive aquarium.

Letting off steam

On the other side of I-95 (exit 22) from the IGFA Fishing Hall of Fame, **Boomers** *(1700 NW 1st St, Dania Beach, 33004; 954 921 1411; www.boomersparks.com/site/dania)* is an old-fashioned fun park, with high-speed go-karts, mini-golf, laser tag, and a huge video arcade.

The Lowdown

🌐 **Map reference** 10 H2

Address 300 Gulf Stream Way, Dania Beach, 33004; 954 922 4212; www.igfa.org. Bass Pro Shops Outdoor World: 200 Gulf Stream Way, Dania Beach, 33004; 800 227 7776; www.basspro.com

🚆 **Train** Tri-Rail to Fort Lauderdale Airport station, then walk to the museum

ℹ️ **Visitor information** Dania Beach Chamber of Commerce, 102 W Dania Beach Blvd, Dania Beach, 33004; 954 926 2323; www.dania beachchamber.org

🕐 **Open** 10am–6pm Mon–Sat & noon–6pm Sun

💲 **Price** $30–40; under 3s free

👫 **Age range** 5 plus

⏱️ **Allow** 1–2 hours

🍴 **Eat and drink** SNACKS Jaxson's Ice Cream Parlor *(128 S Federal Highway, US-1, Dania Beach, 33004; 954 923 4445; www.jaxsonsicecream.com)* is a vintage ice cream shop that also serves burgers, hotdogs, and sandwiches. REAL MEAL Islamorada Fish Company *(220 Gulf Stream Way, Dania Beach, 33004; 954 927 7737; restaurants.basspro.com/fishcompany/DaniaBeach)*, next door to the IGFA Fishing Hall of Fame, offers fresh seafood dishes.

The tropical pool area in the Seminole Indian Hard Rock Hotel and Casino

⑤ Seminole Indian Hard Rock Hotel and Casino

Florida's Native Americans and a Hard Rock Cafe

For a different perspective on Florida's history and culture, visit the Seminole Hard Rock Hotel and Casino near Hollywood. In 1979, the Seminole became the first Native American tribe to develop gaming as a form of income and in 2004 the tribe purchased the Hard Rock Cafe franchise. Today,

The Lowdown

🌐 **Map reference** 10 H2

Address 1 Seminole Way, 33314; 954 315 9112; www.seminole hardrockhollywood.com

🚗 **Car** Rent a car from Fort Lauderdale Airport.

🕐 **Open** Seminole Okalee Indian Village: 9:30am–5:30pm Wed–Sun. Hard Rock Cafe: 11am–midnight Sun–Thu & 11am–2am Fri–Sat

💲 **Price** Seminole Okalee Indian Village: $40–48; under 4s free

👫 **Age range** 5 plus

⏱ **Allow** 2–3 hours

🍽 **Eat and drink** SNACKS Ben & Jerry's (5725 Seminole Way, 33314; 954 321 5144; scoop shops.benjerry.com/scoopshops/hardrockhollywood) serves some of the most unusual flavors of ice cream. REAL MEAL Johnny Rockets (5740 Seminole Way, 33314; 954 316 1915 www.johnnyrockets.com) offers juicy hamburgers, hand-dipped shakes, and freshly baked apple pie in a 1950s-style diner. It also has a kids' menu.

the million-dollar revenues from the complex finance health care, education, full senior care, and modern community centers.

Head to the **Seminole Okalee Indian Village**, on the north side of the complex, to buy souvenirs from the Seminole arts and crafts shop. Unless there are special presentations scheduled in the village, older kids may prefer the restaurants and shops in the hotel complex. These include the **Hard Rock Cafe** itself, the Florida oak-smoked barbecue at Renegade Barbeque Company, and Wetzel's Pretzels. Hip kids' clothing store Brats and the Seminole Store are among the shops on site.

If there is time, take in one of the wide range of concerts and shows at the Hard Rock Live, or enjoy a dip in the lagoon-style pool.

Letting off steam

A short drive south from the complex, the **Topeekeegee Yugnee Park** (3300 N Park Rd, 33021) has picnic areas, basketball courts, playgrounds, and a 2-mile (3-km) loop of paved pathways for walking, jogging, skating, and biking. In summer, visit the Castaway Island Water Park, located within the park.

Browsing through a variety of cowboy hats at Grif's Western, Davie

⑥ Davie

Cowboys, children's art and a trip to the stars

Lying 20 miles (32 km) inland, this Fort Lauderdale suburb is the unlikely venue for some intriguing family attractions. Somewhat bizarrely, Davie is more like a cowboy outpost than a typical Florida town, a legacy

The Lowdown

🌐 **Map reference** 10 H2

Address Grif's Western: 6211 Orange Dr, 33314; 954 587 9000; grifswestern.com. Old Davie School Historical Museum: 6650 Griffin Rd, 33314; 954 797 1044; odshm.ch2v.com. Young at Art Children's Museum: 751 SW 121 Ave, 33325; 954 424 0085; www.youngatartmuseum.org. Buehler Planetarium & Observatory: 3501 Davie Rd, Broward College campus, 33314; 954 201 6681; www.iloveplanets.com

🚗 **Car** Rent a car from Fort Lauderdale Airport.

🕐 **Open** Grif's Western: 10am–9pm Mon–Sat & 11am–5pm Sun. Old Davie School Historical Museum: 9am–5pm Mon–Fri & 10am–4pm Sat. Young at Art Children's Museum: 10am–5pm Mon–Thu (till 6pm Fri–Sat), 11am–6pm Sun. Buehler Planetarium: 8–10pm Wed, Fri & Sat (public viewings); check website for show timings.

💲 **Prices** Old Davie School Historical Museum: $24–34. Young at Art Children's Museum: $50–62, under 1s free. Buehler Planetarium: free on public viewing nights; shows range $4–6

👫 **Age range** 5 plus

⏱ **Allow** A day

🍽 **Eat and drink** SNACKS La Spada's Original Hoagies (2645 S University Dr, 33328; 954 476 1099; www.laspadashoagies.com) offers some of the best sandwiches in southern Florida. REAL MEAL Pizza Loft (3514 S University Dr, 33328; 954 916 8880; www.thepizzaloft.com) is a family-friendly pizza joint.

🎪 **Festival** Bergeron Rodeo Grounds hosts 6 to 8 rodeos (davieprorodeo.com; Feb & Mar)

of the Western settlers who came here in the early 20th century. Kids will love watching the town rodeo, held intermittently between February and November. There is even a rodeo for kids in June. Fans of the Wild West should visit **Grif's Western**, the leading seller of cowboy boots, hats, and saddles in the state. Stop by the **Old Davie School Historical Museum**, a restored 1918 schoolhouse, with exhibits that bring Florida's pioneer history to life. Younger children will get more out of the **Young at Art Children's Museum**, which explores the history of art through five child-friendly themes. Finally, do not miss the **Buehler Planetarium &**

Observatory, where planetarium shows are followed by star-gazing sessions. On a clear night, Jupiter, or even Saturn's rings, might be visible.

Letting off steam

Zip off to **Tree Tops Park** (*3900 SW 100th Ave, 33328; 954 357 5130; www.broward.org/Parks*), which has playgrounds, hiking trails, and guided horse-rides.

⑦ Flamingo Gardens

The home of pink flamingos

This botanical garden, smothered with subtropical plants and trees, is a serene preserve that attracts butterflies and hummingbirds in winter. The gardens are set up with families in mind – children are encouraged to touch and smell herbs and plants in the Fragrance Garden. But, inevitably, most kids will be asking, "where are the flamingos?" Fear not, the on-site Everglades Wildlife Sanctuary is home to 83 species of Florida's native birds and animals, including

Visitors aboard a tram tour in Flamingo Gardens, Davie

alligators, panthers, bobcats, otters, eagles, and pink flamingos. Around 250 birds, including plenty of noisy waders, can be seen inside the huge Free-flight Aviary. For a change of pace, visit the Wray Home Museum, restored to its appearance in the 1930s, when it was the home of Floyd and Jane Wray, the founders of the gardens.

Take cover

If it rains, head for the **Old Davie School Historical Museum** (*see p84*), located 6 miles (10 km) east of Flamingo Gardens. The museum houses artifacts and photographs that tell the story of the journey of the pioneers into the Everglades.

A flock of wading birds in Flamingo Gardens, Davie

The Lowdown

🌐 **Map reference** 10 G2
Address 3750 S Flamingo Rd, (between Griffin Rd and I-595), Davie, 33330; 954 473 2955; www.flamingogardens.org

🚗 **Car** Rent a car from Fort Lauderdale Airport.

🕐 **Open** 9:30am–5pm daily; Jun–Oct: closed Mon

💲 **Price** $56–72; under 3s free

🚩 **Guided tours** Guided tours of Wray Home Museum take place 10am–4pm daily. Narrated tram tours of the gardens depart on the hour 11am–4pm daily.

👫 **Age range** 5 plus

🦊 **Activities** Live Wildlife Encounter Shows (weather permitting) at 12:30pm, 1:30pm & 2:30pm daily.

⏱ **Allow** 2–3 hours

🍽 **Eat and drink SNACKS** Publix Countryside Shops (5630 S Flamingo Rd, Cooper City, 33330; 954 434 2803; www.publix.com) is the nearest major supermarket to Flamingo Gardens. **REAL MEAL** Marola's Trattoria (5822 S Flamingo Rd, Cooper City, 33330; 954 434 3420; marolas.com), a family-friendly Italian restaurant, serves salads, pasta, and pizza.

Picnic under $25; **Snacks** $25–50; **Real meal** $50–80; **Family treat** over $80 (based on a family of four)

A butterfly on foliage in Butterfly World, Coconut Creek

⑧ Butterfly World
Birds, butterflies, and bugs

Few places are as enchanting as this nature park, located in Tradewinds Park, where hundreds of brilliantly colored butterflies flutter through tropical greenhouses, and exotic birds nestle in the palms. Inside the Tropical Rain Forest Aviary, bright blue, amber, and yellow butterflies land gently on children's hands and shoulders. Kids also love the Lorikeet Encounter, where multicolored parrots feed from cups of nectar right out of visitors' hands.

The Tinalandia Suspension Bridge, which sways as kids romp across it, is another favorite, while the main attractions inside the blossom-filled Jewels of the Sky Aviary are the fearless hummingbirds, which feed on nectar in the flowers. Do not miss the Bug Zoo, where giant water bugs, creepy spiders, and mean-looking wasps are sure to elicit gasps of horror/pleasure.

Letting off steam
Kids can run around in **Tradewinds Park** (www.broward.org/Parks/Trade windsPark), an expanse of green that has playgrounds, picnic areas, and a fishing lake. Pony rides and trips in a model steam train are also available.

⑨ Boca Raton
A Mediterranean fantasy

This lovely city started to develop during the Florida land boom of the 1920s, when famous architect Addison Mizner built the ultra chic pink building called the Boca Raton Resort & Club. Kids will probably spot this fortress from the car. Mizner inspired the Mediterranean Revival style of architecture that still dominates downtown and gives Boca Raton a Continental feel.

Younger kids will find the **Boca Raton Children's Museum** enticing. Set within a 1913 driftwood Cracker cottage – the simple abode of early Florida farmers – it has many hands-on exhibits that will keep children occupied for hours. The KidsCents Bank exhibit shows how a bank works, with teller windows and a working vault, while Imogene's Closet, a display of child-sized pioneer clothing and old-fashioned

Elevated viewing platform in the Gumbo Limbo Nature Center, Boca Raton

dolls, gives a feel of Boca Raton's history. Nearer to the ocean, take a stroll around **Gumbo Limbo Nature Center**, where boardwalks wind through a tropical hardwood hammock and a mangrove forest. Spot ospreys, and brown pelicans, and the occasional manatee lurking in the warm waters.

Letting off steam
There are plenty of public beaches in Boca Raton, but parking tends to be expensive. The **Red Reef Park**, next to the Gumbo Limbo Nature Center on Highway-A1A, is good for swimming, sunbathing, and snorkeling. The nearby **Delray Beach** is a cheaper alternative.

The Lowdown

🌐 **Map reference** 10 H1
Address Boca Raton Children's Museum: 498 Crawford Blvd, 33432; 561 368 6878; www. cmboca.org. Gumbo Limbo Nature Center: 1801 N Ocean Blvd, 33432; 561 338 1473; www.gumbolimbo.org

🚗 **Car** Rent a car from Fort Lauderdale Airport.

ℹ️ **Visitor information** Boca Raton Chamber of Commerce, 800 N Dixie Hwy, 33432; 561 395 4433; www.bocaratonchamber.com

🕐 **Open** Boca Raton Children's Museum: noon–4pm Tue–Sat. Gumbo Limbo Nature Center: 9am–4pm Mon–Sat, noon–4pm Sun

💲 **Prices** Boca Raton Children's Museum: $20–30; under 1s free. Gumbo Limbo Nature Center: free; $5 donation per person

🚩 **Guided tours** Gumbo Limbo Nature Center runs guided walks to observe sea turtles laying eggs (May–Jul) and eggs hatching (Jul–Aug).

👫 **Age range** 5 plus

🕐 **Allow** A day

🍴 **Eat and drink** PICNIC 4th Generation Organic Market (75 SE 3rd St, 33432; 561 338 9920; www.4thgenerationmarket.com) stocks salads, sandwiches, wraps, and desserts. Enjoy the picnic in the Red Reef Park. REAL MEAL Tom Sawyer Restaurant & Pastry Shop (1759 NW 2nd Ave, 33432; 561 368 4634; www.tomsawyer restaurant.com; 7am–2pm daily) is an old-fashioned diner with excellent breakfasts. It also serves soups, salads, and seafood.

The Lowdown

🌐 **Map reference** 10 H1
Address Tradewinds Park, 3600 W Sample Rd, Coconut Creek, 33073; 954 977 4400; www. butterflyworld.com

🚗 **Car** Rent a car from Fort Lauderdale Airport.

🕐 **Open** 9am–5pm Mon–Sat & 11am–5pm Sun

💲 **Price** $90–100; under 2s free

👫 **Age range** All ages

🎨 **Activities** Download the coloring book at www.butterflyworld.com/ FlyingColorsBook.pdf and find out about the great variety of butterflies.

🕐 **Allow** 2 hours

🍴 **Eat and drink** SNACKS The Lakeside Café (on site) is the best place for sandwiches, salads, iced drinks, and coffee. REAL MEAL Lime Fresh Mexican Grill (Promenade at Coconut Creek, 4425 Lyons Rd, 33073; 954 586 2999; www.lime freshmexicangrill.com), a short drive away, offers kids' menus and great tacos.

Japanese-style schoolboy's bedroom at the Morikami Museum, Delray Beach

⑩ Morikami Museum and Japanese Gardens
A day out in the Far East

Southern Florida is an unlikely place for an outpost of classical Japan, but this museum and its beautifully landscaped grounds give visitors an authentic taste of the Far East. See six beautiful Japanese gardens, a Shinto shrine, a teahouse, and a museum – the legacy of a Japanese agricultural colony established in Boca Raton in the early 20th century.

The main section of the museum displays Japanese art, but kids might find this hard-going; aim instead for the Yamato-kan house, where the Japan Through the Eyes of a Child exhibit offers a taste of modern Japanese life specially designed for younger kids. Explore a Japanese classroom, a shopping street, and a typical home complete with *tatami* mats (straw mats used to cover floors), a huge bathtub, and a high-tech toilet. There is also a mock train station with a bullet train compartment. The gardens, with zigzag bridges, hidden waterfalls, Zen-inspired rock gardens, and many bonsai trees, are ideal for strolling.

Letting off steam

The museum and gardens form part of the greater **Morikami Park**, a public space featuring Lake Biwa and Saki Pavilion. Visitors can picnic here, and there is also a playground and a nature trail.

The Lowdown

- 🌐 **Map reference** 8 H6
  Address 4000 Morikami Park Rd, Delray Beach, 33446; 561 495 0233; www.morikami.org
- 🚗 **Car** Rent a car from West Palm Beach Airport.
- 🕐 **Open** 10am–5pm Tue–Sun
- 💲 **Price** $42–52; under 5s free
- 👫 **Age range** All ages
- ⏱ **Allow** At least 2–3 hours
- 🍴 **Eat and drink** SNACKS Cornell Café *(on site; 11am–3pm Tue–Sun)* is an open-air place selling pan-Asian snacks, drinks, light meals, and desserts. REAL MEAL Henry's *(16850 Jog Rd, 33446; 561 638 1949; henrysofboca raton.com)* offers contemporary American and Continental cuisine just outside the gardens.
- 🎉 **Festival** Hatsume Fair, spring festival (Mar)

Stone sculptures and flower beds in the Japanese Gardens, Delray Beach

Picnic under $25; **Snacks** $25–50; **Real meal** $50–80; **Family treat** over $80 (based on a family of four)

⑪ Palm Beach

Hang out with America's mega-rich

One of the wealthiest places in the US, Palm Beach is peppered with dreamy mansions, pristine gardens, and upscale shopping streets. The town was founded in the 1890s, when Henry Flagler brought his railroad south and built two luxury hotels here. In the 1920s, Addison Mizner added Mediterranean-style homes and plazas, lending the town a refined European air. Ever since, it has attracted tycoons, sports stars, and even royalty.

Impressive facade of The Breakers

Key Sights

① **Lake Trail** Bike or walk along this tree-shaded 3-mile (5-km) path that borders the waters of Lake Worth to take in scenic lake views and admire Palm Beach mansions.

② **Green's Pharmacy** Open since 1937, this old-fashioned diner is known for its breakfasts, burgers, and ice cream sodas. Hit the pharmacy section for all sorts of beach gear, toys, and old-style sweets.

③ **The Breakers** Established by Henry Flagler in 1896, this hotel is a spellbinding place to visit for a guided tour. The present Italianate building dates from 1926.

④ **Episcopal Church of Bethesda-by-the-Sea** This Neo-Gothic church was built in 1926. Stroll in its lush Cluett Memorial Garden, amid the cloisters, with gazebos and a fountain pond filled with colorful koi.

[Map showing: WELLS RD, Lake Trail ①, BRADLEY PLACE, N COUNTY RD, OCEAN BLVD, Green's Pharmacy ②, SUNRISE AVENUE, ROYAL POINCIANA WAY, Breakers Ocean Golf Course, Lake Worth, The Breakers ③, Episcopal Church of Bethesda-by-the-Sea, Atlantic Ocean, COCOANUT, BARTON AVE, ④, COCOA NUT, S COUNTY RD, Society of the Four Arts ⑤, ⑥, ROYAL PALM WAY, Norton Museum of Art 1 mile (2 km), PERU, SOUTH OCEAN BLVD, WORTH AVENUE. Scale: 0 meters 600, 0 yards 600]

⑤ **Society of the Four Arts** While art exhibitions are held inside this Italianate building, the beautifully landscaped grounds contain a series of lush botanical gardens, and a selection of elegant modern sculptures.

⑥ **Norton Museum of Art** This museum houses several masterpieces by great artists such as Picasso and Gauguin, as well as modern American art by Jackson Pollock, Georgia O'Keeffe, and glass artist Dale Chihuly.

Letting off steam

Spend time on the wide, clean **public beach** off Ocean Boulevard. Further afield, little ones will enjoy Playmobil toys at the **Playmobil FunPark** (8031 N Military Trail, 33410; 561 691 9880; store.playmobilusa.com).

Eat and drink

Picnic: under $25; Snacks: $25–50; Real meal: $50–80; Family treat: over $80 (based on a family of four)

PICNIC Publix on Palm Beach (135 Bradley Pl, 33480; 561 655 4120; www.publix.com) is a great

Prices given are for a family of four

place to pick up delicious goodies for a picnic on the beach or in Cluett Memorial Garden.

Dining in the charming courtyard of Pizza Al Fresco

SNACKS Sprinkles Ice Cream & Sandwich (279 Royal Poinciana Way, 33480; 561 659 1140; 9am–10pm Sun–Thu, 9am–11pm Fri–Sat) offers luscious ice cream in several flavors.

REAL MEAL Pizza Al Fresco (14 Via Mizner, 33480; 561 832 0032; pizzaalfresco.com) has courtyard seating and serves fabulous brick-oven pizza and baked pasta.

FAMILY TREAT Charley's Crab (456 S Ocean Blvd, 33480; 561 659 1500; www.muer.com) offers fine seafood right on the beach. Try the Alaskan king crab or the filet mignon.

Shopping

Teenagers might like to window shop in **Worth Avenue** *(www.worth-avenue.com)* in downtown Palm Beach, which is packed with designer stores and art galleries. Try Palm Beach's high-class thrift stores, such as **Church Mouse** *(378 S County Rd, 33480; 561 659 2154)* for more affordable bargains.

Find out more

DIGITAL Check out *www.pbpulse.com* for information on events, dining, shopping, arts and culture.

Next stop...

POLO AND SWIMMING The Palm Beach area is famous for polo. For fun tournaments held on weekends (Jan–Apr), visit the **International Polo Club of Palm Beach** *(3667 120th Ave S, Wellington, 33414; 561 282 5290; www.international poloclub.com).* **Peanut Island** *(www.pbcgov.com/parks/peanut island),* in the middle of Lake Worth, is a country park good for swimming and snorkeling. It is home to John F. Kennedy's Cold War bunker. The park also has a campground, and picnic areas with grills.

A polo match in progress at the International Polo Club of Palm Beach

The Lowdown

🌐 **Map reference** 8 H5
Address Green's Pharmacy: 151 North County Rd, 33480; 561 832 4443. The Breakers: 1 South County Rd, 33480; 888 273 2537; *www.thebreakers.com.* Episcopal Church of Bethesda-by-the-Sea: 141 South County Rd, 33480; 561 655 4554; *www.bbts.org.* Society of the Four Arts: 2 Four Arts Plaza, 33480; 561 204 5687; *www.fourarts.org.* Norton Museum of Art: 1451 S Olive Ave, West Palm Beach, 33401; 561 832 5196; *www.norton.org*

🚗 **Bus** Palm Tran bus 44 *(www.pbcgov.com/palmtran)* from airport to downtown West Palm Beach. Palm Tran bus 41 (Mon–Sat) from downtown Palm Beach to West Palm Beach Tri-Rail station *(www.tri-rail.com).*
Car Metered parking available on the Palm Beach seafront

ℹ️ **Visitor information** 1555 Palm Beach Lakes Blvd, Suite 800, West Palm Beach, 33401; 800 544 7256; *www.palmbeachfl.com*

🕐 **Open** Green's Pharmacy: 7am–5pm Mon–Sat, 7am–3pm Sun.

Episcopal Church of Bethesda-by-the-Sea: 8am–5pm daily. Society of the Four Arts: 10am–5pm daily. Norton Museum of Art: 10am–5pm Tue, Wed, Fri & Sat, 10am–9pm Thu & 11am–5pm Sun

💲 **Prices** Episcopal Church of Bethesda-by-the-Sea and Society of the Four Arts: free. Norton Museum of Art: $34–44; under 12s free

🎫 **Guided tours** Norton Museum of Art offers summer tours at 2pm Fri–Sun; check website. The Breakers offers a historical tour; call ahead for reservations

🏃 **Activities** Download puzzles and games at *www.norton.org.* Rent bikes from Palm Beach Bicycle Trail Shop ($15 per hour, $29 half a day & $39 for 24 hours) and ride around Lake Worth.

⏱️ **Allow** 1–2 days

Good family value?
Palm Beach is an expensive town, but it does not cost a cent to explore its pristine streets and shops, or enjoy its lovely beaches.

⑫ Flagler Museum
A palace fit for a merchant prince

While traveling along the east coast of Florida, it is impossible not to hear about Henry Flagler, the man who probably did more to develop the state than any other. Before Flagler's East Coast Railway reached Miami in 1896, most of Florida was a wilderness. By the time the trains made it to Key West in 1912, the region was firmly established as a winter getaway. Flagler's lavish Palm Beach home, Whitehall, is now the Flagler Museum, a fascinating monument to the man and his legacy.

Grand piano in the Drawing Room

Key Features

 Illustrated area Constructed in 1902.

Extension Added in 1925.

Pavilion Added in 2005.

Yellow Roses Room

Music Room Flagler employed his own organist to play a 1,249-pipe Odell organ in this room, a favorite with Mrs. Flagler for holding parties.

Entrance

Master Suite

Drawing Room

Flagler-Kenan History Room Learn about Flagler's achievements as a founding partner in Standard Oil and as a developer of Florida's east coast here. An 18-carat gold replica of the telegram announcing the completion of his Key West Railway is also on display.

The Grand Hall Seven types of marble were used to create the largest and grandest room built in America's Gilded Age. It contains a bust of Caesar Augustus and a portrait of Henry Flagler himself.

West Room Part of the 1925 hotel extension, this room originally served as the dining room. Look out for the medieval crests that circle the walls below the ceiling.

Vacationers at a public beach, Palm Beach

Letting off steam

The Flagler Museum lies on the route of the **Lake Trail** (see p88), while the beach is a short drive away on South Ocean Boulevard.

Prices given are for a family of four

Eat and drink

Picnic: under $25; Snacks: $25–50; Real meal: $50–80; Family treat: over $80 (based on a family of four)

PICNIC Amici Market (155 North County Rd, 33480; 561 832 0201; www.myamicimarket.com) is a gourmet market and deli just north of the museum. Picnic on the beach.

SNACKS Toojay's Original Gourmet Deli (313 Royal Poinciana Way, 33480; 561 659 7232; www.toojays.com) tempts with chicken noodle soup, overstuffed sandwiches, potato pancakes, and vegetable quesadillas. There is also a good kids' menu.

REAL MEAL Palm Beach Grill (340 Royal Poinciana Way, 33480; 561 835 1077; www.hillstone.com; dinner only), a short walk from the museum, serves excellent seafood. Do sample their Key lime pie.

FAMILY TREAT Buccan (350 South County Road, 80304; 561 833 3450; buccanpalmbeach.com) is the place for a real splurge. The tapas plates are perfect for sharing and there are plenty of creative pizzas on the menu, as well as more innovative dishes such as grilled quail with jalapeño biscuit. An extensive wine list is available too.

The Lowdown

🌐 **Map reference** 8 H5
Address 1 Whitehall Way, Palm Beach, 33480; 561 655 2833; www.flaglermuseum.us

🚌 **Bus** Palm Tran bus 41 connects downtown Palm Beach with West Palm Beach Tri-Rail station (Mon–Sat).

🕐 **Open** 10am–5pm Tue–Sat, noon–5pm Sun

💲 **Price** $46–72; under 5s free (kids 6–12: $3)

🚩 **Guided tours** Free guided tours run 11am–2pm Tue–Sat and at 12:30pm & 2:30 pm on Sun. Free audio guides are also available.

👫 **Age range** 7 plus

👫 **Activities** Pick up the free *Tour & Activity Guide for Kids* at the entrance, which is designed to engage and entertain children as they tour the museum. The guide features questions to be answered and items to be drawn; and includes

a pencil. At the Museum Store, kids receive a souvenir penny and two quarters for the Penny Stretching Machine.

⏱️ **Allow** 2 hours

♿ **Wheelchair access** Yes

🍴 **Café** Café des Beaux-Arts (on site; Thanksgiving–Easter: 11:30am–2:30pm Tue–Sat & noon–3pm Sun) serves a set lunch, which is more like an elaborate afternoon tea with sandwiches and cakes.

🚻 **Restrooms** Outside the Café des Beaux-Arts and on the first floor next to the West Room

Good family value?

Though there are no family tickets, the entrance charge is relatively low. Kids are well-catered for with the great activity guide, friendly docents, and plenty of curious, rare objects to see.

Master Suite Henry Flagler and his wife shared this, the most lavish bedroom in the house. The furniture and gold color are in French Louis XIV style.

Drawing Room Flagler used delicate aluminum leaf, coated with shellac, to highlight the plaster ornaments in this gorgeous room.

Henry Flagler's private Railcar No. 91 The Flagler Kenan Pavilion has Flagler's very own "palace on wheels," with a bedroom, a bathroom, guest quarters, and a kitchen.

Lily pond in the gardens at the Society of the Four Arts, Palm Beach

Find out more

DIGITAL Read about the house and the life of Henry Flagler on www.flaglermuseum.us, the official website. Find more on Flagler at www.keyshistory.org/flagler.html.

Next stop...

GLIMPSES OF THE GILDED AGE Head up the road to the beautifully landscaped grounds of the **Society of the Four Arts** (see p88) or walk across the street to **The Breakers** (see p88), the extravagant hotel built by Henry Flagler in 1896.

KIDS' CORNER

Do you know...

Visit the Flagler-Kenan History Room and see if you can answer these questions:

1 When was Henry Flagler born?

2 Which company made the original gold telegram? (Hint: it's a girl's name.)

3 Which town in Florida did Flagler's railway reach in 1912?

Answers at the bottom of the page.

FLAGLER'S LONG-LOST RAIL CAR

Henry Flagler's private Railcar No. 91 wasn't always at the Flagler Museum. In 1935 it was sold to a railway in Georgia; 14 years later it was sold again. By the time it was rediscovered in 1959 it was being used as a dormitory for farm workers in Virginia! It took another nine years to restore it at the museum.

Color it pretty

Did you visit the Yellow Roses Room? Flowery wallpaper was popular in the early 1900s. Draw the most colorful wallpaper pattern you can think of – try to use at least three shapes and three colors.

Dream house

Flagler's mansion had 75 rooms, including 22 bathrooms. If you could design a mansion or a palace, how many rooms would you have? What kind of rooms would you include? Draw a floor plan of your dream house. Be sure to mark the front door on the plan.

Answers: **1** 1830. **2** Tiffany **3** Key West.

A rare Florida panther in Palm Beach Zoo, West Palm Beach

⑬ Palm Beach Zoo

Pyramids, an interactive fountain, and wild things

This wildlife park has an intriguing array of themed areas and plenty of showstopping animal attractions, including eagles, panthers, black bears, otters, tigers, and alligators. Don't miss the stunning Harriet W. & George D. Cornell Tropics of the Americas exhibit – a re-creation of the Central and South American rain forest, where jaguars and giant anteaters pad around Mayan pyramids. The zoo, with its naturalistic environments and friendly, informative staff, is especially good for families. There are plenty of things to touch and climb onto, and opportunities to feed pelicans.

The Lowdown

- 🌐 **Map reference** 8 H5
- 🏠 **Address** 1301 Summit Blvd, West Palm Beach, 33405; 561 547 9453; www.palmbeachzoo.org
- 🚌 **Bus** Palm Tran bus 45 connects West Palm Beach and the Tri-Rail station with the zoo (Mon–Sat only).
- 🕐 **Open** 9am–5pm daily
- 💲 **Price** $64–76; under 3s free
- 👫 **Age range** All ages
- 🏃 **Activities** Watch Wings over Water bird show 11am Mon–Fri and 11am & 2pm Sat–Sun, as well as Wild Things Show 1pm Mon–Fri & noon Sat–Sun.
- ⏱ **Allow** At least 2–3 hours
- 🍽 **Eat and drink** SNACKS The zoo concession stand (on site; closes 4pm) offers cold drinks, ice cream, hot dogs, and other snacks. REAL MEAL Tropics Café, (on site; closes 3pm) serves salads, roast chicken, pasta, and healthy snacks for kids such as raisins, applesauce, and granola bars.

The daily Wild Things Show features a rainbow boa, singing dogs, and a pygmy hedgehog named Xena. Be sure to bring the kids' bathing suits – they get to cool off in the water jets at the Interactive Play Fountain. Kids also love taking rides on the Wildlife Carousel and browsing the outdoor gift shop.

Take cover

If it rains, head to the **South Florida Science Museum** (4801 Dreher Trail North, 33405; 561 832 1988; www.sfsm.org), located next door to the zoo. The museum features more than 50 hands-on exhibits, a planetarium, aquariums, and natural history displays.

A demonstration in progress at South Florida Science Museum, Palm Beach

⑭ Lion Country Safari

Journey to the African savanna

A wildlife preserve, Lion Country Safari does a fine job of re-creating the African plains, with elephants, giraffes, chimpanzees, zebras, ostriches, and lions roaming free. This is a drive-through safari park, with a 4-mile (6-km) road and 900 wild animals, which means visitors are confined to their cars. In addition to the African areas, there are sections dedicated to the South American pampas and the Gir Forest in India.

The chimpanzees live on a five-island system: try to spot Little Mama, who was born in Africa around 1938 and is the oldest chimpanzee in captivity. She is thought to have been a performer in the traveling entertainment show Ice Capades when she was young, and she still likes to wear a shawl!

The Lowdown

- 🌐 **Map reference** 8 G5
- 🏠 **Address** 2003 Lion Country Safari Rd, Loxahatchee, 33470; 561 793 1084; www.lioncountrysafari.com
- 🚗 **Car** Rent a car from Palm Beach Airport.
- 🕐 **Open** 9:30am–5:30pm daily
- 💲 **Price** $96–110; under 3s free. Parking $6 per vehicle
- 👫 **Cutting the line** Book online and get $2 discount on tickets and free parking.
- 🚩 **Guided tours** VIP private tours, insider tour, and photo-guided tour are available; check website for details.
- 👫 **Age range** 3 plus
- 🏃 **Activities** Go for boat rides on the Safari Queen. The preserve holds Flamingo talks 2pm daily and Alligator chit chat 3pm daily.
- ⏱ **Allow** Half a day to a full day
- 🍽 **Eat and drink** SNACKS Safari Snacks (on site) offers pizza, hot dogs, funnel cakes, and ice cream. REAL MEAL Sneaky Pete's Bar & Grill (5088 Seminole Pratt Whitney Rd, Loxahatchee, 33470; 561 333 1179) is a family-friendly diner located close to the safari.

Antelopes resting in shade at Lion Country Safari, Loxahatchee

Kayaking in John D. MacArthur Beach State Park, near Juno Beach

After the safari, families can stretch their legs at Safari World. This is a theme park with interactive fountains, a Ferris wheel, and a petting zoo, as well as camel rides and a giraffe-feeding exhibit.

Letting off steam

Bring bathing suits to cool off in **Safari Splash** inside the Lion Country Safari. Kids can play a round of mini-golf, or slide down the bouncy waterslide. Paddleboats are available by the lake in the park.

⑮ Juno Beach: Loggerhead Marinelife Center

Saving turtles and feeding fish

The sands of Juno Beach, 13 miles (21 km) north of West Palm Beach, make for a pleasant visit any time, but this small seaside town is enhanced by the family-friendly Loggerhead Marinelife Center. The focus here is the Sea Turtle Hospital, where sick and injured turtles are cared for. See feeding, medication being given, and even physical therapy sessions, depending on the time of day.

The center's exhibit hall chronicles turtle life cycles and Florida's coastal ecosystems. There are also five small aquariums with fish, corals, and anemones. Catch the 30-minute Dr. Logger show, which reveals the life of a sea turtle, highlighting not just its diet and habits, but the threats it faces in an interactive way that engages kids of all ages. At Hatchling Tales, younger kids are entertained with ocean-inspired stories and crafts, and there is also a weekly marine-related Kids' Story Time. In June and July, there are turtle

The Lowdown

- 🌐 **Map reference** 8 H5
- 🏠 **Address** 14200 US-1, Juno Beach, 33408; 561 627 8280; *marinelife.org*
- 🚗 **Car** Rent a car from Palm Beach Airport.
- ℹ️ **Visitor information** Northern Palm Beach County Chamber of Commerce, 800 North US-1, Jupiter, 33477; 561 746 7111; *npbchamber.com*
- 🕐 **Open** 10am–5pm Mon–Sat & 11am–5pm Sun
- 💲 **Price** Free; turtle walks $15 per person
- 🚩 **Guided tours** The center runs a 1-hour guided tour at noon every Sunday.
- 👫 **Age range** All ages
- 👫 **Activities** Find kids' corner activities and puzzles to download at *www.marinelife.org*. There is fish feeding 3pm Tue, Thu & Sat and turtle feeding noon Tue & Fri
- ⏱️ **Allow** 1–2 hours; more time for activities
- 🍴 **Eat and drink** SNACKS Hurricane Café (*14050 US-1, 33408; 877 775 2559; www.hurricanecafe. com*) has outdoor seating and great selections for kids. REAL MEAL Captain Charlie's Reef Grill (*12846 US 1, 33408; 561 624 9924*) is justly famous for its seafood.

walks – expeditions to watch the turtles as they crawl ashore to lay eggs under cover of darkness. Reservations for this are essential, and accepted from May onward.

Letting off steam

Just south of Juno Beach, **John D. MacArthur Beach State Park** (*10900 Jack Nicklaus Dr, 33408; 561 624 6950; www.macarthurbeach.org*) offers plenty of outdoor activities, with a nature walk, a pretty beach with dunes, and kayak rental.

⑯ Vero Beach
Let's hunt for treasure!

North of Palm Beach, the cities, resorts, and grand mansions give way to the less developed Treasure Coast, which boasts waters where manatees can be spotted, great sweeps of sandy beaches, and seaside towns such as Vero Beach. Much of the area's appeal lies in its state parks and sandy barrier islands, but there are plenty of museums and wildlife-related activities to keep families busy.

Trial Scene by Tom Otterness, Vero Beach Museum of Art

Key Sights

① Sebastian Inlet State Park The wild and enchanting beaches here lure plenty of surfers and swimmers, and the McLarty Treasure Museum provides a cultural diversion.

② Mel Fisher's Treasure Museum Dedicated to Mel Fisher, a modern treasure hunter, this museum displays Spanish booty dredged up from the 1715 fleet wrecked just offshore.

③ Environmental Learning Center Learn about the mangroves and wetlands of the Indian River Lagoon here, with hands-on exhibits, boat tours, and touch tanks full of local sea life.

④ Riverside Children's Theatre Watch plays and musicals performed by kids for kids here – from Roald Dahl's The Twits, to The Wiz, and a jazz version of The Nutcracker.

⑤ Driftwood Resort This bizarre-looking hotel – a giant beach shack right on the water – is worth a visit even for non-guests. The entire edifice was built in 1935 from ocean-washed timbers and planks.

⑥ Vero Beach Museum of Art See modern art in a variety of media, from the stunning glasswork of Dale Chihuly to the horse sculptures of Deborah Butterfield.

⑦ Indian River Citrus Museum Citrus farming has been an important part of life in Florida since the 1860s, and this museum chronicles the struggles and successes of the early pioneers.

⑧ McKee Botanical Garden This lush, blossom-smothered garden features an extensive subtropical jungle laced with streams, ponds, and trails dating back to the 1920s.

The Lowdown

🌐 **Map reference** 8 G2
Address Sebastian Inlet State Park: 9700 S State Rd A1A, Melbourne Beach, 32951; www.floridastateparks.org. Mel Fisher's Treasure Museum: 1322 US-1, Sebastian, 32958; www.melfisher.com. Environmental Learning Center: 255 Live Oak Dr, 32963; www.discoverelc.org. Riverside Children's Theatre: 3280 Riverside Park Dr, 32963; riversidetheatre.com. Driftwood Resort: 3150 Ocean Dr, 32963; www.thedriftwood.com. Vero Beach Museum of Art: 3001 Riverside Park Dr, 32963; www.verobeachmuseum.org. Indian River Citrus Museum:

2140 14th Ave, 32960; www.veroheritage.org/CitrusMuseum.html. McKee Botanical Garden: 350 US-1, 32962; mckeegarden.org

🚃 **Train** Amtrak from West Palm Beach. **Car** Rent a car from Palm Beach Airport.

ℹ **Visitor information** Indian River County Chamber of Commerce, 1216 21st St, 32960; 772 567 3491; www.indianriverchamber.com; 9am–5pm Mon–Fri

🕐 **Open** Sebastian Inlet State Park: daily (McLarty Treasure Museum: 10am–4pm daily). Mel Fisher's Treasure Museum: 10am–5pm Mon–Sat & noon–5pm Sun;

closed Sep. Environmental Learning Center: 10am–4pm Tue–Fri, 9am–noon Sat (till 4pm in winter) & 1–4pm Sun. Riverside Children's Theatre: check website for shows. Vero Beach Museum of Art: 10am–4:30pm Mon–Sat & 1–4:30pm Sun. Indian River Citrus Museum: 10am–3pm Tue–Fri. McKee Botanical Garden: 10am–5pm Tue–Sat & noon–5pm Sun

💲 **Prices** Sebastian Inlet State Park: $8 per vehicle, $2 per pedestrian or cyclist. Mel Fisher's Treasure Museum: $20–24. Environmental Learning Center: $20–30; under 12s free. Riverside Children's Theatre: tickets $40–50. Vero

Prices given are for a family of four

The tranquil Treasure Shores Beach Park, Vero Beach

Letting off steam

About 10 miles (16 km) north of Vero Beach lies **Treasure Shores Beach Park** *(11300 Hwy-A1A, 32963)* which also has a playground for little ones. **Humiston Park** *(3000 Ocean Dr, 32963; 772 231 5790)*, closer to downtown, also has a playground, but the beach here is smaller and hemmed in by development. Lifeguards are on duty 9am–5pm in summer and 10am–3pm in winter.

Eat and drink

Picnic: under $25; Snacks: $25–50; Real meal: $50–80; Family treat: over $80 (based on a family of four)

PICNIC Publix at Vero Mall *(1255 US-1, 32960; 772 778 1984; www.publix.com)* offers a huge selection of fresh groceries, a deli, and an in-store bakery. The beach is a short drive away.
SNACKS The Barefoot Cafe *(2036 14th Ave, 32960; 772 770 1733; www.thebarefootcafe.com)* has seating, but mostly caters to a take-out crowd with a tasty menu of healthy wraps, soups and salads.

Beach Museum of Art & Indian River Citrus Museum: free. McKee Botanical Garden: May–Oct: $22–28; Nov–Apr: $28–38

Guided tours The Environmental Learning Center runs daily Trek & Tracks nature walks in its grounds.

Age range All ages

Activities Download the McKee Botanical Garden's Children's Guide at www.mckeegarden.org.

Allow 2 days

Good family value?
Low entrance charges make this town suitable for all budgets. The beaches offer endless fun for kids.

Playground for kids in Humiston Park, Vero Beach

REAL MEAL The Lemon Tree *(3125 Ocean Dr, 32963; 772 231 0858; www.lemontreevero.com)* overlooks the ocean and is an especially good place for a diner-style breakfast or lunch. It also offers a kids' menu.
FAMILY TREAT Ocean Grill *(1050 Sexton Plaza, 32963; 772 231 5409; www.ocean-grill.com; closed Sun lunchtime)* is a local legend situated right on the beach. It serves classic seafood and has a great kids' menu.

Island-style decor of the Barefoot Cafe, Vero Beach

Find out more

DIGITAL Visit www.kidsrecyclingzone.com and www.naturerocks.org, which are fun sites with an environmental theme. Older kids might want to check out 1715treasurefleet.com for more on the Spanish treasure fleet.

Next stop...

FORT PIERCE Head 15 miles (24 km) south to Fort Pierce *(see p96)* for a day to learn about Florida's marine life at the Manatee Observation & Education Center and Harbor Branch Ocean Discovery Center.

KIDS' CORNER

Tables, trees, and Tikis

You might think that the McKee Botanical Garden is just full of plants and trees, but if you look hard enough you might find some special things:
1 Somewhere in the garden is a wooden table – not just any table, but the biggest mahogany table in the world!
2 A Tiki is a large Polynesian carving of a scary face usually made on Pacific islands. But there is one here guarding a secret seating area: can you find it?
3 There is a strange-looking tree called "the dragon tree." Can you see why it is called that?
4 The pineapples you can eat look green and yellow. You can see tiny pink pineapples in the gardens. Don't try to pick them!

TREASURE QUEST

Take a sketchbook and draw your own treasure island map. Add scary names such as Blood Valley, Skull Cave, and Terror River. Make sure you mark the treasure with a special symbol, and draw arrows to show how to find it.

What lies beneath

The Spanish treasure fleet of 1715, sailing from Cuba to Spain, was made up of 12 galleons loaded with silverware, and lots of gold. As the fleet sailed past Florida, it was hit by a fierce hurricane that wrecked 11 of the ships. Over 1,000 sailors were drowned, and many more died of starvation. Much of the treasure was never recovered – experts think that treasure worth $550 million remains hidden on the seabed.

⑰ Fort Pierce

On top of the lagoon, and deep beneath the sea

Much of Fort Pierce is industrial, but there are a few attractions on the outskirts. The **Manatee Observation & Education Center**, overlooking the Indian River Lagoon, is the favored grazing spot of the local manatee population. The best time to see them is from mid-November to early April. Dolphins and pelicans are also regular visitors. The center houses a butterfly garden and hands-on exhibits that provide information about manatees, butterflies, their habitats, and more.

Just 5 miles (8 km) north of Fort Pierce, the Harbor Branch Oceanographic Institute is a well-equipped deep-sea research center belonging to Florida Atlantic University. Visit the **Ocean Discovery Center** to learn about the incredible work done in the underwater labs – developing food aquaculture and

deep-ocean exploration. The interactive exhibits are educational, but still fun for kids 7 plus. There is also a small aquarium for little ones.

Letting off steam

Head to **Fort Pierce Inlet State Park** *(905 Shorewinds Dr, 34949; 772 468 3985; www.floridastateparks.org)*, on the other side of the North Causeway (Hwy-A1A). It has a small unspoiled beach.

⑱ Hutchinson Island

Bathtubs on the beach

This island is a slim, 20-mile (32-km) stretch of mangroves, scrub, and idyllic sandy beaches. It has only one road, Highway-A1A, which runs from north to south. The best attractions lie at the southern end of the island, across from the town of Stuart. **Bathtub Reef Park** is a popular destination for families. At low tide,

Fishing along the shore of Hutchinson Island

a series of exposed reefs just offshore create a protected, bathtub-like swimming area ideal for kids. A short drive north, the **Elliott Museum**, in eco-friendly premises, charts the history of the area with interactive exhibits and hands-on learning experiences. The museum also has a collection of over 50 vintage cars.

The Lowdown

🌐 **Map reference** 8 H3
   Address Stuart 34996.
   Bathtub Reef Park: 1585 SE McArthur Blvd. Elliott Museum: 825 NE Ocean Blvd; 772 225 1961; *www.elliottmuseumfl.org*. Florida Oceanographic Coastal Center: 890 NE Ocean Blvd; 772 225 0505; *www.floridaocean.org*

🚗 **Car** Rent a car from Palm Beach Airport.

ℹ **Visitor information** Stuart/Martin County Chamber of Commerce, 1650 S Kanner Hwy, 34994; *www.stuartmartinchamber.org*

🕐 **Open** Elliot Museum: reopening in 2013. Florida Oceanographic Coastal Center: 10am–5pm Mon–Sat & noon–4pm Sun

💲 **Price** Florida Oceanographic Coastal Center: $20–40; under 3s free

👫 **Age range** All ages

👫 **Activities** The Florida Oceanographic Coastal Center offers a children's activity pavilion, stingray feeding program, and lagoon fish feeding program.

🕐 **Allow** Half a day to a full day

🍽 **Eat and drink** SNACKS The Chef Shack *(899 N E Ocean Blvd, 34996; 772 334 0820)* serves grouper sandwiches and burgers. REAL MEAL Shuckers Restaurant *(9800 S Ocean Dr, Jensen Beach, 34957; 772 229 1224; islandbeachresort.net)* has pasta and seafood.

Rocky shoreline of Fort Pierce Inlet State Park, Fort Pierce

The Lowdown

🌐 **Map reference** 8 G3
   Address Manatee Observation & Education Center: 480 N Indian River Dr, 34950; 772 466 1600; *www.manateecenter.com*. Ocean Discovery Center: 5600 US-1, 34946; 772 242 2417; *www.fau.edu/hboi/OceanDiscoveryCenter.php*

🚌 **Bus** Greyhound bus from Miami and Jacksonville. It's best to drive.

ℹ **Visitor information** St Lucie County Chamber of Commerce, 482 N Indian River Dr, 34950; 772 468 9196; *www.stluciechamber.org*

🕐 **Open** Manatee Observation & Education Center: check website. Ocean Discovery Center: 10am–5pm Mon–Fri & 10am–2pm Sat

💲 **Prices** Manatee Observation & Education Center: $4–14;

under 6s free. Ocean Discovery Center: free

🚩 **Guided tours** Indian River Lagoon Wildlife Boat Tours at Manatee Observation & Education Center; call 772 460 6445.

👫 **Age range** All ages. Ocean Discovery Center: 7 plus

👫 **Activities** Manatee Observation & Education Center runs family-friendly kayak tours every Sat Jan–May.

🕐 **Allow** Half a day to a full day

🍽 **Eat and drink** SNACKS Uncle Carlo's Gelato *(141 Melody Lane, 34950; 772 672 4401)* has gelato, cookies and paninis. REAL MEAL 12A Buoy *(22 Fisherman's Wharf, 34950; 772 672 4524)* is a fish shack with an old Florida vibe and an outdoor deck.

The **Florida Oceanographic Coastal Center** across the street from the museum, takes a practical approach to learning about Florida's marine life, offering a stingray touch tank, a huge game fish lagoon, and a looping nature trail to the Indian River Lagoon.

Letting off steam

Just across Ocean Boulevard from the Elliott Museum, **Stuart Beach** is a tranquil stretch of sand with lifeguards, boardwalk access points, parking, a snack bar, and restrooms.

⑲ Jupiter Island

Turtle walks and blowing rocks

A long, thin strip of pine, sand, and scrub, Jupiter Island is 17 miles (27 km) of affluent homes and wonderfully pristine beaches. The only north–south thoroughfare on the island is Beach Road, but with the sea blocked from view most of the way, it is not especially scenic, so plan to make several stops.

The northern end of the island is protected within **Hobe Sound National Wildlife Refuge**, a major nesting site for sea turtles and best experienced on an organized turtle walk. At other times, stroll up the 2-mile (4-km) beach trail to Peck Lake, looking out for scrub jays, gopher tortoises, and tiny snakes. The refuge's small nature center, on US-1, has a few exhibits, including tanks with baby alligators, and there is a short nature trail that leads down to the shores of the Indian River Lagoon.

Toward the southern end of the island, **Blowing Rocks Preserve** contains a limestone outcrop that covers much of the beach – it is fun to watch the waves driving under the rocks and spraying out at the top.

The Hawley Education Center across the road has displays on Jupiter Island habitats and more trails into the thick mangroves on the lagoon.

Letting off steam

Visit **Jonathan Dickinson State Park** (16450 SE Federal Hwy, Hobe Sound, 33455; 772 546 2771; www.florida stateparks.org), located south of Stuart. It has a swath of pine scrub, mangroves, and river swamps just across the water from Jupiter Island.

The Lowdown

🌐 **Map reference** 8 H4
Address Hobe Sound National Wildlife Refuge: 13640 SE Federal Hwy, Hobe Sound, 33475; 772 546 6141; www.fws.gov. Blowing Rocks Preserve: 574 South Beach Rd, Hobe Sound, 33455; 561 744 6668; www.nature.org

🚗 **Car** Rent a car from Palm Beach Airport.

ℹ️ **Visitor information** Northern Palm Beach County Chamber of Commerce, 800 US-1, 33477; 561 746 7111; npbchamber.com

🕐 **Open** Hobe Sound National Wildlife Refuge: sunrise–sunset daily. Blowing Rocks Preserve: 9am–4:30pm daily

💲 **Prices** Hobe Sound National Wildlife Refuge: $5 per car per day. Blowing Rocks Preserve: $8–18; under 12s free

🧍 **Age range** All ages

🤸 **Activities** Hobe Sound National Wildlife Refuge runs turtle hikes. Call 772 546 2067 for details.

⏱️ **Allow** A day

🍴 **Eat and drink** SNACKS Harry & the Natives (11910 SE Federal Hwy, 33455; harryandthenatives.com) has fish sandwiches and gator burgers. REAL MEAL Flash Beach Grille (9126 SE Bridge Rd, 33455; www.flashcatering.com) serves mermaid pasta & popcorn shrimp.

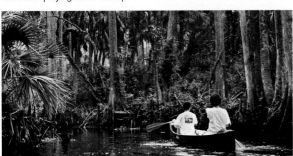

Visitors canoeing down the river in Jonathan Dickinson State Park

Picnic under $25; **Snacks** $25–50; **Real meal** $50–80; **Family treat** over $80 (based on a family of four)

Where to Stay on the Gold and Treasure Coasts

This region offers plenty of choice in family-friendly lodging, from budget motels to luxury resorts on the beach. Finding campgrounds close to the beach is tough, but state parks often have good camping options. There is a wide range of self-catering apartments and cottage rentals to choose from too.

AGENCIES

Boca Valley Realty
www.bocavalleyrealty.com
This agency offers a wide choice of lodging in southern Florida, including Boca Raton and Miami.

Vacation Rentals
www.vacationrentals.com
This website lists over 13,000 properties across Florida, from vacation homes and beach houses to condos and apartments.

Boca Raton   Map 8 H6

RESORT
Boca Beach Club
900 S Ocean Blvd, 33432; 561 447 3000; www.bocabeachclub.com
This plush place sits right on the beach and offers lots of activities, as well as the dedicated Camp Boca for kids. Rooms and suites are stylish, with plenty of amenities, but no kitchen. There is also a Family Room and tennis clinics for ages 3 to 18.
ⁿ ⁣⁣⁣⁣ $$$

HOTEL
Ocean Lodge
531 N Ocean Blvd, 33432; 561 395 7772; www.oceanlodgeflorida.com
Just off the beach, this hotel has spotless rooms, granite kitchenettes and dining areas, as well as flat-screen TVs and barbecue grills. There is a coin-operated laundry on site.
ⁿ ⁣⁣ $$

Fort Lauderdale   Map 10 H1

RESORTS
Harbor Beach Marriott Resort & Spa
3030 Holiday Dr, 33316; 954 525 4000; www.marriottharborbeach.com
A luxurious beachfront property with large, comfy suites, this resort has a private beach and a complimentary Surf Club for kids with a Hawaiian surf

simulator, a clubhouse, and two Xbox 360s. Resort activities include beach sports and face-painting.
ⁿ ⁣⁣⁣⁣ $$$

Lago Mar Resort & Club
1700 S Ocean Lane, 33316; 954 523 6511; www.lagomar.com
This sprawling beachfront property has 164 suites with refrigerators and microwaves. Centrally located and with its own secure, private beach, it offers beach volleyball, shuffleboard, and a giant outdoor chessboard.
ⁿ ⁣⁣⁣⁣ $$$

Palm-fringed pool at Birch Patio, Fort Lauderdale

HOTELS
Birch Patio
617 N Birch Rd, 33304; 954 563 9540; www.birchpatio.com
This retro-looking hotel is a 5-minute walk from the beach, with spacious, modern efficiency apartments. Free parking, a coin-operated washer and dryer, and two barbecue grills are available. Kids under 12 stay free.
ⁿ ⁣⁣⁣ $

Premiere Hotel
3110 Belmar St, 33304; 954 566 7676; www.premierehotel.com
Located close to the beach, this hotel offers efficiency rooms with two beds and fully equipped kitchens, as well as suites. Although this is an older property, everything is spotless.
ⁿ ⁣⁣ $

Fort Pierce/Port St. Lucie   Map 8 G3

RESORT
Club Med Sandpiper Bay
4500 SE Pine Valley St, Port St Lucie, 34952; 772 398 5100; www.clubmed.us
This all-inclusive resort is especially fun for families, with a Baby Welcome program, Baby Club Med, beautifully furnished family rooms and heaps of kids' programs at the Kidz Village.
ⁿ ⁣⁣⁣⁣ $$$

HOTEL
Holiday Inn Express
7151 Okeechobee Rd, Fort Pierce, 34945; 772 464 5000, www.hiexpress.com
Located close to the Florida Turnpike and I-95, and a 10–15-minute drive into downtown Fort Pierce, this hotel is suitable for a one-night stay. Rooms are modern and can lodge up to four.
ⁿ ⁣ $

CAMPING
Savannas Campground
1400 E Midway Rd, Fort Pierce, 34982; 772 464 7855; www.stlucieco.gov/parks/savannas.htm.
This county-run campsite is situated 7 miles (11 km) south of downtown Fort Pierce. It lies on reclaimed marshland beside the Indian River, and offers both primitive pitches and some with electricity and water.
ⁿ ⁣⁣⁣⁣ $

Hutchinson Island   Map 8 H3

RESORT
Hutchinson Island Marriott Beach Resort & Marina
555 NE Ocean Blvd, Stuart, 34996; 772 225 3700; www.marriott.com
Just across the causeway from Stuart, this resort has rooms with pull-out sofa beds for kids, and

well-equipped kitchens. Family-friendly activities are planned each week.

🌊 🍽 🛏 ⊙ ⊘ $$

Juno Beach
Map 8 H5

HOTEL
Hampton Inn Jupiter
13801 US-1, 33408; 561 626 9090; hamptoninn.hilton.com
This convenient, family-friendly hotel, near the Loggerhead Marinelife Center, offers "Two Queen Deluxe" rooms that accommodate up to five and are equipped with a microwave. Breakfast is included. A coin-operated laundry is on site.

🌊 🔋 🛏 ⊙ $$

Palm Beach
Map 8 H5

RESORT
The Breakers
1 S County Rd, 33480; 888 273 2537; www.thebreakers.com
A fabulous option for families, this resort has a self-contained Family Entertainment Center, babysitting services, and a variety of kids' camps. All rooms are luxuriously furnished; standard rooms are big enough for most families with young children.

🌊 🍽 🛏 ⊙ ⊘ $$$

HOTELS
Palm Beach Historic Inn
365 S County Rd, 33480; 561 832 4009; www.palmbeachhistoricinn.com
This charming old guesthouse offers clean rooms with two double beds, as well as four spacious suites with a king bed, trundle bed, VCR, and refrigerator. Breakfast is included.

🌊 🛏 $$

The Chesterfield
Cocoanut Row, 33480; 561 659 5800; www.chesterfieldpb.com
A historic hotel with bright and luxurious rooms that lodge two adults and two children. Kids aged 12 and under stay and eat free when sharing a room with parents.

🌊 🍽 🛏 ⊙ $$$

Vero Beach
Map 8 G2

RESORTS
Driftwood Resort
3150 Ocean Dr, 32963; 772 231 0550; www.thedriftwood.com
The most atmospheric place to stay on the Treasure Coast offers spacious rooms and villas. Families can go for a large two-room suite in the "Breakers" section. Kids will love the scavenger hunts and shuffleboard.

🌊 ☕ 🛏 ⊙ ⊘ $

Disney's Vero Beach Resort
9250 Island Grove Terrace, 32963; 407 939 7828; www.disneybeach resorts.com/vero-beach-resort
A plush resort set on the beach, this has elegant studios that sleep four, villas, and three-bedroom cottages that sleep up to 12. There is a 163-ft (50-m) spiral waterslide, a children's wet play area, treasure hunts, and sing-a-long campfires.

🌊 🍽 🛏 ⊙ ⊘ $$$

Vero Beach Hotel & Spa
3500 Ocean Dr, 32963; 772 231 5666; www.verobeachhotelandspa.com
This family-friendly luxury resort has one-, two- and three-bedroom suites, all with kitchens. The "Kimpton Kids" program provides babysitting, cribs, and high chairs.

🌊 🍽 🛏 ⊙ ⊘ $$$

MOTEL
Comfort Suites Vero Beach
9050 Americana Way, 32963; 772 257 3400; www.comfortsuites.com
This excellent motel off I-95 is just 12 miles (19 km) from the beach. All rooms come with flat-screen TVs, microwaves, and refrigerators. There is a coin-operated laundry, and breakfast is included.

🌊 ⊙ $

CAMPING
Sebastian Inlet State Park
9700 S State Rd A1A, Melbourne Beach, 32951; 321 984 4852; www.floridastateparks.org
The park's attractive tent and RV campground is just a short stroll from the beach. All 51 sites have water and electrical hook-ups. There is a Bedtime Story Camper Lending Library for kids aged 4 to 9.

🌊 $

West Palm Beach
Map 8 H5

MOTEL
Best Western Palm Beach Lakes Inn
1800 Palm Beach Lakes Blvd, 33401; 561 683 8810; www.bestwestern westpalm.com
Across from the Palm Beach Mall, which is about 15 minutes from downtown, this motel has standard rooms arranged around a central pool area. All rooms have microwaves and refrigerators, and rollaway beds are available on request.

🌊 ⊙ $

CAMPING
Lion Country Safari KOA Campground
2003 Lion Country Safari Rd, Loxahatchee, 33470; 561 793 9797; www.lioncountrysafari.com
This campground, adjacent to Lion Country Safari, has tent sites with water and electricity, a grill and picnic table, as well as cabins, which offer a bit more comfort. There is a general store, playground, and laundry, and plenty of sports are on offer.

🌊 ⊙ $

Price Guide
The following price ranges are based on one night's accommodation in high season for a family of four, inclusive of service charges and additional taxes.

$ Under $150 **$$** $150–300 **$$$** over $300

A double room with a view of the ocean in The Breakers, Palm Beach

Key to symbols *see back cover flap*

Orlando
and the Parks

With more than a dozen theme parks, central Florida might seem like one big roller coaster, but there is also much natural and cultural beauty to explore. Orlando and its upscale "suburb," Winter Park, have museums, world-class restaurants, festivals, and sporting events that enhance the joy of the thrill rides, and add to the experience of visiting this colorful area.

Highlights

Walt Disney World® Resort
See Walt Disney's vision come alive in four famous theme parks *(see pp106–17)*.

Universal Studios Florida® and Universal's Islands of Adventure®
Meet the Simpsons™ or visit Harry Potter's™ Hogwarts™ at these entertainment theme parks *(see pp118–21)*.

SeaWorld®, Aquatica, and Discovery Cove®
Applaud performing whales at SeaWorld®, swim with dolphins at Discovery Cove®, and hop aboard thrilling water rides at Aquatica *(see pp122–3)*.

Wet 'n Wild®
Spend the day getting soaked at the country's first – and still one of its best – water park thrill ride attractions *(see pp124–5)*.

Orlando and Winter Park
Visit museums of art and science, watch championship basketball, and marvel at leaping alligators – a combination possible only in Orlando *(see pp127–31)*.

LEGOLAND®
At this LEGO®-themed park, kids can learn how many LEGO® blocks it would take to build the Statue of Liberty, and how they could do it at home *(see pp132–5)*.

Left *The iconic Sorcerer Mickey Hat at Disney's Hollywood Studios®*
Above right *Massive LEGO® giraffe at the entrance to the thrilling Imagination Zone, LEGOLAND®*

The Best of
Orlando and the Parks

The fantasylands, wild animals, movie history, and world culture of the Walt Disney® theme parks have been drawing millions of visitors since 1971. Universal Studios Florida® adds to the adventure, celebrating movies and the world of Harry Potter™, along with the water wonderlands of SeaWorld® and Wet 'n Wild®. The city of Orlando, and its suburb Winter Park, have excellent historical museums, cultural sites, and entertainment options.

The wonderful world of Disney

Look up in **Magic Kingdom®** *(see pp108–9)* to see the soaring castle towers where Cinderella and Beauty's Beast live, or get an adrenaline rush on the Space Mountain®, Splash Mountain®, and Big Thunder Mountain® coasters. Ride with Ariel on Under the Sea: Journey of the Little Mermaid, and on a flying carpet in The Magic Carpets of Aladdin.

Soarin'™ lets visitors glide over the Californian landscape in **Epcot®** *(see pp110–11)*, while Test Track allows them to design and test custom vehicles, and Mission: Space® goes beyond the atmosphere. World Showcase displays the cultures of 11 countries in a 2-mile (3-km) circle and features booming *taiko* drummers in the Japan Pavilion, and the Off Kilter bagpipe band in the Canada Pavilion.

Visit Muppets, living toys, and Indiana Jones™ in **Disney's Hollywood Studios®** *(see pp114–15)*. All Kermit fans will love Muppet*Vision 3D,

and thrills await at the Rock 'n' Roller Coaster® Starring Aerosmith. At **Disney's Animal Kingdom®** *(see pp112–13)*, Festival of the Lion King blends music and theater. Take the Kilimanjaro Safaris® to see lions and wildebeests.

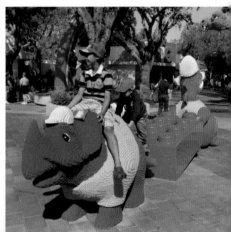

Right Kids playing with LEGO® dinosaurs, LEGOLAND®
Below Riding the Kali River Rapids, Disney's Animal Kingdom®

Above Crazy curves and weird shapes of the Cat in the Hat's™ Seuss Landing, Universal Studios Florida®

Movie magic

Universal Orlando® Resort presents entertainment for the whole family. Once a single movie park, today it features the amazing **Universal Studios Florida®** *(see pp118–19)* and **Universal's Islands of Adventure®** *(see pp120–21)*. Men In Black™ and The Simpsons™ rides bring movies and TV to life at **Universal Studios Florida®**, while the Shrek 4-D show reintroduces the big green ogre. Over at **Universal's Islands of Adventure®** kids can cast a spell aboard Harry Potter and the Forbidden Journey™ or travel at 40 mph (64 km/h) on The Incredible Hulk Coaster®.

Culture vultures

International Drive *(see p126)*, Orlando's bustling strip of restaurants and hotels, features **Wonderworks** *(see p126)*, which includes a simulated earthquake and an upside-down building, and the fascinating **Ripley's Believe It or Not! Odditorium** *(see p126)*. **Downtown Orlando's** *(see p130)* big draw is the 20,000-seat **Amway Center** *(see p130)*, home of NBA basketball, arena football, concerts, and circuses. Check out the fine restaurants and music clubs nearby, as well as the charming Lake Eola Park, which has plenty of space to run around. While **Downtown Orlando** holds the **Orlando Museum of Art** *(see p130)* and the **Orlando Science Center** *(see pp128–9)*, **Winter Park** *(see p130)* is home to the world's best collection of Tiffany art at the **Morse Museum** *(see p130)*, and a wonderfully casual main street filled with shops and restaurants called Park Avenue. The highlight of **Winter Park** is the **Scenic Boat Tour** *(see p131)* that winds through the picturesque lakes and canals of this historic area, with views of grand mansions and beautiful natural life.

The best of the rest

While **Wet 'n Wild®** *(see pp124–5)* boasts some of the most thrilling water rides with The Storm and Mach 5, big water shows with big sea animals, such as One Ocean with Shamu the whale, are the highlights at **Seaworld®** *(see pp122–3)*. **Discovery Cove®** *(see pp122–3)* offers a relaxed resort-like experience, and a close encounter with dolphins.

Kids can walk through the amazing LEGO® city replicas at Miniland USA in **LEGOLAND®** *(see pp132–5)*, unearth Egyptian treasures in the Lost Kingdom Adventure, and have an exciting driving experience at the Ford Jr. Driving School.

Left The dazzling Tiffany Chapel exhibit in the Morse Museum, Winter Park

Orlando and the Parks

Orlando is the undisputed theme park capital of the world, with Walt Disney World® Resort, Universal Orlando® Resort, LEGOLAND®, and the water parks making the city a family-oriented fantasyland. But the city has a lot more to offer. International Drive is chock-full of kid-friendly attractions and good restaurants, and sports fans will delight in the spectacular basketball arena at Amway Center. With so many sights spread out over the city, it is best to hire a car to get around.

Scenic view of a lakefront mansion, Winter Park

Places of interest

SIGHTS

1   Walt Disney World® Resort
2   Universal Studios Florida®
3   Universal's Islands of Adventure®
4   SeaWorld®, Aquatica and Discovery Cove®
5   Wet 'n Wild®
6   International Drive
7   Gatorland
8   Orlando Science Center
9   Loch Haven Park
10 Downtown Orlando
11 Winter Park
12 Winter Park Scenic Boat Tours
13 LEGOLAND®

Kids playing with an interactive exhibit at Orlando Science Center

The TriceraTop Spin in DinoLand U.S.A., Disney's Animal Kingdom®

The Lowdown

🚗 **Getting there and around**
Air Fly to Orlando International Airport (www.orlandoairports.net) or Orlando Sanford International Airport (www.orlandosanford airport.com). **Bus** Greyhound (1 800 231 2222; www.grey hound.com) has stations across Orlando. Red Coach (1 877 733 0724; www.redcoachusa.com) has terminals near Orlando International Airport. Megabus (1 877 462 6342; us.megabus. com) has a downtown terminal near the Lynx main station. See Walt Disney World® (see pp106–7) for transportation across parks. **Train** Amtrak (1 800 872 7245; www.amtrak.com) has stations in Orlando and Winter Park. **Car** Rental chains, such as Avis (www. avis.com) and L&M (www. lmcarrental.net), are located at the airport and across Orlando.

ℹ️ **Visitor information** Orlando Visitor Center, 8723 International Dr, Orlando, 32819; 407 363 5872; www.visitorlando.com

🛒 **Supermarkets** Publix (www. publix.com) is the premier supermarket with outlets throughout the region. The upscale organic food chain Whole Foods (www.wholefoods market.com) also has branches in Orlando and Winter Park. **Markets** Downtown Orlando Farmers' Market, located near Lake Eola, offers seasonal produce, ethnic foods, and local crafts and artwork every Sun.

🎊 **Festivals** Walt Disney World® Marathon (Jan). Zora Neale Hurston Festival of the Arts; www.zorafestival.com (Jan). Universal Studios Florida® Mardi Gras (mid-Feb–Apr). Orlando International Fringe Theatre Festival; www.orlandofringe.org (May). Epcot® International Flower & Garden Festival (Mar–May). Seaworld® Viva La Musica; www.tinyurl.com/ SWViva (Apr–May). Disney® Star Wars™ Weekends (May–Jun). Universal® Summer Nights (Jun–Aug). Walt Disney World® Night of Joy (Sep). Mickey's Not-So-Scary Halloween Party (Sep–Oct). Universal® Halloween Spooktacular (Oct). Epcot® International Food & Wine Festival (Sep–Nov). LEGOLAND® Christmas Bricktacular (Dec). Universal® Grinchmas (Dec). For festivals across Walt Disney World®, visit disneyworld.disney. go.com/special-events. For Universal Studios® and Islands of Adventure® festivals, visit www.universalorlando.com/ Events/Year-Round-Events.aspx.

➕ **Pharmacies** Walgreens (www.walgreens.com) and CVS (www.cvs.com) are the two major pharmacies in the region; some of their branches in cities are open 24 hours.

🚻 **Restrooms** All major attractions, shopping malls, and gas stations have public restrooms.

LEGO® pirates at the entrance to Pirate's Cove, LEGOLAND®

① Walt Disney World® Resort
The house of The Mouse

Walt Disney changed Orlando from a sleepy cattle-rearing and orange-growing town into a family vacation hot spot. Spread over four exciting theme parks, the resort's attractions are based on cartoon animals invented 80 years ago, as well as characters out of 3-D movies. While Magic Kingdom® and Disney's Hollywood Studios® play with the imagination, Epcot® showcases world culture and Disney's Animal Kingdom® entertains with animal-themed rides.

DinoLand, U.S.A., Disney's Animal Kingdom®

Key Sights

① **Magic Kingdom®** Splash down a 52-ft (16-m) high mountain, learn the ways of a pirate, or wander through Cinderella Castle at the best known of the Disney parks.

② **Epcot®** This park is divided into two sections: the modernistic Future World, with the iconic Spaceship Earth ride, and the World Showcase, which features the attractions, shops, and cuisines of 11 countries.

③ **Disney's Animal Kingdom®** Besides thrill rides, musical shows and parades, and animals from Africa and Asia in re-creations of their natural habitats, this unique zoo also has dizzying roller coasters zipping through mountains.

⑤ **Water Parks** Cool off aboard one of the world's tallest waterslides at Blizzard Beach, a snow-covered ski resort. The tropical Typhoon Lagoon has water-soaked attractions to suit all ages, including a surf pool with 6-ft (2-m) waves.

④ **Disney's Hollywood Studios®** High-speed rides, thrilling stunt and stage shows, and film extravaganzas – from The Muppets to Beauty and the Beast – lure visitors of all ages to this theme park.

Prices given are for a family of four

The Lowdown

🌐 **Map reference** 6 E6
Address 4600 N World Dr, Lake Buena Vista, 32830; 407 939 6244 or 407 939 1289 (for tickets); *disneyworld.disney.go.com*

🚗 **Bus** Lynx bus 50, 56, 302 & 306 ($2 one way) from Downtown Orlando to the Ticket and Transportation Center (TTC). Free airport shuttle for resort guests. Free Disney buses connect every park. **Taxi** Water taxis from the TTC to Magic Kingdom®, Epcot®, Downtown Disney®, and resorts. **Train** Monorails from the TTC to Magic Kingdom®, Epcot®, and resorts. **Car** From Orlando International Airport take South exit (FL 417S – toll) to Osceola Pkwy West (Exit 3) to Disney exits. Parking $14/day

🕑 **Open** Parks open from between 9am and 11am to between 5pm and 1am. Hours vary by park and season; check website for details. Every day, one theme park opens an hour early and closes two hours later for guests staying at the Walt Disney World® Resort hotels – Extra Magic Hours.

💲 **Prices** $344–56 per park; under 3s free. The Park-Hopper® Pass for visiting multiple parks can be bought for an additional $140. Multiday tickets range from 2 days ($590–680; under 3s free) to 5, 7, 14 and 21 days. Check website for vacation plans at Disney hotels that include discounted park prices, and for offers on park tickets.

👥 **Cutting the line** Parks are busiest in mid-Feb, mid-Mar–late Apr,

⑥ **Disney's Fort Wilderness Resort & Campground** This resort offers some of the best kid-centered dining options. Mickey's Backyard BBQ offers a chance to dance with Mickey Mouse.

⑦ **Downtown Disney®** Live music at the House of Blues, the thrilling Cirque du Soleil®-La Nouba™ show, and video games at the DisneyQuest® Indoor Interactive Theme Park are some of the highlights of this entertainment and shopping complex.

⑧ **Winter Summerland Miniature Golf Course™** Play putt-putt in two Santa Claus-themed courses: the sunny Sand Course or the wintry Snow Course.

Colorful exterior of Pizzafari restaurant, in Disney's Animal Kingdom®

Eat and drink

Each park has a multitude of dining options, from fast-snack carts to full-service restaurants and themed dinner shows *(see individual entries for details)*. Signature restaurants throughout the parks require a credit card for reservations; if the reservation is not canceled at least 24 hours ahead, there is a $10

charge per person. Restaurants that request full prepayment will not make a refund unless the reservation is canceled sufficiently in advance.

Shopping

Find everything from toys and kids' apparel to housewares, and jewelry in the park's shops. Kids will love the Captain Jack-themed gifts near the Pirates of the Caribbean® ride in Magic Kingdom®, and carved animal toys in Animal Kingdom®.

Find out more

DIGITAL Visit *www.wdwmagic.com/walt-disney-world-history.htm* to learn about the history of Walt Disney World® Resort. The website has a timeline that highlights events in the park's story. Younger kids will like *www.disney.co.uk/disney-junior*.

Memorial Day weekend (May), mid-Jun–Labor Day (Sep), Thanksgiving weekend (Nov) & Christmas week–New Year's Day. **FASTPASS** tickets allow visitors to reserve a time slot for the 21 attractions covered in this system by inserting a park ticket into a FASTPASS machine at ride entrance.

Guided tours The 7-hour Backstage Magic tour takes visitors behind the scenes at three Disney parks – Epcot®, Disney's Hollywood Studios® and Magic Kingdom® – and shows how thrill rides, landscaping, and parades are put together; tickets include lunch at Wilderness Lodge.

Age range The parks are most suitable for ages 7 and above.

Younger kids will enjoy Magic Kingdom® the most, as well as some parts of Disney's Animal Kingdom® and Disney's Hollywood Studios®. Age and height restrictions apply for most rides.

Activities Some Disney resorts run kids' programs that feature supervised activity centers. There are playgrounds, tennis courts, and a marina with watercraft rental.

Allow At least a day for each park

Wheelchair access Yes

Cafés Many across the park

Restrooms Across the park

Good family value?

Although expensive, Disney is every child's dream come true and an unforgettable experience.

Riding the monorail

There are 12 trains in the Walt Disney World® Monorail System, riding on almost 215 miles (346 km) of tracks high above the Seven Seas Lagoon™ and Epcot®. The loop around the lagoon stops at three Disney hotels; ride the complete circle and see if you can name them all.

① **Walt Disney World® Resort continued ▶**

Magic Kingdom®
Let the enchantment begin!

A world full of the romance of princesses and magicians, and the frights of haunted houses – with a few nerve-testing roller coasters thrown in – Magic Kingdom® is the most popular Disney park. Divided into six areas, it is filled with rides and attractions that show off Walt Disney's best-loved characters, and a Disney-style cartoon version of the future.

Balloon vendor at Main Street, USA®

Key Features

Entrance

④ **Frontierland®** Ride a runaway mining car through the Wild West, then board a sailing ship to look for hidden treasure on Tom Sawyer Island.

⑤ **Splash Mountain®** This log flume ride runs through swamps and caves before plummeting 52 ft (16 m) down into a pond.

⑥ **Liberty Square** Themed around the Colonial era, this area features the thrilling Haunted Mansion® and the educative Hall of Presidents.

③ **Fantasyland®** Attractions in this delightful area include the Storybook Circus, with the Great Goofini Coaster.

① **Main Street, USA®** Shop, dine, and see dazzling parades at Main Street. Visitors can board a steam train or a horse-drawn trolley from here for a relaxing trip around the park.

② **Adventureland®** A mix of tropical jungles and colonial buildings, this area features the ever popular Pirates of the Caribbean® and the Magic Carpets of Aladdin carousel.

⑦ **Cinderella Castle** This most photographed Disney attraction houses glass murals depicting the fairy tale. At night, spectacular shows illuminate the stunning castle in a riot of colors.

⑧ **Tomorrowland®** From the sharp turns and steep drops of Space Mountain® to the humor of Monsters, Inc. Laugh Floor, this area is filled with attractions for all ages.

The Lowdown

🌐 **Map reference** 6 E5
Address 1180 Seven Seas Dr, Lake Buena Vista, 32830; 407 939 6244; *disneyworld.disney.go.com*

🚗 **Bus, water taxi, or monorail** from the TTC and resorts *(see p106)*

🕐 **Open** From between 8am and 9am to between 8pm and 1am. Check the park's "Calendar" page for seasonal variations and Extra Magic Hours.

💲 **Price** *see p106*

👫 **Cutting the line** Avoid Mon and Thu, when the park is busiest.

🚩 **Guided tours** The 4½-hour Keys to the Kingdom walking tour ($74 per person) highlights the behind-the-scenes workings of Magic Kingdom®, including a walk through the legendary underground tunnels. The tour is for ages 16 and above.

👫 **Age range** All ages

🎭 **Shows** Kids will love Mickey's PhilharMagic, a 12-min 3-D movie, and Country Bear Jamboree, a musical revue featuring singing bears. One-eyed monster Mike Wazowski will have

kids laughing at the interactive Monsters, Inc. Laugh Floor comedy show; contact the Guest Relations office (407 939 6244) for times.

⏱ **Allow** Half a day to 2 days

♿ **Wheelchair access** Yes

🍴 **Eat and drink** SNACKS The Lunching Pad *(in Tomorrowland®)* serves hot dogs, chips, and beverages. FAMILY TREAT Cinderella's Royal Table *(inside Cinderella Castle)* offers the experience of dining with Disney princesses and family,

Top 10 Attractions

1. **BUZZ LIGHTYEAR'S SPACE RANGER SPIN®**
   Shoot a laser cannon at aliens from a spinning XP-37 Space Cruiser on this ride in Tomorrowland®.

2. **SPLASH MOUNTAIN®**
   A theme park in itself, this water-soaked ride in Frontierland® has a track running through swamps, caves, and bayous.

3. **PIRATES OF THE CARIBBEAN®**
   Find Captain Jack Sparrow aboard a boat cruise in Adventureland®, meet pirates, and see blazing cannons before plunging down a 14-ft (4-m) high waterfall.

4. **HAUNTED MANSION®**
   Ride through dark and dusty rooms looking for – or trying to avoid – 999 ghosts, ghouls, and goblins in Liberty Square.

5. **STITCH'S GREAT ESCAPE!™**
   This slightly scary audio and video extravaganza in Tomorrowland® recruits riders as Galactic Federation Security Agents to guard an alien called Stitch.

with a choice of breakfast, lunch, and dinner menus.

Shops Visit the shops at Main Street, USA® for Disney souvenirs.

Restrooms Many throughout the park – the least crowded ones are next to the Pirates of the Caribbean® gift shop, near the Town Hall on Main Street, USA®, and in Tomorrowland®.

Good family value?
Colorful parades, thrilling rides, and spectacular fireworks make this park a treat for all ages.

6. **TOMORROWLAND® SPEEDWAY**
   Drive mini gas-powered sports cars around a 2,000-ft (609-m) long track on this exciting ride.

7. **ENCHANTED TIKI ROOM**
   Hundreds of singing Animatronic® birds – from crooning parrots to *Aladdin's* wisecracking Iago and *The Lion King's* Zazu – delight the audience at this musical show in Adventureland®.

8. **SPACE MOUNTAIN®**
   Climb into a rocket ship to blast into outer space and spiral through a black hole on this intense ride in Tomorrowland®.

9. **BIG THUNDER MOUNTAIN RAILROAD®**
   Zip through an abandoned Wild West-themed mine, with extreme twists and steep drops, on board this dizzying roller coaster in Frontierland®.

10. **MAGIC CARPETS OF ALADDIN**
   Work the controls of a flying carpet to ride high or low around a giant genie bottle in Adventureland®. Watch out for the spitting camels!

Epcot®
Back to the future

The Experimental Prototype Community of Tomorrow (Epcot®) was Walt Disney's neighborhood of the future, designed to connect people with technology. Enjoy exploring the history of science and technology in this complex of two different, but connected, parks. Future World takes visitors from the bottom of the sea to the outer reaches of space, while World Showcase introduces the cultures of 11 countries through their food, architecture, and music.

Guests enjoying the Test Track ride

Key Features

Main Entrance

World Showcase Entrance

Monorail

① **The Seas with Nemo & Friends** In this tribute to the world's oceans, the eponymous ride leads to the majestic Carribean Coral Reef, a 5.7 million gallon (22 million liter) saltwater aquarium home to 6,000 underwater inhabitants.

② **The Land** Parasail over Californian landscapes in the Soarin'™ flying simulator, and take the Living with the Land boat tour through a simulated rain forest to experimental working greenhouses.

③ **Imagination!** Make a dragon sing just by moving, operate the world's largest digital camera, and watch Figment create mischief in Journey into Imagination.

④ **Innoventions** Learn how science affects daily life in this interactive museum of the technology of the past and future. Design a roller coaster and then "ride" it at The Sum of All Thrills™ in Innoventions East.

⑤ **World Showcase** These country-specific pavilions have architectural models and replicas from Mexico, Norway, China, Germany, Italy, the United States, Japan, Morocco, France, the United Kingdom, and Canada. They house a variety of ethnic restaurants and shops.

⑥ **Universe of Energy** Ellen's Energy Adventure, starring Ellen DeGeneres, is a 45-minute journey by film – featuring animatronic dinosaurs and theater seats that move – of the history of energy production and the search for new energy resources.

The Lowdown

🌐 **Map reference** 6 F6
Address 1510 North Ave of the Stars, Orlando, 32830; 407 824 4321; *disneyworld.disney.go.com/parks/epcot*

🚌 **Bus** From all Disney locations. **Monorail** From TTC to Future World. **Taxi** Water taxis from several resorts; check website. Epcot® has two entrances; park at a resort and take the water taxi to avoid the "front door" lines.

🕐 **Open** Future World: 9am–9pm & World Showcase: 11am–9pm. Check the park's "Calendar" page for seasonal variations and Extra Magic Hours.

💲 **Price** see p106

👪 **Cutting the line** The park is most crowded on Tue and Fri; it

⑦ **Mission: SPACE®** This motion simulation thrill ride blasts off on a realistic training mission for space travel, which leads to the Advanced Training Lab for testing of skills in space-related games, and culminates in a landing on Mars.

Prices given are for a family of four

Top 10 Attractions

1. **SPACESHIP EARTH**
   This ride travels through the 40,000-year history of communications, from hieroglyphs to computers, while Project Tomorrow, an interactive play area, lets guests play virtual reality games.

2. **TEST TRACK**
   On this Future World ride, kids go through rigorous crash tests before riding a self-designed car along a three-story high track at 65 mph (105 km/h).

3. **MISSION: SPACE®**
   Dodge meteors, feel the force of twice the Earth's gravity, and train for a Mars landing on this motion simulation ride.

4. **SOARIN'™**
   Hang-glide over California in this ultra-realistic simulator ride in the Land Pavilion, suspended in a giant panoramic movie theater filled with the sights, sounds and feeling of flying.

5. **THE SEAS WITH NEMO & FRIENDS**
   Join Dory and Marlin in their search for Nemo on the sea floor aboard a "clamobile," among live fish and colorful coral reefs in this massive saltwater tank of the Seas Pavilion.

6. **ELLEN'S ENERGY ADVENTURE**
   Ellen DeGeneres and Bill Nye, the Science Guy, travel through time, exploring the history of energy and taking visitors from the Big Bang to laser views of outer space.

7. **JOURNEY INTO IMAGINATION WITH FIGMENT**
   A flying dragon explores and plays with sight, smell, sound, touch, and taste in this whimsical tour of the senses, in the Imagination! Pavilion.

8. **MAELSTROM**
   Board a Viking ship as it sails through fjords, swamps, and seas, battling rebel trolls and plundering pirates, in the Norway Pavilion.

9. **TURTLE TALK WITH CRUSH**
   Interact with Crush, Finding Nemo's surfing turtle, about the wonders of the ocean at this live 3-D show at the Seas Pavilion.

10. **ILLUMINATIONS: REFLECTIONS OF EARTH**
    This nightly sound and light show uses spectacular fireworks and lasers to tell the history of the world.

KIDS' CORNER

Find the chatterboxes!

There are three talking water fountains and a talking trash can in Epcot®. See if you can find them.

....

Answer at the bottom of the page.

Thirsty?
Club Cool in Innoventions West is the coolest place in Epcot®, offering free samples of soda from all over the world. Try lemon soda from Israel and a Japanese bubbly vegetable drink.

PEEK-A-BOO!

A surprise treat awaits at the Germany Pavilion. Stand in the middle of the square to see hidden cuckoo clocks emerge from almost every building to strike the hour.

Go around the world

1 Be sure to get a World Showcase Passport, which you can have stamped at each "country" you visit.

2 Make your way through the hedge maze in the hidden park behind the United Kingdom Pavilion.

3 Don't miss the acrobat show in front of the China Pavilion, the juggling waiters of Serveur Amusant™ outside the France Pavilion, and the drummers of Japan.

....

---

is busiest during the Flower & Garden Festival (early Mar–mid-May) and Food & Wine Festival (late Sep–mid-Nov).

🚩 **Guided tours** Behind the Seeds is a 1-hour walking tour of Living with the Land greenhouses. There are several tours inside the The Seas Pavilion. Check website for prices. Call 407 939 8687 for reservations.

🧍 **Age range** 3 plus

🎭 **Shows** Watch the World Showcase Players in the United Kingdom Pavilion, Circle of Life in the Land Pavilion, and Phineas & Ferb: Agent P's World Showcase Adventure.

⏱ **Allow** At least 6 hours

♿ **Wheelchair access** Yes

🍴 **Eat and drink SNACKS** Electric Umbrella Restaurant *(in Future World)* has meatball subs and cheeseburgers. **FAMILY TREAT** Coral Reef Restaurant *(in Living Sea)* offers fresh seafood with views of a live coral reef.

🛍 **Shops** Regional choices in World Showcase, notably Der Teddybar in the Germany Pavilion, and kimonos, chopsticks, and candy in the Japan Pavilion.

🚻 **Restrooms** At every pavilion and restaurant. Baby care center between the Mexico Pavilion and Test Track.

Good family value?

Though pricey, the variety of rides and informative tours will engage kids of all ages, and grown-ups.

Disney's Animal Kingdom®

Explore the world's jungles

Disney invented the term "notazoo" to describe Animal Kingdom®, and it is certainly different from a traditional zoo. Families can see Asian tigers padding through ruins, daintily swimming hippos, and majestic mountain gorillas, all of whom live here happily. In addition, there are thrilling rides for the adventurous, and lots more to entertain everyone.

Primeval Whirl® in DinoLand U.S.A.

Key Features

2 miles
(3 km)

Entrance

① **Camp Minnie-Mickey** Resembling a summer camp, this is the place to meet Mickey and Minnie, and enjoy the live-action Festival of the Lion King show.

② **Discovery Island®** Wooden bridges and cave-like tunnels lead to giant tortoises, lemurs, kangaroos, and other exotic creatures. There is also a glass-paneled viewing area where playful otters can be seen.

⑦ **DinoLand, U.S.A.** Travel under the sea with Finding Nemo – The Musical, and into the prehistoric past on the TriceraTop Spin carousel and Primeval Whirl® – two facing coasters with spinning cars.

③ **The Tree of Life** This 145-ft (44-m) tall structure is decorated with around 325 super realistic animal carvings. It also houses the It's Tough to be a Bug® show.

④ **Disney's Animal Kingdom Lodge** This majestic lodge, located close to the park, has a six-story lobby with a view of the surrounding savannas, and some of the best African cuisine around.

⑤ **Rafiki's Planet Watch** Pet the goats, sheep, and llamas in the Affection Section, then head to Habitat Habit! to meet frisky South American cotton-top tamarins.

⑥ **Asia** The Asia section of the park thrills with the Expedition Everest® roller coaster, and is the setting for tigers, Komodo dragons, and a bird show.

⑧ **Africa** Explore the African savanna in the Kilimanjaro Safaris® Expedition, walk along the Pangani Forest Exploration Trail® to the gorilla habitat, and then take the steam-powered Wildlife Express Train.

Top 10 Attractions

17

1. **FESTIVAL OF THE LION KING**
   This elaborate 30-minute musical show in Camp Minnie-Mickey features puppets, dance, and music, and occasionally invites children from the audience to dance along.

2. **PANGANI FOREST EXPLORATION TRAIL®**
   Walk this self-guided trail in Africa to see massive silverback gorillas, exotic birds, meerkats, and hippos.

3. **KALI RIVER RAPIDS®**
   Enter a lush rain forest, in a ride that leads through steaming geysers and misty waterfalls, on

the churning Chakranadi River in the Asia section, before dropping down a 30-ft (9-m) waterfall for a soaking good time *(left)*.

4. **THE AFFECTION SECTION**
   This petting zoo is the only place in Animal Kingdom® where kids can touch and feed a variety of friendly, domesticated animals, such as goats, chickens and sheep.

5. **FINDING NEMO – THE MUSICAL**
   Watch performers dressed as giant colorful fish bring the much-loved animation to life with music, puppets, and Elton John tunes, in this live 30-minute show at DinoLand, U.S.A.

Prices given are for a family of four

The Lowdown

🌐 **Map reference** 6 E6
Address 1375 E Buena Vista Dr, Lake Buena Vista, 32830; 407 824 4321; www.disney world.disney.go.com/parks/animal-kingdom

🚌 **Bus** Lynx 301 from Downtown Orlando. Disney buses connect from TTC and resort hotels.

🕐 **Open** From between 8 and 9am to between 5 and 8pm. Check the park's "Calendar" page for seasonal variations and Extra Magic Hours.

💲 **Price** see p106

👫 **Cutting the line** Avoid Mon–Wed, when park is busiest.

🚶 **Guided tours** Backstage Safari ($288–98), a 3-hour inside look at the care and feeding of the animal inhabitants, ages 16 and above. Wild Africa Trek ($756–66), small group excursions into Pangani Forest for close encounters with animals. Call 407 939 8687 to reserve.

👫 **Age range** All ages

⏱ **Allow** 6 hours–2 days

♿ **Wheelchair access** Yes

🍵 **Eat and drink** REAL MEAL Tusker House Restaurant (in Africa) has an extensive buffet of modernized African cuisine. FAMILY TREAT Sanaa (in Disney's Animal Kingdom Lodge) offers an extraordinary blend of African and Indian food. Dine while enjoying the view of the animals in their habitats.

🛍 **Shops** Zawadi Marketplace gift shop (in Disney's Animal Kingdom Lodge) has African clothing, masks, and toys. Mombasa Marketplace (in Africa) sells African art, wines, jewelry, and musical instruments.

🚻 **Restrooms** Throughout the park. Baby Care Center near Discovery Island

Good family value?

With several outdoor adventures alongside shows for the young ones, there's something for everyone at Animal Kingdom®.

---

6. IT'S TOUGH TO BE A BUG!®
Inside The Tree of Life, see what it means to be a bug, as A Bug's Life characters turn this 3-D movie into a creepy, crawly experience.

7. KILIMANJARO SAFARIS®
Hop aboard a jungle taxi to ride across a dry savanna in Africa, within feet of live zebras, giraffes, rhinos, and elephants.

8. PRIMEVAL WHIRL®
Spin on two dipping, twisting coasters that go back to the age of the dinosaurs, in DinoLand, U.S.A.

9. EXPEDITION EVEREST®
A leaping Abominable Snowman interrupts this hair-raising coaster as it goes up a treacherous

mountain in Asia, at which point the car slams into reverse, to travel downhill at 50 mph (80 km/h).

10. THE TREE OF LIFE
Spot elephants, iguanas, lemurs, sea horses, and serpents among the 325 animals carved into this exquisite manmade tree in Discovery Island® (below).

---

① Walt Disney World® Resort continued ▶

Disney's Hollywood Studios®

Hollywood magic meets the wizardry of Disney

From adventuring treasure hunters and swashbuckling spacemen to living toys and friendly monsters, the attractions at Hollywood Studios® immerse visitors in the history of Hollywood, Disney-style. Opened in 1989 as a working film and TV production facility, today the park features shows and rides based on famous films and TV shows.

Arched entrance leading to the park

Key Features

Entrance

① **Hollywood Boulevard** Kids will love the Pixar Pals Countdown to Fun! parade, with characters from *A Bug's Life* and *Toy Story*, which begins here, and leads visitors to the Sorcerer's Hat, the icon of Disney's Hollywood Studios®.

② **Sunset Boulevard** Ride a runaway elevator on The Twilight Zone Tower of Terror™ or zoom away on the Rock 'n' Roller Coaster® Starring Aerosmith, before ending the day at a fireworks show.

③ **Echo Lake**
The American Idol®
Experience re-creates
the TV show with new
singing stars chosen by the
audience. The Indiana Jones™ Epic
Stunt Spectacular! offers pyrotechnics
of another sort.

⑤ **Star Tours®** The most popular attraction in this park, Star Tours® uses characters and scenes from the *Star Wars*™ films and leads guests on a multiple-storyline intergalactic adventure in the Backlot.

⑥ **Animation Courtyard**
Meet Disney and Pixar
characters before
the Magic of Disney
Animation show. Puppets
take the stage for
Playhouse Disney Live
on Stage!, and during
the Voyage of the Little
Mermaid live show.

⑦ **Pixar Place** Board
a spinning car in Toy
Story Mania!®, to practice
pie-throwing and play
ring toss with Toy Story
characters, and giant
green Army men.

④ **Streets of America** Movie history buffs will enjoy the Lights, Motors, Action!® Extreme Stunt Show®, while the *Honey, I Shrunk the Kids*: Movie Set Adventure lets kids play and crawl as if shrunk to bug size.

The Lowdown

🌐 **Map reference** 6 F6
Address 351 South Studio Dr, Lake Buena Vista, 32830; 407 824 4321; *disneyworld.disney.go. com/parks/hollywood-studios*

🚌 **Bus** Lynx bus 303 from Downtown Orlando to Disney's Hollywood Studios®. Disney buses run from the TTC. **Taxi** Water taxis from BoardWalk and Yacht Club Resorts, as well as Swan and Dolphin resorts.

🕐 **Open** 9am–10pm daily. Check the park's "Calendar" page for seasonal variations and Extra Magic Hours.

💲 **Price** *see p106*

👥 **Cutting the line** Busiest days are Sun and Wed. Star Wars™ Weekends (May–Jun) and Christmas are the busiest periods.

👫 **Age range** 4 plus

🎭 **Shows** Disney Channel Rocks *(in Hollywood Boulevard)* features

music from Hannah Montana and other favorites. Fantasmic! *(in Sunset Boulevard)* combines lasers, water, and fireworks with dozens of Disney characters.

⏱ **Allow** 3–8 hours

♿ **Wheelchair access** Yes

🍴 **Eat and drink** SNACKS Fairfax Fare *(in Sunset Boulevard)* has salads and specialty hot dogs. REAL MEAL Sci-Fi Dine-In *(in Backlot)* has sci-fi movies playing while families sit at

Prices given are for a family of four

Top 10 Attractions

1. **STAR TOURS®**
   Board a Starspeeder 1000 and ride along with C-3PO and R2-D2 from *Star Wars™* through a 3-D universe.

2. **INDIANA JONES™ EPIC STUNT SPECTACULAR!**
   Amid explosions and fire, daredevil stunt artists re-enact scenes from *Raiders of the Lost Ark* in this 30-minute show in the Backlot.

3. **BEAUTY AND THE BEAST LIVE ON STAGE**
   The magic and romance of the film are re-created in this kid-friendly live show in Sunset Boulevard, featuring dancing, music, brilliant colors, and hilarious characters.

4. **VOYAGE OF THE LITTLE MERMAID**
   Experience the land of Ariel and friends in this 15-minute live show in Animation Courtyard, in which water, lasers, music, and glow-in-the-dark puppets re-create scenes from the movie.

5. **TOY STORY MANIA!®**
   Located in Pixar Place, this carnival-themed ride is straight out of the beloved *Toy Story*

car-shaped tables and eat burgers, pasta, and steaks.

🏷️ **Shops** Each attraction has its own gift shop. Tatooine Traders, the *Star Wars™* store, is one of the most popular.

🚻 **Restrooms** Throughout the park

Good family value?
It's a little expensive, like all Disney parks, but with rides and shows geared to kids of all ages, this is an excellent place to spend a day.

movies. Kids can shoot virtual darts and eggs at 3-D targets, as Woody, Buzz, and Jessie offer helpful hints and cheer them on.

6. **LIGHTS, MOTORS, ACTION!® EXTREME STUNT SHOW®**
   Leaping jet skis, crashing cars, plummeting stunt men, and lots of explosions and fireballs characterize this 33-minute Streets of America show, which puts the spotlight on driving very fast.

7. **MUPPET*VISION 3D**
   Join Jim Henson's creations on a 17-minute, multiscreen kids' delight while Kermit, Miss Piggy, and Fozzie sing, dance, and play along inside the theater, in Streets of America.

8. **THE TWILIGHT ZONE TOWER OF TERROR™**
   Take a ride on an out-of-control elevator in the Hollywood Tower Hotel, where guests are taken to a height of 170 ft (52 m) in a dizzying combination of lifts and faster than gravity drops.

9. **MAGIC OF DISNEY ANIMATION**
   Go behind the scenes with real Disney animators and discover the tricks of making cartoons like *Mulan*, *Aladdin* and *The Lion King*, in Animation Courtyard.

10. **ROCK 'N' ROLLER COASTER® STARRING AEROSMITH**
    Rock out on this very fast, very loud roller coaster in Sunset Boulevard, where guests sit in souped-up limousines and are launched from a full stop to 60 mph (96 km/h) in 2.8 seconds, upside down, in the dark.

① **Walt Disney World® Resort continued ▶**

Blizzard Beach
A water park – with snow

Walt Disney World® Resort's creatively designed winter ski resort-turned adventure park looks like a snowy wonderland, and has plenty of thrilling rides. The waterslides of Summit Plummet shoot straight down 120 ft (37 m) at 60 mph (97 km/h) and the twisty-turny double slides of Downhill Double Dipper are 50 ft (15 m) tall and 200 ft (61 m) long. Try the family white-water raft ride Teamboat Springs, which drops down 1,200 ft (366 m) of waterfalls, or take a water-slicked bobsled ride down Mt. Gushmore on the eight-lane Toboggan Racers. The **Winter Summerland** mini-golf course is right at the entrance.

Take cover
If inclement weather threatens, head to the **Coronado Springs Resort** (disneyworld.disney.go.com/resorts/coronado-springs-resort). It has many dining options, including Pepper Market, which offers buffet-style breakfast and lunch,

The Lowdown

- **Map reference** 6 E6
  Address 1524 W Buena Vista Dr, Lake Buena Vista, 32830; 407 824 4321; disneyworld.disney.go.com/parks/blizzard-beach
- **Bus** Disney bus from the TTC and resort hotels
- **Open** Hours vary by season; check website for details.
- **Price** $180–220; under 3s free. Combined annual Park Hopper pass for Blizzard Beach and Typhoon Lagoon $360–370; under 3s free. Winter Summerland: $44–54; under 3s free
- **Cutting the line** The park is least crowded from mid-Feb to mid-Mar, and mid-Sep to early Nov.
- **Age range** 2 plus. Swim diapers required for toddlers.
- **Allow** 2–6 hours
- **Wheelchair access** Yes
- **Eat and drink** SNACKS Cooling Hut (near the entrance) offers pretzels, nachos, muffins, tuna sandwiches, and popcorn. REAL MEAL Lottawatta Lodge (straight ahead from the entrance) serves chili dogs, chicken wraps, french fries, salads and burgers.
- **Restrooms** Throughout the park

The thrilling 90-ft (27-m) high Slush Gusher ride, Blizzard Beach

and the quick-service restaurant Café Rix, which serves salads, paninis, and freshly baked goods.

Typhoon Lagoon
Ten ways to get really soaked

This Disney water park has everything from gentle raft rides for the whole family to daredevil waterslides for the fearless. The tropical island theme is reflected in the park's lush palm trees and the white-sand beach. Visitors can snorkel among benign sharks in Shark Reef, while the Surf Pool with its 6-ft (2-m) waves tempts experienced board riders. The roller-coaster-like slides of Crush 'n' Gator let three people take the plunge, and the slides of Gang Plank Falls can take four people for a wet ride. Go over the edge at the three raft rides of Mayday Falls, the winding waterways of Storm Slides, or the five-story high-speed drop of Humunga Kowabunga.

Take cover
Getting wet is the whole point of a water park, but an escape can be found at **Downtown Disney®**

The Lowdown

- **Map reference** 6 F6
  Address 1195 E Buena Vista Dr, Lake Buena Vista, 32830; 407 824 4321; disneyworld.disney.go.com/parks/typhoon-lagoon
- **Bus** Disney bus from the TTC and resort hotels
- **Open** Hours vary by season; check website for details
- **Price** $180–220; under 3s free. Combined annual Park Hopper pass for Blizzard Beach and Typhoon Lagoon $360–370; under 3s free
- **Cutting the line** The park is least crowded from mid-Feb to mid-Mar, and mid-Sep to early Nov.
- **Age range** 2 plus. Swim diapers required for toddlers.
- **Allow** 2–6 hours
- **Wheelchair access** Yes
- **Eat and drink** SNACKS Surf Doggie Hot Dog Cart (near the shallow end of Surf Pool) serves hot dogs and turkey legs. REAL MEAL Typhoon Tilly's (between Shark Reef and Castaway Creek) offers shrimp, fish, and salads.
- **Restrooms** Throughout the park

(see p117). It has shops, restaurants, an extensive LEGO® Imagination Center, and a massive movie theater.

Disney's Fort Wilderness Resort & Campground
Hoop-Dee-Doo!

More than just a themed camping resort, the Disney's Fort Wilderness Resort & Campground (see p137) offers visitors the opportunity to hike, ski, and take horse-drawn carriage rides. Families can sit by the campfire and sing along with

Scuba diving in Shark Reef, Typhoon Lagoon

Chip and Dale behind the Meadow Trading Post. The superb Artist Point restaurant will please fine dining enthusiasts and kids will enjoy the antics at the dinner show Hoop-Dee-Doo Musical Revue.

Letting off steam
Kids will have fun climbing and sliding at **Creekside Meadow** and at the **Bay Lake** in the beach area.

The Lowdown

- 🌐 **Map reference** 6 F6
  Address 901 Timberline Dr, Lake Buena Vista, 32830; 407 824 2900; disneyworld.disney.go.com/resorts/wilderness-lodge-resort
- 🚌 **Bus** Disney bus from the TTC and resort hotels
- 💲 **Price** Hoop-Dee-Doo Musical Revue: $170–220
- 🔫 **Guided tours** A 45-min guided trail rides around Fort Wilderness ($42 horseback; $35 carriage ride). Wilderness Back Trail Adventure is a 2-hour Segway tour of the grounds ($90 per person).
- 👫 **Age range** 3 plus
- 🏃 **Activities** Rent a bike or pontoon boat or take a pony ride at the Tri-Circle-D Ranch. Cub's Den has supervised activities for kids aged 3 to 12 from 4:30pm to midnight.
- ⏱ **Allow** 1–3 hours
- ♿ **Wheelchair access** Yes
- ☕ **Eat and drink** SNACKS The Roaring Fork (in Disney's Wilderness Lodge) has sandwiches, burgers, and omelets. FAMILY TREAT Artist Point (in Disney's Wilderness Lodge) serves specialties from the Pacific Northwest, including seafood, sirloin, and game.
- 👫 **Restrooms** In all comfort stations

Downtown Disney®
Everything here is really big

Three distinct areas make up Downtown Disney®: West Side, Marketplace, and Pleasure Island. Besides some superb dining options, West Side is home to Cirque du Soleil®-La Nouba™, the five-story DisneyQuest® Indoor Interactive theme park, and the 24-screen AMC. Marketplace has the world's largest Disney merchandise outlet, a Harley-Davidson store, a gigantic LEGO® Imagination Center, and a three-story Planet Hollywood®. To sample world cuisine, head to Pleasure Island, which includes the Raglan Road Irish Pub and Paradiso 37.

Letting off steam
Take a quick trip on the Disney bus system to the **Typhoon Lagoon** (see p116).

A variety of plush toys in the World of Disney® store, Downtown Disney®

The Lowdown

- 🌐 **Map reference** 6 F6
  Address 1590 E Buena Vista Dr, Lake Buena Vista, 32830; 407 828 3800; disneyworld.disney.go.com/destinations/downtown-disney
- 🚌 **Bus** Disney bus from the TTC and resort hotels
- ⏱ **Open** Hours vary; check website
- 💲 **Price** Cirque du Soleil®-La Nouba™: $280–512; under 3s free. DisneyQuest®: $152–176; under 3s free. AMC Downtown Disney®: check website for details.
- 🏃 **Activities** Play interactive virtual reality games such as virtual jungle cruise, Buzz Lightyear's Astroblasters, and design-your-own roller coaster at DisneyQuest®. Splitsville (in West

Side) combines family bowling and billiards with dining. The Characters in Flight ($60–70; under 3s free), a hot-air balloon ride, takes 29 guests a breathtaking 400 ft (122 m) above Downtown Disney®
- ♿ **Wheelchair access** Yes
- ☕ **Eat and drink** SNACKS Earl of Sandwich (1750 E Buena Vista Dr, 32830; 407 938 1762; www.earlofsandwichusa.com) offers soups, salads, and sandwiches. FAMILY TREAT Fultons Crab House (1670 Buena Vista Dr, 32830; 407 934 2628; www.fultonscrabhouse.com) serves some of the freshest fish in town.
- 👫 **Restrooms** At all restaurants, some shops, and Cirque du Soleil®

② Universal Studios Florida®
Rock 'n' roll and lots of aliens

This Universal Orlando® Resort theme park takes movies and television very seriously, but in a fun way. See Hollywood's history come alive through classic horror films, characters from famous movies, and some vintage cartoon creatures that younger guests may never have seen before. The thrilling rides, based on mummies, earthquakes, and animated ogres, incorporate state-of-the-art technology in themed zones.

Universal Globe at the entrance to Universal Studios Florida®

Key Features

Hollywood Learn about movie and TV greats, like Lucille Ball at Lucy: A Tribute, and meet a cyborg time traveler at Terminator 2®: 3-D Battle Across Time.

Woody Woodpecker's KidZone® Everything young kids could hope for is here, from Woody Woodpecker's Nuthouse Coaster® and the E.T. Adventure®, to the Curious George Goes to Town playground, with its cartoonish buildings and plenty of activities for toddlers.

Production Central Shrek 4D lets guests ride a dragon, while Despicable Me Minion Mayhem hosts a dance party. But the highlight is the thrilling 17-story-high Hollywood Rip Ride Rockit® coaster.

New York Experience a tornado first hand at TWISTER...Ride it Out®, escape the undead in Revenge of the Mummy®, or dance in the streets to the music of The Blues Brothers® Show.

San Francisco Classic Hollywood horror films such as *Frankenstein®*, *Dracula®*, and the *Wolfman®* come to life at Beetlejuice's Graveyard Revue™, while guests face realistic fears in Disaster!: A Major Motion Picture Ride... Starring You! and the interactive Fear Factor Live show.

World Expo Wily aliens await in the streets of New York in MEN IN BLACK™: Alien Attack™, and Bart and the gang hang out at Krustyland at the simulated The Simpsons Ride™.

The Lowdown

🌐 **Map reference** 6 F5
Address 6000 Universal Blvd, Orlando, 32819; 407 363 8000, or 407 224 7840 (for tickets); *www.universalorlando.com*

🚗 **Bus** Lynx bus 40 ($2 one way) from Downtown Orlando.
Car From Orlando International Airport to Interstate 4 East. Parking $15 per day. Park at Loews Royal Pacific Resort to take the free water taxi to CityWalk®.

🕐 **Open** Park usually open 9am–7pm; closing times vary; check website for seasonal hours. Universal CityWalk®: 11am–2am

💲 **Price** $352–62. $492–502 park-to-park pass for both parks. Multiday packages available; check website for details.

👫 **Cutting the line** The park is busiest Tue–Fri. Avoid visiting in the months of Mar–Aug, Oct, and late Nov–Dec. Hotel guests get a free Express Pass that helps in avoiding queues, and provides unlimited access to certain rides.

🚶 **Guided tours** VIP guided walking tours with Express Pass to rides: $600 one park; $740 both parks.

🎭 **Shows** Littles ones adore the big purple dinosaur at A Day in the Park with Barney™. Families love

Universal's Horror Make-Up Show, and older kids will get a kick out of Fear Factor Live.

👫 **Age range** 3 plus. Age and height restrictions apply for most rides.

🕐 **Allow** 1–2 days

♿ **Wheelchair access** Yes

🚻 **Restrooms** Throughout the park

Good family value?
Every moviegoer's dream, this park brings blockbuster movies to life and offers a variety of rides and attractions for both kids and adults.

Prices given are for a family of four

Letting off steam

Enjoy a round of sci-fi and horror film-themed golf at CityWalk's® **Hollywood Drive-in Golf™** course.

Eat and drink

Picnic: under $25; Snacks: $25–50; Real meal: $50–80; Family treat: over $80 (based on a family of four)

PICNIC Richter's Burger Co. *(in San Francisco)* has cheeseburgers, salads, and sandwiches to take away.
SNACK Kid Zone Pizza Company *(in Woody Woodpecker's KidZone®)* has pizza, chicken, and salads.
REAL MEAL International Food & Film Festival *(in World Expo)* offers Asian, Italian, and American dishes.
FAMILY TREAT The Kitchen *(at Hard Rock Hotel)* has fine dining with a rock 'n' roll attitude.

Cafeteria-style restaurant sign of the International Food & Film Festival

Shopping

Everything movie- and cartoon-related can be found at **Woody Woodpecker's KidZone®**, in stores such as **The Barney® Store**, **E.T.'s Toy Closet**, and **Universal's Cartoon Store**, while stores such as the Simpsons'™ **Kwik-E-Mart** have customized goodies. There are also acres of shopping in **CityWalk®**.

Top 10 Attractions

1. **THE SIMPSONS RIDE™**
   There are many surprises and twists on this flying, crashing visit to the Krustyland carnival with the Simpson family, in World Expo.

2. **MEN IN BLACK™: ALIEN ATTACK™**
   Join the famous alien hunters in their underground headquarters, and then ride through the streets of New York blasting escaped aliens – who may shoot back.

3. **TERMINATOR 2®: 3-D BATTLE ACROSS TIME**
   Join forces with Terminator robots in this live show that pits humans against futuristic cyborgs in Hollywood.

4. **DISASTER! A MAJOR MOTION PICTURE RIDE... STARRING YOU!**
   Escape from the hypocenter of an earthquake in this stunt ride through the subway tunnels of San Francisco, where exploding trucks and trains add to the excitement of the chase.

5. **REVENGE OF THE MUMMY®**
   The mummy awakes, along with fiery fireballs, and attacks in total darkness during the coaster's twists and turns in this New York ride.

6. **SHREK 4-D**
   Ride on a fire-breathing dragon, plunge over a churning waterfall with Shrek, Fiona, and Donkey, and gallop through a haunted forest in Production Central's hilarious motion simulation movie adventure.

7. **DESPICABLE ME MINION MAYHEM**
   The mischievous minions, as well as other characters from the hit film, join guests on a tour of Gru's house in this Production Central ride that ends in a wild dance party.

8. **WOODY WOODPECKER'S NUTHOUSE COASTER®**
   Visit the woodpecker's Nut Factory for a wacky kid-friendly ride full of small thrills, silly jokes, and gentle ups and downs.

9. **HOLLYWOOD RIP RIDE ROCKIT®**
   Pick your music and then strap in to a high-tech car on Orlando's highest coaster, which climbs 17 stories above the park before plummeting at 65 mph (104 km/h).

10. **E.T. ADVENTURE®**
    Bring E.T. back to his home on this part movie, part virtual flying bike ride that ends with a personalized farewell from E.T. himself.

③ Universal's Islands of Adventure®

Where superheroes hang out

When the snow-covered Wizarding World of Harry Potter™ opened here in 2010, Potter fanatics snatched up a year's worth of Butterbeer™ and Ollivanders™ wands in six weeks, and it continues to be a popular draw. But there's a lot more at this Universal Orlando® Resort theme park, including some of the stunning pyrotechnics, fastest roller coasters, and rides for younger kids, inspired by everyone's favorite movies.

The Pharos Lighthouse at the entrance

Key Features

Wizarding World of Harry Potter™ Explore Hogwarts™ Castle, ride a dual-headed dragon and the one-of-a-kind Hippogriff™, enjoy a thrilling Quidditch™ match, or shop in Hogsmeade™ Village.

Lost Continent® Witness legends, myths, and heroes at the Eighth Voyage of Sindbad® Stunt Show, or talk to the Mystic Fountain, which squirts water in reply.

Marvel Super Hero Island® Meet your favorite superheroes and villains on the Amazing Adventures of Spider-Man® 3D ride, the Incredible Hulk Coaster, and Doctor Doom's Fearfall®.

Jurassic Park® Dinosaur-fueled excitement awaits, from the 14-story drop inside the Jurassic Park River Adventure® to the fun of the sky-high Pteranodon Flyers®.

Toon Lagoon® Children love the crashing log-ride adventure of Dudley Do-Right's Ripsaw Falls® and the water-based action of Popeye and Bluto's Bilge-Rat Barges® and Me Ship, The Olive.

Seuss Landing™ From the house of The Cat In The Hat™ to the spinning fun of the Caro-Seuss-el™ and One Fish Two Fish Red Fish Blue Fish™ rides, this is the place for Dr. Seuss fans. Don't miss the High in the Sky Seuss Trolley Train Ride!™.

Take cover

Blue Man Group, the colorful show at **Universal CityWalk®**, is a great indoor escape from the coaster thrills and waiting in line at Hogwarts™.

Eat and drink

Picnic: under $25; Snacks: $25–50; Real meal: $50–80; Family treat: over $80 (based on a family of four)

PICNIC Blondie's *(in Toon Lagoon®)* has towering made-to-order sandwiches for the family, with fresh meat, vegetables, and a variety of cheeses and dressings.
SNACKS The Watering Hole *(in Jurassic Park®)* has hot dogs, nachos, and chicken wings, as well as soft drinks.

Prices given are for a family of four

REAL MEAL Three Broomsticks™ *(in Wizarding World of Harry Potter™)* offers authentic British food such as fish and chips, Cornish pasties, and shepherd's pie.
FAMILY TREAT Mythos Restaurant® *(in Lost Continent®)*, built inside a rocky cliff, is one of the best

The award-winning Mythos Restaurant® in Lost Continent®

restaurants in Orlando. It serves great soups and appetizers, excellent seafood, and fabulous desserts.

Shopping

The Wizarding World of Harry Potter™ has fun stuff, from Chocolate Frogs™ at **Honeydukes™** to screaming yo-yos at **Zonko's™ Joke Shop**. Kids will also enjoy the shops at Toon Lagoon®, Marvel Super Hero Island®, Seuss Landing™, and Jurassic Park®.

Find out more

DIGITAL Visit www.mugglenet.com and www.universalorlando.com/harrypotter for insider information.

Top 10 Rides

1. INCREDIBLE HULK COASTER
Dive underwater and rocket upside down on this thrilling coaster on Marvel Super Hero Island®.

2. HARRY POTTER AND THE FORBIDDEN JOURNEY™
Fly a broomstick with the Hogwarts gang in the Wizarding World of Harry Potter™, an amazing 3D experience that is one of the most popular attractions here.

3. DRAGON CHALLENGE™
Choose a Chinese Fireball or a Hungarian Horntail dragon on this upside-down, dual roller coaster ride in the Wizarding World of Harry Potter™.

4. POSEIDON'S FURY®
Travel to a legendary past with titans, giants, and walls of water and flames, and a dazzling live-action show, in the Lost Continent®.

5. AMAZING ADVENTURES OF SPIDER-MAN®
Spidey and his friends swing off the page in this 3-D living comic book on Marvel Super Hero Island®.

6. POPEYE AND BLUTO'S BILGE-RAT BARGES®
Head to Toon Lagoon® for a ride along rapids on giant rafts, as onlookers shoot water cannons.

7. JURASSIC PARK RIVER ADVENTURE®
Journey on a river, past quiet lagoons, before the raptors attack and the only escape from a giant T-Rex is an 85-ft (26-m) dark plunge.

8. THE HIGH IN THE SKY SEUSS TROLLEY TRAIN RIDE™
The storytelling trolley in Seuss Landing™ roams over carousels and roller coasters, and even through the Circus McGurkus Café.

9. THE CAT IN THE HAT™
Join Red Fish Blue Fish, and Things One and Two on this wacky tour of The Cat's home in Seuss Landing™.

10. PTERANODON FLYERS®
Fly under the outstretched wings of a pteranodon as it glides over the playground in Jurassic Park®.

The Lowdown

🌐 **Map reference** 6 F5
Address 6000 Universal Blvd, Orlando, 32819; 407 224 4233 or 407 224 7840 (for tickets); www.universalorlando.com

🚗 **Bus** Lynx bus 40 ($2 one way) from Downtown Orlando to Universal Studios® parking garage. Park at Loews Royal Pacific Resort and take the free water taxi to Universal CityWalk®. **Car** Rent a car from Orlando.

🕐 **Open** 9am–6pm daily; check website for variations. Universal CityWalk®: 11am–2am daily

💲 **Price** $350–500; call for current prices. Multiday packages are available; check website for details and discounts.

👥 **Cutting the line** The least crowded months are mid-Jan–Feb, Sep & early Nov. The busiest days are Mon–Fri. A Universal Express pass to skip lines for rides is available; check website for details and discounts. An Unlimited Express Ticket allows unlimited skipping of lines; check website for details.

👫 **Age range** 7 plus

⏱ **Allow** 1–2 days

🚻 **Restrooms** Throughout the park

Good family value?
Although expensive, the park has something to offer everyone, and Harry Potter™ fans will be thrilled to see the books brought to life.

④ SeaWorld®, Aquatica, and Discovery Cove®

A splashing good time

SeaWorld®, and its sister parks Aquatica and Discovery Cove®, are located close to each other, and provide opportunities for families to learn about marine life while having fun. Kids will enjoy the entertaining seals and penguins, the impressive sharks and killer whales, and the thrilling rides at SeaWorld® and Aquatica, while Discovery Cove®, a resort-like park, allows visitors to snorkel and interact with dolphins.

Shamu the whale, the mascot of SeaWorld®

Key Features

Thrill Rides SeaWorld® offers some of the fastest, wettest rides in town, such as the high-flying Manta, the upside-down Kraken, and Journey to Atlantis, a flume-ride and roller-coaster hybrid – filling the air with screams of delight.

Discovery Cove® Swim with dolphins, take an underwater stroll in a diving helmet, and meet otters and marmosets.

SeaWorld® for Kids Shamu: Close Up gives kids a chance to look a killer whale in the eye, and the Dolphin Nursery lets them see newborn dolphin calves.

Shows Leaping whales and playful dolphins are the stars at SeaWorld®, in spectacular shows like One Ocean, and in wacky adventures in Sea Lion and Otter Stadium.

The Animals Feed bottlenose friends at Dolphin Cove, pet velvety rays in the Stingray Lagoon, and play with sea lions at Pacific Point Preserve, in SeaWorld®.

Undersea Life SeaWorld®'s the Manta Aquarium holds 3,000 animals, from sea horses to octopuses. In Shark Encounter, see thousands of sharks through glass.

Aquatica This water park features giant surfing pools, zooming underwater mazes, and racing rapids, as well as Loggerhead Lane, the laziest river in town.

Prices given are for a family of four

The Lowdown

🌐 **Map reference** 6 F6
Address SeaWorld®: 7007 SeaWorld Dr, Orlando, 32821; 407 351 3600; www.seaworld orlando.com. Aquatica: 5800 Water Play Way, Orlando, 32821; 1 888 800 5447; www.aquatica byseaworld.com. Discovery Cove®: 6000 Discovery Cove Way, Orlando, 32821; 1 877 557 7404; www.discoverycove.com

🚗 **Car** Rent a car from Orlando International Airport. Parking: SeaWorld® $14; Aquatica $12; Discovery Cove® free

🕐 **Open** SeaWorld®: 9am to between 6 and 10pm. Aquatica: 9am–6pm. Discovery Cove®: 9am–5:30pm. Check websites.

💲 **Prices** SeaWorld®: $310–20; under 2s free. Aquatica: $185–95. Discovery Cove®: $800–$1,435 (inclusive of meals; cheapest in Sep). SeaWorld®/Aquatica 14-day unlimited entry: $485–95. Add $120 to Discovery Cove® for unlimited 14-day access to SeaWorld®

and Aquatica. SeaWorld® All Day Dining Deal: $90–100.

👫 **Cutting the line** The Quick Queue pass gives front-of-the line access to Manta, Kraken, Journey To Atlantis, and Wild Arctic ($60–100). The parks are busiest late May–Sep and Nov. Thu–Sun are crowded.

🚩 **Guided tours** There is a 90-minute SeaWorld® Behind the Scenes tour and a 6-hour VIP tour with lunch.

👪 **Age range** 2 plus. Age and height restrictions apply for most rides.

🕐 **Allow** 1–3 days

♿ **Wheelchair access** Yes

👫 **Restrooms** Across the parks. Diaper-changing tables in restrooms near SeaWorld®'s front entrance.

Good family value?
Though pricey, the three parks have many entry options that ensure a great family experience.

Letting off steam

Shamu's Happy Harbor is a great place for kids to burn off energy, with plenty of shady spots for parents.

Eat and drink

Picnic: under $25; Snacks: $25–50; Real meal: $50–80; Family treat: over $80 (based on a family of four)

PICNIC Mango Joe's *(near Wild Arctic, SeaWorld®)* has delicious fajita sandwiches, wraps, and salads for a quick picnic in the park.
SNACKS Captain Pete's Island Eats *(in Dolphin Cove, SeaWorld®)* serves funnel cakes and hot dogs in a breezy island atmosphere.
REAL MEAL Seafire Inn *(in Waterfront, SeaWorld®)* has stir-fry and pasta, as well as fish and chips.
FAMILY TREAT Sharks Underwater Grill *(in Shark Encounter, SeaWorld®)* serves exceptional seafood with a view of a massive glass-walled shark tank.

Shopping

Across the parks, visit **Emporium** for hats, **Coconut Bay Traders** for souvenirs, and **Fins** for plush toys.

Find out more

DIGITAL Watch Shamu and the SeaWorld® penguins on webcams at *www.tinyurl.com/7t2umlf*.

Guests enjoying a seafood meal at Sharks Underwater Grill, SeaWorld®

Top 10 Attractions

1. ONE OCEAN
Join Shamu the killer whale star for a music-filled spectacular in SeaWorld®, especially in the seating area aptly named the Soak Zone.

2. MANTA
Ride this manta ray-shaped suspended coaster in SeaWorld® that includes an up-close encounter with manta rays and other sea life.

3. JOURNEY TO ATLANTIS
Travel through the ruins of a sunken city on this part-boat, part-roller coaster in SeaWorld®, and explore dark passageways before being plunged into the waters below.

4. KRAKEN
This spiraling, upside-down, high-speed monster of a thrill ride suspends riders high above the Serpent's Lagoon in SeaWorld®.

5. ANTARCTICA – EMPIRE OF THE PENGUIN
Get up close with penguins and see what it's like to live on ice on this magical SeaWorld® ride, where the adventure is different every time.

6. DOLPHIN COVE
Interact with bottlenose dolphins during feeding time in this massive but peaceful lagoon in SeaWorld®.

7. SHAMU'S HAPPY HARBOR
Younger kids will love this SeaWorld® mini-park that has boat rides, teacup spinners, an octopus carousel, and the Shamu Express teeny coaster.

8. DOLPHIN PLUNGE
This thrilling Aquatica ride has side-by-side enclosed tubes that slide through the underwater home of black-and-white dolphins.

9. TURTLE TREK
Witness the journey of a sea turtle in the world's first 3-D, 360-degree domed theater, surrounded by giant aquariums and thousands of fish, in SeaWorld®.

10. WALHALLA WAVE & HOOROO RUN
In these two connected Aquatica waterslides, guests can ride through a six-story tunnel maze, which then takes them over the edge and racing to the bottom.

KIDS' CORNER

See more at SeaWorld®
1 Stop by the SeaWorld® Information Center (right of entrance turnstiles) to find out when you can help feed the dolphins, sharks, and whales.
2 Head to the Lakeside Patio to dance with Shamu at the all-day Shamu's Party Zone.
3 Climb the 400-ft (122-m) rotating Sky Tower for a bird's-eye view of Orlando, Walt Disney World® Resort, and Universal Orlando®.

"Secret" events
Shamu & Crew sign autographs at the SeaWorld® front gate from 9am to noon, and pirates invade the Sea Lion and Otter Stadium 30 minutes before the Clyde and Seamore Take Pirate Island show.

TRICK A GROWN-UP!
Tell your parents to sit in the front row on the Journey to Atlantis coaster, but don't tell them how wet they'll get!

Whirlwind spin
Aquatica's quiet Loggerhead Lane lazy river has a thrilling secret: from the island in the middle, climb the tower and dive into Tassie's Twisters – a series of lightning-fast tubes that spin into a giant bowl – for a dizzying ride back into the river.

5 Wet 'n Wild®
A watery world of wonders

Created by the founder of SeaWorld® in 1977 and now owned by Universal Orlando®, the immensely popular Wet 'n Wild® claims to be the world's first water park. The park's large kids' area and tranquil Lazy River contrast with its insanely high-speed rides and the all-you-can-ride beach-party atmosphere. Its many multi-person water rides – more than at any other water park in the area – give families the chance to get drenched together.

Entrance to Wet 'n Wild®

Key Features

① **The Surge and Disco H2O™** Hop onto the Surge, a five-story tube ride with plenty of sharp twists and steeply banked curves, or go for the funky Disco H2O™, a multi-person ride through enclosed flumes filled with flashing lights and disco music.

② **The Flyer and Mach 5** Mount a four-person toboggan at the Flyer for a watery adventure ride round hairpin turns and banked curves, or brave it alone on Mach 5, a 1,700-ft (518-m) high flume ride that ends with an exhilarating splash.

③ **Blastaway Beach** The huge water playground is built around a 60-ft (18-m) high sand castle, with pools, waterfalls, soakers, and slides for the whole family.

④ **The Black Hole™: The Next Generation** Pilot a two-person "hydra capsule" down a dark tunnel filled with pulsating lights and eerie sounds.

⑤ **Bomb Bay** Look out for the trap door on the floor of the 76-ft (23-m) high Bomb Bay, which sends riders down a nearly vertical slide, or try a free-falling bobsled of a waterslide at Der Stuka.

⑥ **Surf Lagoon** Float on the crest of 4-ft (1-m) high waves in this giant wave pool that features a spectacular waterfall. A lovely picnic area overlooks the lagoon.

⑦ **Brain Wash™** Climb aboard this dizzying tube ride that winds through a tunnel with crazy lights and strange videos and then heads for a 53-ft (16-m) vertical drop into a huge domed funnel that shoots riders out at the bottom.

⑧ **Wakezone** Indulge in extreme water sports such as wakeskating, two-person tubing, and knee-skiing across a huge lake at this attraction.

⑨ **Lazy River and Bubba Tub** Drift down the Lazy River as it meanders through an "old Florida" of boat docks and orange groves. Next to it is Bubba Tub, a six-story triple-dip slide that is fun for all the family.

⑩ **The Storm** This thrilling attraction takes riders down a water-soaked chute into a high-speed spin around an enormous bowl before leading to a high-pressure drop into the pool.

Entrance

Prices given are for a family of four

The Lowdown

🌐 **Map reference** 6 F5
Address 6200 International Dr,
32819; 407 351 1800; *www.wet
nwildorlando.com*

🚗 **Bus** Lynx bus 8 from Downtown
Orlando. **Car** Rent a car from the
airport; $10 parking

🕐 **Open** 9:30am–5pm, or later.
Wakezone: May–Sep: noon–
dusk; but hours vary; check
website. Park may close due to
bad weather; call ahead of visit.

💲 **Price** $184–94; under 3s free.
Admission is half-price in the
afternoon (hours vary with
season). The Length-of-Stay
Pass ($196–206; under 3s free)
allows unlimited visits for 14
consecutive days. Additional
$44.95 charge for Wakezone.
Towels and lockers are available.

Multipark tickets available;
check website for details.

🚻 **Cutting the line** The park
is quietest on Mondays. Buy
an Express Pass for quicker
access to rides.

👫 **Age range** 3 plus. Most
rides have a minimum height
restriction of 48 in (122 cm).
Wakezone has a minimum height
restriction of 56 in (142 cm).

⏱ **Allow** Half a day to 2 days

♿ **Wheelchair access** Limited

🚻 **Restrooms** By the main entrance
and in every restaurant

Good family value?
It's not cheap but, with a mix of
extreme and gentle rides, Wet 'n
Wild makes for an exciting day out.

Take cover
Head 1 mile (2 km) northeast to
Festival Bay Mall (*5250 International
Dr, Orlando, 32819; 407 351 7718;
www.shopfestivalbaymall.com*)
to try its indoor, glow-in-the-dark
miniature golf. The mall also has
a 20-screen movie theater.

Eat and drink
*Picnic: under $25; Snacks: $25–50;
Real meal: $50–80; Family treat:
over $80 (based on a family of four)*

PICNIC Bubba's BBQ *(in Surf
Lagoon)* offers BBQ chicken, and ribs,
that can be eaten in the Sundeck
picnic area above Surf Lagoon.
SNACKS Carnival Treats *(in The
Flyer)* tempts with funnel cakes,
cotton candy, and ice cream.
REAL MEAL Surf Grill *(in The
Surge)* offers hot dogs, Big Kahuna
hamburgers, and taco salads, as
well as adult beverages.

FAMILY TREAT Bonefish Grill
*(7830 West Sand Lake Rd, Orlando
32819; 407 355 7707; www.bone
fishgrill.com)* serves shrimp tacos,
fish and chips, and other seafood.
The restaurant also has a wine list.

Shopping
The **Breakers Beach Shop** *(on
site)* sells sportswear, swimsuits,
hats, sunscreen, sunglasses, and
disposable cameras.

Next stop...
ORANGE BLOSSOM BALLOONS
Take off in a hot-air balloon with
Orange Blossom Balloons *(407 894
5040; www.orangeblossomballoons.
com)* for a ride above the theme
parks, orange groves, and untouched
landscape of Orlando at sunrise.
Flights depart from various spots
in the Disney area.

Orange-striped Carnival Treats stand near the Flyer, Wet 'n Wild

⑥ International Drive

Watch out for falling buildings

With Universal Studios Florida® at one end and SeaWorld® at the other, I-Drive features great attractions for kids. It is hard to miss the upside-down building of **Wonderworks** and its science-oriented exhibits, including a re-creation of the 1989 San Francisco earthquake. **Monkey Joe's** has wall-to-wall bouncing fun for ages 4 to 12, and an adult lounge for parents. The dramatically tilted building of **Ripley's Believe It or Not! Odditorium** contains the world's largest collection of weird stuff, such as shrunken heads, dinosaur fossils, wax statues, and a four-eyed man. For a quiet interlude, watch the ducks waddle through the **Peabody Hotel** at 11am and 5pm.

Letting off steam

Head to **Fun Spot Action Park** (5551 Del Verde Way, 32819; 407 363 3867; www.funspot.tuten

Bizarre-looking building housing Wonderworks, International Drive

graphics.com) for go-karts, bumper cars, Ferris wheels, and tilt-a-whirls. Or try the 14-slide water park at the **Coco Key Resort** (7400 International Dr, 32819; 407 351 2626; www.cocokeyorlando.com).

⑦ Gatorland

Toothy critters

Opened in 1949, Gatorland offers old Florida-style entertainment. Walk through a giant alligator's mouth to see snakes, lizards, Florida deer, and spiders before heading for Alligator Island, which is home to hundreds of Florida gators, along with several Nile crocodiles. Kids will like the Swamp Walk, at the southern end of the park, which offers a chance to walk through an unspoiled Cypress Swamp on the lookout for real alligators. The Gatorland Express train rolls through the park and ends at the Gator Wrestling arena, where genuine Florida cowboys catch

The Lowdown

🌐 **Map reference** 6 F5
Address Wonderworks: 9067 International Dr, 32819; 407 351 8800; www.wonderworks online.com. Monkey Joe's: 9101 International Dr, 32819; 407 352 8484; www.monkeyjoes. com. Ripley's Believe It or Not! Odditorium: 8201 International Dr, 32819; 407 345 0501; www. ripleys.com/orlando. Peabody Hotel: 9801 International Dr, 32819; 407 352 4000; www. peabodyorlando.com

🚗 **Car** Rent a car from the airport.

🕐 **Open** All sights open daily; times vary.

💲 **Price** Wonderworks: $90–100; under 4s free. Monkey Joe's: $27–37; under 3s free. Ripley's Believe it or Not! Odditorium: $66–76; under 4s free

👫 **Cutting the line** I-Drive is quieter on weekdays.

👫 **Age range** 4 plus

⏱ **Allow** 2–8 hours

☕ **Eat and drink** SNACKS McDonald's (6875 West Sand Lake Rd, 32819; tinyurl.com/btarxwk) at I-Drive has a two-story playroom and a huge aquarium. FAMILY TREAT Benihana (12690 International Dr, 32821; benihana.com) thrills kids with at-the-table Japanese cooking.

The Lowdown

🌐 **Map reference** 6 F6
Address 14501 South Orange Blossom Trail, 32837; 800 393 5297; www.gatorland.com

🚌 **Bus** Lynx bus 4 from main terminal in Downtown Orlando. **Car** Interstate 4 exit #72 to Beachline Expressway east. Exit State Rd 441

🕐 **Open** 10am–5pm daily

💲 **Price** $84–94; under 3s free

👫 **Cutting the line** Spring and fall are the best times to visit.

🔫 **Guided tours** The 2-hour Trainer for a Day program teaches kids 12 plus how to handle snakes, baby gators, and other reptiles.

👫 **Age range** 4 plus

⏱ **Allow** 2–6 hours

♿ **Wheelchair access** Yes

☕ **Eat and drink** SNACKS Gatorland Snack Bar (front entrance) serves hot dogs and ice cream. REAL MEAL Pearl's Smokehouse (last stop on the Gatorland Express train) offers pizza, salad bowls, and even deep-fried gator tail.

🛍 **Shop** The Gatorland gift shop (on site) sells plush toys, books, and gator-themed apparel.

👫 **Restrooms** In the gift shop, at the restaurant, and at front gate

alligators by hand and climb onto the snapping animals' backs. But the best part is the Gator Jumparoo Show, where the largest alligators in the world jump 4–5 ft (1–1.5-m) out of a wading pool to snap food away from their trainer's hand.

Letting off steam

Get wet under oddly shaped animal jets, a bucket tree for younger kids, and shooting bird-shaped fountains in **Gator Gully Splash Park** (on site).

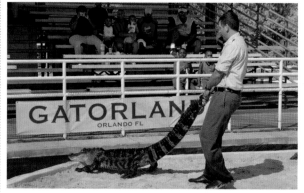
A gator wrangler wrestling an alligator, Gatorland

Orlando, Winter Park, and around

Entertainment, gardens, and the promise of warm winters have been luring visitors to Orlando since the 1880s. About an hour's drive from both east and west coasts, it usually escapes the worst of the hurricane season while benefitting from pleasant temperatures in winter. Bordering greater Orlando, Winter Park's appeal lies in its great museums, cafés, and scenic waterways.

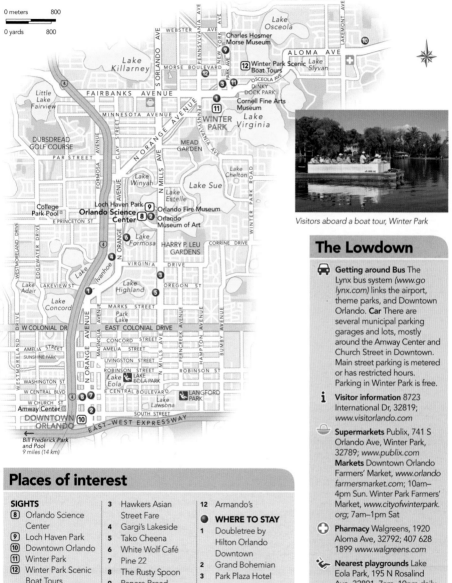

Visitors aboard a boat tour, Winter Park

The Lowdown

🚌 **Getting around Bus** The Lynx bus system (*www.go lynx.com*) links the airport, theme parks, and Downtown Orlando. **Car** There are several municipal parking garages and lots, mostly around the Amway Center and Church Street in Downtown. Main street parking is metered or has restricted hours. Parking in Winter Park is free.

ℹ **Visitor information** 8723 International Dr, 32819; *www.visitorlando.com*

🛒 **Supermarkets** Publix, 741 S Orlando Ave, Winter Park, 32789; *www.publix.com* **Markets** Downtown Orlando Farmers' Market, *www.orlando farmersmarket.com*; 10am–4pm Sun. Winter Park Farmers' Market, *www.cityofwinterpark. org*; 7am–1pm Sat

➕ **Pharmacy** Walgreens, 1920 Aloma Ave, 32792; 407 628 1899 *www.walgreens.com*

🔭 **Nearest playgrounds** Lake Eola Park, 195 N Rosalind Ave, 32801, 7am–10pm daily. Langford Park, 1808 E Central Blvd, 32803; 5am–sunset daily

Places of interest

SIGHTS
8. Orlando Science Center
9. Loch Haven Park
10. Downtown Orlando
11. Winter Park
12. Winter Park Scenic Boat Tours

EAT AND DRINK
1. Ethos Vegan Kitchen
2. SUBWAY
3. Hawkers Asian Street Fare
4. Gargi's Lakeside
5. Tako Cheena
6. White Wolf Café
7. Pine 22
8. The Rusty Spoon
9. Panera Bread
10. Tibby's New Orleans Kitchen
11. Powerhouse Café
12. Armando's

WHERE TO STAY
1. Doubletree by Hilton Orlando Downtown
2. Grand Bohemian
3. Park Plaza Hotel

⑧ Orlando Science Center

Explore the past and the future

Walking across the glass bridge from the parking garage into the Science Center's spaceship-like rotunda is like stepping into another world. Science-hungry kids and curious adults alike will enjoy the interactive exhibits, live programs, and films on giant screens. Hands-on learning and tricks teach kids about the small wonders of science, while astronomy exhibits and an observatory let them consider the enormity of the universe.

Exterior of Orlando Science Center

Key Features

- **Level 4** DinoDigs, Our Planet, Our Universe, Science Stations
- **Level 3** SimMan, Careers for Life
- **Level 2** Science Park, All Aboard, Darden Adventure Theater, The Science Store
- **Level 1** NatureWorks, KidsTown, Dr. Phillips CineDome

① **NatureWorks** Exhibits of animal habitats and diverse ecosystems start with an exhibit on Florida's natural fish and alligator habitats.

② **DinoDigs** Find fossils buried in the Dig Pit, look into a triceratop's eye, and see life-size replicas of a T-Rex and a 40-ft (12-m) long plesiosaur skeleton.

③ **Science Park** Kids can get their hands on electricity-powered cars, a giant Tesla coil, and air cannons here.

④ **KidsTown** Young visitors float boats on a multilevel waterfall, work at an orange juice factory, and repair pint-size cars in the Super Service Center in this play area.

⑤ **Our Planet, Our Universe** Explore the stars, and learn how planets were formed, what happens when galaxies collide, and why the sky is blue.

⑥ **All Aboard** In this gallery, kids can play engineer in a child-size steam train, travel the world in a wooden biplane, and take off in a mini-space shuttle.

⑦ **Dr. Phillips CineDome** Watch films about the bottom of the sea and the Grand Canyon on this spectacularly huge screen.

Swans on the grassy banks in Lake Eola Park, south of the Orlando Science Center

Letting off steam

Kids can tire themselves out harvesting plastic oranges and loading crates by hand in the juice factory in KidsTown. **Lake Eola Park**, 3 miles (5 km) south, offers lots of running space, a jogging lane around the lake, and boating.

Prices given are for a family of four

Eat and drink

Picnic: under $25; Snacks: $25–50; Real meal: $50–80; Family treat: over $80 (based on a family of four)

PICNIC Ethos Vegan Kitchen
(601-B S New York Ave, 32804; 407 228 3898; www.ethosvegankitchen.com) has meat-free sandwiches and salads to take away for a picnic at **Loch Haven Park** (see p130).

SNACKS SUBWAY (Level 1) is a sandwich shop that also has fresh salads and kids' meals.

REAL MEAL Hawkers Asian Street Fare (1103 Mills Ave, 32803; 407 237 0606) presents a menu of street food delights from China, Vietnam, Malaysia, and Singapore in small plates for everyone to share.

The Lowdown

🌐 **Map reference** 6 F5
Address 777 E Princeton St, Orlando, 32803; 407 514 2000; www.osc.org

🚗 **Bus** Lynx bus 125 from Downtown Orlando. **Car** Rent a car from Downtown Orlando and head onto Interstate 4, exit 85. Parking $5

🕐 **Open** 10am–5pm Mon–Tue & Thu–Sat. Hours vary; check website. Crosby Observatory: Sat

💲 **Price** $58–68. $125–35 for an annual family membership

👫 **Cutting the line** Visit on weekdays during summer to avoid crowds.

🚩 **Guided tours** The Overnight Adventures program ($160–170) has workshops, IMAX® films,

access to the Crosby Observatory, meals, and an overnight stay in the Center.

👫 **Age range** 3 plus

👫 **Activities** Hands-on Early Childhood Workshops let younger kids explore ocean life, the five senses, and more.

🕐 **Allow** 1–3 hours

☕ **Café** SUBWAY (see p128)

🛍 **Shop** The Science Store (Level 2) sells puzzles, interactive science kits, and toys.

👫 **Restrooms** On each level near the elevator

Good family value?

From dinosaurs to space exploration, this museum has a great variety of exhibits and activities for the whole family.

Science Live! Mad scientists in training will enjoy conducting experiments at Dr. Dare's Lab, and observing images of Earth, the Moon, and Mars projected on the hovering Science on a Sphere globe that hangs high above the audience.

The Crosby Observatory This silver dome on top of the Orlando Science Center hides a custom telescope powerful enough to see Saturn's rings, Jupiter's moons, and distant stars.

FAMILY TREAT Gargi's Lakeside (1414 N Orange Ave, Orlando, 32804; 407 894 7907; www.gargis lakeside.com) is a popular place for authentic Italian food. Located in a beautiful park, it overlooks picturesque Lake Ivanhoe, and has a playground for kids.

SUBWAY on Level 1 of the Orlando Science Center

Next stop…

Head for the **Orlando Museum of Art** (see p130) in Loch Haven Park, close to the Orlando Science Center, to see ancient Aztec pottery share space with contemporary American art, along with African handicrafts and fascinating touring exhibitions.

⑨ Loch Haven Park
Art in the green

This extensive park is a cultural mecca, home to the Orlando Science Center *(see pp128–9)*, and several theaters and museums. The **Orlando Shakespeare Theater** performs plays by the Bard and modern playwrights, as well as children's theater and productions from the Orlando International Fringe Theatre Festival. Across the parking lot, the multiple galleries of the **Orlando Museum of Art** hold American contemporary art, glass works by Dale Chihuly, and large collections of African handicrafts. Behind the Shakespeare Theater is the small **Orlando Fire Museum**, with rebuilt engines, and pumpers dating from 1911.

Letting off steam
Cool off at the **College Park Pool** *(2411 Elizabeth Ave, 32804; 407 246 2764)*, located just a few minutes away from Loch Haven Park.

Strolling along a lush lawn in Harry P. Leu Gardens, Downtown Orlando

The Lowdown

- 🌐 **Map reference** 6 F5
- **Address** Orlando Shakespeare Theater: 812 E Rollins St, 32803; *orlandoshakes.org*. Orlando Museum of Art: 2416 North Mills Ave, 32803; *www.omart.org*. Orlando Fire Museum: 819 E Rollins Rd, 32803; *www.cityof orlando.net/fire/Museum.html*
- 🚌 **Bus** Lynx bus 102 from Winter Park **Car** Rent a car from the airport.
- 🕐 **Open** Orlando Shakespeare Theater & Orlando Museum of Art: closed Mon. Orlando Fire Museum: Fri–Sat
- 💲 **Price** Orlando Shakespeare Theater: prices vary with events; check website. Orlando Museum of Art: $26–36; under 3s free
- 🚶 **Cutting the line** Avoid visiting during the Orlando International Fringe Theatre Festival in May.
- 👉 **Guided tours** Free docent-led tours of Orlando Museum of Art at 1:30pm Thu
- 🚻 **Age range** 4 plus
- ⏱ **Allow** 2–8 hours
- 🍴 **Eat and drink** SNACKS Tako Cheena *(932 N Mills Ave, 32803; 321 236 7457)* has tacos stuffed with exotic fillings. REAL MEAL White Wolf Café *(1829 N Orange Ave, 32804; 407 895 9911; whitewolfcafe.com)* serves pasta dishes, steaks, and seafood.
- 🚻 **Restrooms** In all attractions

⑩ Downtown Orlando
Basketball, great food, and pretty gardens

The heart of Orlando is the corner of Church Street and Orange Avenue – a section filled with nightclubs, restaurants, and bars. Visit the **Amway Center** for its concerts and circuses, and to watch the NBA team Orlando Magic. But there's more to downtown Orlando than basketball. Church Street's restaurants serve some of the best food in town, and Lake Eola has an iconic fountain and an easy, mile-long walking path. The **Orlando History Center** houses exhibits representing Orlando's past, present, and future. Nearby are the vast **Harry P. Leu Gardens**, with roses, azaleas, a giant bamboo collection, and more.

Letting off steam
Dubsdread *(www.historical dubsdread.com)* welcomes kids aged 17 and under to play golf.

The Lowdown

- 🌐 **Map reference** 6 F5
- **Address** Amway Center: 400 W Church St, 32801; 407 440 7000; *www.amwaycenter.com*. Orlando History Center: 65 E Central Blvd, 32801; 407 836 8500; *thehistory center.org*. Harry P. Leu Gardens: 1920 N Forest Ave, 32803; 407 246 2620; *www.leugardens.org*
- 🚌 **Bus** Lynx bus 102 from Winter Park
- 🕐 **Open** Amway Center: check website for events. Orlando History Center & Harry P. Leu Gardens: daily
- 💲 **Prices** Amway Center: check website. Orlando History Center:

⑪ Winter Park
Art and culture in the suburb

Suburban Winter Park became a warm-weather escape for wealthy Northerners in the early 1900s, and today its museums, high-end stores, and great restaurants retain an air of sophistication.

At the north end of the beautiful one-mile stretch of green called Park Avenue stands the **Charles Hosmer Morse Museum of American Art**, which holds the world's largest collection of art, stained glass, jewelry, and furnishings made by

Elegant Tiffany lamps in the Morse Museum, Winter Park

$30–40; under 4s free. Harry P. Leu Gardens: $18–28; under 5s free
- 🚻 **Age range** 2 plus
- ⏱ **Allow** A day
- 🍴 **Eat and drink** SNACKS Pine 22 *(22 E Pine St, 32801; 407 574 2160; pine22.com)* has a build-your-own burger menu with 300,000 possible combinations. REAL MEAL The Rusty Spoon *(55 W Church St, 32801; 407 401 8811; www.therustyspoon. com)* uses organic produce from local farmers for a range of cuisines served in a casual, upscale setting.

Louis Comfort Tiffany (1848–1933). At the south end of Park Avenue is Rollins College, the oldest university in the southeast, which is home to the **Cornell Fine Arts Museum**. The museum has a stellar collection of American and European art.

Letting off steam
Next to Rollins College is **Dinky Dock**, a public park with grills and tables for picnicking, and a sand beach with opportunities to swim.

The Lowdown

- 🌐 **Map reference** 6 F5
  Address Morse Museum: 445 N Park Ave, 32789; 407 645 5311; www.morsemuseum.org. Cornell Fine Arts Museum: 1000 Holt Ave, 32789; 407 646 2526; www.rollins.edu/cfam
- 🚗 **Train** Amtrak train from Downtown Orlando. **Bus** Lynx bus 102 from Downtown Orlando
- ℹ️ **Visitor information** Winter Park Welcome Center & Chamber of Commerce, 151 West Lyman Ave, 32789; 407 644 8281
- 🕐 **Open** Morse Museum & Cornell Fine Arts Museum: closed Mon
- 💲 **Price** Morse Museum: $10–20; under 12s free. Cornell Fine Arts Museum: $20–30
- 👫 **Cutting the line** Avoid visiting during the two annual arts festivals in March and October.
- 🚩 **Guided tours** Morse Museum has docent-led tours during public hours.
- 👫 **Age range** 5 plus
- ⏱️ **Allow** 3–8 hours
- ☕ **Eat and drink** SNACKS Panera Bread (329 N Park Ave, 32789; www.panerabread.com) offers bagels, sandwiches, and a kids' menu. REAL MEAL Tibby's New Orleans Kitchen (2203 Aloma Ave, 32792; tibbysneworleanskitchen.com) has authentic New Orleans gumbo, and po-boy sandwiches.

⑫ Winter Park Scenic Boat Tours
Behind the scenes and houses of Winter Park

The Scenic Boat Tour glides along a chain of magnificent lakes, past some of the finest homes in Florida. The lush canals that connect Lake Osceola, Lake Virginia, and Lake Maitland were renovated in the 1930s especially for tourism, and

Boat cruising along a picturesque canal in Winter Park

the flat-bottom pontoon boats have been plying them ever since. Mansions built by Goodyear and Walgreen, the Rollins College campus, and the home of noted American architect James Gamble Rogers II can be seen on the tour. Decades-old palm trees, bamboo, papyrus, and flowering vines overhang the canals, providing a cool break from the bright sun, but be sure to carry sunscreen and hats. Kids can spot gray herons, sunning anhingas, turtles, and even the rare alligator on the cruise.

Letting off steam
Go 11 miles (18 km) southwest to **Bill Frederick Park and Pool** (3401 S Hiawassee Rd, 32835; 407 246 4486), at Turkey Lake, for boat rentals, largemouth bass fishing, and a wooden playground with a maze of tunnels and swings.

The Lowdown

- 🌐 **Map reference** 6 F5
  Address 312 E Morse Blvd, 32789; 407 644 4056; scenicboattours.com
- 🚗 **Car** Rent a car from the airport.
- 🕐 **Open** 10am–4pm daily. Tours depart on the hour.
- 💲 **Price** $36–48; under 2s free
- 👫 **Cutting the line** Tour early or pick late tours (no reservations), when the sun isn't directly overhead.
- 👫 **Age range** 2 plus
- ⏱️ **Allow** 1 hour
- ☕ **Eat and drink** SNACKS Powerhouse Café (111 E Lyman Ave, 32789; 407 645 3616; www.powerhousecafe.com) serves healthy juices, smoothies, and Middle Eastern snacks. FAMILY TREAT Armando's (463 W New England Ave, 32789; 407 951 8930) serves classic Neapolitan food.
- 👫 **Restrooms** At the boathouse

⑬ LEGOLAND®

Not just another brick in the wall

Built on part of the former site of Cypress Gardens, Florida's oldest theme park, LEGOLAND® has captured everyone's imagination. With 50 acres (20 ha) of attractions, including a section of the original Cypress Gardens park, LEGOLAND® Florida is the biggest of the five parks of its kind across the world. A tribute to the popular little Danish building blocks, this spectacular park is full of roller coasters, rides, and shows that challenge as well as entertain. The inventive and often humor-filled constructions make adults giggle, while children gaze in awe as they discover an entire city made of LEGO® bricks.

LEGO® models of Batman and Robin, Imagination Zone

Key Features

① **The Beginning** This colorful area right at the entrance features the Island in the Sky, a 150-ft (46-m) rotating platform that offers a panoramic view of the park.

② **Fun Town** Stroll past giant sea serpents and the Island in the Sky to enter this area, which is home to the 700-seat Wells Fargo 4D Theater. See how LEGO® bricks are transformed from raw plastic into building blocks in the Factory Tour. Younger kids will enjoy riding the two-tier Grand Carousel.

③ **DUPLO® Village** Playgrounds, planes, and trucks designed for little kids with big imaginations can be found in this play area. Don't miss the DUPLO® Farm, full of play animals, fire engines, and drivable cars.

④ **LEGO® Kingdoms** Little princesses and knights joust and battle wizards in this medieval castle. Climb aboard the Dragon coaster for a ride through the LEGOLAND® castle, before heading to Royal Joust for a quiet time on the cantering LEGO® horses.

Entrance

⑤ **Land of Adventure** Steer around brick jungle beasts on the Safari Trek, or brave the rollicking wooden tracks of Coastersaurus that rumble past giant LEGO® dinos. Shoot back at glowing skeletons and pirates to score points in the Lost Kingdom Adventure.

⑥ **Miniland USA** Marvel at miniature LEGO® replicas of American cities spread over seven themed areas. Look for movie stars in Los Angeles in California and street musicians in Times Square in New York, and see the space shuttle smoke and rumble at the Kennedy Space Center. Then check out the battle of miniature galleons at Pirate's Shores.

Prices given are for a family of four

⑦ LEGO® City Little ones can learn to drive at the Ford Jr. Driving School, steer a boat in hopefully the right direction at the Boating School, and soar in the air on Flying School, a thrilling roller coaster. Rescue Academy gets the whole family to pump, drive, and fight fire in a muscle-powered fire engine.

⑧ LEGO® TECHNIC™ Filled with hair-raising rides on the ground, in the water, and in the air, this area is the most extreme of all the zones in the park. Hop onto the wind-powered speedsters at AQUAZONE Wave Racers to dodge water blasters or cycle the way into the sky on Technicycle.

⑨ Imagination Zone Budding engineers can build and program real MINDSTORM® robots in LEGO® MINDSTORMS® or build and race brick cars at Build & Test. In the LEGO® Hero Factory play area, kids can design their own heroes to fight evil.

⑩ Cypress Gardens Opened in 1936, Cypress Gardens was Florida's first theme park. Although it has been whittled down to its current 39-acre (16-ha) slice of LEGOLAND®, it is still a wonderful place to relax, explore, and marvel at Florida's natural beauty. Tropical trees and plants line the pathways and there are hidden waterfalls and flower gardens at every turn.

⑪ LEGOLAND® Water Park Toddlers will love the DUPLO® Splash Safari with short slides and interactive DUPLO® creatures. Older kids can choose from the 375-ft (114-m) waterslides at Twin Chasers or the playground with a 300-gallon (1,135-liter) bucket drop in Joker Soaker.

⑬ LEGOLAND® continued ▶

KIDS' CORNER

Sharp spotting

It could take hours to find everything tucked in Miniland USA, but here are a few fun things to keep an eye out for:

1 Cats. Find the cats jumping through flaming hoops in Key West, and a lady with kittens on the roof in California.

2 Pirates. Not only is there a big sea battle at Pirate's Shores, but there's also a Las Vegas version at the Treasure Island Hotel.

3 A giant chicken, and men lifting weights in Miami Beach.

4 People turning into babies at the Fountain of Youth in St. Augustine.

5 Penguins and parrots in Central Park in New York.

Brownie points
Take aim at the cobra in the Lost Kingdom ride in Land of Adventure, and keep shooting to rack up tons of extra points!

OLD, OLD TREE

Unsuspecting visitors will be astonished by a massive banyan tree – the giant trunk and roots having grown in this spot since 1939. Look out for the tree's "knobbly knees" for a giggle.

LEGO® mania

1 Kids around the world spend 5 billion hours a year playing with LEGO® bricks.

2 More than 400 billion LEGO® bricks have been produced since 1949. Stacked on top of each other, this is enough to connect the Earth and the Moon ten times over!

3 All the LEGO® bricks sold in one year would circle the world five times.

LEGOLAND®, continued

Facade of the inn housing the award-winning Chalet Suzanne Restaurant, Lake Wales

Letting off steam

Run around in LEGOLAND®, or go to **Rotary Park** *(300–398 6th St NE, Winter Haven, 33881)* to burn off excess energy. The park offers a skate park, a sand volleyball court, and walking paths.

Eat and drink
Picnic: under $25; Snacks: $25–50; Real meal: $50–80; Family treat: over $80 (based on a family of four)

PICNIC Castle Burger *(in LEGO® Kingdoms)* serves burgers and fries. Picnic in the shaded area in the Land of Adventure by the Safari Trek.

Exterior of Cap'n Blackbeard's Burgers, Pirate's Cove

SNACKS Granny's Apple Fries Stand *(in Fun Town)* is the place for a tasty fried snack of apple sticks coated in cinnamon and sugar served with a vanilla cream dip. The **City Stage Snack Bar** *(in LEGO® City)* dishes out hot dogs and chips.
REAL MEAL The Market Restaurant *(in The Beginning)* serves coffee and pastries in the morning,

and rotisserie chicken and Asian fusion dishes later in the day. **Cap'n Blackbeard's Burgers** *(in Pirate's Cove)* offers beef hamburgers, cheeseburgers, and chips.
FAMILY TREAT Chalet Suzanne *(3800 Chalet Suzanne Dr, Lake Wales, 33859; 863 676 6011; www. chaletsuzanne.com; closed Mon)*, an Old Florida landmark, is an inn with

a celebrated dining room. Try the "Romaine Soup," a dish that has been served on the space shuttle. The menu has fresh soups, sandwiches, and delicious steaks, as well as chocolate cream pie and crème brûlée for dessert. There is also a fine wine list.

Shopping
Find everything from LEGO® toy sets and LEGO® exclusives to T-shirts and souvenirs in **The Big Shop** *(near the entrance)*. Head for LEGO® Studios *(in Fun Town)* to pick up *Star Wars™*, *Harry Potter™*, and

Star Wars™ LEGO® sets lining the shelves of LEGO® Studios, Fun Town

The Lowdown

🌐 **Map reference** 7 D1
Address One LEGOLAND Way, Winter Haven, 33884; 877 350 5346; *florida.legoland.com*

🚗 **Bus** Daily shuttle bus (8200 Vineland Rd, Orlando, 32821; *florida.legoland.com/en/buy_ tickets/shuttle*; $5 per person) leaves from Orlando Premium Outlets mall at 9am and returns at park closing. Reserve online.
Car Hire a car from Orlando Airport. Parking $12; preferred parking $20

🕐 **Open** Parks usually open from 10am to between 7pm and 8pm. Closed Tue–Wed year-round except Jun–Aug. Check *florida.legoland.com/ en/Plan/hours* for details.

💲 **Price** $256–72; under 3s free. Additional fee of $28–36 for the Water Park. Buy the Annual Pass ($576–636; under 3s free) for free parking and discounts. Second day add-on available at the park for $15. Discount coupons are sometimes available at fast food outlets, on LEGO® kit boxes, and for

AAA (Automobile Association of America) members. Lockers are available for rent in The Beginning and inside LEGOLAND® Water Park.

🚻 **Age range** 2 plus

🎭 **Show** Big Test Live *(in LEGO® City)* features the City Volunteer Fire Department in a superb interactive show full of music and dance. Shows at 11am, 12:45pm, 2:15pm, & 4pm

⏱ **Allow** 1–2 days

♿ **Wheelchair access** Yes

☕ **Cafés** Many across the park

🛍 **Shops** Many across the park

🚻 **Restrooms** Plenty throughout the park. The Baby Care Center in DUPLO® Village has baby-changing facilities, high chairs, and bottle warmers.

Good family value?
A mix of educative and entertaining attractions, as well as beautiful gardens, makes LEGOLAND® superb for a family destination.

SpongeBob SquarePants LEGO® toys. There are also bins of individual parts for imaginative builders at **Pick a Brick** (in the Factory Tour).

Find out more

DIGITAL LEGO® Club offers "Master builder" videos, how-to instructions, comic books, and a free magazine with discount coupons for toys and park admission. Check out club. lego.com/en-us/LEGOMagazine/default.aspx for more information.

Take cover

If rough weather threatens, head for the **Best Western Park View Hotel** (5651 Cypress Gardens Blvd, Winter Haven; 33884; 863 324 5950; www.parkviewhotelwinter haven.com), located across the street from LEGOLAND®. The hotel has lounge areas, a restaurant, and a poolside bar.

Next stop...

FROM PRETTY GARDENS TO A RANCH Head 8 miles (13 km) southeast of LEGOLAND® to the **Bok Tower Gardens** (1151 Tower Blvd, Lake Wales, 33853; 863 676 1408;

The striking Neo-Gothic and Art Deco Singing Tower, Bok Tower Gardens

boktowergardens.org), a huge botanical garden and bird sanctuary. Named for Edward W. Bok, an influential publisher, the gardens boast the Singing Tower, which is known for its 45-minute live carillon concert at 1pm and 3pm daily. Dotted with camellias, magnolias, and azaleas, these woodland gardens have plenty for families – picnic areas with sandboxes and toys, reading benches, a vine-covered arbor tunnel, and even secret garden areas.

Alternatively, the **Westgate River Ranch** (3200 River Ranch Blvd, Frostproof, 33867; 863 692 1321; wgriverranch.com), 33 miles (53 km) southeast of LEGOLAND® near Lake Wales, holds a live rodeo every Saturday night, with bucking broncos, bull riding, rodeo clowns, and genuine cowboys. Kids will love petting and feeding barn animals such as lambs, calves, and baby goats in the petting farm. There are also pony rides on offer.

Top 10 Rides

1. **LOST KINGDOM ADVENTURE**
   Pick up a laser pistol and get points for firing at ancient Egyptian targets in this dark and slightly scary ride in the Land of Adventure.

2. **COASTERSAURUS**
   Ride this old-fashioned and noisy wooden roller coaster, in the Land of Adventure, as it zooms through a land filled with brick dinosaurs.

3. **BATTLE FOR BRICKBEARD'S BOUNTY**
   Watch this exciting live-action water battle featuring water-skiing pirates on Lake Eloise in Pirate's Cove. Those wanting to get soaked can sit in one of the first five rows.

4. **AQUAZONE WAVE RACERS**
   Daring riders get to control the speed of their jet skis by starting out slowly and then spinning out to dizzying and soaking heights in this LEGO® TECHNIC™ ride.

5. **MERLIN'S CHALLENGE**
   Battle a LEGO® Merlin as the wooden train spins around a roller coaster track in wild and possibly magical circles in LEGO® Kingdoms.

6. **SPLASH OUT**
   Climb to the highest point in the park, then plummet down one of the three 60-ft (18-m) slides to drop into the pool below in LEGOLAND® Water Park.

7. **FLYING SCHOOL**
   Board a suspended coaster and zoom high above LEGO® City on this winding, twisting, and diving ride.

8. **BUILD-A-RAFT RIVER**
   Design and build a one-of-a-kind boat and launch it on a 1,000-ft (305-m) long lazy river in LEGOLAND® Water Park.

9. **WELLS FARGO 4D THEATER**
   Go on a wild ride while trying to dodge wind, rain, and snow in this awe-inspiring theater in Fun Town that screens three different 4-D movies.

10. **TEST TRACK**
    Race a full-size TECHNIC™ car along a twisting roller coaster track full of sharp twists and turns on this ride in LEGO® TECHNIC™.

Where to Stay in Orlando and the Parks

Orlando and the theme parks have lodgings to suit all tastes. Whether a night under the stars in a tent, or the luxury of a family suite in a tower appeals, there's no lack of choice, and most places offer pools, in-room entertainment, and more. Rooms range from standard to suites with kid-friendly themes.

AGENCY

All-Star Vacation Homes
www.allstarvacationhomes.com
This website connects visitors with the private owners of everything from one-bedroom condos to nine-bedroom vacation homes for holiday rental.

Downtown Orlando and Winter Park Map 6 F5

HOTELS

Doubletree by Hilton Orlando Downtown
60 S Ivanhoe Blvd, 32804; 407 425 4455; doubletree1.hilton.com
Overlooking beautiful Lake Ivanhoe, just north of Downtown Orlando, this Hilton hotel offers a heated rooftop pool with whirlpool for adults, children's activities, and a kids' menu at the restaurant. Free shuttle service to downtown restaurants.

🌐 🍴 🛗 🛗 ☼ $

Grand Bohemian
325 S Orange Ave, 32801; 407 313 9000; www.grandbohemianhotel.com
The only AAA Four-Diamond hotel downtown, this splendid building houses a great collection of art. Centrally located, it has a spa, a fitness center, and a heated outdoor pool overlooking the city.

♿ 🌐 🍴 🛗 ☼ $$

Park Plaza Hotel
307 S Park Ave, Winter Park, 32789; 407 647 1072; parkplaza hotel.com
Overlooking the green space of Central Park, this charming hotel has cast-iron railings on flower-bedecked balconies. Complimentary valet parking means quicker access to the sights. Alternatively, simply check out the shops along Park Avenue or walk to the nearby museums.

🌐 🍴 $$$

LEGOLAND® Map 7 D1

HOTELS

Park View Hotel
5651 Cypress Gardens Blvd, Winter Haven, 33884; 863 324 5950; www. westernparkviewhotel.com
A few blocks from LEGOLAND®, this hotel offers family-friendly rooms and suites. There is a fitness center and a Kids' Zone game room on site. There is also a free shuttle service to and from LEGOLAND®.

🌐 🛗 P ☼ $

Lake Roy Beach Inn
1823 Cypress Gardens Blvd, Winter Haven 32884; 863 324 6320; www.lakeroybeachinn.com
Located on an interconnected chain of 14 lakes and canals, this inn offers rooms and suites with kitchenettes, and three-bedroom townhouse suites, which can sleep up to eight people, with full kitchens, and screened-in porches and balconies overlooking Lake Roy.

🌐 🛗 ☼ ☼ $–$$

SeaWorld® Map 6 F5

RESORTS

Floridays Resort Orlando
12562 International Dr, 32821; 407 238 7700; www.floridaysresort orlando.com
Just 6 miles (10 km) from SeaWorld®, and close to outlet mall shopping, this bright, Mediterranean-themed resort offers two- and three-bedroom suites with separate living and dining rooms, and full kitchens, and in-suite grocery delivery, for an escape from the restaurants.

🌐 🍴 ☕ ☼ 🍽 $$

HOTELS

Fairfield Inn & Suites Orlando at SeaWorld®
10815 International Dr, 32821; 407 354 1139; www.marriott.com
Within walking distance of the Kraken roller coaster and Aquatica, this 200-room hotel has a game room, a fitness center, shuttles to SeaWorld® and Universal Studios Florida®, and views of the nightly fireworks. Free "quick pass" bracelets for SeaWorld® are available at the front desk.

♿ 🌐 🍴 🛟 $$

Marriott Harbour Lake
7102 Grand Horizons Blvd, 32821; 407 465 6100; www.marriott.com
Minutes away from SeaWorld®, this hotel offers rooms equipped with DVD players and laundry facilities, as well as suites with full kitchens. There is miniature golf, slide pools, s'mores (toasted marshmallows and chocolate biscuits) at the campfire, a pirate ship in the pool, and a pirate-themed kids' camp.

🌐 🍴 🛗 🛟 ☼ $$

A fully furnished family suite in Floridays Resort Orlando

Universal Orlando® & Wet 'n Wild®
Map 6 F5

HOTELS
The Enclave Suites
6165 Carrier Dr, 32819; 407 351 1155; www.enclavesuites.com
Directly across from Universal Studios Florida®, this hotel has suites with separate Scooby Doo- and Woody Woodpecker-themed rooms, with bunk beds. Watch the Universal fireworks from the balcony.

🍽 🛏 ⊗ 🛶 $

Coco Key
7400 International Dr, 32819; 407 351 2626; www.cocokeyorlando.com
Close to Universal Studios Florida®, this hotel boasts a water park with 14 slides and four pools, as well as a shaded "Minnow Lagoon," a poolside bar, and spacious rooms.

🌙 🍽 🛏 ⊗ $–$$

Holiday Inn Kessler Castle
8629 International Dr, 32819; 407 345 1511; www.thecastleorlando.com
Bunk beds, individual TVs and Xbox games, as well as outdoor "dive-in" movies at the pool make this castle-themed hotel a treat. Walk through the back gardens to TuTu Tango, one of the better casual restaurants in the area. Free parking.

🌙 🍽 🛏 P ⊗ $–$$

Hard Rock Hotel
5800 Universal Blvd, 32819; 407 490 1272; www.hardrockhotelorlando.com
Right on Universal property, this hotel features a pool with an underwater sound system, and supervised kids' activities at Camp Lil' Rock. Some suites have attached themed kids' rooms. Complimentary water taxi and shuttle buses to the parks.

🌙 🍽 🛏 ⊗ $$$

Walt Disney World® Resort

RESORTS
Hyatt Regency Grand Cypress
Map 6 F5
1 Grand Cypress Blvd, 32836; 407 239 1234; grandcypress.hyatt.com
This resort offers everything from standard guestrooms to massive VIP suites. There's a golf course, a huge lake with watersports, and a vast lagoon pool with slides and waterfalls. Kids' programs are available too.

🍴 🌙 🍽 ⊗ 🏊 $$

The Hard Rock Hotel Orlando, with a view of the pool

Disney's Art of Animation Resort
Map 6 E6
1850 Century Dr, Lake Buena Vista, 32830; disneyworld.disney.go.com
Choose from *Nemo-*, *Cars-*, and *Lion King*-themed family suites that can sleep up to six people. Playgrounds, a jogging trail, in-room pizza delivery, and free Disney movies are some of the lures at this Disney resort.

🍴 🌙 🍽 🛏 ⊗ $$–$$$

Marriott Orlando World Center Resort
Map 6 F5
8701 World Center Dr, 32821; 407 239 4200; www.marriott.com
The world's largest Marriott, just outside Walt Disney World® Resort, has 2,000 rooms and suites, six pools, waterslides, a video arcade, and a golf course. There are organized arts and crafts programs, and scavenger hunts for kids.

🌙 🍽 🛏 $$–$$$

Swan and Dolphin Resort
Map 6 E6
1500 Epcot Resorts Blvd, Lake Buena Vista, 32830; 407 934 3000 (Swan) & 407 934 4000 (Dolphin); www.swandolphin.com
Located in Walt Disney World® Resort, these adjoining hotels offer a massive pool grotto, complete with a white-sand beach and waterfalls. The Camp Dolphin club offers programs for kids aged 4 to 12.

🌙 🍽 🛏 ⊗ 🍽 $$–$$$

Disney's Animal Kingdom Lodge
Map 6 E6
2901 Osceola Pkwy, Lake Buena Vista, 32830; disneyworld.disney.go.com
This massive, beautifully designed Disney resort offers views of wild animals grazing on an extensive savanna. Many of the rooms come

with bunk beds. Free Continental breakfast, midday snacks, and evening wine and cheese.

🌙 🍽 🛏 ⊗ $$$

HOTELS
Ramada Maingate West
Map 6 F6
7491 West Hwy 192, Kissimmee, 34747; 407 396 6000; www.ramadamaingatewest.com
Kids get a goodie bag when they check in at this hotel. The attractions include an indoor pool with a waterfall, and nightly karaoke. Some suites have separate themed rooms with bunk beds. Free shuttles to the Universal and Disney parks.

🌙 🍽 🛏 ⊗ $

Best Western Lake Buena Vista
Map 6 F5
2000 Hotel Plaza Blvd, Lake Buena Vista, 32830; 407 828 2424; www.bestwestern.com
This hotel is within walking distance of Downtown Disney® restaurants and shops, as well as the Disney transportation system. Rooms above the sixth floor offer splendid views of the Epcot® fireworks.

🍴 🌙 🍽 P ⊗ $$

Nickelodeon Hotel
Map 6 F5
14500 Continental Gateway, Orlando, 32821; 407 387 5437; www.nickhotel.com
A Nickelodeon Network-themed hotel featuring *Jimmy Neutron* and *SpongeBob SquarePants* at every turn, with an amazing water park, and kids' suites with bunk beds.

🌙 🍽 🔄 ⊗ 🛶 $$

CAMPING
Disney's Fort Wilderness Resort & Campground
Map 6 F6
4510 N Fort Wilderness Trail, Lake Buena Vista, 32830; 407 939 7429; disneyworld.disney.go.com
Bring a tent, drive in with an RV, or rent a rustic but comfortable cabin for a stay in these woods, minutes away from the Disney parks. Attractions include horseback-riding, and nightly marshmallow roasts.

🍴 🌙 🍽 ⊗ 🛶 $–$$$

> **Price Guide**
> The following price ranges are based on one night's accommodation in high season for a family of four, inclusive of service charges and additional taxes.
> **$** Under $150 **$$** $150–300 **$$$** over $300

The Space Coast

Long home to Native Americans, this part of Florida is where Spanish explorers first landed on American soil – and from where man's first voyage to the Moon took off. Today, the area's highlight is the cutting-edge Kennedy Space Center, from where NASA has launched all its space programs since 1968. Here, visitors get a chance to see the shuttles that orbited in space, and meet the astronauts who manned them.

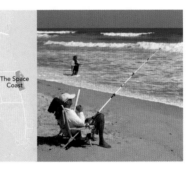

The Space Coast

Highlights

Kennedy Space Center
Become an astronaut and experience what a journey into outer space feels like at this stellar space center, the only one of its kind (see pp144–7).

Merritt Island National Wildlife Refuge
Step back in time to the area where Florida's first inhabitants lived, and where native wildlife thrives today (see pp148–9).

Canaveral National Seashore
Bask in the sun on beautiful, soft white sands that are frequented by migrating sea turtles (see p148).

Brevard Zoo
See animals native to Florida, as well as from lands as far away as Africa and Australia, in this huge zoological park (see p151).

Cocoa Beach and Pier
Take a break at this famous resort, with a white-sand beach, and a pier with restaurants and souvenir shops (see p150).

Brevard Museum of History and Natural Science
Explore this little gem of a museum with exhibits on everything from 7,000-year-old Native American culture to astronauts (see p151).

Left The spectacular Saturn V shuttle displayed at the Apollo/Saturn V Center, Kennedy Space Center
Above right Fishing at Playalinda Beach, Merritt Island National Wildlife Refuge

The Best of
The Space Coast

With beaches located very close to Orlando's major theme parks, the Space Coast is a great destination for families looking for some sand and sun; lively Cocoa Beach is perfect for surfing and swimming. A visit to the Kennedy Space Center offers the thrill of seeing the shuttles that once journeyed into space and learning about astro-history. For a change of pace, visit the region's tranquil wildlife preserves, rich with flora and fauna.

Up in the air and higher

The biggest attraction for sky-gazing visitors is the **Kennedy Space Center** (see pp144–7). From its beginnings in 1969, the center has been the heart of America's space program. With the shuttle orbiter program now closed, there will not be many opportunities to watch a rocket actually take off, but the interactive exhibits and motion-simulation rides at the Shuttle Launch Experience, the Apollo/Saturn V Center, and the United States Astronaut Hall of Fame® make up for it. See rare items from the Moon missions, including the space suit that Apollo 14 Commander Alan Shepard wore on the Moon, in the Apollo Treasures Gallery

Right Splashing in the waters near the Pier, Cocoa Beach
Below A simulated pre-show briefing for visitors at the Shuttle Launch Experience, Kennedy Space Center

Above Kayaking past giraffes in a re-creation of their natural habitat in Brevard Zoo, Melbourne **Right** Roseate spoonbills in Merritt Island National Wildlife Refuge

in the Apollo/Saturn V Center. Admirers of all things aeronautic may also want to catch the Tico Air Show at the **Valiant Air Command Warbird & Vintage Museum** *(see p147)* in Titusville in March, where vintage jets and old biplanes fly overhead.

Fun in the sun

The beaches around Cocoa, Titusville, and Melbourne are a natural draw for families. Some, such as **Cocoa Beach** *(see p150)*, are lined with resort hotels, restaurants and bars, and are popular with sun-lovers and surfing fanatics. By contrast, **Playalinda Beach** *(see p148)*, on the **Canaveral National Seashore** *(see p148)*, is protected by the Parks Department from development. Visitors here can enjoy pristine nature alongside high-tech rockets pointed at the stars.

Florida's wild side

Between the **Canaveral National Seashore** and **Merritt Island National Wildlife Refuge** *(see pp148–9)*, there is a large expanse of wild, untamed Florida. Cypress swamps, flat, windswept prairies, and crystal-clear springs, as well as magnificent scrub oak ridges, are all there, and home to a host of plants and animals, including turtles, manatees, and alligators. Combine all this with the Wild Florida habitat at **Brevard Zoo** *(see p151)*, and families can see hundreds of native animals without having to look far.

In a week

Start with the **Kennedy Space Center**. Check out the Shuttle Launch Experience first, and then take a guided tour before catching an IMAX® movie. The next day visit the center's United States Astronaut Hall of Fame. After lunch, take bathing suits to **Playalinda Beach** for an undisturbed afternoon in the sun. On the third day, follow the **Black Point Wildlife Drive** *(see p148)* at the **Merritt Island National Wildlife Refuge**, enjoy a picnic lunch under the cypress trees, then take a free walking tour of the lagoon with a guide from the Visitor Center. Next head to **Brevard Zoo** to let the kids feed giraffes in the Expedition Africa habitat. An early dinner on the Pier at **Cocoa Beach** is a good way to wrap up the day. The next day, watch the sunrise over the 24 miles (38 km) of **Canaveral National Seashore** beach. Stop at the **Brevard Museum of History and Natural Science** *(see p151)* for a look at prehistoric Florida's inhabitants and a run around the **Imagination Center** *(see p151)*.

The Space Coast

With swamps, flatlands, and beaches, and a temperate to subtropical climate, the Space Coast has more native wildlife than practically anywhere in the US. Due to the high influx of tourists, the major roadways are well kept; however, its location surrounding the Kennedy Space Center and preserves means development is limited. While there is a fairly usable public transportation system, especially along the trolley routes around Cocoa Beach, a car is mandatory for any excursions further afield, and to get here from Orlando. Interstate 95 is the main highway for north–south travel, with US Route 1 the principal road through coastal tourist areas.

Colorful surfboards displayed at the Ron Jon Surf Shop, Cocoa Beach

Visitor Information Center in Merritt Island National Wildlife Refuge

White rhinos in the Expedition Africa exhibit in Brevard Zoo, Melbourne

Building sand castles at Playalinda Beach, Canaveral National Seashore

The Lowdown

🚗 **Getting there and around**
Air Fly into Daytona Beach International Airport (700 Catalina Drive, Daytona Beach, 32114; 386 248 8069; www.flydaytonafirst.com) and Melbourne International Airport (1, Air Terminal Parkway, Melbourne, 32901; 321 723 6227; www.mlbair.com).
Bus Greyhound (1 800 231 2222; www.greyhound.com) is ideal for interstate travel, with stations in Daytona Beach, Titusville and Melbourne. Space Coast Area Transit or SCAT (401 S Varr Ave, Cocoa, 32922; 321 633 1878; www.ridescat.com) local bus service includes a trolley serving Cocoa Beach.
Car Avis (www.avis.com) and Hertz (www.hertz.com) have offices at airports. AAA Taxis (555 Challenger Rd, Cape Canaveral, 32920; 321 868 8888; www.aaataxionline.com) are available throughout Brevard County.

ℹ️ **Visitor Information** Visit the Space Coast tourist center at 430 Brevard Ave, Cocoa Village, 32922; 877 572 3224; www.space-coast.com

🛒 **Supermarkets** Publix (www.publix.com) and Winn-Dixie (www.winndixie.com) are the premier supermarket chains, with outlets throughout this region.

🎏 **Festivals** Ron Jon Easter Surfing Festival, Cocoa Beach; www.eastersurffest.com (mid-Apr). Beach Fest & Beach Sports Championships (Memorial Day, May). Thunder on the Beach: Space Coast Super Boat Grand Prix; powerboat races; www.spacecoastsuperboat.com (mid-May). NKF Pro-Am Surf Festival; surfing competition benefitting the National Kidney Foundation; www.nkfsurf.com (Labor Day, Sep); Brevard Caribbean Festival; live music, good food and family activities; www.brevardcaribbeanfest.com (Labor Day, Sep); Space Coast Art Festival; art competition and exhibition, with kids activities; www.spacecoastartfestival.com (Thanksgiving weekend, Nov)

➕ **Pharmacies** Publix, CVS (www.cvs.com/pharmacy) and Walgreens (www.walgreens.com/pharmacy) are the main pharmacies in the region, with some outlets open 24 hours.

🚻 **Restrooms** Almost all major attractions, restaurants, parks, malls, and most gas stations have public restrooms.

Places of interest

🔲 **SIGHTS**
1 Kennedy Space Center
2 Merritt Island National Wildlife Refuge
3 Cocoa Beach and Pier
4 Ron Jon Surf Shop, Cocoa Beach
5 Brevard Museum of History and Natural Science
6 Brevard Zoo

Spectacular view of the ocean from Turtle Mound, Canaveral National Seashore

① Kennedy Space Center
3-2-1 Blast off!

Every young space cadet dreams of being an astronaut, and this is the place where the dream comes true. Since its opening in 1963, the home of the National Aeronautics and Space Administration (NASA) has launched 135 shuttle missions, 26 manned space flights, and countless rockets from the Cape Canaveral base. The Center's highlight is the permanent display of Atlantis, which ended the shuttle orbiter program in 2011.

A command module on display in the Visitor Complex

Key Features

① **Astronaut Encounter** In this 30-minute show, visitors meet the legendary veteran members of NASA's astronaut teams, who tell stories of their experiences and answer questions.

② **Rocket Garden** Eight vintage rockets from every stage of the US Space Program reach for the stars in this display area, beautifully lit at night. Walk among the real rockets and replicas of space capsules illustrating the Center's history of flight. Touch a 4 billion-year-old moon rock, sit in a Command Module, or climb into replica Mercury, Gemini, and Apollo capsules to see how cramped the travel conditions in these early spaceships were.

Prices given are for a family of four

③ **Exploration Space®: Explorers Wanted** This 10,000-sq ft (3,048-sq m) exhibit features a live theater, interactive experiences, and large-scale multimedia presentations to help kids and adults learn about the future of space exploration. The live Explorers Wanted show runs twice an hour, with children featuring as the Pioneers of Tomorrow, exploring the idea of extraterrestrial travel.

④ **IMAX® Theater** Two massive 50-ft (15-m) movie screens show films featuring footage shot by astronauts during actual missions in space, with sound and 3-D effects so realistic that viewers feel they are in space themselves. Films include *Hubble 3D*, where viewers can "float" alongside astronauts as they build the Hubble Space Telescope, and *Space Station 3D*, which uses film taken by 25 astronauts and cosmonauts of a 3-D journey, from blast-off to docking at the International Space Station.

Entrance

⑤ **United States Astronaut Hall of Fame®** See the world's largest collection of personal astronaut memorabilia, from Gus Grissom's Mercury space suit to the flag flown on the first manned US spaceflight. Within the museum, Science on a Sphere is a three-dimensional view of the Earth and planets, as if seen from outer space.

⑥ **Space Shuttle Plaza** This $100 million exhibit features the space shuttle Atlantis – an Earth orbiter that went into space more than 30 times between 1985 and 2011. This exhibit is one of only three shuttles on display in the world. Its cargo bay door is open and its robotic arm extended.

⑦ **Shuttle Launch Experience®** Ride a thrilling space flight simulator to sample G-forces and zero gravity. After a pre-launch briefing in a replica six-story launch gantry, strap on as the countdown begins, and the sounds, lights, and sensation of being launched into space propel the imagination into orbit.

⑧ **Visitor Complex Exhibits** The Space Center's Visitor Complex has fascinating walk-through exhibits on the US Space Program's major missions. The Early Space Exploration facility showcases key figures from the first space programs, while the Mercury Mission Control Room allows visitors a look at the consoles from which the first eight Mercury missions were monitored.

⑨ **Apollo/Saturn V Center** Explore a reproduction of the Apollo mission control room, marvel at a 370-ft (112-m) tall Saturn V rocket, and see space suits that Apollo 14 astronauts wore in outer space in this tribute to the Apollo Space Program.

① Kennedy Space Center continued ▶

Kennedy Space Center, continued

Letting off steam

Kids can crawl and climb through tunnels, scamper over a rock wall, and command a mini-shuttle in the **Children's Play Dome** (on site), a play area with an outer space theme. If commanding rockets does not use up enough energy, head 8 miles (13 km) south to the **Rotary Riverfront Park** (4141 S Washington Ave, Titusville, 32780), which has a playground and a fishing pier along the Indian River.

Kids exploring the play area in the Children's Play Dome

Eat and drink

Picnic: under $25; Snacks: $25–50; Real meal: $50–80; Family treat: over $80 (based on a family of four)

PICNIC Kloiber's Cobbler Eatery (337 S Washington Ave, Titusville, 32796; 321 383 0689) has sandwiches and salads, which can be enjoyed at the Children's Play Dome. **SNACKS G-Force Grill** (in Astronaut Encounter) serves hot dogs, turkey legs, and nachos. **REAL MEAL The Orbit Café** (next to the IMAX® Theater), the largest eatery in the Kennedy Space

Meeting veteran space explorers at Lunch with an Astronaut

Center, has pizza, barbecue, and sandwiches. Buy a Souvenir Sipper Cup and get free soda refills all day. **FAMILY TREAT Lunch With an Astronaut** (in Astronaut Encounter) gives visitors a rare chance to converse and eat with an actual spaceman. Call 866 737 5235 to make reservations.

Shopping

More than 3,000 space-themed items are available at **The Space Shop** (NASA Central; www.thespaceshop.com; 9am–3pm), including T-shirts, commemorative medals, space-themed LEGO®, and even full replica flight suits.

Find out more

DIGITAL Visit NASA Kids' Club at www.nasa.gov/audience/forkids/kidsclub/flash for contests and

space-themed games featuring Buzz Lightyear for younger kids, and news and pictures taken from space by astronauts for older kids. National Geographic offers an interactive guide to the solar system at science.nationalgeographic.com/science/space/solar-system.

Next stop...

NEARBY SPACE HISTORY
To discover more about space history, head 13 miles (21 km) west to the **US Space Walk of Fame**

Space shuttle model in the US Space Walk of Fame

Timeline

The first American satellite, Explorer 1, is launched		Neil Armstrong and Buzz Aldrin (Apollo 11) walk on the Moon		The space shuttle program begins	Discovery, the first shuttle launched since the Challenger disaster, goes into space	
1958	**1965**	**1969**	**1981**	**1982**	**1986**	**198**
	Edward White is the first American to walk in space		Columbia is the first shuttle in space		The Challenger explodes, killing all its crew	

Prices given are for a family of four

Museum (*4 Main St, Titusville, 32796; 321 264 0434*), with displays on Mercury, Gemini, Apollo, and other shuttles. Or head 12 miles (19 km) east to the **Air Force Space and Missile Museum** (*191 Museum Circle, Patrick Air Force Base, 32925; 321 853 9171*) to see restored items from the US Air Force's space launch

activities. The **Valiant Air Command & Vintage Warbird Museum** (*6600 Tico Rd, Titusville, 32780; 321 268 1941; www.vacwarbirds. org*), 8 miles (13 km) west of the Kennedy Space Center, is for those interested in terrestrial flight. The museum displays, repairs, and flies vintage airplanes.

The Lowdown

🌐 **Map reference** 6 H5
Address State Rd 405, Kennedy Space Center, 32899; 1 866 737 5235; *www.kennedyspace center.com*

🚗 **Car** Rent a car from Orlando.

🕐 **Open** 9am–6pm daily, closed Dec 25 and certain launch days. United States Astronaut Hall of Fame®: noon–6pm daily. Hours vary; check website for timings.

💲 **Prices** $182–252; under 3s free. Unlimited admission annual pass: $212–232; under 3s free. United States Astronaut Hall of Fame®: $100–108; under 3s free

👫 **Cutting the line** Book tickets online and avoid visiting during holidays, the spring break in May, and late fall. Head for the Shuttle Launch Experience in the morning, as the lines get long later in the day.

🚩 **Guided tours** The Center runs KSC Up-Close Tours ($88–100 each; under 3s free), including the Launch Pad Tour, where visitors get a close view of Launch Pad 39-A; the Launch Control Center Tour, which allows visitors to tour Firing Room 4, from where all shuttle launches since 2006 have been controlled; and most adults, are the Vehicle Assembly Building Tour, which allows guests to see at firsthand the area where the shuttles are

assembled for launch using huge bridge cranes. On the Cape Canaveral: Then & Now Tour ($88–100; under 3s free), visitors relive the launch of America's first satellite, and see the launch sites of the Mercury, Gemini, and Apollo programs. The free Rocket Garden tour (10:30am and 4pm daily) shows guests the rockets that helped power American astronauts into space.

👫 **Age range** 6 plus

🤸 **Activities** Kids can ride in a Mars Rover simulator and a slowed-down G-force trainer in the United States Astronaut Hall of Fame®.

🕐 **Allow** 4–8 hours

♿ **Wheelchair access** Yes

🚻 **Restrooms** At the Visitor Complex, IMAX® Theater, and all restaurants

Good family value?
Kids, and most adults, are fascinated by the space program, and the all-inclusive price is a bargain for an all-day experience.

Space shuttle Columbia explodes on re-entry, killing all its crew

NASA's Curiosity Rover lands on Mars

1990	2003	2008	2012	2014

Hubble Space Telescope is launched

NASA's Phoenix probe uncovers the existence of water ice on Mars

NASA plans to test launch the Orion manned spacecraft

② Merritt Island National Wildlife Refuge
The wildest place in Florida

With its dry coastal dunes and boggy marshes, the Merritt Island area is like a theme park built by nature. Established in 1963, the refuge covers an area twice the size of Orlando. More than 1,500 species of plants, mammals, and reptiles are found here, including endangered animals that live nowhere else. Many migratory birds visit between October and April, and many large birds, such as egrets and pelicans, live here year-round.

Manatees in the Observation Area

Key Sights

④ **Black Point Wildlife Drive** Follow the 7-mile (4-km) trail by car or set out on one of the hiking trails and look out for more than 50 species of birds. The connecting 5-mile (8-km) Cruickshank Trail loops through the marsh and back to the drive.

⑤ **Indian River Lagoon** The banks of these waterways, home to Native American tribes for thousands of years, offer the best spots to watch for wintering manatees and bottlenose dolphins.

⑥ **Manatee Observation Area** This deck on the northeast side of Haulover Canal offers close views of these endangered animals. In winter, when the sea temperature falls, several hundred can be seen.

⑦ **Canaveral National Seashore** White-sand beaches, tropical forest, lagoons, and cypress hammock make up this unspoiled 24-mile (39-km) stretch of coastline.

① **Playalinda Beach** This protected beach with pure, soft white sands and undisturbed vistas is one of the few beaches in Florida untouched by big hotels.

② **Visitor Information Center** Exhibits and hands-on presentations on the refuge's wildlife are regularly shown here. Climb the observation tower for fine views.

③ **Oak Hammock and Palm Hammock Foot Trails** The short Oak Hammock Trail is posted with educational signs explaining the area's ecology. The Palm Hammock Trail is a 2-mile (4-km) loop through hardwood forest with areas perfect for spotting songbirds.

Prices given are for a family of four

The Lowdown

🌐 **Map reference** 6 H5
Address SR-402, Titusville, 32782; 321 861 0667; www.fws.gov/merrittisland

🚗 **Car** Rent a car from New Smyrna Beach or Orlando. The refuge begins at the east side of the Max Brewer Causeway.

🕐 **Open** Refuge: sunrise–sunset daily. Visitor Information Center: usually 10am–4:30pm. Hours vary by season; check website. Playalinda Beach: 6am–6pm daily (life guards are on duty May 30– Sept 1: 10am–5pm). Roads, trails, and boat ramps open daily from sunrise to sunset.

💲 **Price** Entry to the park is free, as are fishing permits. Black Point Wildlife Drive and boat docking: $5

🚩 **Guided tours** Driving tours of bird habitats (321 861 5601). Free guided hikes leave from the Visitor Information Center.

🚶 **Age range** 9 plus (for walking trails); driving tours for younger children. Head for the southern end of Playalinda Beach, as the northern end is an unofficial clothing-free area.

🧗 **Activities** The Visitor Center holds crafts workshops for kids.

⏱ **Allow** 1–8 hours

☕ **Café** No

🚻 **Restrooms** At the Visitor Center, Cruickshank Trail stop, and the parking areas at Playalinda Beach.

Good family value?
With free access to one of North America's last unspoiled wild areas, Merritt Island is great for outdoorsy families.

View from the top of Turtle Mound, Canaveral National Seashore

Letting off steam

Merritt Island is a wilderness area, and disturbing the animals here by running and making a noise is frowned upon. Head for **Jetty Park Fishing Pier** in Cape Canaveral to catch and release fish in some of the best waters in the state, or check out **Seminole Rest** and **Turtle Mound** in the middle of the Canaveral National Seashore. These archaeological sites prove the presence of Native Americans here 4,000 years ago.

Eat and drink

Picnic: under $25; Snacks: $25–50; Real meal: $50–80; Family treat: over $80 (based on a family of four)

PICNIC Publix (*125 E Merritt Island Causeway, 32952; 321 452 0288*) stocks picnic supplies. Take your lunch to the Sendler Education Outpost Pavilion, near the Indian River Lagoon. It has picnic tables, running water, and restrooms.
SNACKS Taco City (*2955 S Atlantic Ave, Cocoa Beach, 32931; 321 784 1475; www.tacocity2.com*) has a casual atmosphere and lots of easily-held-by-little-hands Tex-Mex items.
REAL MEAL Grills Seafood Deck & Tiki Bar (*505 Glen Cheek Dr, Cape Canaveral, 32920; 321 868 2226; www.grillsseafood.com*) offers locally caught seafood and outdoor seating in a bay favored by dolphins, 20 miles (32 km) from Merritt Island.
FAMILY TREAT The Fat Snook (*2464 S Atlantic Ave, Cocoa Beach, 32169; 321 784 1190; www.thefatsnook.com*) is a modern Caribbean restaurant that serves interesting dishes such as coffee-rubbed steak and scallops with banana polenta. Call ahead to make reservations.

Shopping

Choose from a variety of hats, caps, T-shirts, totes, badges, pins, and books at the gift shop in the **Visitor Center**.

Find out more

DIGITAL Go to *www.floridabirding trail.com* for a list of 500 sites across Florida ideal for birdwatching.
FILM *The Big Year* (2011), about watching rare birds, and starring Jack Black and Steve Martin, was partly filmed at Merritt Island.

Kids playing in the water near the Pier, Cocoa Beach

Take cover

If rain threatens, head 20 miles (32 km) south to the town of **Cocoa Beach** (*see p150*), which has ample restaurants and shops.

Next stop...

THE BOTANICAL GARDEN Zip 40 miles (64 km) south to the Botanical Garden at Florida Institute of Technology (*facilities.fit.edu/ botanical_gardens.php*). This unique 15-acre (6-ha) garden is dotted with more than 300 species of ferns, palms, and tropical plants.

Vacationers at the famous white-sand Cocoa Beach

③ Cocoa Beach and Pier

Eating, shopping, and fishing above; sunbathing below

The city of Cocoa Beach became famous because of its proximity to the Kennedy Space Center *(see pp144–7)*, but it was popular long before rockets were launched from here. It nestles on a small barrier island bordered by a fertile lagoon and the warm waters of the Atlantic Ocean. Remains of ancient Native American villages prove that Cocoa was home to native Floridians for thousands of years, and shops, restaurants, and museums keep it lively today. The beach, with its soft white sand, stretches into relatively calm waters and has long been a major draw for visitors. There is always plenty of activity, from families building sand castles to surfers, and treasure-hunters with metal detectors. A landmark since 1962, the wooden **Pier** has bars,

restaurants, and stores selling handcrafted gifts. Live concerts and festivals are also held right on the beach.

Take cover

Head for the **Dinosaur Store** *(250 W Cocoa Beach Causeway, 32931; 321 783 7300; www.dinosaurstore.com)*, which has a vast selection of dinosaur teeth and replicas, meteorites, and toys. Kids will like the fake shrunken heads and arcade games.

④ Ron Jon Surf Shop, Cocoa Beach

Always open, always fun

Opened in 1964, this iconic shop has been here so long it has become a tourist destination in its own right. It has lanes lined up for families: shop for swimsuits, board shorts, towels, or flip flops in the fun-looking two-story building

The Lowdown

- 🌐 **Map reference** 6 H6
  Address 4151 North Atlantic Ave, Cocoa Beach, 32931; 321 799 8888; www.ronjons.com
- 🚗 **Car** Rent a car from Orlando International Airport.
- 🕐 **Open** 24 hours daily. Cocoa Beach Surf Museum: 8am–8pm daily
- 👫 **Age range** 6 plus
- 🕐 **Allow** 30 mins–2 hours
- ♿ **Wheelchair access** Yes
- 🍴 **Eat and drink** SNACKS Simply Delicious Café & Bakery *(125 N Orlando Ave, 32931; 321 783 2012)* serves breakfast, sandwiches, and baked goods. REAL MEAL The Shark Pit *(4001 N Atlantic Ave, 32931; www.cocoa beachsurf.com/SharkPit)* has fish tacos, pizza, and a kids' menu.
- 👫 **Restrooms** On both floors

Wide variety of fascinating merchandise in the Ron Jon Surf Shop, Cocoa Beach

fronted by Hawaiian statues. The shop also has a huge selection of kitsch souvenirs, including Ron Jon stickers, tiki statues, keychains and basically everything imaginable with the word "Florida" written on it. Serious surfers, too, shop here, and the assortment of boards and supplies is first-rate. Look out for discount coupons in hotel lobbies before visiting.

Visit the **Cocoa Beach Surf Museum** *(www.cocoabeachsurf museum.org)*, situated just north of the main store building. It screens movies and features exhibits on the history and heroes of surfing.

Letting off steam

Alan Shephard Park *(202 E Cocoa Beach Causeway, 32931; 321 868 3258)*, two blocks away, offers ample opportunities to run around. There is also access to a white-sand beach, and restrooms.

The Lowdown

- 🌐 **Map reference** 6 H6
  Address Pier: 401 Meade Ave, Cocoa Beach, 32931; 321 783 7549; cocoabeachpier.com/cbp
- 🚗 **Car** Rent a car from Orlando International Airport.
- 💲 **Price** Pier: $10 parking fee; check website for details.
- 👫 **Cutting the line** Avoid spring break in Mar, and surfing festivals in Apr and Sep, which draw massive crowds. On July 4, the firework display is spectacular and it might be worth the crush.
- 👆 **Guided tours** Wildside Tours *(www.wildsidetours.com)* runs a

boat excursion from Cocoa Beach to the Banana River Lagoon to spot manatees and birds.
- 👫 **Age range** All ages
- 🕐 **Allow** 2 days
- 🍴 **Eat and drink** PICNIC Cocoa Beach Sunday Farmers' Market *(City Hall, 2 S Orlando Ave, 32931; 321 917 0721; www.cityofcocoabeach.com)* offers local produce and handmade baked goods that can be enjoyed on the beach. REAL MEAL Atlantic Ocean Grille *(on the Pier; 321 783 7549)* offers freshly caught fish and a spectacular view from high above the Atlantic Ocean.

5 Brevard Museum of History and Natural Science

From mastodons to missiles

This charming museum offers a glimpse into the distant past and the technological present of central Florida – from prehistoric fossils to rocket ships. See re-creations of the archaeological dig of the area's oldest site and of ancient Native American villages to get an insight into Cocoa's origins. There are also exhibits on the space program and Brevard County's still-vibrant cattle-ranching. Items from the museum's own holdings about life in Florida are displayed alongside traveling collections.

Letting off steam

The ramped treehouse in the **Imagination Center** (on site) is a high-energy climb and run. The museum's park has nature trails that offer tree-shaded places to cool off.

The Lowdown

- **Map reference** 6 H6
- **Address** 2201 Michigan Ave, Cocoa, 32926; 321 632 1830; nbbd.com/godo/BrevardMuseum
- **Car** Rent a car from Orlando International Airport.
- **Open** 10am–4pm Tue–Sat
- **Price** $21–31; under 4s free
- **Cutting the line** Afternoon is the quietest time to visit.
- **Guided tours** The museum runs a pre-arranged guided tour of the nature trails and exhibits for groups of 15 plus.
- **Age range** 6 plus
- **Activities** There are hands-on activities in the Imagination Center.
- **Allow** 1–3 hours
- **Wheelchair access** Yes
- **Eat and drink** REAL MEAL Jabbers (4360 Grissom Pkwy, Cocoa, 2926; 321 638 4130) offers Cajun and Southern food. FAMILY TREAT Heidelberg Restaurant (7 N Orlando Ave, 32931; 321 783 4559) serves German specialties and great home-made desserts.
- **Restrooms** In the lobby

6 Brevard Zoo

Get up close to bobcats, whistling ducks, and giraffes

As if Florida were not wild enough, this modern, spacious zoo presents even more wild animals and habitats. In the Wild Florida area, see animals native to Florida such as alligators, bobcats, foxes, whistling ducks, and hawks. The zoo also has re-created African, Australian, and South American jungle habitats populated by exotic wildlife. Climb the 16-ft (5-m) high platform in the Expedition Africa zone to look into a giraffe's eye.

Letting off steam

The **Treetop Trek Chutes & Ladders** (on site) activity course runs on rope bridges, tightropes, and zip lines through, around, and 20 ft (6 m) above the zoo.

The Lowdown

- **Map reference** 6 H6
- **Address** 8225 N Wickham Rd, Melbourne, 32940; 321 254 9453; www.brevardzoo.org
- **Car** Rent a car from Orlando International Airport.
- **Open** 9:30am–5pm daily (last admission 4:15pm)
- **Price** $50–60; under 2s free
- **Guided tours** A host of tours are offered inside the zoo and in the connecting wetlands. A behind-the-scenes Wild Encounter tour is also available.
- **Age range** 2 plus
- **Activities** Petting zoo, water park & Cape to Cairo Express train ride
- **Allow** 1–3 hours
- **Wheelchair access** Yes
- **Eat and drink** PICNIC Flamingo Café (on site) offers snacks and refreshments that can be eaten at the picnic tables outside the zoo. SNACKS Whale's Tail (on site) serves sandwiches, pizza, and chicken.

KIDS' CORNER

Listen up, dude!

The sport of surfing has its own language, a mix of words from lots of places including Hawaii and California! See if you overhear any of these words:
1 **Aloha:** hello, goodbye, and what's up, dude?
2 **Bammerwee:** not really good or bad, just okay
3 **Da kine:** Hawaiian for absolutely the best kind of wave
4 **Eat foam:** fall off a surfboard
5 **Gnarly:** an awesome, spectacular thing; the only thing better is gnar-max
6 **Jivel:** everything is going very wrong and not a bit gnarly
7 **Tubular:** very cool
8 **Mahalo:** Hawaiian for thank you

ONLY IN FLORIDA

Gators and manatees aren't the only animals that come from Florida. Unlike most of their fellow fowl, black-bellied whistling ducks live in trees, or even chimneys, and make a high-pitched "pe-che-che" whistle as they fly. You'll recognize them right away by their red bills, long pink legs, and, yes, black bellies.

The Bog People

Find out about the ancient Bog People at the Brevard Museum of History and Natural Science. Living in the swamps near Cape Canaveral more than 8,000 years ago, they had tools, clothing, and houses 3,500 years before there were pyramids in Egypt! More than 160 mummified skeletons have been discovered in the peat bogs around Titusville, and that is why they are called Bog People.

Braving it on a zip line in Brevard Zoo, Melbourne

Picnic under $25; Snacks $25–50; Real meal $50–80; Family treat over $80 (based on a family of four)

Where to Stay on the Space Coast

With more than 2,500 hotels and motels, prices and lodgings in this area range from low and basic to outrageous and ultra-luxurious. While most accommodations trumpet their proximity to the beaches, there are a few hidden gems that offer a unique experience in outdoor living.

AGENCY

Cocoa Beach Best

www.cocoabeachbest.com
Located in the heart of the Space Coast, this agency offers self-catering condominium rentals – from one-bedroom efficiency apartments and tower suites to five-bedroom pool homes – with nightly and weekly rates.

Cape Canaveral Map 6 H6

RESORTS

Radisson Resort at the Port

8701 Astronaut Blvd, 32920; 321 784 0000; www.radisson.com
The closest resort to Port Canaveral allows views of incoming cruise ships from certain balconies. The outdoor recreation area features waterfalls and a hot tub. A microwave and refrigerator are available in each room, and breakfast is free. The Kennedy Space Center is a 30-minute drive away.

ꔷ ◔ $$

Royal Mansions Resort

8600 Ridgewood Ave, 32920; 321 784 8484; www.royalmansions.com
This resort offers oceanfront condo rentals on a private beach. Each apartment has a full kitchen, and outside there is a clubhouse with BBQ grills, hot tubs, and bike rentals, as well as a private walkway to the beach. Breakfast is included. A two-night minimum stay is required.

ꔷ ꔷ P ◔ $$

Ron Jon Cape Caribe Resort

1000 Shorewood Dr, 32920; 321 784 4922; www.ronjonresort.com
Right on the white-sand beach, this resort has a wild water park to tempt guests away from the sand. The resort features mini-golf, tennis and basketball courts, a teen center, and childcare. Air-conditioned villa suites have full kitchens or kitchenettes.

ꔷ ◉ ꔷ ◔ $$–$$$

Pirate-themed water park for kids at International Palms Resort, Cocoa Beach

HOTELS

Residence Inn Cape Canaveral Cocoa Beach

8959 Astronaut Blvd, 32920; 321 323 1100; tinyurl.com/2tp7b3
Set amid lovely landscaped gardens and scenic beachside surroundings, these Key-West-style suites come with free breakfast and an evening social, and light dinner on Mondays through Wednesdays.

ꔷ ꔷ ◓ P ◔ $$

CAMPING

Jetty Park Campground

400 Jetty Rd, 32920; 321 783 7111; www.jettyparkbeachand campground.com
A state-owned site offering over 150 pitches, from "rustic" – a tent beneath the trees – to "improved," with electricity and running water. There is fishing from the pier or beach, and facilities include a bait and tackle shop, laundry, and showers.

◕ ꔷ $

Cocoa Beach Map 6 H6

RESORTS

Beach Island Resort

1125 S. Atlantic Ave, Cocoa Beach, 32931; 321 784 5720; www.beach islandresort.com
This family-friendly resort has one- and two-bedroom accommodations, with fully equipped kitchens and dining rooms. The white-sand beach is a short walk away, and

there is a heated pool and hot tub on the resort premises.

ꔷ ꔷ ꔷ ◓ ◔ $–$$

International Palms Resort

1300 N Atlantic Ave, 32931; 321 783 2271; www.internationalpalms.com
An extensive beachside resort, the Palms offers suites and bunkbed-equipped "family fun rooms." Youngsters will love the game room and pirate-themed water park. Adults can use the gym and fitness center, and tennis and shuffleboard courts. Surfboard rental is available.

ꔷ ◉ ꔷ ◔ ◕ $–$$

Discovery Beach Resort Map 6 H6

300 Barlow Ave, 32931; 321 868 7777; www.discoverybeachresort.com
This condo rental of one-, two-, and three-bedroom suites has views of the beach, perfect for watching giant cruise ships sail by on their way to Port Canaveral. Full kitchens, hot tubs and sauna, tennis and basketball courts, as well as an arcade room, keep everyone busy.

◉ ꔷ ◓ ◔ ◕ $$$

The Resort on Cocoa Beach

1600 N Atlantic Ave, 32931; 321 783 4000; www.theresorton cocoabeach.com
A few minutes from the Kennedy Space Center, this condo rental resort has two-bedroom suites with balconies and ocean views. Along with a fitness center, there are shuffleboard and beach volleyball courts, and screenings of family-friendly movies. Kids can play on the private beach or in the game room.

ꔷ ◉ ꔷ ◔ ◕ $$$

HOTELS

Four Points Cocoa Beach

4001 N Atlantic Ave, 32931; 321 783 8717; www.starwoodhotels.com
Housed within the "World's Largest Surf Complex," this hotel has a bright, surfer-style decor that

makes it look like something from *SpongeBob SquarePants*. Some rooms come with views into the shopping and entertainment area, which offers a huge shark and exotic fish aquarium as well as shops and beach rentals.

🌙 🍴 P ⊘ $

The Inn at Cocoa Beach
4300 Ocean Beach Blvd, 32931; 321 799 3460; www.theinnatcocoa beach.com
Many of the 50 rooms in this French-country-style inn offer both pool and ocean views, while others have Jacuzzi tubs and private balconies with sea views. There are exercise and massage rooms, and a steam bath. Breakfast is free and there is an afternoon wine and cheese bar for adults.

🌙 ⊘ 🌀 $$$

MOTELS
Econo Lodge Space Center
Map 6 H6
3220 N Cocoa Blvd, 32926; 321 632 4561; www.econolodge.com/hotel-cocoa-florida-FL354
This inexpensive motel offers 144 clean, pet-friendly rooms with free breakfast and a shuttle service to the Kennedy Space Center.

🌙 🏦 P ⊘ $

Anthony's on the Beach
3499 S Atlantic Ave, 32931; 321 784 8829; www.anthonysonthebeach.com
Built in 1958, Anthony's is a slice of old Florida beach life. The 19 efficiency rentals have full kitchens and dining areas. The motel is

off the main road and affords a bit of quiet in an otherwise traffic-heavy area. The beach is right outside the door.

🌙 🍴 🍽 🌀 $$

SELF-CATERING
Wakulla Suites
3550 N Atlantic Ave, 32931; 321 783 2230; wakullasuites.com
Family-owned since 1972, this property of two-bedroom suites offers a tropical courtyard setting and a backyard beach with volleyball nets. There is an arcade game room and a lobby snack bar. Beach chair and kayak rentals are available.

🌙 🍴 🍽 P ⊘ $$

Beach Place Guesthouses
1445 S Atlantic Ave, 32931; 321 783 4045; beachplaceguesthouses.com
This complex of 16 guesthouses, is located in a quiet residential neighborhood and is just steps from the beach. The property has three decks with ocean views, hammocks, oversize lounges, and a garden for relaxing.

🌙 🍴 ⊘ 🌀 $$$

Melbourne Beach
Map 8 G1
RESORT
Seashell Suites Resort
8795 S Hwy A1A, 32951; 321 409 0500; www.seashellsuites.com
An interesting combination of luxury resort and eco-friendly environment, this place was built with non-toxic, nature-friendly

materials. A secluded getaway, it offers eight two-bedroom suites, a brick sundeck, and a private beach.

🌙 🍴 ⊘ $$

BED & BREAKFAST
Port d'Hiver Bed and Breakfast
201 Ocean Ave, 32951; 321 722 2727; www.portdhiver.com
This B&B has the air of a boutique hotel. Each of the 11 rooms and suites are individually styled. Room service is available at breakfast. Light hors d'oeuvres are served in the early evening.

🌙 🍴 P ⊘ $$–$$$

Titusville
Map 6 G5
HOTELS
Days Inn Kennedy Space Center
3755 Cheney Hwy, 32780; 321 269 4480; tinyurl.com/7qxxnph
Located closer to Brevard Zoo than the Kennedy Space Center, this pet-friendly hotel offers laundry facilities and a 24-hour front desk service.

🌙 🍴 🍽 ⊘ $

Holiday Inn Titusville-Kennedy Space Center
4715 Helen Hauser Blvd, 32780; 321 383 0200; tinyurl.com/6ln6q4c
Up to four children aged 12 and under eat free at the on-site Bapa's Bistro restaurant with the Kids Eat Free program. In addition, every room comes with a mini-refrigerator and microwave. There is also a fitness center, and cribs are available.

🌙 🍴 🏦 ⊘ $

CAMPING
Manatee Hammock Camp Grounds
7275 South US Hwy 1, 32780; 321 264 5083; tinyurl.com/qn7wqm
Great wildlife viewing opportunities await in the extensive grounds around these 35 campsites, which offer water and electricity, hot showers, and laundry facilities. A two-night minimum stay is required.

🌙 ⊘ $

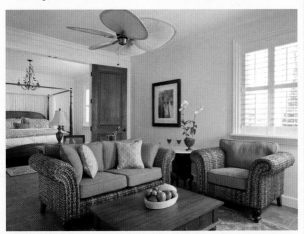

Spacious and elegantly styled suite in Port d'Hiver Bed and Breakfast, Melbourne Beach

Price Guide
The following price ranges are based on one night's accommodation in high season for a family of four, inclusive of service charges and additional taxes.
$ Under $150 **$$** $150–300 **$$$** over $300

The Northeast

The First Coast has been attracting visitors for centuries – the first European to set foot here was Spanish explorer Juan Ponce de León, in 1513. By 1562, Pedro Menendez had established a Spanish colony at St. Augustine. Long before the 1920s tourist boom in Miami, the Northeast's great weather and superb beaches meant it was a mecca for visitors; today's vacationers can add to these a host of newer family attractions.

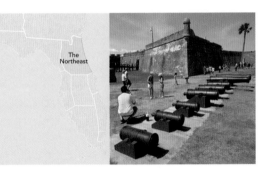

The
Northeast

Highlights

Fernandina Beach
From the shrimp fleet's docks to the Victorian-era homes, historic Fernandina Beach is a great place to stroll, shop, and restaurant-hop (see p166).

Talbot Islands State Parks
Hike through a maritime forest to the beach, investigate the past at a historic plantation, and learn to canoe, at Amelia Island's Talbot Islands park system (see pp164–5).

Jacksonville Zoo and Gardens
Pet the stingrays, feed the giraffes, roar with the jaguars, ride a tiger on the wildlife

carousel, and see animals in their natural habitats in this award-winning zoo with more than 1,500 inhabitants (see pp162–3).

St. Augustine
Walk through this fascinating "Ancient City," founded in 1565, with its historic district allowing a look back into the past (see pp168–9).

Museum of Arts and Sciences (MOAS)
With its planetarium, Ice Age fossils, historic teddy bears, and an interactive children's center, this Daytona Beach museum is always a hit with families (see pp176–7).

Left A canopied street in the historic city of St. Augustine
Above right Row of Spanish cannons at the sprawling 17th-century Castillo de San Marcos, St. Augustine

The Best of
The Northeast

While central Florida has famous theme parks and southern Florida plenty of glamour, the Northeast showcases the state in all its natural beauty. The region has not only many miles of soft-sand beaches, but also remarkably diverse parks where families can swim, shell, hike, fish, and kayak. In addition, numerous attractions, historic sites, and kid-friendly museums keep every member of the family entertained.

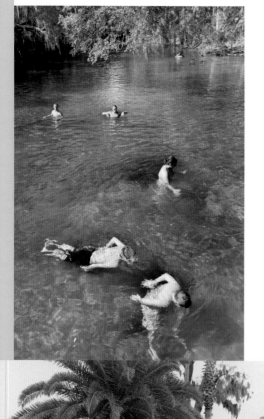

Park it here

Northeastern Florida boasts a number of unusual sights – there are no cookie-cutter parks here. Begin the tour at **Big Talbot Island State Park's** (see p164) Boneyard Beach – its huge windswept skeletons of oaks and cedars create a landscape unlike any other. Head further south to see herds of plains bison and Florida Cracker cows in **Paynes Prairie Preserve State Park** (see p180) near Ocala. Cool off at the nearby **Blue Spring State Park** (see p178), close to Orange City, where manatees like to spend the winter. Round it off by going down all 236 steps into the miniature rain forest at the bottom of the sinkhole known as the **Devil's Millhopper Geological State Park** (see p181) near Gainesville.

Historic encounters

Watch skilled re-enactors bring Florida's history to life at historic sites across the region. At **Fort Clinch State Park** (see p166) in **Fernandina**

Left Snorkelers in the clear waters of Blue Spring State Park in Ocala National Forest *Below* Families go-karting at Adventure Landing, Jacksonville Beach

Above Massive fossilized sharks' jaws at the Florida Museum of Natural History, University of Florida, Gainesville
Right A lioness basking in the sun in the Africa Loop section, Jacksonville Zoo and Gardens, Jacksonville

Beach (*see p166*), soldiers re-create life at the fort during the Civil War. But **St. Augustine** (*see pp168–9*) offers the best opportunity to see life as it was lived in the 1740s. There are several places in the Old Town area that feature costumed actors on a daily basis, and the city also hosts large-scale events regularly. Two of the most popular annual events are the **Sack of St. Augustine** (*see p14*) – with more than 60 buccaneers, Spanish soldiers, and townspeople – and the British Night Watch, when families can join the parade of British guards who march by the light of candles and lanterns to secure the city.

Scientifically speaking

Kids who have an inclination for science will love the Northeast's great museums and research centers. Start a science trek in the **Museum of Science & History** (*see p160*) at **Jacksonville** (*see pp160–61*), then spend an entire day at **Marineland Dolphin Adventure** (*see p172*) south of **St. Augustine**. Although the special programs here can be expensive, they offer rare opportunities such as being a dolphin trainer for a day. Space buffs will not want to miss the planetarium in the **Museum of Arts and Sciences** (*see pp176–7*) in **Daytona Beach** (*see pp174–5*). End the final leg of the trip at the **Florida Museum of Natural History** (*see p180*) in Gainesville – one of the top five natural history museums in the US and the largest "Smithsonian of the south."

The big three

Hit northern Florida's high spots with a trip to its three urban hubs. Begin at **Jacksonville**, which offers the lure of the local NFL team – the Jacksonville Jaguars – as well as real jaguars in its award-winning **Jacksonville Zoo and Gardens** (*see pp162–3*). Kids will also like the fun games and water rides at **Adventure Landing** (*see p160*). A half-hour drive south is **St. Augustine** and its myriad historic sites and outstanding restaurants. Cannon firings at **Castillo de San Marcos** (*see p170*), and the ghost tour at **St. Augustine Lighthouse** (*see p172*) are true kid-pleasers. After a tour of **St. Augustine**, cruise down A1A to **Daytona Beach**, with a stopover at **Washington Oaks Gardens State Park** (*see p173*) for a picnic before heading for the city's famous **Public beaches** (*see p174*) and the **Boardwalk** (*see p174*). Don't miss the **Museum of Arts and Sciences**, a hidden gem with an outstanding interactive children's section.

The Northeast

Some of the most intriguing views of Northeast Florida can be found along SR A1A as it winds through a string of quirky beach towns. Although it is hard to compete with 120 miles (193 km) of white-sand beaches, this region has many other sights worth visiting. Jacksonville and Daytona Beach offer the big-city experience; Fernandina Beach is a quaint town with superb state parks nearby; and St. Augustine boasts a venerable Spanish heritage. Jacksonville is the main transportation hub for the region. Several east–west routes link the coast and I-75, inland.

Splashing in the fountains near the Daytona Beach Boardwalk

The Lowdown

🚌 **Getting there and around**
Air Jacksonville (www.jia.aero) and Daytona Beach (www.flydaytonafirst.com) have international airports. **Train** Amtrak (www.amtrak.com) trains stop at Jacksonville, with two routes south – one inland through Gainesville and Ocala, and another coastal route with stops in Palatka, Daytona, Deland, and Sanford, which is the terminus of the Auto Train Amtrak. **Car** Avis (www.avis.com) and Hertz (www.hertz.com) have offices at airports.

ℹ **Visitor information** Visit the tourist information center at Jacksonville International Airport near the baggage carousel (904/798 9104 or 800/733 2668) for information on Jacksonville, Amelia Island/Fernandina Beach, and St. Augustine.

🛒 **Supermarkets** Publix (www.publix.com) and Winn-Dixie (www.winndixie.com) have outlets throughout this region. **Markets** The Jacksonville Farmers' Market (www.jaxfarmersmarket.com) sells fresh produce from more than 200 farmers from dawn to dusk daily.

🎯 **Festivals** Daytona 500, Daytona Beach; www.daytonainternationalspeedway.com (Feb). Hoggetowne Medieval Faire, Gainesville; www.gvlculturalaffairs.org (Jan). Springing the Blues, Jacksonville Beach; www.springingtheblues.com (mid-Apr). Jacksonville Jazz Festival; www.visitjacksonville.com/jazzfestival (May)

🕐 **Opening hours** Business hours are usually 9am–5pm. Shops open at 10am. Smaller shops may close at 5 or 7pm, but larger stores are often open until 9pm, except Sundays, when stores generally open 11am or noon and close 6 or 7pm. Banks are usually open 8am–3pm Mon–Fri, although many stay open later.

➕ **Pharmacies** Check Publix, Walgreens (www.walgreens.com/pharmacy) or CVS (www.cvs.com/pharmacy) for 24-hour pharmacy locations throughout the region.

🚻 **Restrooms** Almost all major attractions, restaurants, and malls, and most gas stations, have public restrooms.

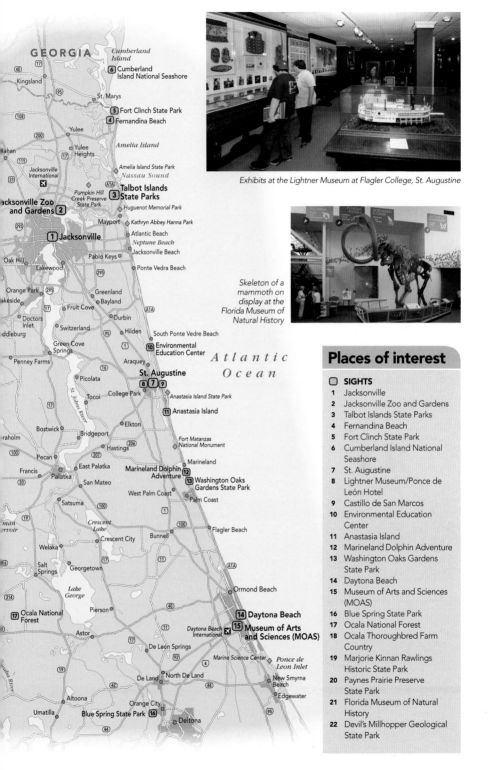

Exhibits at the Lightner Museum at Flagler College, St. Augustine

Skeleton of a mammoth on display at the Florida Museum of Natural History

GEORGIA

Cumberland Island

40
17

Kingsland

95

St. Marys

108

6 Cumberland Island National Seashore

Yulee

200

Yulee Heights

5 Fort Clinch State Park
4 Fernandina Beach

ahan

115

17

Amelia Island

Jacksonville International

23

Amelia Island State Park
Nassau Sound

Pumpkin Hill Creek Preserve State Park

A1A

Talbot Islands
3 State Parks

acksonville Zoo and Gardens 2

Huguenot Memorial Park

295

Mayport

Kathryn Abbey Hanna Park

1 Jacksonville

Atlantic Beach
Neptune Beach

Oak Hill

Lakewood

Pablo Keys

Jacksonville Beach

299

Ponte Vedra Beach

Orange Park

295

Greenland

akeside

17

Fruit Cove

Bayland

A1A

Doctors Inlet

Switzerland

Durbin

ddleburg

Green Cove Springs

95

Hilden

South Ponte Vedre Beach

Penney Farms

16

Araquey

10 Environmental Education Center

Picolata

St. Augustine

8 7 9

Tocoi

College Park

Anastasia Island State Park

17

11 Anastasia Island

Bostwick

Elkton

Bridgeport

206

Fort Matanzas National Monument

raholm

100

Hastings

207

Pecan

East Palatka

Marineland

Francis

Palatka

San Mateo

Marineland Dolphin
Adventure 12

13 Washington Oaks Gardens State Park

20

West Palm Coast

Palm Coast

Satsuma

100

T

man rvoir

19

Crescent Lake

Welaka

Crescent City

Bunnell

Flagler Beach

100

Salt Springs

Georgetown

17

11

A1A

Lake George

16

314

17 Ocala National Forest

Pierson

40

Ormond Beach

Astor

11

14 Daytona Beach

Daytona Beach International

15 Museum of Arts and Sciences (MOAS)

De Leon Springs

92

Marine Science Center

Ponce de Leon Inlet

19

De Land

North De Land

4

42

44

New Smyrna Beach

Altoona

Edgewater

Umatilla

Orange City

95

44

Blue Spring State Park 16

Deltona

Atlantic Ocean

St. Johns River

Places of interest

SIGHTS

1 Jacksonville
2 Jacksonville Zoo and Gardens
3 Talbot Islands State Parks
4 Fernandina Beach
5 Fort Clinch State Park
6 Cumberland Island National Seashore
7 St. Augustine
8 Lightner Museum/Ponce de León Hotel
9 Castillo de San Marcos
10 Environmental Education Center
11 Anastasia Island
12 Marineland Dolphin Adventure
13 Washington Oaks Gardens State Park
14 Daytona Beach
15 Museum of Arts and Sciences (MOAS)
16 Blue Spring State Park
17 Ocala National Forest
18 Ocala Thoroughbred Farm Country
19 Marjorie Kinnan Rawlings Historic State Park
20 Paynes Prairie Preserve State Park
21 Florida Museum of Natural History
22 Devil's Millhopper Geological State Park

① Jacksonville
A city for all seasons

Founded in 1822, Jacksonville flourished as a port and railroad hub in the late 19th century. The largest city in Florida, it has the lion's share of the Northeast's major cultural attractions – museums with outstanding kids' programs, large concert venues, and an award-winning zoo. With great weather almost year-round, the city and its beaches offer plenty to do outdoors, too. Due to the size of the city, it is essential to rent a car to get around.

Cummer Museum of Art and Gardens

Key Sights

① **Cummer Museum of Art and Gardens** Play with digital paint on giant canvases, dance to create colorful patterns, and explore all forms of art at the Art Connections program in this museum.

② **Museum of Science and History (MOSH)** The KidSpace educational play area, a next-generation planetarium, and a schedule of thrilling shows make MOSH a huge draw for families.

③ **Jacksonville Landing** Shop at classy stores, dine in the international food court, and catch exciting events at this entertainment complex.

④ **Museum of Contemporary Art (MOCA)** Five galleries filled with modern and contemporary art, plus interactive fun at the ArtExplorium Loft await visitors at this impressive museum.

⑤ **EverBank Field** From major concerts, symphony performances, and outdoor festivals to NFL football with the Jacksonville Jaguars, this 76,000-seat facility hosts some of the biggest events in Jacksonville.

⑥ **Adventure Landing and Shipwreck Island Waterpark** There is lots to please kids at this theme park, including miniature golf, laser tag, go-karts, and a game arcade, as well as water rides in summer.

The Lowdown

🌐 **Map reference** 4 G3
Address Cummer Museum of Art and Gardens: 829 Riverside Ave, 32204; 904 356 6857; www.cummer.org. Museum of Science and History (MOSH): 1025 Museum Circle, 32207; 904 396 7062; www.themosh.org. Jacksonville Landing: 2 W Independent Dr, 32202; 904 353 1188; www.jacksonvillelanding.com. Museum of Contemporary Art (MOCA): Hemming Plaza, 333 N Laura St., 32202; 904 366 6911; www.mocajacksonville.org. EverBank Field: 300 A Philip Randolph Blvd, 32202;

904 630 3900; www.jaxevents.com/tickets. Adventure Landing: 1944 Beach Blvd, Jacksonville Beach, 32250; 904 246 4386; www.adventurelanding.com

🚌 **Bus** Jacksonville Transportation Authority (JTA) buses and shuttles serve the city and its beaches (www.jtafla.com). **Car** Rent a car from Jacksonville Airport.

ℹ️ **Visitor information** 208 N Laura St, Ste 102, 32202; 904 798 9111; www.visitjacksonville.com

🕐 **Open** Cummer Museum of Art and Gardens & Museum of Contemporary Art (MOCA):

closed Mon. EverBank Field: call 904 630 3900 for event timings or check website. All other sights are open daily.

💲 **Prices** Cummer Museum of Art and Gardens: $32–42; under 5s free. Museum of Science and History (MOSH): $40–46; under 3s free ($5 for all ages Fri). Jacksonville Landing: free. Museum of Contemporary Art (MOCA): $26–32; under 2s free; free for families on Sun. EverBank Field: ticket prices vary. Adventure Landing and Shipwreck Island Waterpark: attractions are individually priced. Waterpark

Lakeside picnic tables in Kathryn Abbey Hanna Park

Letting off steam

Go 15 miles (24 km) east to Atlantic Beach, where **Kathryn Abbey Hanna Park** (*www.tinyurl.com/kahpark*) offers swimming, surfing, biking, and a freshwater lake with a water playground for younger kids. Older kids can opt for canoes and kayaks.

Eat and drink

Picnic: under $25; Snacks: $25–50; Real meal: $50–80; Family treat: over $80 (based on a family of four)

PICNIC Publix at Riverside (*2033 Riverside Ave, 32204; 904 381 8610; www.publix.com*), a few minutes from downtown, has a good deli. Picnic in Memorial Park, just across Riverside Avenue.

SNACKS Cool Moose Cafe and Bistro (*2708 Park St, 32204, 904 381 4242; www.coolmoosecafe.net*), close to the attractions in downtown, has fresh cookies and muffins.

REAL MEAL Singleton's Seafood Shack (*4728 Ocean St, Mayport, 32233; 904 246 4442*) is a simple restaurant that serves tasty seafood dishes. It was well reviewed by The

New York Times and was featured on *Diners, Drive-Ins and Dives.*
FAMILY TREAT Cheesecake Factory (*St. Johns Town Center™, 4663 River City Dr, 32246, www.stjohns towncenter.com*) offers not just delectable cheesecakes, but also sandwiches, pizza, pasta, salads, and steaks.

Shopping

Drop in at **Peterbrooke Chocolatier** (*2024 San Marco Blvd, 32207; 904 398 2488 www.peterbrooke.com*) to pick up gourmet chocolates, and then take a tour of their production facility just down the street. The **St. Johns Town Center™**, a shopping and entertainment venue, houses many kids' apparel stores. Younger children will enjoy the kids' train and the koi pond.

Find out more

DIGITAL In 1864, a Union transport ship named the *Maple Leaf* was sunk by a Confederate torpedo in the St. Johns River, where it stayed until 1989. Take a look at what divers were able to bring up from the bottom more than 100 years later on *www.themosh.org/curator.html.*

Strolling the peaceful American Beach, Amelia Island State Park

Next stop...
BRIDGE TO THE ISLANDS Broward Bridge, across the St. Johns River, is the gateway to **Amelia Island** (*www.amelia island.com*) and **Fernandina Beach** (*see p166*). This impressive bridge is more commonly known as the Dames Point Bridge by locals, and the "bowtie bridge" by kids.

(seasonal): $27.99 for guests 42 in (106 cm) and taller, $22.99 under 42 in (106 cm) tall; under 3s free

Cutting the line Most beaches and attractions are rarely crowded, except on summer weekends.

Age range 4 plus

Allow 2–3 days

Festivals Springing the Blues in Jacksonville Beach (Apr). Jacksonville Jazz Festival (May)

Good family value?
A good mix of inexpensive family-friendly attractions makes the city a great option to suit all budgets.

KIDS' CORNER

A river that flows north!
1 The St. Johns River is unusual because, like the Nile in Africa, it is one of the few rivers that flows south to north.
2 The river averages more than 2 miles (3 km) in width between Palatka and Jacksonville.
3 It drops only 30 ft (10 m)

from its source to the sea, making it one of the laziest rivers in the world.

Sharks' teeth
You shouldn't expect to find an enormous tooth like you would see in a shop, though you might get lucky. Check the patches of small shells along the waterline for something tiny, black, and shiny.

REALLY THE BIGGEST?
Jacksonville is thought to be "the largest city in the US" in terms of square miles. But that's not really accurate – it's just the largest in the contiguous 48 states (the 48 that touch each other). Yakutat, in Alaska, is really the largest city, with 9,459 sq miles (15,223 sq km) of land area.

Saving sand dollars in the sandbank
The wide beaches of Jacksonville are scattered with more than 50 kinds of local shells that are fun to find and save. Look for lightning whelks, olives, angel wings, baby's ear moonsnails, scallops, and even a "Florida jewel box." The best time to find shells is at low tide, especially in late fall, after storms.

② Jacksonville Zoo and Gardens

Into the wild on a walking safari

Opened in 1914, Jacksonville Zoo started out with just one red deer. Today, it has grown into an award-winning regional zoo with more than 1,500 animals; among them are fierce-looking Komodo dragons, playful gorillas and bonobos, docile giraffes, high-spirited elephants in their massive pool, and delightful penguins. Extensive boardwalks with specially designed overlooks meander throughout this huge zoo, allowing visitors to experience a "walking safari."

Entry to the Range of the Jaguar exhibit

Key Features

The Lowdown

- 🌐 **Map reference** 4 G3
  Address 370 Zoo Pkwy, Jacksonville, 32218; 904 757 4463; www.jacksonvillezoo.org

- 🚗 **Bus** Call Jacksonville Transportation Authority (JTA) Ride Request service (904 598 8724). **Car** Rent a car from Jacksonville. Free parking

- 🕐 **Open** 9am–5pm daily

- 💲 **Prices** $50–60; under 3s free. The zoo charges additional fees for Stingray Bay ($1 per person), unlimited train rides ($3 per person), and unlimited carousel rides ($1 per person). Value Tickets include admission, Butterfly Hollow, Stingray Bay, and unlimited train and carousel rides ($74–84; under 2s free).

- 👫 **Cutting the line** Buy tickets online and arrive early to avoid the crowds.

- 🌴 **Guided tours** The zoo offers many Behind the Scene tours. Check website for details.

- 👫 **Age range** 2 plus

- ⏱ **Allow** 4–6 hours

- ♿ **Wheelchair access** Yes

- ☕ **Café** Several in the zoo (see p163)

- 🛍 **Shops** Many throughout the zoo (see p163)

- 🚻 **Restrooms** At the Main Camp Safari Lodge at the entrance

Good family value?
Exciting animals, carousel rides, and a train tour, along with affordable admission prices, make this zoo great for visitors of all ages.

Entrance

① **Wild Florida** Florida's treasured wildlife is the focus of this exhibit. Check out more than two dozen species of reptiles and amphibians in the Reptile House.

② **River Valley Aviary** See a variety of birds, from Inca terns to colorful macaws, in this aviary. Also see the world's smallest deer and the largest freshwater fish.

③ **Stingray Bay** This interactive exhibit allows visitors to observe, touch, and feed stingrays.

④ **Play Park** Kids can cool off in the huge Splash Ground or find their way out of a hedge maze in this park. See penguins at close quarters in the Tuxedo Coast exhibit.

⑤ **Carousel and Zoo Train** The classic Wildlife Carousel with beautiful animal figures is a kid-pleaser. Don't miss a ride around the zoo on the Zoo Train.

⑥ **Asia and Australia** While the Komodo dragon exhibit steals the show at Monsoon Asia, kangaroos and wallabies delight visitors at the Australian Adventure exhibit.

⑦ **Range of the Jaguar** This award-winning jaguar exhibit also features a replica of a Mayan temple that is home to boa constrictors and bushmaster snakes.

⑧ **Africa Loop** Walk along an elevated boardwalk to view African animals, such as pelicans and zebras, in re-creations of their natural habitat. The African Reptile Building has cobras and mambas.

Kids feeding giraffes from the Giraffe Overlook, an elevated viewing area

Take cover

If it rains, head to one of the zoo's many indoor exhibits. The **Discovery Center**, in the Play Park area, runs excellent interactive educational programs for kids.

Eat and drink

Picnic: under $25; Snacks: $25–50; Real meal: $50–80; Family treat: over $80 (based on a family of four)

PICNIC Bring provisions from Jacksonville (see p161) for a picnic adjacent to the parking lot.
SNACKS Main Camp Café (at the entrance), a snack bar, serves popcorn, ice cream, and coffee.
REAL MEAL Palm Plaza Café (in Range of the Jaguar) has tacos, nachos, burritos, sandwiches, and salads on its Southwestern menu. The **Trout River Grille** (near the Gardens of Trout River Plaza) tempts with sandwiches, hot dogs, pretzels, and hamburgers.
FAMILY TREAT Junior's Seafood (9349 N Main St, 32218; 904 751 9180), a local favorite, is a spotlessly kept restaurant and grill, known for its superb food and efficient service. There are seafood dishes, burgers, pastas, and steaks on the menu.

Main Camp Café, a food kiosk in Main Camp Safari Lodge

Mombasa Gift Shop, one of the three gift shops in the zoo

Shopping

Drop in at **Mombasa Gift Shop** (at Main Camp), **Village Market** (in Range of the Jaguar), or **The Kids' Shop** (near the train station) to pick up plush toys, trinkets, apparel, puzzles, and other goodies.

Find out more

DIGITAL Visit www.jacksonville zoo.org/things/kidzone for fun games, coloring pages, and quirky animal trivia.

Next stop...

HUGUENOT MEMORIAL PARK
A horseshoe-shaped peninsula, the Huguenot Memorial Park (10980 Heckscher Dr, 32226; 904 251 3335) is popular with local families, surfers, and windsurfers. The park, 15 miles (24 km) east, is home to a variety of wildlife, and offers plenty of surfing, birdwatching, and windsurfing opportunities. Although the park gets crowded in summer, it can be an enjoyable outing in early spring or late fall. Be sure to check the tide tables (www.srh.weather.gov/jax/tides.shtml) – the shallow tidal pools are great for younger kids. Driving on the beach is allowed, but be warned – it is easy to get stuck in the sand.

(see p161) ... (see p161)

KIDS' CORNER

Penguin quiz
The zoo's Tuxedo Coast is home to Magellanic penguins. Do you know how they differ from other penguins? See if you can figure out if the statements below are true or false:
1 They live on the coastline of Argentina and Chile.
2 They were named for a famous explorer.
3 Only one parent helps keep the egg warm until it hatches.
4 They only eat plants.

Answers at the bottom of the page.

CHEETAH CHAMPS
If all the world's four-legged animals ever enter a race, you should bet on the cheetah to win – they are the planet's champion sprinters, able to run at a speed of 70 mph (113 km/h).

Spot the jaguar
A baby jaguar doesn't have to "grow into" its spots – the kittens are born with plenty of them on their yellowish fur. A jaguar's special markings are called "rosettes." These are open rings that have up to four different dark spots inside them. Some Native American tribes believe the spots are like stars or suns, and that the rosettes look like eclipses swallowing the stars.

Answers: 1 True. **2** True. **3** False. Both parents take turns. **4** False. They eat fish, squid, and crustaceans.

③ Talbot Islands State Parks
Marshes, highlands, and rivers galore

From marshes, highlands, and rivers, to 40 miles (65 km) of Atlantic beaches, this remarkable cluster of state parks offers a great chance to explore a broad range of natural habitats. Families can choose from a wide variety of exciting outdoor adventures such as fishing, canoeing, kayaking, surfing, and beachcombing. Be sure to carry sunscreen, insect repellent, drinking water, and a picnic – the parks do not sell any food or drink.

Aboard the St. Johns River Ferry from Jacksonville

Key Sights

① **Yellow Bluff Fort Historic State Park** Hike and picnic in this small peaceful park, a Civil War site that was used as an encampment by both Confederate and Union soldiers at different times.

② **Fort George Island Cultural State Park** Attractions here include the Ribault Club visitor center and the Kingsley Plantation (see p165) – the oldest plantation home in Florida.

③ **Little Talbot Island State Park** Noted for its stunning beach, the park offers campsites within walking distance of the ocean, complete with picnic pavilions and bathhouses.

④ **Pumpkin Hill Creek Preserve State Park** A vast area of uplands with miles of hiking and biking trails, this park also has great launch sites for kayaking and canoeing.

⑤ **Big Talbot Island State Park** With skeletal remains of oak trees scattered along its shore, Boneyard Beach is this park's best-known attraction.

[Map]
Fernandina Beach 9 miles (14 km)
Fort Clinch State Park 11 miles (17km)
0 km   5
0 miles   5
Amelia Island
⑦ Amelia Island State Park
George Crady Bridge Fishing Pier ⑥
Nassau Sound
Pumpkin Hill Creek Preserve State Park ④
⑤ Big Talbot Island State Park
Little Talbot Island State Park ③
CEDAR POINT ROAD
NEW BERLIN ROAD
Kingsley Plantation
Ribault Club
North New Berlin
Yellow Bluff Fort Historic State Park ①
Fort George Island Cultural State Park ②
Fort George Island
Fort George River
Blount Island

⑥ **George Crady Bridge Fishing Pier** This mile-long pedestrian bridge across Nassau Sound is a favorite with North Florida anglers.

⑦ **Amelia Island State Park** Swim at a beautiful beach, hike through the coastal forest, fish from the shore, and kayak through creeks and marshes in this park.

Take cover
Head for the **Ribault Club** visitor center (www.nps.gov) to check out exhibits on the environment and culture of northeastern Florida.

Eat and drink
Picnic: under $25; Snacks: $25–50; Real meal: $50–80; Family treat: over $80 (based on a family of four)

PICNIC Marché Burette Deli (6800 First Coast Hwy, Amelia Island, 32034; 904 491 4834; tinyurl.com/

7bo7dl3) features gourmet deli items, sandwiches, and more. Picnic on the Amelia Island State Park beach.
SNACKS Long Island Outfitters (13030 Heckscher Dr, 32266; 904 251 0016; www.kayakamelia.com) sells beverages and healthy snacks.
REAL MEAL Sliders Seaside Grill (1998 S Fletcher Dr, 32034; 904 277 6652; www.slidersseaside.com) serves seafood dishes and tasty desserts. There is a playground and sandbox for kids, as well as a tiki bar and live music for grown-ups.

Play area for kids in the informal Sliders Seaside Grill

Prices given are for a family of four

The Lowdown

- **Map reference** 4 H3
- **Address** Yellow Bluff Fort: New Berlin Rd, 32226; 904 251 2320. Fort George Island: 11676 Palmetto Ave, 32226; 904 251 3537. Little Talbot Island, Big Talbot Island, Amelia Island & George Crady Bridge Fishing Pier: State Rd A1A/Heckscher Dr, 32226; 904 251 2320. Pumpkin Hill Creek Preserve: 13802 Pumpkin Hill Rd, 32226; 904 696 5980. Check www.floridastateparks.org for all parks.

- **Car** Rent a car from Jacksonville International Airport.

- **Open** Yellow Bluff Fort, Little Talbot Island, Big Talbot Island, Amelia Island & Pumpkin Hill Creek Preserve: 8am–sunset daily. Fort George Island: 8am–sunset daily. George Crady Bridge Fishing Pier: 24 hours daily

- **Prices** Yellow Bluff Fort, Fort George Island & Pumpkin Hill Creek Preserve: free. Little Talbot Island & Amelia Island: $5 per vehicle & $2 per pedestrian and cyclist. Big Talbot Island: $3 per vehicle. George Crady Bridge Fishing Pier: $2 per person (admission to Amelia Island includes pier access)

- **Cutting the line** Parks are rarely crowded, except on holiday weekends, but book campsites and tours well in advance.

- **Guided tours** Kelly Seahorse Ranch (904 491 5166) offers guided horseback-riding on the beach at Amelia Island. Kayak Amelia (904 251 0016) runs kayak and canoe tours.

- **Age range** All ages for beaches; 5 plus for exhibits and tours

- **Activities** Check websites for ranger programs.

- **Allow** 1–4 hours at each park

- **Wheelchair access** Limited; call 850 245 2157

- **Restrooms** At all parks, except Yellow Bluff Fort and Pumpkin Hill Creek Preserve

Good family value?
With a fantastic mix of outdoor activities, history, and culture, these state parks are a big draw for active families.

FAMILY TREAT Café 4750 (4750 Amelia Island Pkwy, 32034; 904 277 1100; www.ritzcarltonhotel.com), in the Ritz-Carlton on Amelia Island, offers a choice of indoor or terrace dining, and a menu with farm and coastal influences. Reserve ahead.

Shopping
Visit **Island Outfitters** (235 E Gulf Beach Dr, 32328; 850 927 2604; sgioutfitters.com) on St. George's Island for handcrafted necklaces, T-shirts, beach bags, and flip flops.

Next stop...
KINGSLEY PLANTATION Located on the northern tip of Fort George Island, this plantation (www.nps.gov) was named for Zephaniah Kingsley, who owned four major plantations in the area. In 1814, he and his wife Anna Madgigine Jai made the island their main residence, and more than 100 slaves worked on the plantation. Walk the grounds to see the restored slave cabins, the "Ma'am Anna" house, a barn, a kitchen house, and the main clapboard house.

The clapboard house surrounded by trees and lawns, Kingsley Plantation

KIDS' CORNER

Test your "bird brain"
See if you can spot the following birds at the park, using these descriptors:

1 Sandwich tern
These birds have shaggy black crests (crown on the head) and yellow-tipped black bills.

2 Laughing gull
Look out for long, red beaks and reddish-black to black legs.

3 Great blue heron
These herons have very hairy heads, chests and wings, and yellowish bills.

BLACK MASKED BANDITS
If you're camping in northeastern Florida, a raccoon might want to steal your food. Just latching the cooler won't do. In one study, scientists found that it took fewer than ten tries for raccoons to figure out complex locks. Ask a park ranger for advice on keeping your food safe from raccoons.

Digging into the past
Native Americans lived on the Talbot Islands for thousands of years before Europeans arrived, and the area was the site of dozens of little settlements and hunting camps. More than 400 years ago, the Spanish mission San Juan del Puerto was established on Fort George Island, as well as smaller missions called *visitas* (visitors). Archaeologists' explorations indicate that one named "Sarabay" was on Big Talbot Island.

④ Fernandina Beach

Shrimps and small-town charm

Located on Amelia Island, with the Atlantic Ocean on one side and the Amelia River on the other, this quaint and quiet coastal town was the birthplace of the modern shrimping industry in the US. The historic business district, around Centre Street, is bordered by the docks, where visitors can watch the shrimp fleet return at sunset.

Old courthouse in the Historic District, Fernandina Beach

The Lowdown

🌐 **Map reference** 4 H2

🚗 **Car** Rent a car from Jacksonville International Airport.

ℹ️ **Visitor information** 102 Centre St, 32034; 904 277 0717; www.aifby.com

🧍 **Cutting the line** Avoid visiting during holiday weekends.

🚩 **Guided tours** For horse-drawn carriage rides, contact Old Towne Carriage Company (904 277 1555) or Amelia Island Carriages (904 556 2662).

🧍 **Age range** 6 plus

⏱️ **Allow** 2 hours

🍽️ **Eat and drink** *SNACKS* Bright Mornings (105 S 3rd St, 32034; 866 739 2117; www.bright morningscafe.com), a local favorite, offers burgers, salads, and sandwiches. *FAMILY TREAT* Joe's Second Street Bistro (14 S 2nd St, 32034; 904 321 2558; www.joesbistro.com), an award-winning restaurant, serves salads, soups, and entrées.

🎉 **Festival** Isle of Eight Flags Shrimp Festival features pirate parades, exciting contests and music (May).

In the heart of Fernandina Beach, the 50-block Historic District is a neighborhood of gorgeous Victorian-era buildings. Listed in the National Register of Historic Places, the district is filled with shops and restaurants. Stroll the streets on a self-guided or museum-led tour, or take a trolley or a horse-drawn carriage, which kids are sure to enjoy.

Take cover

Visit the **Amelia Island Museum** (www.ameliamuseum.com) to learn about the history of Amelia Island. Housed in an old jail, this small museum's exhibits focus on the Timucuan Indians, the Civil War, railroads, and Spanish missions.

⑤ Fort Clinch State Park

Relive the Civil War

Named for Duncan Lamont Clinch, a general in the Seminole Wars (1816–58), Fort Clinch is more than just a historic military site. In addition to the fort, the site has a beach, trails, and campsites. Begun in 1847 to protect Fernandina Harbor, the fort was built right where the St. Marys River flows into the Atlantic Ocean.

The clean, quiet beach is a major draw for swimmers and sunbathers. Anglers frequent the beach to fish off the pier and the finger jetties, or to make the most of excellent surf fishing opportunities. Outdoor enthusiasts can walk the nature trails or bike the off-road trails.

However, for many families the prime attraction is the chance to see skilled re-enactors – or "living historians," as the park calls them – re-creating living conditions at the fort during the Civil War (1861–65).

The Lowdown

🌐 **Map reference** 4 H2

📍 **Address** 2601 Atlantic Ave, Fernandina Beach, 32034; 904 277 7274; www.floridastateparks.org/fortclinch

🚗 **Car** Rent a car from Fernandina Beach.

🕐 **Open** Park: 8am–sunset daily. Fort: 9am–5pm daily

💲 **Price** Park: $6 per vehicle & $2 per pedestrian or bicyclist. Fort: $2 per person

🧍 **Cutting the line** The park is rarely crowded.

🚩 **Guided tours** Guided nature walks at 10:30am on Saturdays, candlelight tours on Labor Day weekends, and daily Living History programs.

🧍 **Age range** 4 plus

🏃 **Activities** Swimming, nature hikes, biking, fishing & camping

⏱️ **Allow** 2–4 hours

♿ **Wheelchair access** Yes

🍽️ **Eat and drink** *PICNIC* The Happy Tomato Courtyard Café and BBQ (7 S 3rd St, 32034; www.thehappy tomatocafe.com; closed Sat–Sun) is a good place to pick up tasty sandwiches and sides to enjoy near the marina. *SNACKS* The park store sells snacks, and ice cream.

🧍 **Restrooms** At the foot of boardwalks, in the campgrounds, and on the fishing pier.

Watch them perform kitchen and laundry chores, and at times – to the delight of most kids – marching drills and artillery demonstrations.

Letting off steam

Amelia Island's beaches offer plenty of room to run about. Families can choose between the lively **Main Beach Park** (32 N Fletcher Ave, Fernandina Beach, 32034), with a

Kids learning how to work a water pump at Fort Clinch State Park

A wild horse at the Dungeness Mansion in Cumberland Island National Seashore

beachfront playground and barbecue grills, or the peaceful sands of **Peter's Point Beach Park** *(1974 S Fletcher Ave, Fernandina Beach, 32034).*

⑥ Cumberland Island National Seashore

In the lap of nature

Although Cumberland Island is right across the border in Georgia, visitors to Fort Clinch can see its southern edge across Cumberland Sound. Unlike most barrier islands on the Atlantic, Cumberland is not home to golf courses and gated communities, but to pristine beaches, marshes, and

a variety of bird and animal species. The ferry ride from St. Marys is fun; lucky visitors may see dolphins leaping near the boat. The island's tranquil shell-strewn beach is a treat for shell-collectors. Nature-lovers will love the hike trails winding through maritime forests, wetlands, and even historic districts. Look out for herds of wild horses grazing among the ruins of Dungeness Mansion. The island also offers plenty of birdwatching opportunities.

Take cover

Parents might want to plan a visit to see the history exhibits in the **Ice House Museum** *(near the ferry dock; 912 882 4335)* to round off the outing – or during rough weather.

The Lowdown

🌐 **Map reference** 4 H2
Address Camden, Georgia; 912 882 4335; www.nps.gov/cuis

🚗 **Ferry** Ferries depart twice daily from St. Marys. Call ahead to book (912 882 4335). **Taxi** Rent a water taxi, a charter, or a private cruise from Amelia River Cruises & Charters *(1 N Front St, Fernandina Beach, 32034; 904 261 9972; www.ameliarivercruises.com)* or Lang's Charters *(304 Osborne St, St. Marys, 31558; 912 882 9555; www.langcharters.com).*

🕐 **Open** Park: daily. Visitor center: 8am–4:30pm daily

💲 **Price** Park: $8–18; under 16s free

👫 **Cutting the line** Visit on weekdays or in off-season. Arrive early to beat crowds.

🚩 **Guided tours** Free hour-long tours twice daily, at 10am and 12:45pm

👫 **Age range** 6 plus; walking the long distances can be tiring for younger kids.

👫 **Activities** The park runs a free kids' program at 2pm in summer. Kids' activity booklets are available at the Mainland Visitor Center.

🕐 **Allow** At least half a day

♿ **Wheelchair access** Yes

🍽 **Eat and drink** SNACKS Cedar Oak Café and Java Joe'z *(304 Osborne St, St Marys, 31558; 912 882 9555)* has muffins, sandwiches, and coffee. FAMILY TREAT Lang's Marina Restaurant *(307 W St Marys St, St Marys, 31558; 912 882 4432; www.langcharters.com)* serves fresh seafood and has a kids' menu.

👫 **Restrooms** At the visitor center in St. Marys, the ranger station near Cumberland Island dock, Sea Camp Campgrounds, and Plum Orchard

Picnic under $25; **Snacks** $25–50; **Real meal** $50–80; **Family treat** over $80 (based on a family of four)

⑦ St. Augustine
A little bit of Spain

This remarkable city is home to living history museums and elaborate Spanish-style architecture. Its historic district includes 144 blocks, with a wealth of interesting sights, restaurants, and unique shops. Spanning the Matanzas River, the famous Bridge of Lions connects the city to Anastasia Island (see p172), which has a classic striped lighthouse and miles of white-sand beaches.

One of the marble lions on the Bridge of Lions

Key Sights

Oldest Wooden Schoolhouse
350 yards (320 m)

Plaza de la Constitución

Lightner Museum

Villa Zorayda Museum

Bridge of Lions

Oldest House
700 yards (640 m)

Oldest House The González-Alvarez House is the oldest home to survive from the city's Spanish Colonial period. The complex has two museums, an exhibition gallery, and an ornamental garden.

Oldest Wooden Schoolhouse State-of-the-art Audio-Animatronic teachers and pupils re-create life as it was in this cedar and cypress school building more than 200 years ago.

Plaza de la Constitución
Surrounded by historic buildings, this shady square has been a central part of the city's life – from treaty ceremonies to family picnics – for more than 400 years.

Villa Zorayda Museum Built in 1883, this building is a one-tenth scale replica of a portion of the Alhambra in Spain. Now a museum, it houses a superb collection of artifacts from the Middle East.

Bridge of Lions During Florida's land boom in the 1920s – when the city had plenty of money – this historic landmark was built at an exorbitant cost, complete with the marble lions that guard it.

Letting off steam
The grounds of **Castillo de San Marcos** (see p170) offer lots of space to run around. Or visit the **Fort Matanzas National Monument**, a small island fort that guarded St. Augustine from the south, by taking a ferry from the Visitor Center.

Take cover
The eccentric Robert Ripley traveled the world looking for objects that were both weird and wonderful. After his death, his collection became the core of the **Ripley's Believe It or Not! Museum** (19 San Marco Ave,

32084; 904 824 1606; www.ripleys. com/staugustine). It is a good place to while away an afternoon browsing through the astonishing displays.

Entrance to the bizarre Ripley's Believe It or Not! Museum

Eat and drink
Picnic: under $25; Snacks: $25–50; Real meal: $50–80; Family treat: over $80 (based on a family of four)

PICNIC Denoel French Pastry Shop (212 Charlotte St, 32084; 904 829 3974; Wed–Sun) has been a favorite in St. Augustine for several years. Sandwiches can be purchased for a picnic, but it is the chocolate éclairs that hold pride of place.
SNACKS Hyppo (8 Charlotte St, 32084; 904 217 7853; www.the hyppo.com) offers gourmet popsicles with flavors such as "Elvis Presley," a mix of bananas, peanut butter, and honey, and tandoori pineapple.

Prices given are for a family of four

The Lowdown

- 🌐 **Map reference** 6 F1
  Address St. Augustine 32084.
  Villa Zorayda Museum: 83 King
  St; 904 829 9887; *www.villa
  zorayda.com*. Oldest House:
  271 Charlotte St; 904 824 2872;
  *www.staugustinehistorical
  society.org*. Oldest Wooden
  Schoolhouse: 14 St. George St;
  904 824 0192; *www.oldest
  woodenschoolhouse.com*

- 🚗 **Car** Rent a car from Jacksonville
  Airport. Parking is limited in
  tourist areas.

- ℹ️ **Visitor information** St. Augustine
  & St. Johns County Visitor
  Information Center, 10 Castillo
  Dr W, 32084; 904 825 1000;
  www.floridashistoriccoast.com

- 🕐 **Open** Villa Zorayda Museum:
  10am–5pm Mon–Sat & 11am–
  4pm Sun. Oldest House: 9am–
  5pm daily. Oldest Wooden
  Schoolhouse: 9am–4pm daily

- 💲 **Prices** Villa Zorayda Museum:
  self-guided audio tours $28–38;
  under 7s free. Oldest House:
  $18–28 (family ticket). Oldest
  Wooden Schoolhouse: $18–28;
  under 5s free

- 🚩 **Guided tours** Old Town Trolley
  Tours (*167 San Marco Ave,
  32084; 904 829 3800; www.
  trolleytours.com/st-augustine*)
  offers tours of St. Augustine's
  historic district. The Oldest
  House runs free guided tours
  every half hour 9:30am–4:30pm.
  Villa Zorayda Museum offers
  docent-led tours ($40–50; under
  7s free) by reservation only. Call
  904 829 9887 to book. Contact
  St. Augustine Transfer Company
  (*www.staugustinetransfer.com*)
  for carriage tours.

- 🧑‍🤝‍🧑 **Age range** 5 plus. The Villa
  Zorayda Museum and Oldest
  House will be of more interest
  to kids 8 plus.

- ⏱️ **Allow** A day

- 🎊 **Festivals** Rhythm and Ribs
  Festival features live music,
  barbecue, and kids' activities
  (Apr). Nights of Lights celebrates
  the holiday season with art
  shows and parades (Nov–Jan).

Good family value?
A plethora of free, as well as paid,
attractions makes the city a great
place to spend a day.

**REAL MEAL Mango Mango's
Caribbean Grill and Bar** (*700 A1A
Beach Blvd, 32080; 904 461 1077*)
serves casual fare such as mahi
sliders and Carribean island burgers
in a lively beach atmosphere.
FAMILY TREAT The Floridian (*39
Cordova St, 32084; www.thefloridian
staug.com*) offers creative Southern
dishes in a kid-friendly atmosphere.
The menu has vegetarian options.

Shopping
Most kids will enjoy browsing the
shops lining **St. George Street**,
where much of the merchandise on

sale is inexpensive but fun. Choose
from a variety of candles, candies,
T-shirts, and jewelry.

Next stop...
BLACK RAVEN PIRATE SHIP If the
kids have had enough architecture
and highbrow history for a while,
take them to the St. Augustine
Municipal Marina to see the Black
Raven Pirate Ship (*www.blackraven
adventures.com*). Climb aboard
the ship for a tour of the Matanzas
River. The adventure includes a
theatrical show with sword fights,
sea shanties, games, and more.

Shops lining St. George Street in the Historic District of St. Augustine

---

KIDS' CORNER

Beach mouse
The Anastasia Island beach
mouse is an endangered
species and is rarely spotted
these days. Here are some
interesting facts about this
little creature:
1 Home. It usually
digs burrows in the
sand dunes or
lives in the
abandoned homes
of ghost crabs.
2 Food. Sea oats,
other coastal plants, and
small insects make up its diet.
3 Appearance. Its light-colored
coat helps it hide from predators
such as cats, dogs, and raccoons.

ANCHORED TO THE GROUND
The Oldest Wooden Schoolhouse
building may have survived
several centuries, but it is fragile.
In 1937, the city was so worried
it might blow away in a
hurricane that they wrapped a
giant chain around the
house and tied it to
an anchor!

Stone-faced lions
The Bridge of Lions, built at
great expense, is as much a
work of art as a functional bridge.
The "Medici lions" were carved
from Carrara marble – a white
or blue-gray marble often used
in sculpture – and were
a gift to the city from
former mayor
Dr. Andrew
Anderson, who
commissioned
them from
a studio in
Florence, Italy.

⑧ Lightner Museum/Ponce de León Hotel

The charm of bygone days

Commissioned by railroad tycoon Henry Flagler, these gorgeous Spanish Renaissance-style buildings were created as the ultimate luxury hotels. Flagler intended the **Ponce de León Hotel** to be "the world's finest hotel" of its time. Now a part of Flagler College, its splendid carvings and curved arches are worth a look.

The Hotel Alcazar – now the **Lightner Museum** – was not quite as luxurious as the Ponce, but it still offered a three-story ballroom, tropical gardens, a courtyard for concerts, and spa facilities that included everything from Turkish baths to the nation's largest indoor swimming pool. The Lightner now displays an elegant collection of items from the 19th century, including cut glass, furniture, and paintings.

The splendid Victorian Music Room at the Lightner Museum, St. Augustine

The Lowdown

🌐 **Map reference** 6 F1
Address Ponce de León Hotel: in Flagler College, 74 King St, 32084; 904 829 6481; *www.flagler.edu*. Lightner Museum: 75 King St, 32084; 904 824 2874; *www.lightnermuseum.org*

🚗 **Car** Rent a car in St. Augustine.

🕐 **Open** Lightner Museum: 9am–5pm daily. Ponce de León Hotel: tours only

💲 **Price** Ponce de León Hotel: free, except for guided tours. Lightner Museum: $30–40; under 12s free

👫 **Cutting the line** Visit on a weekday morning.

🚩 **Guided tours** Tours of the Ponce de León Hotel from the college's main lobby at 10am & 2pm daily.

👪 **Age range** 8 plus

⏱ **Allow** An hour for the museum

♿ **Wheelchair access** At the Lightner Museum

🍴 **Eat and drink SNACKS** Hot Shot Bakery n' Café (8 Granada St, 32084; 904 824 7898; *www.hotshotbakery.com*) offers freshly baked goods. **REAL MEAL** Café Alcazar (25 Granada St, 32084; 904 825 9948; *www.thecafe alcazar.com*), an elegant lunch spot, is housed in the Alcazar Hotel's former swimming pool.

🚻 **Restrooms** At both sights

Take cover

Children will love the **St. Augustine Pirate & Treasure Museum** (12 S Castillo Dr, 32084; 877 467 5863; *www.thepiratemuseum.com*), which has hundreds of fascinating artifacts, including the world's only known pirate treasure chest. Movie buffs can see Captain Jack Sparrow's sword from *The Black Pearl*. Kids can learn about the Golden Age of Piracy through interactive displays.

⑨ Castillo de San Marcos

Cannons and a castle

After the pirate Robert Searle attacked St. Augustine in 1668, the town's Spanish colonists decided they needed more protection, and in 1672 they began constructing the massive Castillo de San Marcos fort. Built of coquina rock quarried from just across the river on Anastasia Island, it took 23 years to build. The Castillo's design included a seawall

Cannon on the gun deck of Castillo de San Marcos, St. Augustine

The Lowdown

🌐 **Map reference** 6 F1
Address 1 South Castillo Dr, 32084; 904 829 6506 (ext. 227); *www.nps.gov/casa*

🚗 **Car** Rent a car in St. Augustine.

🕐 **Open** 8:45am–5:15pm daily

💲 **Price** $14–28; under 15s free

👫 **Cutting the line** Early weekday mornings are quietest, but most re-enactments and cannon firings are on weekends.

🚩 **Guided tours** There are maps and brochures for self-guided tours.

👪 **Age range** 6 plus

🏃 **Activities** Cannon firings, weapons demonstrations, short films, and ranger programs

⏱ **Allow** 1–2 hours

♿ **Wheelchair access** Yes, except for the upper gun deck

🍴 **Eat and drink SNACKS** Kilwin's (6 St. George St, 32084; 904 823 9226; *www.kilwins.com*) is a great stop for ice cream, fudge, and caramel apples. **REAL MEAL** Casa Maya (17 Hypolita St, 32084; 904 217 3039), in the historic district, is popular for its non-traditional, mostly organic menu. Hours vary; call ahead.

with floodgates that could be opened to fill the moat if an assault threatened. Often attacked, the fort was never taken by force, though it sometimes surrendered when faced with overwhelming odds. For much of its history, this oldest existing masonry fort in the US was used as a military prison.

There are lots of things to do here, such as exploring the gun deck and secret chamber, and

The sanctuary in the Cathedral Basilica of St. Augustine

watching re-enactments. Kids will enjoy the frequent cannon firings on weekends.

Take cover

If inclement weather threatens, head for the **Cathedral Basilica of St. Augustine** *(38 Cathedral Place, 32084; 904 824 2806; www.thefirstparish.org)*. The historic cathedral was built around 1797, and it has a splendid bell tower.

⑩ Environmental Education Center

Marine encounters

A 10-minute drive north of St. Augustine is the Guana Tolomato Matanzas National Estuarine Research Reserve (GTM NERR), an environmental education center that is worlds away from the average handful of exhibits visitors might expect to find there. The $6.2 million center serves as a place for eco-educational activities for the GTM NERR, a water system that protects more than 109 sq miles (282 sq km) along northeastern Florida's coast.

The GTM center presents information about marine creatures in several interesting ways. Visitors can see small specimens in one of the three aquariums. Larger marine creatures are represented by full-scale models. The very largest – a North Atlantic right whale – hangs from the ceiling. There are also interpretive exhibits at the center, a high-tech theater that screens nature films, and an outdoor amphitheater.

The Lowdown

🌐 **Map reference** 6 F1
Address 505 Guana River Rd, S Ponte Vedra Beach, 32082; 904 823 4500; www.gtmnerr.org

🚗 **Car** Rent a car from St. Augustine.

🕐 **Open** Education Center: 9am–4pm daily. GTM trails and beach parking: 8am–sunset daily

💲 **Price** Education Center: $6–16; under 9s free

👫 **Cutting the line** Early mornings and weekdays are best.

🪧 **Guided tours** For family programs or guided trail walks, call 904 823 4500. Ripple Effect Ecotours *(www.rippleeffectecotours.com)* offers kayak and nature tours.

👫 **Age range** All ages

⏱ **Allow** 1–1½ hours

♿ **Wheelchair access** South parking lot accessible

🍴 **Eat and drink** PICNIC Fish Tales Market and Grille *(121 Yacht Club Dr, St. Augustine, 32084; 904 824 0900; www.fishtalesstaug.com)* has boxed lunches that can be eaten at the GTM picnic pavilion. REAL MEAL Barbara Jean's *(15 South Roscoe Blvd, Ponte Vedra Beach, 32082; 904 280 7522; www.barbarajeans.com)* is a hot spot for Southern cuisine. It includes a kids' menu.

👫 **Restrooms** In the Environmental Education Center

Natural exhibits in the Exhibit Hall of the Environmental Education Center

Letting off steam

Just east of the A1A are three walkovers that cross the dunes to an untouched stretch of beach, and on the west side are nature trails, boat launches, places to fish, and 10 miles (16 km) of hiking and biking trails.

KIDS' CORNER

Pirate vocabulary quiz

When it comes to pirate lingo, most of us know what it means to "walk the plank," but have you also heard these terms?

1 Davy Jones' locker
2 Pieces of eight
3 Grog
4 Avast!
5 The Jolly Roger

Answers at the bottom of the page.

IS THAT RIGHT?

Why is the North Atlantic right whale, sometimes seen off St. Augustine's coast, known as the "right whale"? The standard answer is that whalers of the 18th century saw the huge creature as the "right" whale to hunt, but nobody knows if that story is true.

Avast, me hearties!

Not every pirate flew the same flag – in fact, some famous pirates customized the Jolly Roger or designed flags that incorporated their own symbols. In one, the pirate Black Bart is toasting death, and in the other Christopher Moody, an 18th-century pirate, is threatening violence if the victims don't surrender – the hourglass warns them time is running out.

Answers: 1 The imaginary burial place for pirates and sailors at the bottom of the ocean. **2** Silver coins of lesser value found in pirate hoards. **3** A drink of rum and water. **4** Originally meant "hold fast" – as in, stop and pay attention. **5** Pirate flag, customarily with skull and crossbones.

⑪ Anastasia Island
A spooky lighthouse

The 165-ft (50-m) **St. Augustine Lighthouse** is definitely the high point of a visit to Anastasia Island, but there are many other attractions, too. At the northern tip is **Anastasia State Park**, whose 2.5 sq miles (6 sq km) include 4 miles (6 km) of beach with a surf break, a maritime hammock, a tidal salt marsh, and a sheltered lagoon favored by windsurfers. It is possible to fish, hike, or bike around the park, although most beachgoers come here to surf, sail, swim, or just enjoy lazing in the sun.

Energetic families can climb the 219 steps to the top of the lighthouse. Older kids and teens may be interested in a "Dark of the Moon" ghost tour – the lighthouse was featured on *Ghost Hunters*, a paranormal reality TV show. There is also an activity area for younger kids.

Fun at the beach in Anastasia State Park, Anastasia Island

The Lowdown

- 🌐 **Map reference** 6 F1
- **Address** Park: 1340-A State Rd A1A South, 32080; 904 461 2033; *www.floridastateparks. org*. Lighthouse: 81 Lighthouse Ave, 32080; 904 829 0745; *www.staugustinelighthouse.com*
- 🚗 **Car** Rent a car from St. Augustine.
- 🕐 **Open** Park: 8am–sunset daily. Lighthouse: 9am–6pm daily
- 💲 **Price** Park: $8 per vehicle. Lighthouse: $34–44
- 🚶 **Cutting the line** Avoid midday and holiday weekends.
- 🚩 **Guided tours** RippleEffect EcoTours (904 347 1565; *www. rippleeffectecotours.com*) offers kayak/canoe tours. Call lighthouse for information on special tour.
- 👫 **Age range** All ages. For the lighthouse, kids must be taller than 44 in (112 cm), and able to climb alone.
- ⏱ **Allow** Park: 1–2 hours. Lighthouse: at least 1 hour
- ♿ **Wheelchair access** Yes
- 🍽 **Eat and drink** SNACKS Island Beach Shop and Grill *(in Anastasia State Park)* serves snacks and drinks. REAL MEAL O'steen's *(205 Anastasia Boulevard, 32080; 904 829 6974; closed Sun–Mon)* offers fried shrimp and scallops. Call ahead for opening hours.
- 👫 **Restrooms** Park: at beaches and campgrounds. Lighthouse: near the gift shop

Take cover

Head to the 299-seat **World Golf Hall of Fame's** IMAX® theater *(wgf imax.com)*, which has a 3-D digital projection system and the largest digital screen in the southeast. Or go 2 miles (3 km) west to **Whetstone Factory** *(139 King St, St. Augustine, 32084; 904 217 0275)* to learn the candymaker's secrets and do a little taste-testing along the way.

⑫ Marineland Dolphin Adventure
Is Flipper home?

This attraction right on the Atlantic Ocean focuses on research on Atlantic bottlenose dolphins and dolphin encounters. If swimming with dolphins is on the "must-do" list, Marineland may be the high

Visitors taking pictures of a dolphin at Marineland Dophin Adventure

The Lowdown

- 🌐 **Map reference** 6 F2
- **Address** 9600 Oceanshore Blvd, 32080; 904 471 1111; *www. marineland.net*
- 🚗 **Car** Rent a car from St. Augustine.
- 🕐 **Open** 9am–4:30pm daily
- 💲 **Price** $35–45; dolphin programs range from $26 to $550
- 👫 **Age range** 3 plus
- 👫 **Activities** Several dolphin programs; call ahead for details.
- ⏱ **Allow** 1–2 hours
- ♿ **Wheelchair access** Yes
- 🍽 **Eat and drink** SNACKS A small concession stand *(on site)* serves snacks, hot dogs, and drinks. REAL MEAL Thai Korner Restaurant *(1280 Palm Coast Pkwy SW, Palm Coast, 32137; 386 597 2939; www.thaikorner.com)* offers Thai and Japanese food, and has a multiethnic kids' menu.
- 👫 **Restrooms** Near gift shop and main pool area

point of a Florida vacation – a low-key, uncrowded environment where it is possible to get close enough to rub bottlenoses. There are several programs that offer visitors interaction with the dolphins, but these must be booked in advance.

Children will enjoy exploring the dolphins' natural habitat in the adjacent Matanzas River Estuary. A Marineland partner here offers kayak tours that are guided by certified naturalists. The stable tandem- and triple-seat kayaks make the outing possible for complete beginners, and even for kids as young as 6.

Take cover

If inclement weather threatens, visit the **Authentic Old Jail** (167 San Marco Ave, 32084) in St. Augustine. Costumed actors make the tour interesting and fun, if a bit spooky.

⑬ Washington Oaks Gardens State Park

For a fantastic day out

Roses in the ornamental gardens, Ice Age rocks on the beach – the two sides of Washington Oaks Gardens State Park couldn't be more different. Add to that the chance to see manatees hanging out in the river shallows – and this state park is definitely not a run-of-the mill picnic stop. Saltwater anglers can fish from the rocky beach on the east side of A1A. The rocks make it a good place to hunt for sea glass that's been tumbled smooth. Budding anglers can try their hand at freshwater fishing from the seawall on the Matanzas River on the west side of A1A. In the cooler months, this is a good place to spot manatees. The park gardens are also attractive – developed in the 1930s, they include both native and exotic species. In early spring, visitors are greeted by an especially beautiful sight: colorful azaleas and camellias in full bloom.

Take cover

Skate and Shake Skating Center (386 672 8500), 25 miles (40 km) south in Ormond Beach, may be a bit of a drive, but it's a great way for kids to get lots of exercise even when it's pouring outside. Call ahead.

The 19th-century building housing the Authentic Old Jail, St. Augustine

The Lowdown

🌐 **Map reference** 6 F2

Address 6400 N Palm Coast Blvd, Oceanshore, 32137; 386 446 6780; www.floridastate parks.org/washingtonoaks

🚗 **Car** Rent a car from St. Augustine.

🕐 **Open** 8am–sunset daily

💲 **Price** $5 per vehicle

👫 **Cutting the line** The park is rarely crowded.

👪 **Age range** 4 plus

⏱ **Allow** 1–2 hours

♿ **Wheelchair access** Yes. Beach wheelchair with advance notice.

🍴 **Eat and drink** PICNIC Roman's Bagel Deli & Pizza (4255 A1A S, 32080; 904 461 1111; closed Mon) has picnic supplies. REAL MEAL Matanzas Innlet Restaurant (8805 A1A South, 32080; 904 461 6824; www. matanzas.biz) offers boiled shrimp, steamer baskets, big burgers, and a water view.

🚻 **Restrooms** In the visitor center, picnic area, and on the beach

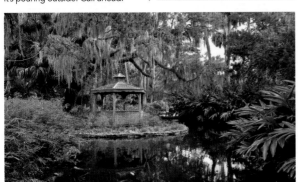

Picturesque view of a gazebo on a pond in Washington Oaks Gardens State Park

⑭ Daytona Beach
Fun on the run

Daytona Beach has been drawing adrenaline junkies since the early 1900s, when automobile racing on the beach's firm sand pushed the boundaries of speed. Although the city is still popular with race fans, it has also become a favorite destination for millions of visitors each year, thanks to its beautiful beaches, superb attractions, and great weather for outdoor activities.

The Southeast Museum of Photography

Key Sights

① **Daytona Lagoon** Although this amusement park is all about water rides from May to October, it also offers exciting year-round "dry attractions" such as laser tag, miniature golf, and go-karts.

② **Daytona Beach Boardwalk** Enjoy old-fashioned arcade games and rides, such as a Ferris wheel, Slingshot, and Hurricane, here. Check out the renovated pier and restaurant.

③ **Public beaches** Car-friendly sands and crowds of festive beachgoers have helped Daytona's 23 miles (37 km) of beaches gain a reputation as "The World's Most Famous Beach."

④ **Halifax Historical Society Museum** This museum features vintage toys and exhibits on Native American culture, along with beach racing. A 20-minute movie covers 130,000 years of local history.

Prices given are for a family of four

⑤ **Southeast Museum of Photography** This is the largest museum of its kind in the southeast, with exhibits, lectures, and seminars, plus Family Photo Fun Days and photo workshops for kids.

⑥ **Daytona International Speedway** Young speed demons will like a tour of the legendary racetrack of the Daytona 500, one of the most famous NASCAR meets.

⑦ **Gamble Place** This Florida Cracker-style property preserves the Citrus-Packing House – the only one in Florida at its original location.

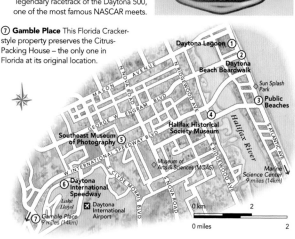

The Lowdown

🌐 **Map reference** 6 G3
Address Daytona Lagoon: 601 Earl St, 32114; *www.daytonalagoon. com*. Daytona Beach Boardwalk: 12 N Ocean Ave, 32118; *www. daytonabeachboardwalk.com*. Halifax Historical Society Museum: 252 S Beach St, 32114; *www. halifaxhistorical.org*. Southeast Museum of Photography: 1200 W International Speedway, 32114; *www.smponline.org*. Daytona International Speedway: 1801 W International Speedway Blvd, 32114; *www.daytonainternational speedway.com*. Gamble Place: 1819 Taylor Rd, Port Orange, 32127; *www.moas.org*

🚍 **Bus** Votran (*www.votran.org*) buses connect sights in the city.
Car Rent a car at Daytona Beach International Airport.

ℹ **Visitor information** Daytona Regional Chamber of Commerce, 126 E Orange Ave, 32115; 386 255 0981; *www.daytonachamber.org*

🕑 **Open** Daytona Lagoon & Daytona Beach Boardwalk: hours vary by attraction and season; check websites. Public beaches: open 24 hours daily to pedestrians and bicyclists & sunrise–sunset to vehicles with driving passes. Halifax Historical Society Museum: 10:30am–4:30pm Tue–Fri & 10am–

The redbrick gift shop next to the Ponce de Leon Inlet Lighthouse

Take cover

The modest **Marine Science Center** (www.marinesciencecenter.com), 11 miles (18 km) southeast of Daytona Beach in Ponce Inlet, has exhibits, aquariums, and guided beach walks.

Eat and drink

Picnic: under $25; Snacks: $25–50; Real meal: $50–80; Family treat: over $80 (based on a family of four)

PICNIC New York Style Bagel Deli and Restaurant *(3344 S Atlantic Ave, 32118; 386 760 0302)* offers deli items, salads, sandwiches, and bakery goods for a beachside picnic.
SNACKS Cow Licks *(2624 S Atlantic Ave, 32118; 386 761 1316)* is the place to chill, with home-made ice cream and Ms. Pac-Man games.
REAL MEAL Rossi's Diner *(2240 S Ridgewood Ave, 32119; 386 760 4564; www.rossisdiner.com)* is a

favorite with locals, thanks to a huge menu, and desserts such as rice pudding and muffins.
FAMILY TREAT Don Vito's Italian Restaurant *(137 West International Speedway Blvd, 32114; 386 492 7935; www.donvitosrestaurant.com)* serves fine, but expensive, Italian fare. The kids' menu has spaghetti and meatballs. The desserts are a hit.

Shopping

Daytona's **Downtown Shopping District** has many antique stores, bookstores, and clothing shops.

Next stop...

PONCE DE LEON INLET LIGHTHOUSE AND MUSEUM Go 10 miles (16 km) south to see the tallest lighthouse in Florida *(www.ponceinlet.org)* on the north bank of Ponce de Leon Inlet.

KIDS' CORNER

Turtles in trouble

Unfortunately, there are many reasons why turtles can end up needing some help at places like the Marine Science Center. Those reasons can include:
1 Upwelling (really cold water rising from the bottom of the ocean that can shock and even kill hatchlings)
2 Washbacks (rough weather pushing baby hatchlings back onto the beach)
3 Illegal fishing equipment (hooks and fishing line that can

get entangled or swallowed by turtles)
4 Red tide (an algae bloom in the water)

PICTURE THIS

When Joseph Niepce took the first photo in 1827, it took 8 hours. Since then, technology has made possible some amazing photographs. One of the most famous photos is "Earthrise," taken by astronaut Bill Anders in 1968 while orbiting the moon. See it on www.nasa.gov.

Lighting up the sky

1 The lighthouse at Ponce de Leon Inlet features a beacon from the 19th century. Can you guess how far out at sea the light could be seen?
2 Do you know how long it takes for the beacon to flash six times?
3 How many bricks did it take to build the lighthouse?

Answers: 1 18 miles (29 km). **2** 15 seconds. **3** 2.5 million.

4pm Sat. Southeast Museum of Photography: closed Mon & during hols. Daytona International Speedway: event hours vary; tours from 10am–4pm daily. Gamble Place: 10am–3pm Fri–Sat
⑤ **Prices** Daytona Lagoon & Daytona Beach Boardwalk: check websites for details; water park: $100–120. Public beaches: call Republic Parking for info at 386 254 4605. Halifax Historical Society Museum: $12–22. Southeast Museum of Photography: free. Daytona International Speedway: for event and race prices, call 1 800 748 7467. Gamble Place: $22–32; under 5s free

Cutting the line VIP tours of the Daytona International Speedway can be booked ahead at $50 per person; call 877 306 7223.
Guided tours Take the 90-min ($78–88; under 5s free) or 30-min ($50–60; under 5s free) All Access Speedway Tour. Gamble House runs tours at 10am, 12pm & 2pm.
Age range 4 plus
Allow At least half a day

Good family value?
Although lodgings can be relatively expensive in this city, the beach, and some sights, are free and many others are moderately priced.

⑮ Museum of Arts and Sciences (MOAS)

Not just another museum

Set in the lush Tuscawilla Preserve, this museum not only houses a superb collection of art, science, and history exhibits, but also allows kids to discover important scientific principles through hands-on exhibits, including the chance to design cars and test their designs by racing against competitors. The domed planetarium is another attraction here, with a Minolta MS-10 sky projector. The preserve also has an environmental education center, trails, and discovery stations.

Mould of the iconic Coca-Cola contour bottle

Key Sights

Entrance

① **"Sumar Special" Indy car**
Housed in the Root Family Museum, the Sumar Special reached the amazing speed of 172 mph (276.5 km/h) in 1957. It was designed by Frank Kurtis and Chapman Root, whose company created the famous Coca-Cola contour bottle.

② **Coca-Cola** The mold of the original Coke bottle is part of Chapman Root's huge collection of historic Coca-Cola memorabilia on display in the Root Family Museum.

③ **Teddy bears** See more than 800 teddy bears, each depicting a different theme or historical period, in the Root Family Museum. Kids will love the large wedding party in full costume, with a bride, a groom, and even a ring bearer.

④ **Giant ground sloth** This 130,000-year-old 13-ft (4-m) tall skeleton of a giant sloth is a major draw in the Bouchelle Gallery of Changing Exhibitions.

⑤ **Planetarium** Located in the West Wing, this facility hosts thrilling solar system-related shows using images from NASA space probes and 3-D special effects.

The Lowdown

Map reference 6 G3
Address 352 South Nova Rd, Daytona Beach, 32114; 386 255 0285; www.moas.org

Car Rent a car from Daytona Beach Airport. Free parking

Open 9am–5pm Tue–Sat & 11am–5pm Sun

Price $40–50; under 6s free. General admission includes regular planetarium shows.

Shows The planetarium hosts laser rock concerts (tickets $5 for one show, $7 for two shows, or $9 for three shows) at 7pm, 8pm & 9pm on second Sat of each month. Limited seating. Tickets can be purchased at the main entrance or in advance. Call 386 255 0285 for information on specific shows.

Cutting the line Visit between 9am and 11am, when the museum is relatively uncrowded.

Guided tours The museum offers pre-scheduled tours.

Age range 6 plus

Activities The Klancke Environmental Education Complex in Tuscawilla Preserve has raised boardwalks and nature trails.

Allow 1–3 hours

Wheelchair access Yes

Shop The small gift shop (by the main entrance) sells mostly art books, which grown-ups might like, as well as snacks.

Restrooms In each of the three wings: West Wing, North Wing, and the Roots Family Museum

Good family value?
A wide range of educative and interactive exhibits make this museum a fun experience for the whole family.

⑥ **Charles and Linda Williams Children's Museum** Kids can race toy cars on the figure-eight track, and also explore numerous exciting hands-on science stations in this museum.

⑦ **Cuban Foundation Museum Collection** Former Cuban president Fulgencio Batista donated the core of the museum's famed Cuban art collection in the 1950s. It is considered to be the best collection outside Cuba.

⑧ **Sculpture Garden** This magical outdoor exhibition area is dotted with works by noted contemporary sculptors such as Ernest Shaw and Juan José Sicre.

Exploring a boardwalk trail through the lush Tuscawilla Preserve

Letting off steam

Burn off excess energy on the nature trails in the **Tuscawilla Preserve**, or relax in its **Sensory Garden**, which has herbs, native wildflowers, a butterfly and hummingbird garden, and a rock garden. The garden serves as the entry to the Klancke Environmental Education Complex.

Eat and drink

Picnic: under $25; Snacks: $25–50; Real meal: $50–80; Family treat: over $80 (based on a family of four)

PICNIC The Cracked Egg Diner (3280 South Atlantic Ave, 32118; 386 788 6772; www.thecrackedegg diner.com) is a great place to pick up subs, sandwiches, salads and fried pickles. Picnic near the pool in the Sensory Garden.

SNACKS Dancing Avocado Kitchen (110 South Beach St, 32114; 386 947 2022; closed Sun–Mon) serves creative breakfast and lunch dishes

with many vegetarian selections. Reasonable prices and a smoothie and juice bar make this restaurant a good choice for snacks and meals.

REAL MEAL Steve's Famous Diner (1584 S Nova Rd, 32114; 386 252 0101; stevesfamousdiner.biz), a popular place near the museum, offers superb fresh-baked breads. The wide-ranging menu has home-made soups, salads, and desserts.

FAMILY TREAT The Cellar (220 Magnolia Ave, 32114; 386 258 0011; www.thecellarrestaurant.com; closed Mon) is a major splurge for Italian cuisine, but the dishes created by chef Sam Maggio have ensured a loyal fan base. The restaurant also has an extensive wine list.

Find out more

DIGITAL Download the free MOAS iPhone app from itunes.apple.com/us/app/moas/id391833573?mt=8 to stroll through the virtual galleries of the museum, get in-depth artist biographies, and check out exhibition and event schedules, as well as ticketing information.

Next stop…

DEVIL'S MILLHOPPER GEOLOGICAL STATE PARK Head 121 miles (195 km) northwest to the Devil's Millhopper Geological State Park (see p181) near Gainesville. A 120-ft (36.5-m) sinkhole, it is one of Florida's most unusual parks. Summer visitors who climb all the steps to the bottom of the sinkhole can experience cooler temperatures and views of diverse wildlife.

Boardwalk leading to the bottom of the sinkhole in Devil's Millhopper

Tubing in Blue Spring State Park, Ocala National Forest

⑯ Blue Spring State Park

Make a splash

When the summer's hottest days roll around, families love to take a refreshing plunge into Blue Spring, where they can swim, snorkel, canoe, kayak, or take a riverboat tour. Certified scuba divers can even dive here. With the onset of winter in mid-November, all water activities stop as Florida's manatees migrate here. The park is a designated

The Lowdown

- 🌐 **Map reference** 6 F4
- **Address** 2100 W French Ave, Orange City, 32763; 386 775 3663; www.floridastateparks/bluespring
- 🚗 **Car** Rent a car from Ocala.
- 🕐 **Open** 8am–sunset daily
- 💲 **Price** $6 per vehicle & $2 per pedestrian and cyclist.
- 👫 **Cutting the line** Arrive early – on weekends, the park often closes by noon because of the crowds.
- 👫 **Age range** All ages
- 🏃 **Activities** Observe manatees from the boardwalk during manatee season. Interpretive programs in the afternoon; call 386 775 3773. St. Johns River Cruises (386 917 0724) offers riverboat tours.
- 🕐 **Allow** 2–4 hours
- ♿ **Wheelchair access** Yes
- ☕ **Eat and drink** SNACKS The snack bar (on site; 386 775 6888; www.myfloridamanatee.com) sells sandwiches, snacks, and drinks. REAL MEAL Texas Roadhouse (2518 Enterprise Rd, 32763; 386 532 7427; www.texasroadhouse.com) is a highly rated steakhouse with a great kids' menu.
- 👫 **Restrooms** Near the parking and picnic areas

Manatee Refuge, and children will delight in watching from the boardwalk as the manatees feed, frolic, and take care of their calves.

Take cover

Head northwest to the excellent **Appleton Museum of Art** (4333 E Silver Springs Blvd, Ocala, 34470; 352 291 4455; www.appletonmuseum.org). The museum's pre-Columbian and African collections are likely to keep kids enthralled for quite a while. The museum's gift shop, which offers art-inspired merchandise, is worth a visit.

⑰ Ocala National Forest

Tarzan's playground

The second-largest National Forest in the country, this 600-sq-mile (1,780-sq-km) jungle could take many years to explore fully – from its sandy Big Scrub to the semitropical Juniper Springs. Among the many attractions that appeal to families, the Yearling Trail takes hikers to Pat's Island, the place where the family in the

A picturesque hiking trail running through Ocala National Forest

The Lowdown

- 🌐 **Map reference** 6 E3
- **Address** North of Orlando between the Ocklawaha and St. Johns Rivers; 352 625 2520; www.fs.usda.gov/ocala
- 🚗 **Car** Rent a car from Ocala.
- ℹ️ **Visitor information** Ocklawaha: 3199 NE Hwy 315, Silver Springs, 34488. Salt Springs: 14100 N State Hwy 19, 32134; 352 685 3070. Pittman: 45621 State Rd 19, Altoona, 32702
- 🕐 **Open** 8am–8pm most sites
- 💲 **Price** Most sites $26–36
- 👫 **Cutting the line** Avoid weekends and holidays.
- 🏴 **Guided tours** Check www.ocalamarion.com for tours by boat, horse, and all-terrain vehicle.
- 👫 **Age range** All ages
- 🕐 **Allow** Half a day
- ♿ **Wheelchair access** Limited
- ☕ **Eat and drink** SNACKS Yomii Frozen Yogurt (2631 Enterprise Blvd, Orange City, 32763; 386 456 5080) offers a selection of self-serve toppings. REAL MEAL Laspada's Original (2200 N Volusia Ave, Orange City, 32763; www.laspadas.com) serves Philly cheese steaks, and Italian hoagies.
- 👫 **Restrooms** At campgrounds

Pulitzer Prize-winning book *The Yearling* (1938) lived. Look out for the endangered Florida black bear on the Florida Black Bear Scenic Highway (State Road 19). The forest is also great for birding – spot bald eagles, ospreys, waterfowl, and owls. Several lakes draw bass anglers, and a full-facility marina rents boats. There are also campgrounds, horse trails, and springs popular for swimming, canoeing, and tubing.

Take cover

The dragsters and vintage cars at the **Don Garlits Museum of Drag Racing** (www.garlits.com), in Ocala, will fascinate kids and car buffs.

⑱ Ocala Thoroughbred Farm Country

Horsing around

With more horses and ponies than anywhere else in the world, Marion County is guaranteed to be a big hit with horse-crazy kids. Watch a polo match or a real rodeo, get a close look at Thoroughbreds – including the famous Rohara Arabians and Young's Paso Finos – at one of the 600 Thoroughbred farms in the area, or explore the countryside on horseback at a ride-for-fun stable. Marion County boasts thousands of national and world champs, plus six Kentucky Derby winners.

Take cover
The carriage museum at **The Grand Oaks Resort** (thegrandoaks.com), in Weirsdale, has rides fit for royalty, but kids may like the life-size horse models as much as the vehicles.

The Lowdown
- **Map reference** 5 D3
- **Car** Rent a car from Ocala.
- **Visitor information** 112 N Magnolia Ave, Ocala, 34475; 352 438 2801; www.ocalamarion.com
- **Price** Varies by tour and activity.
- **Cutting the line** Choose weekdays when possible.
- **Guided tours** Several tours, including by horse, motorbike, all-terrain vehicle, and canoe; check www.ocalamarion.com.
- **Age range** 4 plus
- **Activities** Horse farm tours, horse-riding, and horse shows
- **Allow** 2–4 hours
- **Wheelchair access** Varies, call individual tours and attractions.
- **Eat and drink** SNACKS Stella's Modern Pantry (20 SW Broadway St, 34471; 352 622 3663; closed Mon) gets kudos for desserts, but also offers sandwiches and flatbreads. REAL MEAL Royal Orchid Thai Cuisine (3131 SW College Rd 206, 34474; 352 237 4949) is a local favorite, thanks to an authentic menu and great service.

A room at the house in Marjorie Kinnan Rawlings State Park

⑲ Marjorie Kinnan Rawlings Historic State Park
House of a literary genius

Although she was not a native Floridian, Marjorie Kinnan Rawlings' writings about this area and its people have made her one of the state's best-known authors. She came to live on this farmstead in search of a quiet place to write and fell in love with it, as most visitors do, too. Her books, especially *The Yearling*, which is a favorite among younger readers, help convey the realities of living close to the wilderness in harmony with nature. The park includes her home, furnished as it was when she lived here in the 1930s, a workers' home, a barn, a kitchen garden, and other outbuildings. The home's interior can be viewed only by guided tour.

Letting off steam
Kids can run around the house's extensive grounds to burn off excess energy.

The Lowdown
- **Map reference** 5 D3
- **Address** 18700 S County Rd 325, Cross Creek, 32640; 352 466 3672
- **Car** Rent a car from Gainesville.
- **Open** Park grounds: 9am–5pm daily
- **Price** Park admission: $3 per vehicle. House tours: $10–20; under 5s free
- **Cutting the line** Winter is busy. Fri & Sun mornings are quietest.
- **Guided tours** Hourly tours of house and property Oct–Jul: 10am–4pm Thu–Sun; call 352 466 3672.
- **Age range** 6 plus
- **Allow** 1–2 hours
- **Wheelchair access** Yes
- **Eat and drink** REAL MEAL Blue Highway Pizzeria (204 NE Hwy 441, Micanopy, 32667; 352 466 0062) is a casual eatery where diners can customize their pizza. FAMILY TREAT The Yearling Restaurant (14531 E County Rd 325, Hawthorne, 32640; 352 466 3999; closed Mon–Wed) serves quail and frog legs, along with chicken, steak, and seafood.
- **Restrooms** In the park, adjacent to the historic site

KIDS' CORNER

Manatees talk the talk
While it can't be said that manatees have their own language, they do communicate. Wonder what "Yikes, danger!" or "Mom, I'm lost!" or "Now I'm mad!" would sound like? To find out, go to www.savethemanatee.org/coolstuff.htm and click on "Sounds." The website also has games, stickers, and coloring sheets. Best of all, there's also a webcam that shows manatees at Blue Spring State Park.

THOROUGHLY THOROUGHBRED
A Thoroughbred is a particular breed of horse that is especially good at racing, jumping, and other show events. These beautiful horses are usually about 64 in (163 cm) tall, with a deep chest and a long neck. Those bred to run longer distances are usually smaller, and the ones meant to run shorter distances have bigger muscles.

The fastest two minutes in sports
The Kentucky Derby is a race for 3-year-old Thoroughbreds held each year in Louisville, Kentucky. The race is 1¼ miles (2 km), and the winner is draped with a blanket of roses. The 2012 Derby winner, I'll Have Another, was trained in Ocala.

⑳ Paynes Prairie Preserve State Park

Home on the range, where the deer and the buffalo roam

This 33-sq mile (85-sq km) preserve, 2 hours west of Daytona Beach, is home to deer, bison, wild horses, Florida Cracker cows, and alligators. It is not necessary to hike deep into the wilderness to see its wildlife – the park has multiple observation platforms, including a 50-ft (15-m) high tower for a bird's-eye view. Remember to carry binoculars – 271 species of birds, from bald eagles to sandhill cranes, live here. There is plenty of human history here to explore, too. An audio-visual presentation at the visitor center tells the story of this wilderness, which goes back at least 12,000 years.

The Lowdown

- 🌐 **Map reference** 4 F6
  Address 100 Savannah Blvd, Micanopy, 32667; 352 466 3397; www.floridastateparks.org
- 🚗 **Car** Rent a car from Gainesville.
- 🕐 **Open** 8am–sunset daily. Visitor center: 9am–4pm daily
- 💲 **Price** $6 per vehicle & $2 per pedestrian or cyclist
- 👫 **Cutting the line** Avoid weekends when the University of Florida football team plays at home. The park is less crowded May–Sep.
- 🚩 **Guided tours** Walk and talk programs run Nov–Apr on alternate Thu; call 352 466 4100 for reservations. Free cell phone tour at www.dialanddiscover.com
- 👫 **Age range** 4 plus
- ⏱ **Allow** 2 hours
- ♿ **Wheelchair access** Limited; call 850 245 2157
- 🍴 **Eat and drink** SNACKS Coffee N Cream (201 Northeast 1st St, Micanopy, 32667; 352 466 1101; www.micanopycoffeeshop.com) offers coffee and other drinks, and home-made cookies. Or pick up sandwiches to take to Paynes Prairie. REAL MEAL Pearl Country Store (106A NE Hwy 441, Micanopy, 32667; 352 466 4025; www.pearlcountrystore.com) has barbecue and mac'n'cheese that customers swear by.
- 👫 **Restrooms** At the visitor center and Lake Wauberg campgrounds

Tree-lined drive in Paynes Prairie Preserve State Park, Gainesville

Take cover

Go to **Smiley's Antique Mall** (17020 SE County Rd 234, Micanopy, 32667; 352 466 0707) for Star Wars™ figures and cowboy collectibles.

㉑ Florida Museum of Natural History

Calling all "__ologists!"

For families with kids who love science – whether they want to grow up to be paleontologists, zoologists, or archaeologists – the University of Florida's Museum of Natural History in Gainesville is an astonishing treasure house of information and exhibits. One of American's top five natural history museums, it houses more than 30 million specimens in multiple disciplines. Exhibits at the Hall of Florida Fossils cover the last 65 million years in Florida, from the Eocene era (when the state was underwater) to the arrival of humans about 14,000 years ago. The McGuire Center, the largest research facility on the planet

The Lowdown

- 🌐 **Map reference** 4 F5
  Address SW 34th St & Hull Rd, Gainesville, 32611–2710; 352 846 2000; www.flmnh.ufl.edu
- 🚗 **Car** Rent a car in Gainesville.
- 🕐 **Open** 10am–5pm Mon–Sat & 1–5pm Sun
- 💲 **Price** Free. Butterfly Rainforest: $33–43. Parking $4 per day (cash); free on weekends and holidays
- 👫 **Cutting the line** The museum is not usually crowded.
- 🚩 **Guided tours** Hall of Florida Fossils tours at 11:30am & 2:45pm Sat, 2:45pm Sun
- 👫 **Age range** 4 plus
- 👫 **Activities** Live butterfly releases at 2pm, 3pm & 4pm Sat & Sun, weather permitting. Butterfly-friendly plant sale at 10am–5pm Mon–Sat & 1–5pm Sun
- ⏱ **Allow** 1–2 hours
- ♿ **Wheelchair access** Yes
- 🍴 **Eat and drink** REAL MEAL Satchel's Pizza (1800 NE 23rd Ave, 32609; 352 335 7272; www.satchelspizza. com; closed Sun & Mon) is known for its inventive pizzas. FAMILY TREAT Amelia's (235 S Main St, Suite 107, 32601; 352 373 1919; www.ameliasgainesville.com) serves fresh, home-style Italian food.
- 👫 **Restrooms** Near South Florida People and Environments exhibit, and off the Central Gallery

dedicated to the study of butterflies, includes a screened outdoor exhibit called the Butterfly Rainforest. This contains hundreds of butterflies from all over the world, living in a predator-free environment among waterfalls and tropical plants. On weekend afternoons, when the weather permits, visitors can view live butterfly releases.

Butterfly exhibit in the Florida Museum of Natural History, Gainesville

Steps in Devil's Milhopper Geological State Park leading to the bottom of the sinkhole

Water-Breathing Dragon Fountain in Kanapaha Botanical Gardens, Gainesville

Letting off steam

Head 4 miles (7 km) southwest to **Kanapaha Botanical Gardens** (www.kanapaha.org) to see the hummingbird garden, wildflower meadow, and "children's garden" featuring a treasure wall, a hedge maze, and a koi pond.

㉒ Devil's Millhopper Geological State Park

A sinking sensation

The Devil's Millhopper, in Gainesville, is a sinkhole that appeared when an underground cavern collapsed due to heat and humidity. The sinkhole created a miniature rain forest with many small springs whose streams flow down its sides. On a hot summer day, descending all 236 steps to the sinkhole's lowest point is rewarding for its noticeably cooler temperature. Remember to wear stout shoes if you are up for the walk. Though younger kids may find it exhausting, the walk rewards the energetic ones with sightings of birds from the pinelands and suburbs.

Take cover

Travel 5 miles (8 km) south to check out the Asian wing and gardens of the first-rate **Harn Museum of Art** *(SW 34th St, S Hull Rd, 32611; www.harn. ufl.edu)*. Kids may especially like the Ancient American collection with its Mayan and Aztec works.

The Lowdown

🌐 **Map reference** 4 E5
Address 4732 Milhoppper Rd, Gainesville, 32653; 352 955 2008; www.floridaparks.org

🚗 **Car** Rent a car in Gainesville.

🕐 **Open** 9am–5pm Wed–Sun

💲 **Price** $4 per vehicle & $2 per pedestrian or cyclist

🧍 **Cutting the line** Least crowded Wed–Thu from mid-afternoon on.

🚩 **Guided tours** Guided walk with ranger at 10am every Sat; call 386 462 7905

👫 **Age range** 4 plus

🏃 **Activities** Hiking, picnicking, and wildlife viewing

⏲ **Allow** 2 hours

♿ **Wheelchair access** Yes, limited

🍽 **Eat and drink** PICNIC Schlotzsky's Deli *(4720 Northwest 39th Ave, Gainesville, 32606; 352 372 3354; www.schlotzskys.com)* is a convenient place to pick up sandwiches, sides, and salads for a picnic on the park's grounds. REAL MEAL The Jones Eastside *(401 NE 23rd Ave, Gainesville, 32609; 352 373 6777; www. thejoneseastside.com)* uses fresh local ingredients in a modestly priced farm-to-table menu.

🚻 **Restrooms** At the visitor center

Where to Stay in the Northeast

This region offers a wide variety of accommodations, from award-winning resorts and luxurious hotels to campsites located in beautiful state parks within walking distance of the waves. Northeastern Florida offers plenty of both upscale and budget options to choose from.

AGENCY
Stockton Real Estate
www.stocktonrealestate.com
This local real estate company coordinates short-term rental of individual vacation homes and condos, from oceanfront to golf course locations in Jacksonville and its beaches, Ponte Vedra Beach, and St. Augustine.

Amelia Island   Map 4 H2

RESORTS
Omni Amelia Island Plantation Resort
6800 First Coast Hwy, 32034; 904 261 6161; www.omniameliaisland plantation.com
Spread over 2 sq miles (5 sq km), this resort has 150-plus guest rooms, plus a dazzling beach club and restaurants. Superb supervised kids' programs, along with games, dinner parties, and picnics are offered.
$$$

The Ritz-Carlton, Amelia Island
4750 Amelia Island Pkwy, 32034–5501; 904 277 1100; www.ritzcarlton ameliaisland.com
This oceanfront AAA four-diamond resort has luxurious guest rooms and public spaces. There is a beach, a spa, tennis courts, a fitness center, and stellar programs for kids and teenagers.
$$$

SELF-CATERING
The Villas at Amelia Island Plantation
6800 First Coast Hwy, 32034; 904 261 6161; www.aipfl.com
This huge beach resort offers lodging in rooms, and one-, two-, and three-bedroom villas ideal for families. There's a private beach, golf, a spa, a fitness center, and restaurants.
$$$

CAMPING
Little Talbot Island State Park   Map 4 G3
12157 Heckscher Dr, Jacksonville, 32226; 904 251 2320; www.florida stateparks.org/littletalbotisland
Located off A1A, this campground offers 40 campsites with water, electricity and showers. Laundry facilities and bike rentals are available on site. Reserve ahead.
$

Atlantic Beach   Map 4 H3

RESORT
One Ocean Resort & Spa
One Ocean Blvd, 32233; 904 249 7402; www.oneoceanresort.com
A small but beautiful resort hotel by the ocean, with airy rooms and suites equipped with flat-screen TVs and refrigerators. A personal docent will make reservations, and even enroll kids in the wide variety of programs available.
$$–$$$

Daytona Beach   Map 6 G3

RESORTS
Perry's Ocean Edge Resort
2209 S Atlantic Ave, 32118; 386 255 0581 or 800 447 0002; www.perrys oceanedge.com
Most units in this property come with a full kitchen. The Kids' Beach Suites in the South Tower are a good option for families. There is an atrium pool that allows swimming year round, a fitness center, water aerobics, and bingo for kids.
$

The Hilton Daytona Beach Oceanfront Resort
100 North Atlantic Ave, 32118; 386 254 8200; www.daytona hilton.com
Family suites and the D-Dawg's Kidszone, with arts and crafts, board games, and storytelling, make this oceanfront Hilton resort a great family option. Most of the resort's restaurants offer a kids' menu.
$–$$

Wyndam Oceanwalk Resort
300 North Atlantic Ave, 32118; 800 625 1649; www.oceanwalk.com
Spacious one-, two-, and three-bedroom condos equipped with full kitchens, refrigerators, microwaves, and TVs can be rented at this beachfront resort. Amenities include an outdoor hot tub, activities for kids, and a game room.
$$

Fernandina Beach   Map 4 H2

HOTELS
Amelia Hotel at the Beach
1997 South Fletcher Ave, 32034; 904 206 5200 or 877 263 5428; www.ameliahotelandsuites.com
Across the street from Fernandina's Main Beach, this family-owned hotel features rooms with king-size beds, microwaves, and mini-

The King Terrace Suite at The Hilton Daytona Beach Oceanfront Resort

refrigerators. Kids will love the fresh-baked cookies and milk in the afternoon. Bikes and beach gear can be rented next door. There is also complimentary hot breakfast for all guests.

🌐 🍽 **P** 😊 ☀ **$**

CAMPING
Fort Clinch State Park
2601 Atlantic Ave, 32034; 904 277 7274 or 800 326 3521; www.florida stateparks.org/fortclinch
A fascinating fort and great freshwater and saltwater fishing draw visitors to this campground. Campers can choose between a beach and river location. Facilities include utility hook-ups, laundry, and an on-site store. Reserve well in advance.

🗄 😊 ☀ **$**

Gainesville
Map 4 F5

HOTELS
Hilton UF Conference Center
1714 SW 34th St, 32607; 1 352 371 3600; tinyurl.com/bm8oj4u
Located in the southwestern corner of the Hilton University of Florida (UF) campus, this hotel makes a superb base for visiting the UF museums and other sights. Rooms and suites are comfortably furnished. There is a fitness center, an outdoor pool, a sports bar, and gift shop on site.

🌐 🍴 🍽 ☕ 😊 **$$**

Jacksonville
Map 4 G3

HOTELS
Hampton Inn Beach Boulevard/Mayo Clinic
13733 Beach Blvd, 32224; 904 223 0222; tinyurl.com/bo3jnlh
A 10-minute drive from the beach, this hotel is a great budget choice for its clean airy rooms and suites. There is an indoor heated pool, an on-site convenience store, and free hot breakfast.

🌐 🍴 🍽 **P** 😊 **$**

Omni Jacksonville Hotel
245 Water St, 32202; 904 355 6664; www.omnihotels.com
Located in downtown Jacksonville, a block from riverfront restaurants and shops, this four-diamond Omni boasts a roof-top pool, an upscale restaurant, and kid-friendly services.

🌐 🍴 🍽 ☕ 😊 **$$**

CAMPING
Kathryn Abbey Hanna Park
500 Wonderwood Dr, 32233; 904 249 4700; www.coj.net
Just north of Atlantic Beach, this popular park offers a full-facility campground, with tent and RV sites as well as cabins. A freshwater lake and great bike trails are added perks. Amenities include a general store, laundry, and showers. Reserve ahead.

🗄 **P** 😊 ☀ **$**

Jacksonville Beach
Map 4 H3

HOTEL
Fairfield Inn & Suites Jacksonville Beach
1616 1st St N, 32250; 866 539 0036; tinyurl.com/82ahnvr
Steps away from the beach and local restaurants, this hotel offers suites suitable for larger families and is good for longer stays. Free breakfast.

🌐 🍽 **P** 😊 **$–$$**

Cabin at the campsite in Blue Spring State Park, Ocala National Forest

Ocala
Map 5 D3

HOTEL
Courtyard Ocala
3712 SW 38th Ave, 34474; 352 237 8000; tinyurl.com/7dvptlo
Rooms and suites in this renovated hotel have flat-screen TVs and mini-refrigerators. The on-site restaurant, The Bistro, serves healthy breakfast choices and many dinner options.

🌐 🍽 ☕ **P** 😊 **$**

Orange City
Map 6 F4

CAMPING
Blue Spring State Park
2100 W French Ave, 32763; 386 775 3663; www.floridastateparks.org
This winter home of manatees offers 51 campsites within walking distance of the spring. The sites have water,

electricity, picnic tables, and grills. There is a library of picture books for kids ages 4 to 9.

🗄 **P** 😊 ☀ **$**

Ponte Vedra Beach
Map 4 H4

HOTEL
Sawgrass Marriott Golf Resort & Spa
1000 PGA Blvd, Ponte Vedra Beach, 32082; 386 775 3663; tinyurl.com/ 2qbqty
A top golf resort, this AAA three-diamond property is also terrific for a beach vacation, with a quick shuttle to the oceanfront club. The hotel offers high-quality kids' programs, a great spa, and an on-site restaurant.

🌐 🍽 ☕ 😊 **$$**

St. Augustine
Map 6 F1

HOTEL
Hilton St. Augustine Historic Bayfront
32 Avenida Menendez, 32084 904 829 2277; tinyurl.com/7od9wcd
Located in the historic district, this Hilton hotel makes a great base for exploring the nearby attractions. Rooms come with mini-refrigerators.

🌐 🍴 🍽 ☕ 😊 **$$$**

BED & BREAKFAST
Bayfront Marin House Bed and Breakfast
142 Avenida Menendez, 32084– 5049; 904 824 4301; www.bayfront marinhouse.com
This B&B welcomes kids with family-friendly accommodations, private entrances, and a gorgeous bayfront location. Efficient service.

🧺 🌐 🍽 **P** **$$–$$$**

CAMPING
Anastasia State Park
1340 Florida A1A, 32080; 904 461 2033; www.floridastateparks.org
A short walk from the beach, the campsites include utility hook-ups, grills, fire rings, and picnic tables. The park has a store/restaurant that also rents beach and sports equipment.

🍴 🗄 **P** 😊 ☀ **$**

Key to symbols *see back cover flap*

The Panhandle

The Panhandle has much to offer families besides miles of dazzling white beaches. This was where the Spanish first attempted to colonize Florida, and the region is rich in Spanish and Native American history. This northwest area, bordering the states of Georgia and Alabama, is also more Old South in spirit, with charm galore in cities such as Tallahassee and Pensacola, along with museums and aquariums for rainy days.

Highlights

Grayton Beach
The oldest town on the South Walton, the lanes here are paved with oyster shells and lined with historic cottages and modern beach homes (see p190).

Seaside
Admire pastel-colored cottages with picket fences in the town that was the film location for The Truman Show (see p190).

National Naval Aviation Museum
This museum, in Pensacola's Naval Air Station, traces aviation history with exhibits and hands-on training sessions (see pp196–7).

Gulf Islands National Seashore
Pick a spot to sunbathe on this 150-mile (240-km) paradise of pristine beach and dunes that can be accessed from Pensacola or Fort Walton (see p194).

Mission San Luis
A mission dating to the 1600s is brought to life by re-enacters in this site that was shared by the Spanish and the Apalachee Indians (see p200).

Wakulla Springs State Park
Take a riverboat tour or stand on the observation platform at this park, which has one of the world's deepest springs (see p202).

Left The Blue Angels flight demonstration team performing over Pensacola Beach
Above right Suwannee cooters sunning themselves on a log in Wakulla Springs State Park, Tallahassee

The Best of
The Panhandle

A driving tour is one of the best ways to sample the Panhandle's many fascinating facets. Families can choose between busy beach towns, serene villages, or cities that exude Southern charm. Tallahassee, the state capital, is steeped in history; Pensacola has a marvelous military museum; and Apalachicola offers the ambience of a traditional fishing town. The region's scenic state parks have pristine beaches, and are meccas for wildlife.

Outdoor action

The Panhandle's state parks contain unspoiled beaches and a rare feature – coastal dune lakes, 15 of which are found in the region. The lakes provide beautiful vistas, an abundance of bird life, and opportunities for canoeing or kayaking. **Lake Powell** (see p193), near Panama City, is the largest of the lakes, Western Lake in **Grayton Beach State Park** (see p190) is one of the loveliest, and **Topsail Hill Preserve State Park** (see p191), near Santa Rosa, boasts five scenic ponds. The state parks have miles of trails for hiking and biking. The Panhandle also has uncrowded beaches to escape to. **Shell Island** (see p193), reached by ferry from **St. Andrew's State Park** (see pp192–3) in Panama City, is pure bliss for shell collectors. **St. George Island State Park** (see p203), a

barrier island near **Apalachicola** (see p203), has 9 miles (14 km) of tranquil beach and dunes, and the many miles of the **Gulf Islands National Seashore** (see p194) offer plenty of peace.

Historic highlights

This area provides many opportunities to see some of the best-preserved traces of Florida's first inhabitants. **Indian Temple Mound Museum** (see p191) in Fort Walton marks what was once the center of one of the largest Native American communities. The mound, 17 ft (5 m) tall and 223 ft (68 m) long, is one of the biggest ever found. More Native American lore awaits at **Lake Jackson Mounds Archaeological State Park** (see p199) near **Tallahassee** (see pp198–9). A few miles away is

Below Spanish moss-draped trees shading the reflection pond in Eden Gardens State Park

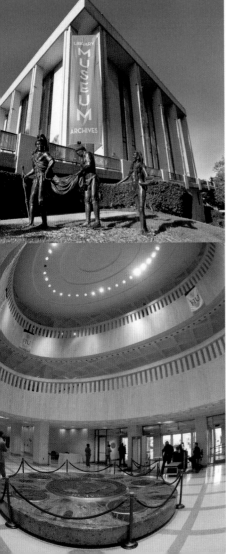

Top National Naval Aviation Museum, Pensacola **Left** *Sculptures from the Indian Heritage Tableau by Bradley Cooley and Bradley Cooley Jr. outside the Museum of Florida History, Tallahassee* **Below** *Rotunda of the Florida State Capitol, Tallahassee*

the **Letchworth-Love Mounds Archaeological State Park** *(see p199)* in Monticello with the tallest recorded ceremonial mound.

Saluting the military

Two major military bases in the Panhandle are home to museums with great family appeal. The **National Naval Aviation Museum** *(see pp196–7)*, at Pensacola's Naval Air Station, has historic planes on display. In addition, there are flight simulators which offer visitors of all ages the thrill of experiencing air combat and stunt flying. For a slice of Pensacola's early military history, visit **Fort Barrancas** *(see p197)*, which dates from the Civil War, and **Fort Pickens** *(see p195)*, once a prison for Apache chief Geronimo. Located at Eglin Air Force base in Fort Walton is the **Air Force Armament Museum** *(see p192)*, with fighters, bombers, and spy planes.

Southern comfort

Visitors looking for Southern charm can head to **Tallahassee** and **Pensacola** *(see pp194–5)*, which show the influence of their southern neighbors. A city of rolling hills and canopy roads, **Tallahassee** has antebellum homes dating from its cotton and tobacco plantation days, such as **Goodwood Museum and Gardens** *(see p198)*, as well as the **Park Avenue Historic District** *(see p198)*, with parks and elegant pre-Civil War architecture. There is no mistaking the Southern sway in the accents and genteel tempo of **Pensacola**, as seen in the historic district's architectural styles, and in entertaining museums with unusual and educational exhibits.

The Panhandle

The Panhandle stretches for some 300 miles (483 km) across the northwest corner of the state, between the Gulf of Mexico and the southern states of Alabama and Georgia. Most families head straight for the beach resorts that extend in an arc between Pensacola and Panama City, but the less-explored interior – a hilly, pine-forested landscape unusual in Florida – also offers plenty of recreation. Though the region is large, excellent highways make it easy to navigate by car: I-10 links Tallahassee and Pensacola, and Highway 98 serves the beach towns.

A parrot at ZooWorld Zoological & Botanical Conservatory

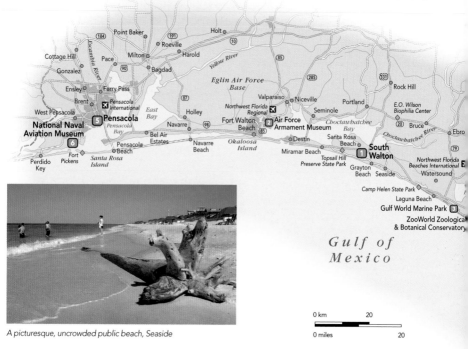

Gulf of Mexico

0 km 20

0 miles 20

A picturesque, uncrowded public beach, Seaside

The Lowdown

Getting there and around
Air Fly to Pensacola Gulf Coast Regional Airport (PNS) (www.flypensacola.com), Northwest Florida Beaches International Airport (ECP) (www.iflybeaches.com) in Panama City, Northwest Florida Regional Airport (VPS) (www.flyvps.com) in Fort Walton Beach, and Tallahassee Regional Airport (TLH) (www.talgov.com/airport).
Car A rental car is essential to get around. Car rentals are available at all airports.

i **Visitor information** See individual entries.

Supermarkets Publix (www.publix.com) is the premier supermarket throughout this region.
Markets Head to Palafox Market, in Pensacola (www.palafoxmarket.com), Tallahassee Downtown Market (www.downtownmarket.com), Tallahassee Farmers' Market, north of I-10 off US 319 (www.localharvest.org/tallahassee-farmers-market-M1165), Okaloosa County Farmers' Market (Apr–Sep) in Fort Walton Beach, or Seaside Farmers' Market in Santa Rosa Beach for fruit, meats, breads, books, and fine art. Most markets are open on Saturdays.

Festivals Pollywoggle Watermelon Music Fest, Panama City; 850 249 3768 (Jun). Blue Angels Air Show, National Naval Aviation Museum (Jul). Wausau Possum Festival; www.wausaupossumfestival.com (Aug). North Florida Fair, Tallahassee (Nov)

Pharmacies Walgreens (www.walgreens.com) and CVS (www.cvs.com) are the two major pharmacies in the region.

Restrooms All major attractions, shopping malls, and gas stations have public restrooms.

Places of interest

At the water's edge in Wakulla Springs State Park, Tallahassee

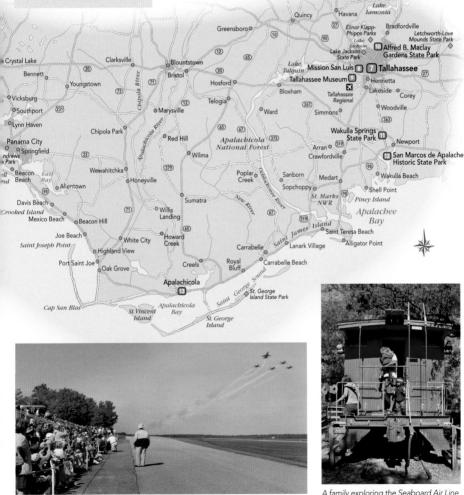

A Blue Angels Air Show in progress at the National Naval Aviation Museum, Pensacola

A family exploring the Seaboard Air Line caboose, Tallahassee Museum

① South Walton
Sparkling beaches and village charm

Lying between the high-rise buildings in Fort Walton and Panama City are 26 miles (42 km) of the finest beaches in Florida. The South Walton shoreline boasts sand that is almost pure quartz crystal, dazzling white to the eye, and soft underfoot. Lined with a string of low-rise, quiet villages, the beaches are great for families. Just under half of the region is preserved as state parks and forests, and opportunities for recreation are plentiful.

Grayton Beach, a charming beach town

Key Sights

① **Baytowne Wharf** This lively enclave along the shores of Choctawhatchee Bay has boutiques, eateries, and the Baytowne Wharf Adventure Zone with a climbing wall and a zip line for adventure-lovers.

② **The Artists at Gulf Place** This cooperative artists' colony and open-air market in Santa Rosa Beach is one of many colorful spots in South Walton where local art is featured.

③ **Grayton Beach** A laid-back town with narrow, oyster-shell-paved lanes, this is the oldest community on the shore. Here, weathered cottages blend with modern beach houses, shaded by pine and oaks.

④ **Grayton Beach State Park** Award-winning beaches, pine forest, and a nature trail through the dunes with views of scenic Western Lake make this park a special retreat.

⑤ **Eden Gardens State Park** The restored, antique-filled Wesley House, a typical Southern mansion of the 19th century, inspires visions of hoop skirts and Scarlett O'Hara in *Gone With the Wind*. Picnic along Tucker Bayou, and explore a nature trail and lush gardens shaded by moss-draped live oaks.

⑥ **Seaside** Developed in the 1980s, this planned village has quaint pastel-colored cottages, and lanes laced with sandy paths that lead to the beach, shops, and restaurants.

⑦ **Timpoochee Trail** Running the full length of Scenic Highway 30A, this superb 23-mile (37-km) bike path winds through the beach communities, along coastal dune lakes, and through picturesque scenery with views of the Gulf of Mexico.

⑧ **Rosemary Beach** Inspired by the Seaside model of a walkable village, this town has a mix of architecture, some with a New Orleans influence, and a wide village green.

The Lowdown

🌐 **Map reference** 1 D3
Address Baytowne Wharf: 9300 US Hwy 98 W, Destin, 32550; www.baytownewharf. com. The Artists at Gulf Place: 40 Town Loop Center, 32459; www.artistsatgulfplace.com. Grayton Beach State Park: 357 Main Park Rd, 32459; floridastateparks.org. Eden Gardens State Park:181 Eden Gardens Rd, 32459; floridastateparks.org

🚗 **Car** Rent a car from Northwest Florida Regional Airport.

🕐 **Open** Grayton Beach State Park & Eden Gardens State Park: 8am–sunset

💲 **Prices** Grayton Beach State Park & Eden Gardens State Park: $5 per vehicle. Baytowne Wharf Adventure Zone: check www.tinyurl.com/BWharfAdv.

🤸 **Activities** Hiking, canoeing, and kayaking in the state parks.

Good family value?
South Walton combines beach fun and sightseeing for the whole family, with few expenses.

Prices given are for a family of four

View of the Gulf of Mexico from Deer Lake State Park, Santa Rosa Beach

Letting off steam

Deer Lake State Park (6350 E County Rd, 30-A, Santa Rosa Beach, 32459; 850 267 8300) and **Point Washington State Forest**, south of Freeport on I-98, have excellent hiking paths. For canoeing and kayaking, head to **Topsail Hill Preserve State Park** (7525 W Scenic Hwy 30-A, Santa Rosa Beach, 32459; 850 267 8330).

Eat and drink

Picnic: under $25; Snacks: $25–50; Real meal: $50–80; Family treat: over $80 (based on a family of four)

PICNIC Modica Market (109 Central Square, Seaside, 32459; 850 231 1214) offers fixings to enjoy a fine picnic at the Seaside beach.

SNACKS Pickles Beachside Grill (2236 Scenic Hwy 30-A, Seaside, 32459; 850 231 5686; www.sweet williamsltd.com) has hot dogs, chili cheese dogs, burgers, fried pickles, and funnel cakes.

REAL MEAL Bud & Alley's (2236 E County Rd, 30-A, Seaside; 850 231 5900; www.budandalleys.com) is a great spot for lunch on the deck with sandwiches and a pizza-pasta bar. There is also a kids' menu.

FAMILY TREAT Fish Out of Water (Watercolor Inn, off Scenic Hwy 30-A, Watercolor, 32459; 850 534 5050) serves up the area's best gourmet dinner fare – fresh seafood, chicken and beef – in comfortable, informal settings with wonderful sea views.

Shopping

Big Mama's Hula Girl Gallery (3031 E Hwy 30-A, Seagrove Beach, 33308; 850 231 6201) is just one of the funky galleries that abound in South Walton's villages, with folk art that will delight all ages. Bargain-hunters can head to **Silver Sands**

Factory Stores (10562 Emerald Coast Pkwy, 32550; 850 654 9771) for popular brands such as Esprit, Gap Kids, and OshKosh B'gosh.

Find out more

FILM The town of Seaside was the set for *The Truman Show*, a satirical comedy starring Jim Carrey, Ed Harris, and Laura Linney.

Take cover

Take a 15-mile (24-km) drive inland to the **E.O. Wilson Biophilia Center** (4956 State Hwy 20, 32439; 850 835 1824; www.eowilsoncenter.org) for nature dioramas, a working beehive, live turtles, snakes, and frogs, as well as films about nature.

Brightly colored interior of Pickles Beachside Grill, Seaside

Next stop...

INDIAN TEMPLE MOUND MUSEUM Located in Fort Walton, the Indian Temple Mound Museum (139 Miracle Strip Pkwy SE, Fort Walton Beach, 32548; 850 833 9595; www.friendsofthemuseums.org) is on the site of a ceremonial and burial earthwork built by early Native Americans of the Mound Builder Culture, who lived between AD 800 and 1400. The museum has objects crafted from stone, bones, shell, and clay from this culture, as well as finds relating to the region's early explorers, and the later settlers.

Inside the cockpit of an aircraft at the Air Force Armament Museum, Fort Walton

② Air Force Armament Museum

Take flight

This museum is located on the Eglin Air Force Base, home of the Air Armament Center (AAC), which is responsible for the development of air-delivered weapons. Start outside the building, where there is a lineup of over 20 military planes to inspect. These date from World War I to the present, and include the SR-71 Blackbird, the fastest plane ever built. It can fly at over 2,200 mph (3,520 kmph)! Inside the museum are four more vintage aircraft and an amazing collection of bombs, missiles, and rockets, as well as interactive displays including one that works the controls of a mock cockpit. Check out other fascinating exhibits, such as "bunker busters," bombs that can hit targets deep underground. There is also a 30-minute film that illustrates the AAC's history and accomplishments.

Letting off steam

Head off 5 miles (8 km) south to **Okaloosa Island**, Fort Walton's beach community. This long strand stretching out to the neighboring town of Destin is accessed by bridges at each end. There is plenty of space on the beach for running around, and quiet picnic areas. The less crowded beaches are closer to Destin. Visit the **Gulfarium Marine Adventure Park** (www.gulfarium.com), a small

The Lowdown

- 🌐 **Map reference** 1 C3
- **Address** 100 Museum Dr (State Rd 85), Eglin Air Force Base, 32542; 850 651 1808; www.afarmamentmuseum.com
- 🚗 **Car** From Fort Walton Beach
- 🕐 **Open** 9:30am–4:30pm Mon–Sat
- 💲 **Price** Free
- 👪 **Age range** 8 plus
- ⏲ **Allow** 2–3 hours
- ♿ **Wheelchair access** Yes
- ☕ **Eat and drink** PICNIC Publix (610 Eglin Pkwy NE, Fort Walton Beach, 32547; 850 862 6789; www.publix.com), one of the Florida-wide supermarket chains, is well stocked with goodies for a picnic at Okaloosa Island. REAL MEAL IHOP (348 SW Miracle Strip Pkwy, Fort Walton Beach, 32548; 850 243 9333; www.ihop.com) serves pancakes day and night, along with omelets, sandwiches, and burgers. The kids' menu features a "Create a Face" pancake with strawberry eyes and a banana smile.

Dolphin at the Gulfarium Marine Adventure Park, Destin

aquarium, and the diminutive but fun **Emerald Coast Science Center** (www.ecscience.org) nearby.

③ Gulf World Marine Park

A kiss from a seal

Dolphins show off flips and leaps, seals kiss willing spectators, and parrots and reptiles perform in the daily live shows that are the specialty of this aquarium. There is also a delightful magic show that features spectacular illusions, comedy acts, special effects, and interactions with the audience. The aquarium's inhabitants include sharks, alligators, penguins, iguanas, and sea turtles. Watch shark and sea turtle feeding sessions, as well as underwater scuba demonstrations, before heading for the stingrays that await visitors in their petting pool.

Letting off steam

Drive 9 miles (14 km) to **St. Andrews State Park** (4607 State Park Lane, 32408; 850 233 5140; www.floridastateparks.org/standrews), on the eastern tip of busy Panama City

The Lowdown

- 🌐 **Map reference** 2 E3
- **Address** 15412 Front Beach Rd, Panama City Beach, 32413; 850 234 5271; www.gulfworldmarinepark.com
- 🚗 **Car** From Fort Walton Beach
- 🕐 **Open** 9am–7pm in summer; 9:30am–5pm rest of the year
- 💲 **Price** $92–112; under 4s free
- 👫 **Activities** Kids aged 5 plus can sign up for the Swim with the Dolphins program. Check website for details.
- 👪 **Age range** All ages
- ⏲ **Allow** 3–4 hours
- ♿ **Wheelchair access** Yes
- ☕ **Eat and drink** PICNIC Publix (23026 Panama City Beach Pkwy, 32413; 850 233 4392; www.publix.com) has all the ingredients for a fine picnic at the beach. REAL MEAL Schooners (5121 Gulf Dr, Panama City Beach, 32408; 850 235 3555; www.schooners.com), an informal eatery on the waterfront, has something for everyone. It serves salads, wings, burgers, grouper sandwiches, and fish tacos.

Beach. The park's beach is relatively quiet, and offers opportunities for canoeing and kayaking, as well as two nature trails. Take the shuttle (850 233 0504) to **Shell Island** for a spot of beachcombing and a rock jetty that creates a shallow area in the water perfect for young kids.

④ ZooWorld Zoological & Botanical Conservatory
A small animal kingdom

This little local zoo offers up-close views of over 250 animals in a tropical garden setting. Children can learn all about parrots, reptiles, and alligators at the live shows, and even pose for pictures with them. The petting zoo houses lots of farm animals for feeding, as well as a camel. A raised walkway allows for a special treat: feeding Sydney the giraffe. The zoo is especially recommended for younger children.

The historic Lodge in Camp Helen State Park

The Lowdown

🌐 **Map reference** 2 E4
Address 9008 Front Beach Rd, Panama City Beach, 32407; 850 233 1243; www.zooworldpcb.net

🚗 **Car** From Fort Walton Beach

🕐 **Open** 9:30am–4pm Mon–Sat & 11am–4pm Sun

💲 **Price** $50–60; under 4s free

🧑‍🤝‍🧑 **Activities** The zoo organizes many educational animal shows; check website for schedule.

🚹🚺 **Age range** 3 plus

⏱ **Allow** 3 hours

☕ **Eat and drink** SNACKS Mike's Café and Oyster Bar (17554 Front Beach Rd, Panama City Beach, 32413; 850 234 1942; www.mikescafeandoysterbar.com) has simple, diner-like decor and lunch choices such as seafood baskets, salads, and sandwiches to please grown-ups, as well as a bargain children's menu. FAMILY TREAT Captain Anderson's Restaurant (5551 N Lagoon Dr, Panama City Beach, 32408; 850 234 2225; www.captanderson.com; closed Sun) is a longtime local dinner favorite for steaks and the freshest of seafood. The restaurant claims to serve the "world's best seafood platter." Kids will find their own special menu.

Letting off steam

Go 14 miles (22 km) northwest to **Camp Helen State Park** (www.floridastateparks.org/camphelen), which is bordered by the Gulf of Mexico on three sides, and by Lake Powell, one of the largest coastal dune lakes in Florida. A private company resort from 1945 until 1984, the huge park offers lots of space for picnicking, as well as swimming, beachcombing, fishing, and hiking.

Wolf Show at the ZooWorld Zoological & Botanical Conservatory, Panama City Beach

⑤ Pensacola
Beaches and the Blue Angels

A distinct Southern accent borrowed from the neighboring state of Alabama, and influences from a colorful past, give Pensacola a unique flavor. The Historic Pensacola Village, its oldest quarter, comprises 27 buildings and museums reflecting 450 years of history. Two of the city's best family attractions are the superb sands of the Gulf Islands National Seashore and tours of the National Naval Aviation Museum (see pp196–7), where the famous Blue Angels stunt flyers practice.

Costumed guides in the Historic Pensacola Village

Key Sights

Museum of Commerce This reconstruction of Pensacola's late 19th- and early 20th-century streetscape features a print workshop, and leather and harness shops.

Pensacola Children's Museum Its many imaginative exhibits and dress-up period clothing make this museum a great place to take younger kids.

Museum of Industry These exhibits depict the industries that helped build the city – fishing, brick-making, lumber, and railroads – including a vintage fishing boat, and a 1905 locomotive.

Seville Square The heart of Pensacola when the area was first settled by the Spanish, this square served as the parade ground for the Fort of Pensacola during British rule in the 1770s.

British Officer's Compound Built during the early years of the American Revolution, this compound's foundations are among the many finds that form Pensacola's Colonial Archaeological Trail.

GOVERNMENT ST

JEFFERSON ST

ZARAGOZA ST

Seville Square

Barkley House

Museum of Industry

Museum of Commerce

Pensacola Museum of Art Once a jail, this building now houses contemporary art, decorative glass, and African tribal art.

Barkley House Built in 1825, this is the oldest surviving example of a "high-house" in the city. Tours of the Historic Pensacola Village include a stop at the house, where visitors can learn about the Barkley family.

Letting off steam

The US 98, leading south to Pensacola Beach on Santa Rosa Island, passes through the community of Gulf Breeze, and the glorious **Gulf Islands National Seashore**. Go to the **Naval Live Oaks** area (www.nps.gov), on the US 98 east of Gulf Breeze, for miles of picturesque nature trails and swimming in Santa Rosa Sound. There is also a campground with a covered picnic pavilion, restrooms, and outdoor showers. Maps are available at the park's **Visitor Center** (1801 Gulf Breeze Pkwy, 32561; 850 934 2600).

Prices given are for a family of four

Enjoying a meal at the popular New Yorker Deli & Pizzeria

Eat and drink

Picnic: under $25; Snacks: $25–50; Real meal: $50–80; Family treat: over $80 (based on a family of four)

PICNIC New Yorker Deli & Pizzeria (3001 E Cervantes St, 32503; 850 469 0029) offers a variety of sandwiches for a picnic in Seville Square.
SNACKS Santino's Pizza (Bruno's Shopping Center, 368 Gulf Breeze Pkwy, Gulf Breeze, 32561; 850 932 1211; www.santinospizza.net) serves pizzas, salads, and brownies.
REAL MEAL Dharma Blue (300 S Alcaniz St, 32501; 850 433 1275) is located in leafy Seville Square, and

offers a wide-ranging menu, from sandwiches to paella. There is an appealing children's menu too. **FAMILY TREAT Fish House** (*600 S Barracks St, 32502; 850 470 0003; www.goodgrits.com*), on the bay, serves the freshest Gulf seafood, with Southern sides such as cheese grits, collard greens, and corn fritters.

Shopping
The **Quayside Art Gallery** (*17 E Zarragossa St, 32502; www.quayside gallery.com*) is southeastern Florida's largest cooperative artists' gallery. Go to the **Blue Moon Antique Mall** (*3721 W Navy Blvd, 32507; 850 455 7377*) for old postcards, toys, jewelry, vintage pottery, and glassware.

Find out more
DIGITAL Learn about Pensacola's history at *www.visitpensacola.com/ articles/pensacola-history*. Visit *uwf.edu/anthropology/research/ colonial/trail* to find out about the discoveries along the Colonial Archaeological Trail.

Next stop...
FORT PICKENS World War II gun emplacements are some of the military artifacts that come to life at Fort Pickens (*www.npa.gov*), 8 miles (13 km) southwest of Pensacola. Completed in 1834, it was the largest of four forts built to defend Pensacola Bay. National Park Service Rangers lead tours at 2pm daily.

Outer walls of Fort Pickens, a massive brick fort at Gulf Islands National Seashore

The Lowdown

🌐 **Map reference** 1 A3
Address Pensacola 32502. Museum of Commerce: 201 E Zaragoza St; 850 595 1559. Pensacola Children's Museum: 115, E Zaragoza St; 850 595 1559. Museum of Industry: 120 E Church St; 850 595 5985. Pensacola Museum of Art: 407 South Jefferson St; 850 432 6247; *www.pensacolamuseumof art.org*. Barkley House: 10 S Florida Blanca St; 850 595 5993, call ahead; *historicpensacola.org*

🚗 **Bus** Escambia County Area Transit (ECAT) buses serve many areas, but the wait between buses can be an hour or more. It's best to rent a car.

ℹ️ **Visitor information** Pensacola Bay Area Convention and Visitors Bureau, 1401 E Gregory St, 32502; 800 874 1234; *www.visitpensacola.com*

🕐 **Open** Tickets for visiting the sights in the Historic Pensacola Village can be purchased at the Tivoli High House Gift Shop (205

E Zaragoza St, 32502; 850 595 5993; 10am–4pm Tue–Sat).

💲 **Price** Historic Pensacola Village: $18–24; under 4s free. An individual visit to the T.T. Wentworth, Jr. Florida State Museum is free.

🚩 **Guided tours** The village runs 1–1½-hour tours at 11am, 1pm & 2:30pm, which include the Lavalle House, the 1871 Dorr House, the 1832 Old Christ Church & the 1890 Lear-Rocheblave House. Walking tours, at 2pm, cover Zaragoza Street and the Barkley House.

👫 **Age range** 6 plus

⏱️ **Allow** 1 day

🎪 **Festival** Blue Angels Air Shows (Jul & Nov)

Good family value?
Reasonably priced tickets, free museum visits and a walk through the historical district, all make Pensacola an exciting destination.

⑥ National Naval Aviation Museum
Spacecraft and fighter planes

Located at the Pensacola Naval Air Station, a training ground for the US Navy and Marine Corps, this museum traces the history of aviation with thrilling displays. Its amazing exhibits include over 150 restored aircraft and spacecraft, dating from the era of the earliest biplanes to the Space Age, and a Mercury space capsule. Hands-on elements include the chance to sit at the controls of a jet trainer, while practice sessions by the daredevil Blue Angel stunt pilots add to the excitement.

A Blue Angel pilot signing autographs

Key Features

■ **Upper Level** Hall of Honor, Medal of Honor, Art Gallery, Flight Adventure Deck, Flight Simulator, and Cockpit Trainers

■ **Main Deck Level** WWII–Korean Aircraft, Sunken Treasure, USS Cabot Flight Deck, Early Aircraft, Modern Aircraft, and Museum Store

Entrance

① **MaxFlight Simulator** High-tech video and real motion simulate the feeling of being on a mission in a high-speed fighter plane.

② **Sunken Treasure** The two aircraft displayed here were used for training during World War II before they sank in Lake Michigan. They were recovered from the lake, remarkably well preserved by the cold water.

③ **Cockpit Trainers** Kids can climb into a cockpit, including that of the A-4 Skyhawk and Corsair II, in this simulated flying experience.

④ **The IMAX® Theater** Four different features are shown daily on one of the largest IMAX® screens in the world. *The Magic of Flight* is a regular on the schedule.

⑤ **Blue Angels** Check out the display of four A-4 Skyhawks, used by the Blue Angels, suspended from the ceiling of a seven-story glass atrium.

⑥ **USS Cabot Flight Deck** See the replica of a flight deck, and the superstructure of a World War II aircraft carrier, complete with fighter planes.

⑦ **Space Capsule Display** Here, space exploration exhibits include a Skylab Command Module, a Mercury capsule, and a Moon Rover vehicle. Astronaut suits and memorabilia are also on display.

⑧ **Biplane** With one wing fixed above the other, biplanes were important early aircraft used in World War I. They are favorites in barnstorming air shows today.

The Lowdown

🌐 **Map reference** 1 A3
Address 1750 Radford Blvd, Suite C, Naval Air Station, 32508; 850 452 3604; www. navalaviationmuseum.org

🚌 **Bus** ECAT bus 57. **Car** Rent a car from Pensacola Gulf Coast Regional Airport.

🕐 **Open** 9am–5pm daily

💲 **Price** Free

👥 **Cutting the line** Arrive early as seats fill up fast for the Blue

Angels practice flights (Mar–Nov: 8:30am Tue–Wed). Pilots often come out afterward to shake hands and sign autographs.

🔫 **Guided tours** Daily 20-min trolley tours of 50 aircraft outdoors at 9:30 & 11am, 1 & 2:30pm. Self-guided tours can be downloaded from the museum's website.

👫 **Age range** 6 plus

🏃 **Activities** Flight Adventure Deck tour at 1pm, 2pm & 3pm Mon–Fri, in which trained volunteers

introduce visitors to hands-on exhibits. Watch the practice flights, weather permitting.

⏱ **Allow** At least 4 hours

♿ **Wheelchair access** Yes

☕ **Café** Cubi Bar Café (see p197)

🚻 **Restrooms** On every level

Good family value?
The free museum is entertaining and watching the Blue Angels is an unforgettable experience.

The kid-friendly Cubi Bar Café at the National Naval Aviation Museum

Letting off steam

If kids need a break, head 8 miles (13 km) west to the **Perdido Kids Park** *(3453 Nighthawk Lane, 32506)* on Perdido Key. An imaginative multilevel wooden play area, it includes climbing areas such as mock forts, a lighthouse, a pirate ship, and Blue Angels planes. There is also a special toddler area, designed for children aged 2 to 5.

Eat and drink

Picnic: under $25; Snacks: $25–50; Real meal: $50–80; Family treat: over $80 (based on a family of four)

PICNIC Winn-Dixie Market *(50 S Blue Angel Pkwy, 32506; 850 458 1375)* offers the makings of a picnic that can be enjoyed on the museum's lawn.
SNACKS Cubi Bar Café *(Main Deck Level)* serves nachos, hot dogs, sandwiches, and salads in a setting similar to the bar area of the famous Cubi Point Officers' Club. Kids love the Whirly Bird, a make-your-own peanut butter and jelly sandwich.
REAL MEAL Roberts Catfish and Seafood *(4539 Saufley Field Rd, 32526; 850 455 1717; www.roberts seafood.webs.com)* offers seafood, burgers, and fried chicken.
FAMILY TREAT Jackson's Steak House *(400 S Palafox St, 32502; 850 469 9898; jacksons.goodgrits.com)*, in Pensacola's Historic District, serves prime steaks with prices to match. Children can order half portions.

Shopping

Everyone will enjoy the **Museum Shop**, which is well stocked with caps and T-shirts for all ages, kids' clothing from infant bodysuits to aviator

jackets, Blue Angels souvenirs, DVDs, flags, posters, and toys. The cute aviator bears wearing goggles, helmet, and scarf are irresistible.

Find out more

DIGITAL Learn about the exciting Blue Angels flight team and see a demo flight on *www.blueangels. navy.mil*. The museum website, *www.navalaviationmuseum.com*, has an electronic scrapbook with photos of important events in aviation history.

Entrance to the historic Fort Barrancas in Pensacola Bay

Next stop...

FORT BARRANCAS Located near the National Naval Aviation Museum, Fort Barrancas *(3182 Taylor Rd, 32508; 850 455 5167; www.forttours.com)* is a two-part fort worth exploring. Its strategic location on a bluff overlooking Pensacola Bay inspired three nations – Britain, Spain, and the US – to build forts here. The Visitor Center screens an informative film. The Spanish Water Battery is a gentle 500-ft (15-m) walk, while the overlook near the fort's entrance offers beautiful views of Pensacola Bay.

⑦ Tallahassee

Tons of Southern charm

Encircled by rolling hills and dotted with pine forests, this state capital has a rich Southern flavor. This former site of an Apalachee Indian settlement is now home to several historical museums. Located in the heart of the city, and spreading over several landscaped blocks, the Capitol Complex offers much to see and do for all ages. Pretty gardens, the nearby beaches, beautiful canopied roads, and a wide choice of dining are further lures to this city.

The canopied Meridian Road, Tallahassee

Key Sights

④ Florida Historic Capitol Museum
See the house and senate chambers, the governor's suite, and the supreme court, all restored just as they were in the state's original columned capitol.

⑤ Park Avenue Historic District
This central chain of green parks is lined with 27 homes that predate the Civil War. Built around 1830, the oldest one, The Columns, houses the James Madison Institute.

① Florida State University
This university is noted for its highly regarded music and theater departments, which stage concerts and plays during the school year.

⑥ Lake Ella
One of Tallahassee's many lakes, Lake Ella is centered by a spraying fountain and circled by a paved walking trail. The surrounding park has picnic tables and some quaint shops.

⑦ Goodwood Museum and Gardens
Discover what life was like for kids in the South long ago in this 1834 plantation house, where much of the original art and furnishings have been restored.

② Museum of Florida History
Prehistoric mastodons, Native American exhibits, and a replica riverboat brings the state's past to life in this excellent museum.

③ Florida State Capitol
Built in 1977, this tower houses art exhibits on the main floor. The 22nd floor observation deck offers views for miles around.

Prices given are for a family of four

The Lowdown

🌐 **Map reference** 3 A3
Address Florida State University: 600 W College Ave, 32306; www.fsu.edu. Museum of Florida History: 500 South Bronough St, 32399; www.museumoffloridahistory.com. Florida Historic Capitol Museum: 400 South Monroe St, 32399; www.flhistoriccapitol.gov. Goodwood Museum and Gardens: 1600 Miccosukee Rd, 32308; www.goodwoodmuseum.org

🚗 **Car** Rent a car from the Tallahassee Regional Airport.
Bus Star Metro (talgov.com) buses cover much of the city.

ℹ️ **Visitor information** Tallahassee Visitor Information Center, 106 E Jefferson St, 32301; 800 628 2866; www.visittallahassee.com

🕐 **Open** Museum of Florida History and Florida Historic Capitol Museum: 9am–4:30pm Mon–Fri, 10am–4:30pm Sat & noon–4:30pm Sun. Goodwood Museum and Gardens: 10am–4pm Mon–Fri & 10am–2pm Sat

💲 **Prices** Museum of Florida History & Florida Historic Capitol Museum: free. Goodwood Museum and Gardens: $18–24; under 3s free

🚩 **Guided tours** Florida State Capitol's Welcome Center has self-guided tour brochures.

⏱️ **Allow** 2–3 days

🚻 **Restrooms** In the museums and public parks

Good family value?
Most attractions are free and the city offers a unique look at American history.

Dog Et Al, a popular spot for hot dogs in Tallahassee

Letting off steam

Tallahassee has an excellent park system with wooded areas and lakes. **Tom Brown Park** (*1125 Easterwood Dr, 32312*) has tennis courts, and nature trails. The **Elinor Klapp-Phipps Park** (*4000 N Meridian Rd, 32308*) offers 10 miles (16 km) of trails, including Bluebird and Butterfly trails.

Take cover

Visit the **Challenger Learning Center** (*200 S Duval St, 32301; 850 645 7827; www.challengertlh.com*), which features shows such as Hubble Space Telescope at its IMAX® Theater.

Eat and drink

Picnic: under $25; Snacks: $25–50; Real meal: $50–80; Family treat: over $80 (based on a family of four)

PICNIC Publix Super Market (*1700 N Monroe St, 32303; 850 222 1975; www.publix.com; 7am–11pm daily*) has ingredients for a picnic that can be savored with a view at Lake Ella.
SNACKS Dog Et Al (*1456 S Monroe St, 32301; 850 222 4099; 10am–6pm Mon–Sat*) serves great hot dogs with a variety of toppings.
REAL MEAL Romano's Macaroni Grill (*1498 Apalachee Pkwy, 32301; 850 877 1706; www.macaronigrill.com; 11am–10pm daily*) has pizza, pasta, and classic Italian dishes. It also has a kids' menu.
FAMILY TREAT Mozaik (*1410 D1 Market St, 32312; 850 893 7668; www.dinemozaik.com*) offers New American cuisine made with fresh local ingredients.

Shopping

Head for **Market Square** (*1415 Timberlane Rd, 32312; 850 906 2453*), where kids will like the toys and the soda fountain treats at Lofty Pursuits. **Governor's Square Mall** (*1500 Apalachee Pkwy, 32301; 850 877 8106*) has stores such as Justice, for tweens, and Lids, a world of sports team caps.

Find out more

DIGITAL Learn about Florida's ancient Native American settlements and ceremonial mounds at *lostworlds. org/ancient_civilizations_florida*.

Pathway at Lake Jackson Mounds Archaeological State Park

Next stop...

MOUNDS OF HISTORY Head 6 miles (7 km) north to **Lake Jackson Mounds Archaeological State Park** to learn about Native American history. The site of an important ceremonial center, it has two remaining large mounds and one smaller mound. Visitors can hike the nature trails and picnic near the two large mounds. Go 22 miles (35 km) east to **Letchworth-Love Mounds Archaeological State Park**, which has one of the largest surviving mounds in Florida. The mound is a truncated pyramid and rises over 42 ft (13 m). Visit *www.florida stateparks.org* for more details.

Animal fur on display next to the chief's dais, Mission San Luis

A re-enactor dressed as a blacksmith in Mission San Luis

⑧ Mission San Luis
Time travel back to the 1600s

Costumed interpreters bring to life a reconstruction of one of Florida's rarest sites: a 1600s mission that was shared by Spanish settlers and the native Apalachee Indians. This unusual cooperation worked because the Spanish needed labor and provisions while the Apalachee Indians wanted peace and prestige. The arrangement lasted until 1704,

The Lowdown

- 🌐 **Map reference** 3 A3
  Address 2100 West Tennessee St, 32304; 850 245 6406; www.missionsanluis.org
- 🚗 **Car** Rent a car from Tallahassee Regional Airport.
- 🕐 **Open** 10am–4pm Tue–Sun
- 💲 **Price** $14–20; under 6s free
- 🎭 **Activities** Choose from musket firing demonstrations (11am–noon Sat), Historical Happenings presentations, Colonial crafts for children, archaeology lab tours, historic gardening tours, blacksmithing, and historical cooking classes. Check website for schedules.
- 👫 **Age range** 6 plus
- ⏱ **Allow** 2–3 hours
- 🍴 **Eat and drink** PICNIC Publix Super Market (800 Ocala Rd, 32304; 850 575 6997; www.publix.com) offers the makings for a lunch to be enjoyed at picnic tables in the Mission grounds. REAL MEAL Wells Brothers (1710 W Tharpe St, 32303; 850 942 6665; www.wellsbrothersbarandgrill.com) serves salads, sandwiches, burgers, and burritos.
- 🎉 **Festival** Winter Solstice Celebration, a festival of Native American culture (Dec)

when both groups fled from British invaders. See the enormous, five-story Indian Council House with its palm-thatched roof. It stands next to a Franciscan church that was constructed by the Apalachee Indians under Spanish supervision. The defensive fort, El Castillo de San Luis, has been re-created, and a Spanish home and working gardens portray everyday life in a community of 1,600 people. The excellent on-site museum traces the archaeological excavations of the area and displays artifacts found during the digs, such as tools and pottery.

Letting off steam

While the paths of the vast grounds provide plenty of scope for exercise, any excess energy can be expended on a nature trail in the wooded area behind the Spanish home. Pick up a brochure in the Visitor Center to identify some of the dozens of butterfly species that can be spotted here.

⑨ Tallahassee Museum
A farm, a plantation, and a zoo – in a museum

Popular with children, this sprawling, multifaceted museum can entertain for hours. Visit farm animals such as cows, sheep, goats, and pigs in the Big Bend Farm, an 1880s farm complete with reconstructed and restored buildings. The garden grows crops such as corn, cotton, and sugarcane. The museum also has a zoo that features Florida wildlife in natural habitats – there are black bears, a red wolf, a black

The Lowdown

- 🌐 **Map reference** 3 A3
  Address 3945 Museum Dr, 32310; 850 575 1636; www.tallahasseemuseum.org
- 🚗 **Car** Rent a car from Tallahassee Regional Airport.
- 🕐 **Open** 9am–5pm Mon–Sat, 11am–5pm Sun
- 💲 **Price** $30–36; under 3s free
- 🎭 **Activities** The museum offers family and youth programs; check website for schedule.
- 👫 **Age range** All ages
- ⏱ **Allow** 4 hours
- ♿ **Wheelchair access** Yes
- 🍴 **Eat and drink** PICNIC Metro Deli (104 1/2 South Monroe, 32301; 850 224 6870; www.metrodelis.com) has a Metro Box Lunch that offers a choice of sandwiches or wraps, chips, a cookie and a drink. Enjoy it in the museum's spacious grounds. REAL MEAL The Trail Break Café (on site) has a variety of sandwiches and a "Bug Bites" children's meal which includes a toy, a drink, chips, and a choice of corn dog, chicken nuggets, grilled cheese, or a hot dog.
- 🎉 **Festival** Jazz and Blues Festival (late Mar)

A bobcat in the zoo within the Tallahassee Museum grounds

panther, bobcats, playful river otters, and a Florida alligator. Other attractions include a restored plantation that has an original home, a kitchen, and a slave cabin – a dwelling that tells of a time when slaves were brought from Africa against their will to work the fields on Southern plantations. Families can take a walk on the nature trail, head indoors to experience the hands-on exhibits in the Discovery Center, or discover underwater life in the Fleischmann Natural Science

An elegantly furnished room in Maclay House, Alfred B. Maclay Gardens State Park

building. The latter has two small freshwater aquariums and an observation window to watch birds feeding outside.

Letting off steam
The zoo's paths, and the many acres of grounds, provide plenty of opportunities for walking. If any energy is left, take advantage of the museum's wooded nature trail.

⑩ Alfred B. Maclay Gardens State Park
A floral wonderland

Alfred B. Maclay, a New York financier, and his wife Louise planned the gardens in the grounds of their winter home in 1923. This blooming oasis, with over 200 varieties of plants, is a vision in late winter and early spring, when camellias, dogwoods, and azaleas are in flower. The season lasts from January to April, with the beauty at its peak in March. Brick walkways and pine needle paths make for a serene stroll through landscapes that include a walled garden, ponds, fountains, and a lovely lake. Look for the narrow path leading to a secret garden. This secluded spot shelters small plants and has pretty wrought-iron benches that are perfect for a break. Lake Hall provides opportunities for swimming, fishing, canoeing, and kayaking, and two nature trails through the woods overlook the lake. Still furnished as it was when the owners were in residence, the Maclay House is open for visits from January through April.

Take cover
A short drive south is **Books-a-Million** (3521 Thomasville Road, 32308; 850 893 3131; www.books amillion.com), a bookstore well stocked with choices to please all ages, from tots to teens, as well as a range of genres for adults. Be prepared to be wheedled into a purchase.

The Lowdown

🌐 **Map reference** 3 A3 **Address** 3540 Thomasville Rd, 32309; 850 487 4556; www.florida stateparks.org/maclaygardens	👫 **Age range** 5 plus
	⏱ **Allow** 2–3 hours
🚗 **Car** Rent a car from Tallahassee Regional Airport.	☕ **Eat and drink** PICNIC The Fresh Market (1390 Village Square Blvd, Ste 4, 32312; 850 907 1392; www.thefreshmarket.com) offers gourmet fixings for a picnic. Pavilions and grills along the Lake Hall shore provide the perfect setting for a picnic. REAL MEAL Red Elephant Pizza and Grill (1872 Thomasville Rd, Suite A, 32303; 850 222 7492; www.redelephant pizza.com) serves pizza, burgers, sandwiches, and desserts. It also has a kids' menu.
⏲ **Open** Gardens: 9am–5pm daily	
💲 **Price** $18–28; under 2s free. $6 per vehicle for parking and additional fee Jan–Apr, when gardens are in bloom	
🚩 **Guided tours** From Jan–Apr, guided tours are offered on most Sat and Sun. A Gardens Walking Tour brochure is available at the Ranger Station.	

⑪ Wakulla Springs State Park

Gator gazing, swims, and walks

A popular location for *Tarzan* movies in the past, Wakulla is home to one of the world's deepest natural springs. Spot alligators, turtles, and birds of all shapes and sizes on one of the park's daily ranger-led riverboat tours. An observation platform offers superb views of the springs, and a safe area has been set aside for swimming; their calm waters are also great for snorkeling. A 6-mile (10-km) hiking trail weaves through a hardwood forest of magnolia oak, beech, and hickory, as well as a longleaf pine forest. Be sure to decide in advance how far to walk, as this is not a loop trail. Built in Mediterranean style in the 1930s, the park's handsome Wakulla Springs Lodge is on the National Register of Historic Places.

Take cover

If it rains, head for the **Wakulla Springs Lodge** and enjoy a treat at the Soda Fountain.

Tour boats at the jetty in Wakulla Springs State Park

Entrance to the elegant Wakulla Springs Lodge, Wakulla Springs State Park

The Lowdown

🌐 **Map reference** 3 A4
📍 **Address** 465 Wakulla Park Dr, Wakulla Springs, 32327; 850 561 7276; www.floridastateparks.org/wakullasprings

🚗 **Car** Rent a car from Tallahassee.
🕐 **Open** 8am–sunset daily
💲 **Price** $26–32, under 2s free
🚩 **Guided tours** The park offers 40–60-min guided riverboat tours that offer plenty of wildlife viewing opportunities. Glass-bottom boat tours are also available.
👫 **Age range** 5 plus
🧗 **Activities** Swimming, biking, and hiking
⏱ **Allow** 3–4 hours
☕ **Eat and drink** SNACKS Soda Fountain (*in Wakulla Springs Lodge; 850 421 2000; www.wakullaspringslodge.com*) boasts the world's longest marble counter top, and has milk shakes, sodas, hot dogs and sandwiches. *REAL MEAL* Ball Room Restaurant (*in Wakulla Springs Lodge*) serves breakfast, lunch, and dinner. Navy Bean Soup and Southern fried chicken are among the specialties. There are lovely views from the arched windows.

⑫ San Marcos de Apalache Historic State Park

Biking, hiking, birds, and a historic fort

This state park is situated in the tiny historic fishing town of St. Marks on Apalachee Bay. The flags waving over the entrance mark a site fought over by Spanish, English, American, and Confederate forces. Though the first Spanish settlement here was built in 1528, the original fort, now a National Historic Landmark, was built in 1679. The fort was later replaced by a stone fortress. A museum in the park exhibits pottery and tools unearthed near the original fort; and displays and a video reveal the site's colorful history.

Although a small town today, St. Marks was once a major port. Built in 1830 to bring cotton from Tallahassee plantations, the railroad is known today as the **Tallahassee-**

The Lowdown

🌐 **Map reference** 3 A4
📍 **Address** 148 Old Fort Rd, St. Marks, 32355; 850 925 6216; www.floridastateparks.org/sanmarcos

🚗 **Car** Rent a car from Tallahassee.
ℹ️ **Visitor information** St. Marks Visitor Center, 15 Old Palmetto Path, St. Marks, 32355; 850 925 0400; www.cityofstmarks.com
🕐 **Open** 9am–5pm Thu–Mon
💲 **Price** Free. Museum: $8–12, under 5s free
🚩 **Guided tours** The parks offers a self-guided trail winding through the historic ruins. Guided tours available with two weeks' notice.
👫 **Age range** 6 plus
🧗 **Activities** Families can hike trails and explore the fort ruins.
⏱ **Allow** 2 hours
🍴 **Eat and drink** PICNIC Bo Lynn's Grocery (*850 Port Leon Dr, 32355; 850 925 6156*) stocks provisions for a picnic in the state park or the refuge. *REAL MEAL* Riverside Café (*69 Riverside Dr, 32355; 850 925 5668*) is an informal eatery where the menu ranges from wings and burgers to full dinners. Grouper sandwiches are one of the favorites here.
🎉 **Festival** St. Marks Stone Crab Festival (mid-Oct)

St. Marks Historic Railroad Trail State Park, a paved 16-mile (26-km) trail for hikers and bikers ending at the St. Marks waterfront.

Letting off steam

Only the Everglades can boast more species of birds than the **St. Marks National Wildlife Refuge** (*www.fws.gov/saintmarks*), located 5 miles (3 km) southwest of the state park. The refuge has forests, swamps, marshes, and a salt water estuary, which explains the huge variety of birds. It also has Florida's second-oldest lighthouse, built around 1830. The Visitor Center has road and trail maps, including part of the Florida National Scenic Trail.

⑬ Apalachicola
Oyster town

A major seaport when cotton was coming down from northern Florida's plantations, this quaint little town waned after the Civil War (1861–65). But it has a wonderfully walkable Historic District, with many beautifully restored homes and warehouses. Start with the walking tour map from the Information Center and take a look at the town's 50-plus pre-Civil War buildings, many of which house gift shops and restaurants. Today, the town relies on the sea for its livelihood, and is famous for its oysters. A variety of boat trips take visitors out into Apalachicola Bay.

Palm trees lining the path to the lighthouse, St. George Island State Park

Letting off steam

Located about 15 miles (24 km) east of Apalachicola on a barrier island, **St. George Island State Park** (*www.floridastateparks.org/stgeorge island*) boasts 9 miles (14 km) of pristine, dune-backed beach, with pavilions for picnics, as well as a lighthouse. The 2½-mile (4-km) trail to Gap Point meanders through a pine forest to Apalachicola Bay. The 1-mile (2-km) East Slough Trail offers boardwalks and resting benches.

Jetty at Apalachicola Bay, near the town of Apalachicola

The Lowdown

🌐 **Map reference** 2 G5

🚗 **Car** Rent a car from Tallahassee.

ℹ **Visitor information** 122 Commerce St, 32320; 850 653 9419; *www.apalachicolabay.org*

🎣 **Guided tours** Backwater Guide Service (*Scipio Creek Marina, 32320; 850 899 0063*) offers guided fishing and wildlife tours. Alternatively, learn how to tong and cull your own oysters on Captain Doug's oyster boat with Affordable Fishing (*604 Wilderness Rd, Eastpoint, 32320; 850 524 5985*)

👫 **Age range** All ages

🧗 **Activities** Kids will enjoy Grady Market (*76 Water St, 32320; 850 653 4099; www.jegrady.com*) with its ships and maritime memorabilia. Browse through toys, games, and

souvenirs at Kids Port (*21 Ave C, 32320; 850 653 2899*). Stop at the John Gorrie Museum (*46 6th St, 32320; 850 653 9347*) to see the ice-making machine that Gorrie patented in 1851, marking the beginning of air conditioning.

⏱ **Allow** A day

☕ **Eat and drink** SNACKS Old Time Soda Fountain (*93 Market St, 32320; 850 653 2606*) has a vintage 1950s-style interior. The menu offers sandwiches, as well as sodas and ice cream. REAL MEAL Boss Oyster (*River Inn, 123 Water St, 32320; 850 653 9364*) is the place to try the town's specialty – it offers oysters in 17 different ways. Kids can go for seafood pizza.

🎉 **Festival** Florida Seafood Festival (early Nov)

Rails to trails

Modern highways and airplane services have meant that many older railroad tracks are no longer needed. Formed in 1986, the Rails to Trails Conservancy works to change the flat beds where rails used to be into paved paths for bikers and hikers. So far 20,000-plus miles (32,186 km) of rail-trail have been opened across the US.

Picnic under $25; **Snacks** $25–50; **Real meal** $50–80; **Family treat** over $80 (based on a family of four)

Where to Stay in the Panhandle

From beach bungalows and condo resorts to city hotels, the Panhandle offers a wide range of accommodations. The numerous cottages and low-rise condos within walking distance of South Walton's beaches are especially appealing for families.

AGENCIES

Beach Rentals of South Walton
www.brswvacations.com
This agency offers lodging options across South Walton, including the villages of Seagrove, Grayton Beach, and Santa Rosa.

Rosemary Beach Rentals
www.rosemarybeach.com
This website has links to agencies with properties ranging in size from two to seven bedrooms.

Apalachicola   Map 2 G5

HOTEL
Water Street Hotel & Marina
329 Water St, 32320; 888 211 9239; www.waterstreethotel.com
A modern choice in a vintage town, this is a small all-suite hotel with a prime location by the water. Family suites have rooms with a queen bed, plus a small adjoining room with a bunk or full bed, as well as kitchens, balconies, and washer-dryers.
📶 🍴 P ⊘ $$

BED & BREAKFAST
Coombs House Inn
80 Sixth St, 32320; 888 244 8320; www.coombshouseinn.com
Three elegant Victorian homes make up this charming 23-room inn. Some suites have kitchenettes and private verandas. Guests are treated to daily breakfast, and afternoon tea, and wine on weekend evenings. Chairs, towels, and umbrellas are provided for excursions to St. George Island.
📶 🍴 P 🌀 $–$$

Pensacola   Map 1 A3

HOTELS
Crowne Plaza-Pensacola Grand Hotel
200 E Gregory St, 32501; 877 270 1393; www.pensacolagrandhotel.com
The former 1912 L&N railroad passenger depot, furnished with antiques, is this hotel's old-fashioned lobby and restaurant, but its 15-story glass tower beyond is strictly modern. Many rooms offer views of the Historic Pensacola Village. There is a fitness center on site.
📶 🍴 P ⊘ $–$$

New World Inn
600 S Palafox St, 32501; 850 432 4111; www.newworldlanding.com
This 15-room boutique hotel, located in the historic district, features a grand staircase and lofty rooms with attractive, traditional decor. Free Continental breakfast.
📶 🍴 P $$

MOTEL
Suburban Extended Stay Pensacola
3984 Barrancas Ave, 32507; 850 453 4140; www.suburbanhotels.com
A convenient option if visiting the Naval Aviation Museum, this motel is well equipped and provides free internet access. Laundry facilities, barbecue grills, and a fitness room are available. Despite the name, extended stays are not required.
📶 🍴 P ⊘ $

BED & BREAKFAST
Lee House Bed & Breakfast
400 Bayfront Pkwy 32501; 850 912 8770; www.leehousepensacola.com
With its classic Southern columns and spacious public rooms, Lee House offers modern comforts. Several of the eight suites can accommodate four. Enjoy breakfast with views of Pensacola Bay and Seville Square on the expansive porches.
📶 P $$

Pensacola Beach   Map 1 B3

RESORT
Portofino Island Resort and Spa
10 Portofino Dr, 32561; 877 484 3405; www.portofinoisland.com
This luxurious resort, situated along 8 miles (13 km) of pristine beach within the Gulf Islands National

A well-lit luxurious room in Sandestin Golf and Beach Resort, South Walton

Seashore, offers spacious two- and three-bedroom apartments equipped with washer-dryers. There are whirlpools, a spa, and special programs for kids and teens.
🛏 🍴 P ⊘ 🌀 $$$

MOTEL
Days Inn Pensacola Beachfront
Via De Luna Dr, 32561; 850 934 9780; www.daysinn.com
Located right on the beach, this basic motel offers rooms with microwaves, refrigerators, and coffee-makers. Amenities include laundry facilities, a pool, and free Continental breakfast.
📶 P ⊘ 🌀 $–$$

South Walton

RESORT
Sandestin Golf and Beach Resort   Map 1 C3
9300 Emerald Coast Pkwy, Destin, 32550; 800 267 8000; www.sandestin.com
This excellent resort features a 7-mile (11-km) beach, tennis courts, a fitness center, and biking trails. Lodging options range from high rises to cottages in beach, bay, and golf communities. Baytowne Wharf, a pedestrian village within the resort, offers shops, dining, and fun activities including a zip line. The resort has programs for children and teens.
📶 🍴 🛏 P ⊘ $–$$$

CONDO RESORTS

The Inn at Gulf Place   Map 1 D3
95 Laura Hamilton Blvd, Santa Rosa Beach, 32548; 888 909 6807; www.gulfplacefl.com
Across the road from the beach, this small complex offers rooms that sleep four, or one-bedroom condos with full kitchens and balconies. There are tennis courts, a hot tub, and a washer-dryer on site.

🐾 🔁 🗂 P ✪ $–$$

The Village of South Walton   Map 2 E4
10343 E Scenic Hwy 30A, Seacrest Beach, 32413; 877 808 4323; www. villageofsouthwaltonbeach.com
This four-story condo resort offers lodgings ranging from studios to three-bedroom units with washer-dryers, TV, and DVD players. The resort has its own shopping center, and a spray fountain for splashing, and offers easy access to the big Seacrest Village pool.

🍽 🔁 🗂 P ✪ $–$$$

WaterSound Resort   Map 1 D3
6652 E County Hwy 30A, Watersound, 32413; 800 413 2363; www. watersoundvacationrentals.com
A beach home community spread over an extensive area that includes the towering dunes along the Gulf of Mexico, this resort offers a beach club with a free-form pool and tennis courts. Lodgings vary from individual homes to condo units.

🍽 🔁 🗂 ✪ 🌀 $–$$$

HOTEL

30-A Suites   Map 1 D3
6904 Hwy 30A West, Santa Rosa Beach, 32459; 850 499 5058; www.30asuites.com
Spacious and attractively furnished, this 15-suite boutique hotel offers rooms with walk-in closets, and private balconies. Although the

hotel is recommended for families traveling with teens, younger kids are also welcome in its nearby two-bedroom condos.

🐾 🔁 🗂 $$

INN

Watercolor Inn   Map 1 D3
34 Goldenrod Circle, Santa Rosa Beach, 32459; 866 426 2656; www. watercolorresort.com
This luxurious 60-room inn near the Gulf of Mexico offers large rooms with king-size beds and queen sofa sleepers, a mini-refrigerator, and balconies with fabulous views. Bikes and kayaks are complimentary.

🐾 🍽 P ✪ $$–$$$

CAMPING

Grayton Beach State Park   Map 1 D3
Off Scenic Hwy 30A, Grayton Beach, 32459; 800 326 3521 (reservations); www.floridastateparks.org
Famous for its beautiful beaches, this state park offers full camping facilities plus 30 modern two-bedroom cabins accommodating six. Cabins have central heating and cooling, kitchen, an outdoor grill, as well as an initial set of linen and towels. Minimum two-night stay in cabins on weekends.

🔁 🗂 🌀 $

Topsail Hill Preserve State Park   Map 1 D3
7525 W Scenic Hwy 30A, Santa Rosa Beach, 32459; 800 326 3521; www.floridastateparks.org
This scenic park offers ample choices from a fully equipped campground and tent sites to one-bedroom bungalows and

The scenic pool at Watercolor Inn, Santa Rosa Beach

two-bedroom cabins. Cabins have full kitchens. Guests can take a free tram to the beach.

🔁 🗂 ✪ $

Tallahassee   Map 3 A3

HOTELS

Doubletree Hotel
101 S Adams St, 32301; 850 224 5000; www.doubletree.hilton.com/ tallahasee
Located close to Florida State Capitol and the Capitol Museum, this full-service downtown hotel is a good choice for families. Rooms are comfortable, and cribs and high chairs are available. The on-site restaurant has a children's menu.

🐾 🍽 ✪ P $–$$

Governor's Inn
209 South Adams St, 32301; 850 681 6855; www.thegovinn.com
Originally a livery stable, this boutique 41-room hotel near Florida State Capitol has rooms named for former Florida governors. The rooms are spacious, with two queen beds.

🐾 🍽 🔁 $$

MOTEL

Cabot Lodge
1653 Raymond Diehl Rd, 32308; 850 386 7500; www.cabotlodge thomsvilleroad.com
This friendly motel is convenient for the I-10 highway. Executive rooms are equipped with a microwave and mini-refrigerator. Complimentary features include breakfast, daily newspaper, evening cocktails, and computers in the lobby.

🐾 P ✪ 🗂 $

> **Price Guide**
>
> The following price ranges are based on one night's accommodation in high season for a family of four, inclusive of service charges and additional taxes.
>
> **$** Under $150 **$$** $150–300 **$$$** over $300

Camped RVs in Topsail Hill Preserve State Park, Santa Rosa Beach

Key to symbols *see back cover flap*

The Gulf Coast

Florida's Gulf Coast feels as if it could have been designed with families in mind. Alongside some of the state's best beaches, it has a major theme park and a spectacular aquarium, mermaids and manatees, and top museums for kids. Chic towns such as Tampa, St. Petersburg, and Sarasota offer world-class attractions and entertainment for adults. And there is still room for an abundance of unspoiled wild Florida.

The Gulf Coast

Highlights

Ringling Museum, Sarasota
See the elaborate estate on the bay created by circus legend John Ringling, and marvel at the world's largest miniature circus (see pp224–5).

The Dalí Museum, St. Petersburg
Discover this surreal museum, with unique art and architecture to fascinate all ages (see pp220–21).

Busch Gardens, Tampa
Ride on thrilling roller coasters, then say hello to hippos and lions, living as they would in the wild, at this exciting park (see pp214–15).

The Florida Aquarium
Go underwater without getting wet at the Coral Reef Gallery, a mammoth grotto where more than 2,300 fish are on the move (see p216).

Siesta Key
Take a walk on the beach that features on every list of "best in the US," and is known for its superb white sand (see p213).

Myakka River State Park
Explore these untouched lands that preserve Florida's lush natural landscape and diverse wildlife at its best (see p227).

Left *Howard Bros. Circus model at the Tibbals Learning Center in the Ringling Museum, Sarasota*
Above right *Giraffes and zebras in the Edge of Africa habitat at Busch Gardens, Tampa*

The Best of
The Gulf Coast

The Gulf Coast is an area ripe for exploration. The cities clustered around Tampa Bay have distinct personalities and are famous for their winning combination of family attractions, wildlife, and abundant beaches. All these lie within a 100-mile (160-km) area and can easily be visited on a driving tour. With so much packed into a compact area, this beautiful part of the coast should not be missed.

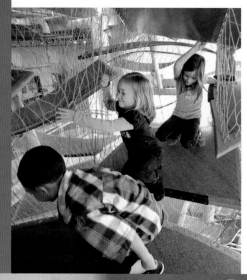

Tale of three cities

Each of the three major cities in the Tampa Bay area has its own lures, and is less than an hour's drive from the others. **Tampa** (see pp214–19), the region's port and business hub, is sometimes overlooked in favor of beach locations, but its riches include the **Busch Gardens** (see pp214–15), with its thrilling rides and animals, **The Florida Aquarium** (see p216), the Cuban flavor of **Ybor City** (see p218), major league sports, and the **Museum of Science and Industry** (see p217) – the biggest science museum in the southeast, with a special section for kids. **Sarasota** (see pp224–7) is an upscale community of about 60,000 people, with museums and performing arts venues that rival those of cities many times its size, plus some of the state's best beaches.

Left Water's Journey exhibit in the Glazer Children's Museum
Below An intricately carved circus wagon in the Ringling Museum

Above One of the many beautiful white-sand beaches along the Gulf Coast

St. Petersburg *(see pp220–23)* is more serene, with a beautiful boulevard by the sea and the world-famous **The Dalí Museum** *(see pp220–21)*, as well as **St. Pete Beach** *(see p212)*, a distinct area about 10 miles (16 km) from downtown.

Wet and wild

Ever seen a manatee up close or "mermaids" doing acrobatics underwater? Drive from **Tampa** to see manatees drawn to the warm waters in winter and get even closer to these marine mammals in a floating observatory at the **Homosassa Springs Wildlife State Park** *(see p219)*. Costumed "mermaids" have been performing their antics to applauding crowds at **Weeki Wachee Springs State Park** *(see p215)* since 1947. **The Florida Aquarium** has daily dolphin cruises to view some of the 500 wild dolphins that live in Tampa Bay and Swim with the Fishes, an in-water reef experience, offers guests aged 6 plus a watery adventure indoors in the aquarium's replica coral reef.

The circus is in town

The excitement of Sarasota's old days comes to life at the **Tibbals Learning Center** *(see p224)* in the **Ringling Museum** *(see p224–5)*, which boasts the biggest model circus in the world. See this amazing handmade replica of the Ringling Bros. and Barnum & Bailey circus in its heyday, with its eight main tents, including a big top with three rings and four stages full of tiny model clowns, aerialists, and showgirls. Other exhibits focus on the most exciting circus acts, acrobats, aerialists, animals, and clowns.

Try out circus skills, such as walking a tightrope (safely close to the ground). Younger kids who are being taught circus arts show off their skills at the **PAL Sailor Circus** *(see p37)* in late December.

Treats for tots

Finding attractions for younger children away from the beach can be a challenge, but not on the Gulf Coast. Younger kids will enjoy the friendly **Lowry Park Zoo** *(see p216)* in **Tampa**. With some 2,000 animals, there is plenty to see here, and lots of chances for close-up encounters and feeding the animals. Another kids' favorite is the **Sarasota Jungle Gardens** *(see p225)*, with cool, shady paths, a Kiddie Jungle with a playground, and delightful shows such as parrots on roller skates. Tampa's **Glazer Children's Museum** *(see p218)* features fun experiences including flying a mock airplane or cooking as a chef. The **Great Explorations Children's Museum** *(see p223)* in **St. Petersburg** has crafts programs even for toddlers, along with plenty of attractions for older kids.

Right Manatee at Homosassa Springs Wildlife State Park, one of the best places for viewing these fascinating marine mammals

The Gulf Coast

This region stretches for hundreds of sandy miles along the western border of Florida, with a host of exciting stops along the way. From beaches and manatee-watching to circus tricks, roller coasters, animal parks, and one of Florida's most famous theme parks, the Gulf Coast has loads to keep families entertained. The cities welcome with aquariums and kid-friendly museums to intrigue all ages. Excellent roads make it easy to tour it all by car.

Circus exhibits in the Ringling Museum, Sarasota

Places of interest

THE GULF COAST
1 Gulf Coast Beaches
2 Busch Gardens, Tampa
3 The Florida Aquarium
4 Lowry Park Zoo
5 Museum of Science and Industry
6 Ybor City
7 Glazer Children's Museum
8 Manatee Viewing Center
9 The Dalí Museum, St. Petersburg
10 Bayshore Drive and The Pier
11 Museum of Fine Arts
12 Great Explorations Children's Museum
13 Ringling Museum, Sarasota
14 The Aquarium at Mote Marine Laboratory
15 Marie Selby Botanical Gardens
16 G.WIZ – The Science Museum

Alligator basking in Homosassa Springs Wildlife State Park

Kids splashing in the waves on Venice Beach, south of Sarasota

A thrilling floorless roller coaster at Busch Gardens, Tampa

The Lowdown

🚐 **Getting there and around**
Air Fly to Tampa (www.tampa airport.com) or Sarasota (www. srq-airport.com) airports. Tampa has a comprehensive local bus service, as well as a trolley by day connecting downtown attractions, and a streetcar running from the city center to Ybor City.
Bus Tampa, St. Petersburg and Clearwater have Greyhound bus connections from other major cities in Florida. **Trolley** Sarasota, Bradenton, and Clearwater have a trolley service from town to the beach. Clearwater's Jolley Trolley (clearwaterjolleytrolley.com) links beaches from Clearwater south to St. Petersburg, and also runs north to Tarpon Springs on weekends. However, schedules may not be convenient or reliable, and many sites and restaurants are not covered.
Car A car is by far the best way to get around, although it is possible to manage some parts of the region with public transportation. Numerous car rental agencies can be found at both airports. Keep dimes and quarters handy for parking meters.

ℹ **Visitor information** See individual entries.

🍴 **Supermarkets** Publix (www. publix.com) is the premier supermarket here, with outlets throughout the region.
Markets St. Petersburg Saturday Morning Farmers' Market, First Ave South and First St, on the waterfront, 33701; 727 455 4921; www.saturdaymorning market.com; Oct–May: 9am–1pm. Tampa Downtown Farmers' Market, 200 and 300 blocks on Twiggs St; www.tampa downtownmarket.com; Oct–May: 10am–2pm Fri. Ybor City Saturday Market, Centennial Park, 8th Ave and 19th St, 33605; 813 241 2442; www.ybormarket. com; 9am–3pm Sat year-round. Sarasota Farmers' Market, corner of State and Lemon Streets; 941 225 9256; www.sarasotafarmers market.org; 7am–noon Sat year-round. Downtown Clearwater Farmers' Market, Station Square Park, 500 and 600 blocks of Cleveland St; 727 461 7674; www.clearwaterfarmersmarket. com; Oct–May: 9am–2pm Wed

🎭 **Festivals** Gasparilla Pirate Festival, Tampa: lavish costumed parades; www.gasparillapirate fest.com (late-Jan). Florida Strawberry Festival, Plant City; www.flstrawberryfestival.com (late-Feb–mid-Mar). Highland Games, Dunedin (Apr). Medieval Fair, Sarasota; sarasotamedieval fair.com (Nov)

➕ **Pharmacies** Walgreens (www.walgreens.com) and CVS (www.cvs.com) are the two major pharmacies in the region; some of their city branches are open 24 hours.

🚻 **Restrooms** All major attractions, shopping malls, and gas stations have public restrooms.

① Gulf Coast Beaches

Soft sands and warm sunshine

For many visitors, the Gulf Coast's fabulous barrier beaches are the biggest attractions; reached via causeway bridges, they encompass some 35 miles (56 km) of soft sand, lapped by the gentle waves of the Gulf of Mexico. Clearwater Beach and St. Pete Beach, lined with hotels, are convenient for families. At Sarasota most development has been kept away from the beachfront. Several islands off the coast offer unspoiled sands ideal for beachcombers.

Surf kayaking at Turtle Beach, Siesta Key

Key Sights

③ St. Pete Beach This beach stretches for 7 miles (11 km) and is ideal for strolling. Lined with hotels, it is popular with families, and has excellent watersports.

① Caladesi Island Accessible only by boat, the island has a state park and an uncrowded beach ideal for beachcombing.

④ Pass-a-grille This public beach at the quieter end of St. Pete Beach offers great sunset views. Bring quarters for parking.

⑤ Fort De Soto Park There are three sugar-sand beaches and a nature preserve with trails here *(see p223)*.

⑥ Anna Maria Island Located at the quiet northern end of Bradenton, this island has picturesque beaches and a laid-back feel.

② Clearwater Beach Favored by active beachgoers, this resort beach has volleyball courts and watersports concessions. Sunset brings a nightly celebration with music and street performances.

⑦ Bradenton Beach This small island appeals to families with its beaches as well as the quaint town, with its historic pier, and a variety of shops, restaurants, and lodging.

⑧ Longboat Key This is an upscale resort island with lovely beaches and golf courses, but limited public access.

The Lowdown

🌐 **Map reference** 7 A1–3 and 7 B3–4

🚗 **Car** Rent a car from one of the rental agencies at Sarasota International Airport to get around the region.

ℹ️ **Visitor information** Caladesi Island: 727 469 5918; *www.florida stateparks.org/caladesiisland.* Clearwater Beach: 727 469 5918; *www.visitclearwaterflorida.com.* St. Pete Beach: 727 582

2267; *www.stpetebeach.org.* Pass-a-grille: 727 363 9247; *www. visitpassagrille.com.* Fort de Soto Park: 727 552 1862; *www.pinellas county.org/park/05_ft_desoto. htm.* Anna Maria Island: 941 778 1541 *www.annamariaisland chamber.org.* Bradenton Beach: 941 778 1005; *www.cityof bradentonbeach.com.* Longboat Key and Lido Key: 941 383 2466; *www.longboatkeychamber.com/ visitor.* Siesta Key: 941 349 3800;

www.siestakeychamber.com. Venice Beach: 941 486 2626; *www.venicegov.com*

💲 **Prices** Caladesi Island: $6 per boat; $42–56 ferry. Fort De Soto Park and Pass-a-grille: $5 parking

👫 **Age range** All ages

🤸 **Activities** Various watersports – snorkeling, canoeing, and kayaking – can be enjoyed at beaches such as Caladesi Island, St. Pete Beach, Lido Key, and

⑨ Lido Key This barrier island offers spacious beaches in three sections – dunes and trails to the north; resorts in the center; and a handsome shaded beachfront park to the south.

⑩ Siesta Key Justly popular, this small island is famous for its dazzling white-quartz sand that stays cool even on the hottest days.

⑪ Venice Beach A bounty of sharks' teeth lures sharp-eyed beachcombers to this beach.

Siesta Key. There is fishing at Fort De Soto Park and on Anna Maria Island, while Venice Beach is perfect for beachcombing and coral reef diving.

🕐 **Allow** 1–3 days

Good family value?
The Gulf Coast beaches and islands offer a range of sporting and leisure options for the whole family at a reasonable price.

KIDS' CORNER

Sand craft
To make a fine sandy souvenir, pack up some sand and shells in a plastic container with a lid to take home from the beach. Spread glue on cardboard and cover it with sand, then glue shells in a pattern you like. Or make a border on a plain wooden frame for a picture or a mirror. Try to find enough scallop shells of the same size, since they look great as borders.

Bucket race
Here's a silly beach game to play with friends and family. Set up two buckets away from the water's edge and see who can fill the bucket first by carrying water from the sea using only their hands.

WHAT IS A SEA SHELL?
The shells you see were home to sea creatures who have moved on. Some of the prettiest are scallop shells. Others may have held sea snails, crabs, or mussels. Caladesi Island State Park is a good place to look for shells on the Gulf Coast.

Sandy facts
A beach is made up of super-tiny, loose specks of rock that gather at the shore and are carried onto the land by waves or ocean currents. Strong waves carry the sand farther inland and pile it into dunes. Underwater coral reefs are one source of sand. The finest white sand, found on beaches like Siesta Key, is made of pure quartz crystal that has washed down from mountains far away then been carried to the sea by rivers.

② Busch Gardens, Tampa
Rocking roller coasters and roaring animals

This granddaddy of Florida theme parks still thrills with its daring roller coasters, African safari, water adventures, and lively musical shows. The grounds are divided into themed locations, such as the Congo and Timbuktu – each featuring animals native to those countries – while the Serengeti Plains are home to rhinos, giraffes, and more. Even the most adventurous will be challenged aboard the scream-inducing roller coasters, and little ones can enjoy their own special kingdom.

Flamingos in Busch Gardens, Tampa

Key Features

④ **Iceploration** This entertainment on ice features lavishly costumed, world-class ice skaters, amazing aerial performers, master puppeteers, and animal stars.

⑤ **Serengeti Railway** Take this train for a relaxing ride through all the major areas in the park.

⑥ **Sesame Street Safari of Fun** Aimed at pre-schoolers, this features rides and shows starring Sesame Street favorites.

⑦ **Cheetah Run** Get a close-up view of the world's fastest animals from these floor-to-ceiling, glass-paneled viewing areas.

⑧ **King Tut's Tomb** This is a detailed re-creation of the riches-filled burial chambers of Egypt's "boy king." Young ones can hunt for replicas of the finds.

Entrance

① **Gwazi** This wild, wooden roller coaster is actually two coasters in one. Traveling at 50 mph (80 km/h), its "lion" and "tiger" cars run on lines which pass each other by mere inches six times along the route.

② **Edge of Africa** This walking safari experience on the southern edge of the Serengeti Plains offers sightings of hippos, lions, hyenas, lemurs, and other exotic African animals in naturalistic habitats.

③ **Cheetah Hunt** Designed for speed, this roller coaster climbs more than 10 stories above the African landscape before plunging 130 ft (40 m) into an underground trench. It set a park record for distance with 4,429 ft (1,350 m) of track.

The Lowdown

🌐 **Map reference** 7 B1
Address 10165 N McKinley Dr, Tampa, 33612; 888 800 5447; *seaworldparks.com/en/busch gardens-tampa*

🚌 **Bus** Hartline bus 18 (*hartline.org*) from downtown to Busch Blvd. Shuttle Express available from Orlando to Busch Gardens

🕐 **Open** 10am–6pm Mon–Fri & 9am–7:30pm Sat–Sun. Hours may vary with season; check website.

💲 **Price** $324–34; under 5s free with a Preschool Pass that can be downloaded from the website.

👥 **Cutting the line** The Quick Queue pass ($34.99 per person; prices vary with season) gives access to the head of the line on each ride. Book tickets online to avoid waiting lines at the entrance and get $10 discount, with a second day for free. Ride lines are shortest near park opening and closing times.

🎫 **Guided tours** Insider tours with keepers, as well as Safari tours

👪 **Age range** 3 plus. Stop by Guest Relations to pick up kids' wristbands with space to

Prices given are for a family of four

Letting off steam

With climbing nets, bridges, crawl tubes, and a multilevel maze, **Treetop Trails** (on site), a three-story play area in the Jungala area, gives kids plenty of exercise. If any energy remains, head for **Adventure Island** (www.adventureisland.com), a tropical-themed water park just across the street. This features Riptide, a 55-ft (17-m) slide, Wahoo Run, a river raft ride, and twisting spirals on the Aruba Tuba run.

Eat and drink

Picnic: under $25; Snacks: $25–50; Real meal: $50–80; Family treat: over $80 (based on a family of four)

PICNIC Kenya Kanteen (in the Nairobi Village area) serves hot dogs that can be enjoyed on the patio overlooking the Serengeti Plains.
SNACKS Crown Colony Café (in the Egypt Village area) offers pizza by the slice, salads, and sandwiches.
REAL MEAL Zambia Smokehouse (in the Morocco Village area) has barbecued chicken and ribs, and mac and cheese.

Diners at the casual Crown Colony Café in the Egypt Village area

FAMILY TREAT Crown Colony Restaurant (in the Egypt Village area) has all-you-can eat family-style fried chicken dinners and more formal fare such as steak or salmon. A kids' menu is also available.

Plush toys for sale at a store in the Moroccan Village area

Shopping

Throughout the park, shops tempt with attractive souvenirs. Find legions of plush animals at the **Sahara Trading Company** (in the Timbuktu Village area). Sesame Street favorites are the lure at **Abby Cadabby's Treasure Hut** (in Safari of Fun) and teens like the surf garb and cool sunglasses at **Casablanca Outfitters** (in the Moroccan Village area). **Caravan Crossing** (in the Nairobi Village area) stocks beach towels, backpacks, and T-shirts.

Find out more

DIGITAL Explore the real Serengeti Plains of Africa at www.serengeti. org. Go to www.eyewitnesstohistory. com/tut.htm to find out about the amazing discovery of King Tut's tomb in Egypt. Learn how to make a mini-coaster at home on pbskids.org/ zoom/activities/sci/rollercoaster.html.

Next stop...

WEEKI WACHEE SPRINGS STATE PARK About 40 miles (64 km) north of Busch Gardens, the Weeki Wachee Springs (6131 Commercial Way, Weeki Wachee, 34606; 352 592 5656; weekiwachee.com) is where mermaids await. They aren't real mermaids, of course, but families have been enjoying the acrobatic antics of costumed swimmers since 1947. The arena is a natural spring so deep that the bottom has never been found. Seats are built into the limestone sides of the spring.

A diver amid reefs and exotic fish at The Florida Aquarium, Tampa

③ The Florida Aquarium

Fishy fun – from sharks to sea horses

Florida's largest aquarium is a great outing for all ages. In the Coral Reef Gallery, get a close-up view of a colossal and colorful underwater world that is usually only seen by deep-sea divers. Discover Florida's freshwater creatures, such as otters, alligators, and snakes, in the Wetlands exhibit, while the Ocean Commotion has predators including sharks, a giant Pacific octopus, and a lionfish. Children will love the sea horse exhibit, which shows off these adorable creatures that come in a surprising number of varieties. At the touch tank in the lobby, kids can pet a starfish and feel other sea creatures.

Letting off steam

If children get restless, head to **Explore A Shore**, an extensive outdoor water adventure zone in The Florida Aquarium. They can climb a pirate ship, build sand castles, and careen down slippery slides while the grown-ups relax in the shade. There is a separate area for toddlers.

④ Lowry Park Zoo

Ride a camel and feed a giraffe

This major zoo, with 2,000 animals on 56 lush acres (23 ha), is interesting for all ages, but is especially recommended for younger kids. It allows lots of close-up encounters, including camel and pony rides, feeding giraffes and rhinoceroses, a petting zoo, and a special viewing area for watching manatees swimming underwater. The animals are divided into seven sections that include Asia Domain, Safari Africa, and Florida Wildlife Center. The zoo also has a Jungle Carousel, the Tasmanian Tiger Family Coaster, and the gentle Gator Falls Flume Ride.

The Lowdown

- **Map reference** 7 B1
  Address 701 Channelside Dr, Tampa, 33602; 813 273 4000; www.flaquarium.org
- **Trolley** TECO (tecolinestreetcar.org) Line Streetcar Route 8
- **Open** 9:30am–5pm daily
- **Price** $84–94
- **Cutting the line** Book tickets online and get discounts.
- **Guided tours** Behind the Scenes and Feeding tours, as well as the dolphin-spotting cruise are offered for an additional fee.
- **Age range** 2 plus
- **Activities** Shows begin every few minutes and feature coral reef divers, otters at play, stingray feedings, and a Penguin Promenade. Check the daily schedule in the lobby.
- **Allow** At least 4 hours
- **Eat and drink** SNACKS Café Ray (on site) offers sandwiches, wraps, panini, and salads. It also has a kids' menu. REAL MEAL Taverna Opa (615 Channelside, Space 123, 33602; 813 443 4221; www.tavernaopa.com/tampa) serves Greek specialties, as well as burgers and sandwiches.

The Lowdown

- **Map reference** 7 B1
  Address 1101 West Sligh Ave, Tampa, 33604; 813 935 8552; www.lowryparkzoo.com
- **Bus** Hartline buses 41 and 45 stop at the zoo.
- **Open** 9:30am–5pm daily
- **Price** $86–96 (including rides, except camel and pony rides). Stroller rentals $7.50 single, $10 double
- **Cutting the line** Lines can be long in early afternoon and on weekends.
- **Guided tours** Go for safari tram rides through the Safari Africa exhibit.
- **Age range** 2 plus
- **Activities** The zoo offers animal feedings, animal keeper talks, and birds of prey shows.
- **Allow** At least 4 hours
- **Eat and drink** SNACKS Stephanno's Pizzeria (6607 N Florida Ave, 33604; 813 232 9486) sells pizza by the slice and sandwiches on foccacia bread for heartier appetites. REAL MEAL Bohio Verde (8114 N Florida Ave, 33694, 813 932 1712) gives the chance to sample Cuban fare and also has a menu for children who prefer dishes like chicken nuggets.

A white tiger lounging in the Asian Gardens habitat area in Lowry Park Zoo, Tampa

Lying down on a bed of nails in the Museum of Science and Industry, Tampa

Letting off steam

The Aussie-themed **Woolshed Playground** in the zoo's Wallaroo Station works off energy with slides, tunnels, and ladders. It includes a cooling water play area, and kids can also splash around in the waters of the Manatee Fountain near the entrance.

Kids splashing in the water play area in Wallaroo Station, Lowry Park Zoo

⑤ Museum of Science and Industry

America's largest science center for kids

Allow lots of time for the massive Museum of Science and Industry (MOSI), an imaginative scientific playground that offers some 450 hands-on exhibits to keep all ages engaged in learning and fun. Experience the impact of hurricane winds, and ride a high wire bike on a cable suspended 30 ft (9 m) above the ground. Dinosaur fans will find skeletons of the largest articulated bones ever discovered. This huge complex includes a butterfly garden, a backwoods forest preserve, an IMAX® dome theater,

and a planetarium. The separate interactive science center for children, Kids in Charge, is the largest of its kind in the country. Children are encouraged to investigate, create, and get involved in activities such as lying down on a bed of nails to learn why it does not hurt, and pulling in a tug of war to find out how levers work.

Letting off steam

MOSI's outdoor **Backwoods Forest Preserve** offers plenty of room to work off excess energy, and its multilevel **Sky Trail® Ropes Course** is designed with challenges for all ages.

The Lowdown

🌐 **Map reference** 7 B1
Address 4801 Fowler Ave, Tampa, 33617; 813 987 6080; *mosi.org*

🚌 **Bus** Hartline bus 5 from downtown

🕐 **Open** 9am–5pm Mon–Fri & 9am–6pm Sat–Sun

💲 **Price** $90–100; under 5s free (including IMAX® film, planetarium show, and Kids in Charge)

👫 **Cutting the line** Book tickets online or by phone

👫 **Age range** 5 plus

🏃 **Activities** The museum offers Weekend Family Escape classes and workshops.

⏱ **Allow** At least 4 hours

🍽 **Eat and drink** SNACKS Mel's Hot Dogs (*4136 E Busch Blvd, 33617; 813 985 8000; closed Sun*), a Tampa tradition, serves hot dogs plain and fancy. REAL MEAL Antonio's Pasta Grille (*11401 North 56th St, 33617, 813 914 8899*) has Italian favorites, including pizza and paninis.

Picnic under $25; **Snacks** $25–50; **Real meal** $50–80; **Family treat** over $80 (based on a family of four)

Facade of the yellow-brick building housing the Ybor City Museum State Park, Tampa

⑥ Ybor City
Cuban flavor in a cloud of cigar smoke

This Tampa neighborhood is named for Don Vicente Martinez Ybor, whose cigar-making business opened here in 1886, spawning the most vibrant Cuban community in the US. Head to the **Ybor City Museum State Park**, housed in a historic bakery, to find out more about Ybor City's history, and to see how workers lived. Though the cigar industry has waned, Ybor City still makes for a colorful visit. Stroll along 7th Avenue, where the old architecture remains, along with the many cafés and shops that have opened more recently. The Saturday morning market in Centennial Park draws crowds for its farm-fresh produce, Cuban coffee, arts and crafts, and live music.

Letting off steam
The **Ybor City Museum State Park** has a formal garden with paths for strolls. If children need a break, drive 2 miles (4 km) to Tampa's **Bayshore Boulevard** on the west shore of Hillsborough Bay – a 7-mile (10-km) promenade for walkers, runners, and bikers advertised as "the world's longest sidewalk."

The Lowdown

- 🌐 **Map reference** 7 B1
- **Address** Ybor City Museum State Park: 1818 North Ave, Tampa, 33605; 813 247 6323; floridastateparks.org/yborcity/
- 🚋 **Trolley** TECO line streetcar from downtown Tampa to Ybor City
- ℹ️ **Visitor information** The Visitor Information Center, Centro Ybor, 1600 East 8th Ave, Tampa, 33605; 813 241 8838; www.ybor.org
- 🕐 **Open** Ybor City Museum State Park: 9am–5pm daily
- 💲 **Price** Ybor City Museum State Park: $16–26; under 5s free
- **Guided tours** Self-guided audio walking tours of the neighborhood are available from the museum.
- 👫 **Age range** 8 plus
- **Activities** The museum runs guided tours of a Casita – a cigar worker's house – on the hour 11am–3pm Mon–Sat.
- ⏱️ **Allow** 2 hours
- 🍴 **Eat and drink** SNACKS La Tropicana Café (1822 E 7th Ave, 33605; 813 247 4040) is a favorite for authentic Cuban sandwiches, snacks, and other treats. FAMILY TREAT Columbia Restaurant (2117 E 7th Ave, 33605; 813 248 4961) is Florida's oldest restaurant and well worth a splurge for fine Cuban/Spanish cuisine and flamenco entertainment.

⑦ Glazer Children's Museum
Big fun for small kids

Tampa's newest museum offers young children the chance to learn through discovery and play in mock settings – from a firehouse and a vet's office to a bank. Flying an airplane, shopping for groceries, and serving as a waiter are some of the experiences that kids will enjoy. In Tug Boat Tots, children aged 3 and under can explore a boat, play

The Lowdown

- 🌐 **Map reference** 7 B1
- **Address** 110 W Gasparilla Plaza, Tampa, 33602; 813 443 3861; www.glazermuseum.org
- 🚌 **Bus** Hartline buses 30 and 70
- 🕐 **Open** 9am–5pm Mon–Fri, 9am–6pm Sat & 1pm–6pm Sun
- 💲 **Price** $50–60
- **Cutting the line** Advance tickets can be ordered online, but there is rarely a queue.
- 👫 **Age range** 3 plus
- **Activities** Special programs are scheduled frequently; check website for details.
- ⏱️ **Allow** 2–4 hours
- ♿ **Wheelchair access** Yes
- 🍴 **Eat and drink** SNACKS Tiny Bites Café (on site) has sandwiches, snacks, and a kids' menu with favorites like peanut butter and jelly, and grilled cheese sandwiches. REAL MEAL Five Guys Burgers and Fries (777 N Ashley Dr, 33602; 813 463 1999), nearby, serves little burgers for small prices and has plenty to satisfy heartier appetites too.

Budding architects in the Design + Build area in Glazer Children's Museum, Tampa

at fishing, and listen to stories. The museum also features water play, as well as arts and crafts activities.

Letting off steam
The Glazer Museum is located in **Curtis Hixon Waterfront Park** (600 N Ashley Dr, 33602), which offers a playground and a scenic paved waterside path. The playground has a unique feature – an interactive NEOS 360 Ring, which combines video games with aerobic exercises.

Sculpture of a manatee by Silas Beach, Homosassa Springs Wildlife State Park

⑧ Manatee Viewing Center

Florida's favorite mammal, close up

The Florida manatee is a swimming mammal and an endangered species whose closest relative is the elephant. It has a huge, seal-like body, flippers, and a flat tail, and can weigh as much as 1,000 lb (450 kg) and grow as long as 10 ft (3 m). These gentle creatures need warmth and, in cooler months, they flock to the warm water generated at the Tampa Electric Company's Big Bend Power Station. They can be seen close up from the viewing platform at the Manatee Viewing Center, which is situated within the power station. Manatees are also drawn year-round to the warm springs at **Homosassa Springs Wildlife State Park** *(4150 S Suncoast Blvd, Homosassa, 34446, 352 628 5343; www.floridastateparks.org/ homosassasprings)*, located 87 miles (140 km) from Tampa. Here, manatees can be seen from the park's underwater observatory. The park is also home to a variety of wildlife, such as bears, alligators, otters, deer, flamingos, and more.

Letting off steam

The viewing center's **Tidal Walk** to the Tampa Bay Estuary works off energy and also offers a chance to see native coastal plants and birds. At the end of the walkway is another view of manatees swimming – in the plant's discharge canal.

The Lowdown

🌐 **Map reference** 7 B2
Address 6990 Dickman Rd, Apollo Beach, 33572; 813 228 4289; www.tampaelectric.com/manatee

🚗 **Car** Rent a car from Tampa Airport. Parking is available.

🕐 **Open** Nov 1–Apr 15: 10am–5pm daily

💲 **Price** Free

👫 **Age range** All ages

🧍 **Activities** There is lots of fun stuff for kids on www.tampaelectric.com/manatee/funstuff/webcam2.

⏱ **Allow** 1 hour

🍴 **Eat and drink** SNACKS San Remo Pizza Restaurant (6426 N US 41, 33572; 813 645 9742) is a pleasant, family-run spot serving *calzones*. REAL MEAL Circles Waterfront Dining (1212 Apollo Beach Blvd, 33572, 813 641 3275; closed Sun) provides great views along with a varied menu and plenty of choices for children.

KIDS' CORNER

Watch out for....

When you visit Ybor City, head for:
1 The Visitor Information Center. The Centro Ybor at 1600 East 8th Avenue is housed in the world's largest cigar box along with the Ybor City Museum.
2 José Martí Park. Located on the corner of 8th Avenue and 13th Street, this park honors José Martí, Cuba's greatest freedom fighter. The Pedroso family bought the land and donated it to what is now the independent Republic of Cuba as a memorial to Martí. So, technically, you are standing on Cuban soil.

FAMOUS CIGAR SMOKERS

Though smoking isn't good for you, a lot of famous people have been photographed smoking cigars. They include past US presidents Bill Clinton and John F. Kennedy, Britain's former prime minister Winston Churchill, and Cuba's former president, Fidel Castro.

Massive manatees

To get enough nourishment for their mammoth bodies, manatees spend 6 to 8 hours a day feeding. How much do you think you would weigh if you ate for that long? Full-grown manatees can eat 100 lb (45 kg) to 150 lb (68 kg) of food per day – and they are vegetarians. They only eat green things growing in the ocean. Would you like that many vegetables in your diet?

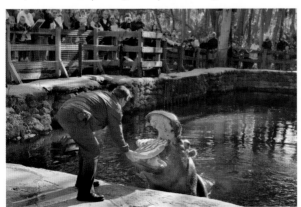

Lu, the hippo, enjoying his birthday cake, Homosassa Springs Wildlife State Park

Picnic under $25; **Snacks** $25–50; **Real meal** $50–80; **Family treat** over $80 (based on a family of four)

⑨ The Dalí Museum, St. Petersburg

The Surreal world of Salvador Dalí

The whimsical creations of Spanish artist Salvador Dalí, with his use of optical illusions and dreamlike canvases, intrigue all ages. Brought to St. Petersburg in 1982 by businessman A. Reynolds Morse and his wife, Eleanor, this is the biggest collection of Dalí's works outside Spain. The 2,140 pieces are housed in a concrete building wrapped in a fantastic geodesic "wave."

Aerial view of the spectacular Dalí Museum and Avant-Garden

Key Features

Third Floor Permanent collection, and a special exhibitions gallery

Second Floor Business, research, and meeting rooms

First Floor Theater, gift shop, and café

① **West Entrance** The austere west facade of the museum gives no hint of the surprises inside. The entry through a dim, grotto-like space leads to a light-flooded three-story atrium.

② **East facade**
The undulating windows on the museum's east facade are made of 1,062 triangular glass panes, of which no two are alike. They infuse the interior with light and offer visitors a unique view of St. Petersburg's waterfront.

③ **Helical staircase** The staircase spirals toward the skylight, leading visitors to the galleries on the third floor. While a permanent gallery holds the paintings, another gallery has Dalí's sculptures and films.

④ **The Discovery of America by Christopher Columbus** This painting, over 5 ft (1.5 m), is one of eight "masterworks" in the collection. Each painting has its own gallery for best viewing.

⑤ **Avant-Garden** The museum's waterside garden is a wonder, with boulder outcrops, eerie tropical plantings, a "golden rectangle" with multicolor paving, and a labyrinth. Some of the curved benches are draped with melting clocks.

⑥ **The Disintegration of Persistence of Memory** With its melting watches, this is one of Dalí's most famous paintings.

⑦ **The Hallucinogenic Toreador** Painted in the years 1969–70, this is one of Dalí's dreamlike paintings, employing optical illusions that are especially engaging to young viewers.

Prices given are for a family of four

The Lowdown

🌐 **Map reference** 7 A2
Address 1 Dalí Blvd, St. Petersburg, 33701; 727 823 3767; www.thedali.org

🚌 **Trolley** The Downtown Looper trolley line ($0.50 per person; under 5s free) has a stop at the museum.

🕐 **Open** 10am–5:30pm Mon–Sat (till 8pm Thu) & noon–5:30pm Sun

💲 **Price** $56–84; under 5s free ($7 for ages 6–12 & $15 for ages 13–18)

👪 **Cutting the line** Order tickets online to avoid queuing. Use the online coupon to save on adult admission.

🚩 **Guided tours** The museum runs daily tours on the half hour at 10:30am–3:30pm, as well as at 5:30pm and 6:30pm Thu. Tours run at 12:30pm–3:30pm Sun.

👫 **Age range** 5 plus

👫 **Activities** Dilly Dally with Dalí children's programs are held on weekdays during museum hours, and at 12:30–4pm Sun. There are arts and crafts at 11:45am–4:30pm on Sat and storytelling at 11:15am Tue–Thu.

⏱ **Allow** 2–3 hours

♿ **Wheelchair access** Yes

☕ **Café** Café Gala (on site) serves soups, salads, and tapas.

🛍 **Shop** On the first floor (see p221)

👫 **Restrooms** On the first and third floors

Good family value?

The Dalí introduces kids to Surrealist art. Although expensive for a family visit, the museum is a memorable experience.

Wide variety of apparel and bags in the wonderful Dalí Museum Store

Letting off steam

The **Albert Whitted Park**, near the museum and adjacent to a small city-owned airport, offers an aviation-themed playground, and a "control tower" to watch airplanes taking off.

Eat and drink

Picnic: under $25; Snacks: $25–50; Real meal: $50–80; Family treat: over $80 (based on a family of four)

PICNIC Mazzaros Italian Market *(2909 22nd Ave N, 33713; 727 321 2400; www.mazzarosmarket.com)* has wonderful fixings for a picnic to be enjoyed in a park by Tampa Bay.
SNACKS Hangar Restaurant & Flight Lounge *(540 1st St SE, 33701; 727 823 7767; www.thehangarst pete.com)*, in Albert Whitted Airport, offers sandwiches and snacks to go.

Outdoor seating at the Moon Under Water, St. Petersburg

REAL MEAL The Moon Under Water *(332 Beach Dr NE, 33701; 727 896 6160; www.themoonunder water.com)* serves standard British pub grub such as fish and chips, plus salads. There is also a kids' menu.
FAMILY TREAT St. Pete Brasserie *(533 Central Ave, 33701; 727 823 3700; www.stpetebrasserie.com)* offers French favorites, and has a fixed-price four-course dinner. Kids can order *pommes frites* (chips).

Shopping

The **Dalí Museum Store** stocks irresistible merchandise inspired by Dalí imagery. There is home ware, trendy Art to Wear in form of jewelry, scarves, fashion apparel, totes, and more. Kids will like the puzzles and books on optical illusions.

Find out more

DIGITAL Check out *academickids. com/encyclopedia/index.php/ Surrealism* for a good introduction to Surrealism.

Next stop...

CRYSTAL RIVER ARCHAEOLOGICAL STATE PARK
A 2-hour drive north of St. Petersburg, this National Historic Landmark *(www.floridastateparks.org/crystal riverarchaeological)* is one of the best places to see glimpses of the lives of ancient Native Americans in Florida. Once an important ceremonial center for burying the dead and conducting trade, this huge site has six burial mounds, temple platform mounds, and a midden, which is a mound containing shells, bones, and other relics dating as far back as 1,600 years ago.

Burial mounds in Crystal River Archaeological State Park

The Pier, one of the most popular attractions in St. Petersburg

⑩ Bayshore Drive and The Pier

Is that building the right way up?

The Dali Museum (*see pp220–21*) anchors one end of St. Petersburg's extensive system of handsome waterfront parks, which stretch for some 23 blocks on Bayshore Drive beside Tampa Bay. The city's best-known landmark, **The Pier**, extends

The Lowdown

- 🌐 **Map reference** 7 A2
  Address The Pier: 800 2nd Ave NE, St. Petersburg, 33701; 727 821 6443; www.stpetepier.com
- � **Trolley** The St. Pete trolley ($2, under 5s free) runs to The Pier.
- 🕐 **Open** The Pier: 10am–8 pm Mon–Thu, 10am–9 pm Fri–Sat & 11am–7pm Sun
- 💲 **Price** The Pier: free
- 👫 **Age range** All ages
- 👫 **Activities** Many concerts and special events are held at the Pier. Check website for details.
- ⏱ **Allow** 2 hours
- ☕ **Eat and drink** SNACKS The Dockside Eatery (*on the first floor of The Pier; 727 821 6443*) is a food court serving everything from Chinese food and gyros to sandwiches, pizza, and ice cream. *FAMILY TREAT* Columbia Restaurant (*on the fourth floor of The Pier; 727 822 8000*), a branch of Tampa's famous restaurant chain, tempts with festive Cuban/Spanish meals. It also offers panoramic views of Tampa Bay.

from the center of the parks into the bay. Its five-story, upside-down-pyramid-shaped building includes shops, a small aquarium, restaurants, and a food court. Sightseeing boat tours of the bay also leave from The Pier. However, a new building called The Lens, has been selected to replace The Pier after its design won the St. Petersburg Pier International Design Competition. At the northern end of Bayshore Drive, the restored Renaissance Vinoy Resort is worth a stop to see photo displays of what life was like here in the posh 1920s.

Letting off steam

Energetic kids will find plenty of room to run on the park paths that stretch the length of **Bayshore Drive**. They are the perfect place for a bike ride, too. Wheel Fun Rentals (*at The Pier; 727 820 0375; www.wheelfunrentals.com*) rents out a wide variety of bikes. Visit the nearby **Demen's Landing Park** (*1st St, 33701*), with a playground and nice spots for a picnic. The park also offers open lawns for frisbees, a game of catch, or kite-flying. Walk over to the **South Straub Park** (*1st Ave N, 33701*), which has a rock sculpture that kids love to climb.

⑪ Museum of Fine Arts

Small museum, great artists

Housed in a handsome building overlooking Tampa Bay, this museum is located in the center of the bayside park system. While introducing kids to fine art can be difficult if the museum is big and

The Lowdown

- 🌐 **Map reference** 7 A2
  Address 255 Beach Dr NE, St. Petersburg, 33701; 727 896 2667; www.fine-arts.org
- � **Trolley** The St. Pete trolley
- 🕐 **Open** 10am–5pm Mon–Sat, till 8pm Thu & noon–5pm Sun
- 💲 **Price** $54–68; under 6s free
- 🚩 **Guided tours** The museum runs docent-led tours at 11am, 2pm Tue–Sat and 2pm Sun.
- 👫 **Age range** 7 plus
- 👫 **Activities** There are children's programs every third Saturday of the month.
- ⏱ **Allow** 2 hours
- ☕ **Eat and drink** SNACKS MFA Café (*on site; 727 822 1032; closed Mon*), an airy space in the museum, offers a nice selection of sandwiches and salads. *FAMILY TREAT* Parkshore Grill (*300 Beach Dr NE, 33701; 727 896 3463; www.parkshoregrill.com*) has outdoor seating overlooking the Vinoy Yacht Basin. It also has a handsome dining room, with an open kitchen. The varied American menu ranges from crab cakes to steaks. There is also a well-priced kids' menu.

View of the stately building housing the Museum of Fine Arts, St. Petersburg

overwhelming, this museum is small enough to suit short attention spans. It contains an excellent collection of art by many great artists – Cézanne, Monet, Renoir, Rodin, and O'Keeffe, to name but a few. Other galleries introduce ancient and Asian art, and the museum has a sculpture garden, a Steuben glass gallery, and a fine photography collection.

Letting off steam

Run around in the bayside park around the museum, or take a trip 12 miles (19 km) southwest to the

Fort De Soto Park (www.fortdesoto. com). A great day's getaway, this is a county park of five interconnected islands with beautiful beaches and a cool historic fort to explore. The islands are home to mangroves, wetlands, and palm hammocks, as well as numerous species of birds. Fishing piers, hiking trails, and canoe, kayak, and bike rentals provide plenty of activities. There are restrooms, a food concession, and outdoor showers to wash away beach sand.

Picturesque view of the Fort De Soto Park

⑫ Great Explorations Children's Museum

Create a robot, run a pizzeria

Kids take charge here, in little re-creations of grown-up domains such as a pizza parlor, a fire engine house, a veterinary office, and a supermarket. There is a pretend

orange grove where they can pick, pack, and ship oranges, plus turn them into orange juice. A treehouse built for climbing, a lab for making moving robots, and the chance to create animation using a digital video recorder are among the favorite activities in this museum.

Letting off steam

Go to the **Sunken Gardens** (1825 4th St N, 33704; 727 551 3102; www. stpete.org/sunken), adjacent to the museum. This long-established attraction has paved paths to stretch young legs, cascading waterfalls, and some 50,000 exotic plants and flowers from around the world.

The Lowdown

- 🌐 **Map reference** 7 A2
- **Address** 1925 4th St N, St. Petersburg, 33704; 727 821 8992; www.greatexplorations.org
- 🚌 **Bus** PSTA (www.psta.net) city bus 4 stops near the museum. Check website for routes.
- 🕐 **Open** 10am–4:30pm Tue–Sat & noon–4:30pm Sun; closed Mon
- 💲 **Price** $40–50
- 👫 **Age range** 2 plus
- 🏃 **Activities** The museum hosts many special Saturday programs. Check the current schedule on the website.
- ⏱ **Allow** 2 hours
- ☕ **Eat and drink** SNACKS Panera Bread (1908 4th St N, 33704; 727 895 5441) stocks delicious breads that make fine sandwiches. The desserts are tasty. REAL MEAL Fourth Street Shrimp Store (1006 4th Ave N, 33701; 727 822 0325) is set in a former service station and has a funky ambience. It serves great seafood and there is a children's menu too.

Meandering path through lush greenery at the Sunken Gardens, St. Petersburg

Picnic under $25; **Snacks** $25–50; **Real meal** $50–80; **Family treat** over $80 (based on a family of four)

⑬ Ringling Museum, Sarasota
The greatest show on Earth!

Built in 1925, the art museum holding multimillionaire circus owner John Ringling's famous art collection is just one part of his vast estate beside Sarasota Bay. Ringling's original collection of 600 paintings has grown to over 2,000 objects, including Asian and contemporary art. Peppered with gardens, the estate boasts America's only authentic 18th-century European theater, as well as the exquisite Ringling home and two museums filled with circus nostalgia and fun.

Circus Poster in the Ringling Museum of Art

Key Features

① Cà' d'Zan The Ringlings' restored Venetian-style palazzo, completed in 1926, has a bathtub carved from a huge single block of marble. Look up at the ballroom's ceiling – it has a painting by children's book illustrator Willy Pogany, showing dancing couples from all over the world.

② Circus Museum Established after Ringling's death, this documents the rich history of the circus, and also features colossal parade wagons, sequined costumes, and Ringling's private rail car.

③ Historic Asolo Theater This restored theater serves as the venue for film screenings and concerts. Built in Italy in 1798, it was moved to the Ringling estate in the 1940s.

④ Ringling Museum of Art Now Florida's official state museum, this houses priceless Old Master paintings. Look out for Rubens' *Gathering of the Manna* – it is hard to say whether the figure of Moses has rays of light or horns coming from his head.

⑤ Courtyard of the Museum of Art Find casts of original antiquities and Renaissance sculptures, including the towering *David* by Michelangelo, along with two replicas of Roman fountains. The *Fountain of the Tortoises* is a favorite with kids.

Entrance

⑥ Tibbals Learning Center Kids can walk a safe tightrope, fire a miniature cannon, dress up as a circus clown, and try to fit into a midget car here. The handmade miniature Howard Bros. Circus model fills an entire room, with eight tents and 152 wagons, and is very detailed, right down to the smallest dishes in the mess tent.

The Lowdown

🌐 **Map reference** 7 B3
Address 5401 Bay Shore Rd, Sarasota, 34243; 941 359 5700; *www.ringling.org*

🚗 **Bus** Sarasota County Area Transit (SCAT) bus 99 arrives hourly from downtown (*www.scgov.net/scat*).

🕐 **Open** 10am–5pm daily & till 8pm Thu (museums only)

💲 **Price** $60–70 (Thu: $30–40). Free entry to the Ringling Museum of Art on Mon.

👥 **Cutting the line** Call 941 358 3180 for advance ticketing

information and 941 360 7399 to book tickets for the Historic Asolo Theater.

🚩 **Guided tours** Hourly docent-led tours of the Ringling Museum of Art and the Circus Museum. The first floor of Cà' d'Zan can be visited on guided tours only.

👫 **Age range** 6 plus; the Cà' d'Zan is not recommended for younger kids due to its narrow walkways.

🤸 **Activities** Check website for Center Ring Saturdays and shows at the Historic Asolo Theater.

⏱ **Allow** At least half a day

♿ **Wheelchair access** Yes

🍴 **Café** Banyan Café, opposite the Circus Museum, serves hot dogs and chicken fingers.

🛍 **Shop** In John M. McKay Visitors Pavilion (see p225)

🚻 **Restrooms** In every building

Good family value?
Kids will enjoy the Museum's attractions, especially the Circus Museum, though it is expensive.

Sculptures and blooming rose beds in Mable's Rose Garden

Letting off steam

The vast grounds of the Ringling estate have many paths for working off excess energy and beautiful gardens to admire. John Ringling's wife, Mable, was an avid gardener and her **Rose Garden**, patterned after an Italian circular design, is one of the estate's prettiest spots. When the 1,200 rose bushes are in bloom, the scents are delightful. Kids will have fun finding **Mable's Secret Garden**, the **Dwarf Garden**, and the estate's **Millennium Tree Trail**.

Blue Dolphin Café in the historic St. Armands Circle, Sarasota

Eat and drink

Picnic: under $25; Snacks: $25–50; Real meal: $50–80; Family treat: over $80 (based on a family of four)

PICNIC Publix *(1044 N Tamiami Trail, 34236; 941 366 3270)* has picnic fixings and snacks to enjoy at the outdoor tables in the grounds near the Rose Garden.
SNACKS St. Armands Circle, the shopping area developed by John Ringling on Lido Key, has many good choices. **Venezia** *(373 St. Armands Circle, 34236; 941 388 1400; venezia 1966.com)* serves tasty pizza.
REAL MEAL Blue Dolphin Café *(470 John Ringling Blvd, 34236; 941 388 3566; bluedolphincafe. com)*, an informal diner, offers a kids' menu for breakfast and lunch.

FAMILY TREAT Café L'Europe *(431 St. Armands Circle, 34236; 941 388 4415; www.cafeleurope. net)* is a traditional French favorite for a special night out. The kids' menu has salads, chicken fingers, and Key lime pie.

Shopping

The **Museum Store** delights kids with souvenirs such as juggling balls, clown noses, and puzzles of museum sites. Grown-ups will find scarves with Venetian themes from Cà' d'Zan, interesting jewelry, and home accessories. **St. Armands Circle** is lined with dozens of shops of all kinds, plus conveniently located ice cream parlors for a break.

Find out more

DIGITAL See *www.ringling.com* to learn more about the history of the Ringling circus, the best circus acts, animal care, and other interesting topics. Discover what it takes to be a clown at *www.allaboutclowns.com*.

Next stop...

SARASOTA JUNGLE GARDENS
One mile (2 km) south of the Ringling Museum, the Sarasota Jungle Gardens *(www.sarasota junglegardens.com)* have been pleasing families since the 1940s. There are trails through 10 acres (4 ha) of lush tropical vegetation and a "kiddie jungle" with an imaginative playground. Grown-ups and kids will like feeding the flamingos. Shows geared for kids feature alligators, snakes, birds of prey, and tropical birds – parrots on roller skates are a favorite.

⑭ The Aquarium at Mote Marine Laboratory

Close encounters of the marine kind

From seeing shark habitats, a dolphin lagoon, and a 23-ft (7-m) giant squid to getting up close with sea turtles and manatees and feeling a stingray's velvety back in a touch

Children observing tropical fish at The Aquarium at Mote Marine Laboratory

pool, The Aquarium at Mote Marine Laboratory, has it all. Attached to a major marine research facility, The Aquarium showcases the Lab's work and includes exhibits that feature real scientific studies on coral reefs and with other species. The chance to see exhibits where sea horses are hatched and raised, or learn how injured sea creatures are healed and returned to the wild at Mote's Dolphin & Whale Hospital and the Sea Turtle Rehabilitation Center, are exceptional opportunities that make a visit to this aquarium unique.

Letting off steam
A large swath of parkland with great views bordering Sarasota Bay, the **Ken Thompson Park** *(1700 Ken Thompson Pkwy, 34236)*, nearby, has swings for kids, a fishing pier, and lots of green lawn for games and picnics.

⑮ Marie Selby Botanical Gardens

Forest, fish, and an enchanted garden

The more than 6,000 orchids are the showstoppers, but not the only lures, at this beautiful world of exotic plants. While known for its epiphytes – plants such as orchids that grow on other plants – the gardens also include bamboo and banyan groves, hibiscus, ferns, tropical fruits, cactus, native Florida plants, a mangrove forest, and eight plant-filled greenhouses. Kids are welcomed here and encouraged to wander the paths and run on the great lawn. Check out the weird plants that live on trees, feed the fish in the koi pond, and conduct

The Lowdown
- **Map reference** 7 B3
- **Address** 811 South Palm Ave, Sarasota, 34236; 941 366 5731; www.selby.org
- **Bus** SCAT bus 17 on Tamiami Trail (US 41) stops nearby.
- **Open** 10am–5pm daily
- **Price** $46–68; under 6s free
- **Age range** 5 plus
- **Activities** Little Sprouts is a fun interactive program for pre-schoolers, with stories and games.
- **Allow** 2 hours
- **Eat and drink** SNACKS Local Coffee + Tea Cafe *(on site)* serves snacks, sandwiches, and desserts. REAL MEAL Hillview Grill *(1920 Hillview St, 34239; 941 952 0045; closed Sun)* offers a varied American menu, including burgers, salads, and main courses.

a plant hunt, which can be printed out from the website, with one of the children's guides.

A short drive 1 mile (2 km) north is the **Sarasota Children's Garden** *(www.sarasotachildrens garden.com)*, a magical world where a tunnel leads to a space filled with whimsical sculptures of friendly dragons and octopuses, a pirate ship with rigging to be climbed, a maze to be explored, a tree fort, and a fairy garden for tea parties.

Take cover
If raindrops fall, the Kids' Corner in the **Historic Selby House** on site is the perfect shelter. This interactive space is filled with plant-themed books, puzzles, activities, and crafts. A volunteer is often on hand to help.

The Lowdown
- **Map reference** 7 A3
- **Address** 1600 Ken Thompson Pkwy, Sarasota, 34236; 941 388 4441; www.mote.org
- **Car** Rent a car from Sarasota Airport.
- **Open** 10am–5pm daily
- **Price** $58–68; under 4s free
- **Guided tours** The 90-minute Morning Rounds tour allows up to three guests aged 10 plus to get an up-close look at feeding and care of the animals.
- **Age range** All ages
- **Activities** Play interactive games at the Immersion Cinema (on site). Check website for current schedule of family programs. The aquarium also offers Eco-Boat tours of the Sarasota Bay.
- **Allow** 3 hours
- **Wheelchair access** Yes
- **Shop** The gift shop sells toys, plush birds, T-shirts, and puzzles.
- **Eat and drink** SNACKS Deep Sea Diner *(on site)* is fine for snacks or a light lunch. REAL MEAL The Old Salty Dog *(1601 Ken Thompson Pkwy, 34236; 941 388 4311)*, nearby, is one of Sarasota's best family choices, with an informal menu and an outdoor deck for watching the boats go by.

Kids' Corner in the Historic Selby House in the Marie Selby Botanical Gardens

Prices given are for a family of four

The fascinating exterior of G.WIZ – The Science Museum

⑯ G.WIZ – The Science Museum

Amazing adventures and fantastic facts

Create a bolt of lightning, float a beach ball in air, build a bridge with magnetism, play a laser harp, make an animated video, gaze at a hissing cockroach from Madagascar – the science adventures are nonstop at this creative museum. A robotics lab and medical lab are sources of fantastic facts and "Sid the Science Kid" challenges pre-schoolers with a fun quiz. Those interested in mechanics can drop by Machine Village to see how levers, pulleys, and gears work.

Letting off steam

G.WIZ is in the middle of **Bayfront Park**, where there are lots of activities and families can happily while away an afternoon. Alternatively, for a wilderness experience just 9 miles (14 km) outside Sarasota, head for **Myakka River State Park** *(www.myakkariver.org)*. Here, the wild and scenic Myakka River flows through miles of untouched wetlands, prairies, and woodlands. Admire its beauty from a canopy walkway high above the ground, a boardwalk across Upper Myakka Lake, a tram tour through the backcountry, airboat tours, or on hiking trails, and watch out for wildlife such as alligators and armadillos.

The Lowdown

🌐 **Map reference** 7 B3
Address 1001 Blvd of the Arts, Sarasota, 34236; 941 309 4949; www.gwiz.org

🚗 **Bus** SCAT bus 99 stops two blocks away and runs hourly from downtown.

🕐 **Open** 10am–5pm Mon–Sat & noon–5pm Sun (Sep–Feb: closed Mon)

💲 **Price** $50–60; under 3s free

🧍 **Age range** 5 plus

🤸 **Activities** A variety of talks and programs are held at the museum. Check website for current schedule.

⏱ **Allow** 2 hours

♿ **Wheelchair access** Yes

🍴 **Eat and drink** PICNIC Morton's Gourmet Market *(1924 S Osprey Ave, 34239; 941 955 9856)* stocks goodies for picnics that can be enjoyed in Bayfront Park. REAL MEAL Mattison's City Grille *(1 Lemon St at Main St, 34236; 941 330 0440; closed Sun)*, downtown, has outdoor seating on Sarasota's pleasant Main Street and a menu offering everything from pizza to steak.

The pristine landscape of Myakka River State Park

Where to Stay on the Gulf Coast

A major draw for families, the Gulf Coast offers everything from campsites and budget motels to luxurious condos. Numerous all-suite properties afford extra space and even modest lodgings usually offer air-conditioning and swimming pools – welcome features in the warm climate.

AGENCIES

Find Vacation Rentals
www.findvacationrentals.com/florida.html
This website provides condo listings throughout the state, including the Gulf Coast.

Florida Vacation Connection
3720 Gulf of Mexico Dr, Longboat Key, 34228; 877 702 9980; flavacationconnection.com
Use this reservation service for vacation rentals, ranging from beachfront resorts to condos, on Longboat Key and Lido Key, Sarasota's choice beach locations.

Bradenton Beach Map 7 A3

HOTEL
Bridgewalk, a Landmark Resort
100 Bridge St, 34217; 941 779 2545; www.silverresorts.com
Bradenton's historic Bridge Street is charming, and this well-appointed property is right across the road from the beach. The hotel has suites and apartments with kitchens, with shops and restaurants next door. The free Bradenton trolley takes guests to the town and other Gulf Coast beaches.
🛎 ⚙ 🍽   **$$**

St. Pete Beach Map 7 A2

HOTELS
Plaza Beach Hotel
4506 Gulf Blvd, 33706; 800 257 8998; www.plazabeachresorts.com
For families who want to be on the beach, this small, low-key resort of just 39 suites is right on the sands. The good-size suites come with full kitchens. Besides the pool, kids will find mini-golf, shuffleboard, and other games here. Beach cabanas and beachside BBQ grills are free, as is the Wi-Fi service.
🛎 🐟 🍽 ⚙ 🌀   **$–$$**

Don CeSar Beach Hotel
3400 Gulf Blvd, 33706; 727 360 1881; www.loewshotels.com/en/Don-CeSar-Hotel
A luxury landmark since it opened in 1928, this cotton-candy pink palace by the sea is hard to miss. The building is well maintained and enjoys a beachfront location.
🛎 🍽 ⚙ 🌀 ⚙   **$$$**

St. Petersburg Map 7 A2

RESORT
Renaissance Vinoy Resort
501 5th Ave NE, 33701; 727 894 1000; www.marriott.com
This beautifully restored historic hotel blends the grandeur of the past with modern conveniences, including a lavish pool, tennis, golf and spa, and a highly regarded restaurant. It overlooks Tampa Bay and makes a good base for visiting nearby sights.
🛎 🍽 ⚙ ⚙   **$$$**

INNS & SUITES
Hampton Inn & Suites St. Petersburg
80 Beach Dr NE, 33701; 727 892 9900; www.stpetehamptonsuites.com
This property offers good-size rooms with refrigerators, microwaves, and DVD players. There is a laundry facility, as well as free Wi-Fi and hot breakfasts. Guests can check e-mail at the business kiosk.
🛎 ⚙   **$$**

BED & BREAKFAST

Dickens House Bed and Breakfast
335 8th Ave Northeast, 33701; 727 822 8622; www.dickenshouse.com
Bed and breakfast fans, with kids aged 9 plus, will love this warm 1912 Craftsman-style home. It serves sumptuous breakfasts and is located two blocks from the waterfront parks. Amenities include refrigerators in rooms and a computer for guests.
🛎 P   **$–$$**

CAMPING
Fort De Soto Park
3500 Pinellas Bayway S, Tierra Verde, 33715; 727 552 1862; www.fortdesoto.com
This beautiful park, 12 miles (19 km) southwest of St. Petersburg, offers tent camping just steps from the beach and full-service RV hook-ups. There are fishing piers, hiking trails, and canoe, kayak, and bike rentals, as well as a fort to explore.
P ⚙ 🛶   **$**

Sarasota Map 7 B3

HOTELS
Siesta Key Banyan Tree Resort and Vacation Rentals Map 7 B4
378 Canal Rd, Siesta Key, 34242; 800 732 7231; siestakeybanyanresort.com
Studio apartments and one-, two-, and three-bedroom condos are available by the week here. All units

Don CeSar Beach Hotel, a renowned beachfront luxury hotel

Camping near the water at Fort De Soto Park

have full kitchens. The award-winning Siesta Key Beach and Siesta Key Village are within walking distance.

🛒 🗄 ⊘   **$–$$**

Lido Beach Resort
700 Ben Franklin Dr, 34236; 941 388 2161; www.lidobeachresort.com
This resort offers the choice of a tower with spacious condo suites or a low-rise hotel. Even basic hotel rooms have kitchenettes with microwaves and refrigerators. Check website for discounts.

📶 🔋 🗄 ⊘ ◑   **$$–$$$**

Ritz-Carlton Hotel
1111 Ritz-Carlton Dr, 34236; 941 309 2000; www.ritzcarlton.com
The most elegant accommodation in Sarasota welcomes kids with board games at the concierge desk, assorted games at the pool, and a children's menu. Shuttles take guests to a private club on Lido Beach with counselor-supervised kids' programs.

📶 🍽 🔋 ⊘ ◑   **$$–$$$**

INN & SUITES
La Quinta Inn & Suites
1803 N Tamiami Trail, 34234; 800 233 1234; www.lq.com
A well-kept motel within an easy drive of the Ringling Museum or the beach, La Quinta has rooms with mini-refrigerators and pillow-top beds. Free Internet access and Continental breakfast are offered.

📶 P ⊘   **$**

Regency Inn and Suites
4200 N Tamiami Trail, 34234; 941 954 5775; www.regencyinnandsuites sarasota.com
This budget motel offers 14 rooms with refrigerators and microwaves, and 20 one-bedroom suites with full-size kitchens. Its location on the main highway is convenient for visiting the city's best attractions.

📶 🗄 ⊘   **$**

Holiday Inn Lido Beach
233 Ben Franklin Dr, 34236; 877 410 6667; www.holiday inn.com
This property boasts an unmatched location directly across the road from Lido Beach. Amenities include an indoor fitness center. The enclosed-rooftop dining room offers great views, and kids eat free.

📶 🍽 🔋 ⊘   **$$**

CAMPING
Myakka River State Park Cabins and Camping   Map 7 B4
13208 State Rd 72, 34241; 941 361 6511; www.myakkariver.org
Stay near the city but in the heart of unspoiled nature in these five rustic but comfortable log cabins lodging up to six people. Amenities include linen and blankets, kitchen utensils, and microwaves.

🛒 🗄 ◑ 🎣   **$**

Tampa   Map 7 B1

HOTELS
Hampton Inn-International Airport/Westshore
4817 W Laurel St, 33607; 813 287 0778; www.hamptoninn.hilton.com
Among the hotels clustered near Tampa Airport, where expressway connections make it easy to reach downtown, the Hampton Inn is one of the best. The spacious rooms are equipped with refrigerators and microwaves. Free breakfast.

📶 🔋 ⊘   **$**

Wingate By Wyndham
3751 E Fowler Ave, 33612; 813 979 2828; www.wingatehotels.com
This hotel is a good base for visiting Busch Gardens, and offers a free daily shuttle to the park. Rooms have refrigerators and microwaves, and the full breakfast buffet and Wi-Fi are free. The outdoor pool and indoor hot tub are refreshing after a day out in the theme park.

📶 P ⊘   **$**

Embassy Suites Tampa Airport/Westshore
555 N Westshore Blvd; 813 875 1555; www.embassysuites.com
This all-suite property stands out for families, as it provides a full living room with sofa bed and the privacy of a separate bedroom, plus two

TVs. Rooms have refrigerators and microwaves. The cooked-to-order breakfast and nightly cocktails are free.

🛒 📶 🔋 🛒 ⊘   **$$**

Embassy Suites Tampa Downtown Convention Center
513 South Florida Ave, 33602; 813 769 8300; www.embassysuites.com
This excellent family choice has the added plus of a downtown location served by the TECO trolley, making it easy to get to The Florida Aquarium or the Glazer's Children's Museum.

📶 🔋 🛒 ⊘   **$$**

Westin Tampa Harbour Island
725 S Harbour Island Blvd, 33602; 813 229 5000; www.starwood hotels.com
On a private island but just a footbridge away from downtown, the luxurious Westin has spacious rooms with oversize windows, many of which overlook Tampa Bay.

📶 🍽 P ⊘   **$$$**

Westin Tampa Harbour Island, a luxury waterfront hotel in downtown Tampa

CAMPING
Hillsborough River State Park   Map 7 B2
15402 US 301 N, Thonotossa, 33592; 800 326 3521; www.stateparks.com
This state park on the river 12 miles (19 km) north of Tampa has a 108-site campground for tents and RVs. Most sites have electricity and all have water. The park offers swimming, fishing, hiking, and biking trails.

⊘ ◑ 🎣   **$**

Price Guide
The following price ranges are based on one night's accommodation in high season for a family of four, inclusive of service charges and additional taxes.

$ Under $150 **$$** $150–300 **$$$** over $300

The Lower Gulf Coast, Everglades, and Keys

Florida's southernmost tip offers an irresistible package for families interested in history, culture, watersports, and nature. Lying close to the Caribbean islands, the Keys also share some of the former's characteristics. The Everglades are the culmination of the state's wilds, and have a Native American heritage. In the Fort Myers-Naples area, the barrier islands boast some of the state's best beaches, while Naples is famous for arts and golf.

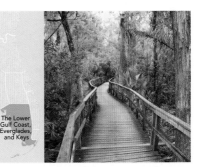

The Lower Gulf Coast, Everglades, and Keys

Highlights

Sanibel Island
Collect shells at this famous island and enjoy its safe beaches, family resorts, and great museums *(see p238)*.

Edison and Ford Winter Estates
Stimulate inventive young minds at the homes, gardens, and laboratories of two of America's greatest geniuses *(see p236)*.

Everglades National Park
Hike, bike, kayak, and boat around this mysterious land of mangrove forest, forgotten islands, wetlands, and a river of grass that teems with rare wildlife *(see pp242–3)*.

John Pennekamp Coral Reef State Park
Visit this undersea park to see brilliantly colored coral reefs by snorkel or aboard a glass-bottom boat *(see p251)*.

Key West
Head to this legendary island town to experience its eccentricity and unique spirit *(see pp246–7)*.

Fort Myers River District
Take in local history and culture in downtown Fort Myers, which has historic buildings, museums, galleries, and monthly street parties *(see p236)*.

Left *Signboards at the entrance to Robbie's Marina, Islamorada*
Above right *Wooden boardwalk winding through the swamp forest, Fakahatchee Strand State Preserve*

The Best of The Lower Gulf Coast, Everglades, and Keys

The great outdoors, history, and culture make this region a well-rounded destination with plenty for everyone. Families can get their fill of sunny beaches, warm seawaters, and watersports such as fishing, boating, jet-skiing, kayaking, and paddleboarding during their stay in this area. Massive national and state parks, as well as wildlife preserves, provide opportunities to hike, bike, and get close to nature.

In and on the water

Flanked by the Atlantic Ocean, Florida Bay, and the Gulf of Mexico, this area demands getting wet – or at least wetting a line. **Key Largo** (see pp250–51) is a good place to initiate kids into the wonderful world of underwater sightseeing. Ease them into it with a glass-bottom boat tour at **John Pennekamp Coral Reef State Park** (see p251). When they are ready to jump in, try the snorkeling tours offered by the park, or sign up with one of the numerous operators in town. Fishing in the Atlantic can get rough, so begin gently with a backwater Everglades fishing excursion from **Flamingo Visitor Center** (see p242) or in **Everglades City** (see p245). Head to Sanibel Island for an educational sea life cruise into **J. N. "Ding" Darling National Wildlife Refuge** (see p239).

Right Christ of the Deep, John Pennekamp Coral Reef State Park *Below* Anhinga and alligator, Everglades National Park

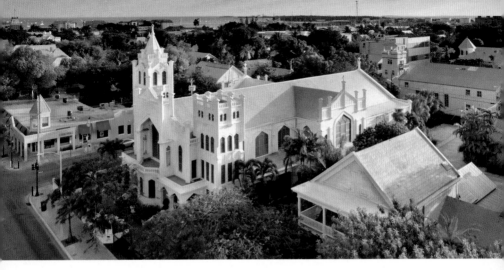

Above Aerial view of Duval Street, a famous shopping and dining hub in the heart of Old Town in Key West

Wildlife-watching

Alligator sightings are practically guaranteed at **Royal Palm Visitor Center** (see p242) to the east of **Everglades National Park** (see pp242–3) and at **Shark Valley Visitor Center** (see p242) in the west, while white-tailed deer, and raccoons also make occasional appearances. At **Flamingo Visitor Center**, saltwater crocodiles often sun themselves on the boat ramp. Birdwatchers should be able to tick off dozens of bird species from their "life list" of sightings in the **Everglades National Park** and **Big Cypress National Preserve** (see pp244–5). Other birding hot spots include **Tigertail Beach** (see p241) on **Marco Island** and **Corkscrew Swamp Sanctuary** (see p240) north of **Naples** (see p240).

Rambling around the Keys

With five to seven days to spend in the Florida Keys, start with a trolley tour in **Key West** (see pp246–7). Spend the remainder of the day walking around the Old Town and exploring the **Key West Aquarium** (see p246) and the **Eco-Discovery Center** (see p246) before hitting the beach at **Fort Zachary Taylor Historic State Park** (see p246). However, don't miss sunset at Mallory Square. Heading north, families can bike or kayak into **National Key Deer Refuge** on **Big Pine Key** (see p248), then factor in some quality beach or snorkeling time at **Bahia Honda State Park** (see p248). **Marathon** (see p249) merits a day of exploration: go to **Crane Point** (see p249) in the morning and either **Pigeon Key** (see p249) or **Sombrero Beach** (see p249) in the afternoon. Devote the remaining days to kayaking and snorkeling in **Islamorada** and **Key Largo** (see p250).

History hot spots

Local history runs deep throughout the region. One of Florida's oldest commercial ports, **Key West** holds the most treasures in its Old Town. **Pigeon Key** has the historic remains of the operation to build a railroad to Key West. The **Museum of the Everglades** (see p243) tells the story of the building of Tamiami Trail through the Everglades' wetlands and swamps. The **Marco Island Historical Museum** (see p241) focuses on the island's past as an ancient Calusa Indian capital. The **Edison and Ford Winter Estates**, in **Fort Myers** (see pp236–7), shed light on the lives of the two scientists who vacationed there. The **Southwest Florida Museum of History** (see p236) explores the area's fishing, cattle-ranching, and baseball heritage.

Left Cyclists heading towards Pigeon Key on the historic Seven-Mile Bridge

The Lower Gulf Coast, Everglades, and Keys

Florida tapers off to its narrowest and flattest at its southern tip. While barrier islands rim the shoreline along the Gulf Coast, sandy beaches, mangrove estuaries, saltwater marshes, and the shallow Florida Bay make up the unique Everglades. Further south are the Florida Keys, a string of islands that rest on a bed of coral and limestone from ancient reefs. The Tamiami Trail (Highway 41), known as "Alligator Alley" when it passes through the Everglades, connects the areas in this region. Interstate 75 is a faster route between Fort Myers and Naples.

Informative displays in the Bailey-Matthews Shell Museum, Sanibel Island

The Lowdown

Getting there and around
Air Southwest Florida International Airport (RSW), in Fort Myers, serves most of the major and low-fare airlines from destinations in and outside Florida. A couple of carriers fly small planes between Fort Myers and Key West. Several taxi companies service the airport and provide transportation throughout the region. Naples and Key West have small airports with a limited service. Most visitors to Key West fly into Miami International Airport (MIA) and drive to the Keys. **Car** Several rental car agencies are based at RSW. Note that all cars, including rentals, need a transponder device to use for the toll road from Miami to the Keys. Check www.sunpass.com/rentalcar for details.

Visitor information See individual entries.

Supermarkets Publix (www.publix.com) is the major chain here with outlets throughout this region. There is also Winn-Dixie, which is slightly more affordable.

Markets Different communities host farmers' markets on various days, sometimes only in the winter or spring season. Contact tourist offices for details.

Festivals Edison Festival of Light, Fort Myers: junior parade with floats and street performers; www.edisonfestival.org (Feb). Conch Republic Independence Celebration, Key West; www.conchrepublic.com (Apr)

Opening hours Some facilities in the Everglades area close in summer and the fall. Many restaurants in the Everglades and Keys close for a month in the fall.

Pharmacies Walgreens (www.walgreens.com) pharmacies in Fort Myers and Naples stay open 24 hours. However, in the Keys, CVS (www.cvs.com) and Walgreens do not stay open all night. Be sure to stock up on medical supplies before visiting the Everglades and Keys.

Restrooms All major attractions, fast-food restaurants, shopping malls, supermarkets, and gas stations have public restrooms.

Breathtaking view of Long Pine Key Lake, Everglades National Park

Places of interest

SIGHTS

1 Fort Myers
2 Sanibel and Captiva Islands
3 Upper Islands
4 J. N. "Ding" Darling National Wildlife Refuge
5 Corkscrew Swamp Sanctuary
6 Naples
7 Marco Island
8 Everglades National Park
9 Biscayne National Park
10 Miccosukee Indian Village
11 Big Cypress National Preserve
12 Everglades City
13 Key West
14 Big Pine Key
15 Bahia Honda State Park
16 Marathon
17 Islamorada
18 Key Largo
19 John Pennekamp Coral Reef State Park

The Busy Beehives exhibit in the Imaginarium Science Center, Fort Myers

Feeding tarpons at Robbie's Marina, Islamorada

① Fort Myers
Sunny skies and island beaches

Born out of the Seminole Wars that drove Native Americans into the Everglades, Fort Myers grew slowly along the Caloosahatchee River. In 1885, Thomas Edison saw bamboo growing here, and, hoping to use it as filament for his new invention, the light bulb, he built a winter home, putting Fort Myers on the map. Today, the Historic Downtown District draws visitors to its museums, theaters, shops, and restaurants. A trolley service links Fort Myers' main sights.

Pirate manatee at Manatee Park

Key Sights

④ **Art of the Olympians Museum** This museum in the Historic River District is the only one in the world to link sport and art. It features hands-on activities for kids.

⑤ **Cape Coral** Enjoy a day of fun at the Sunsplash Family Waterpark and Greenwell's Bat-a-Ball and Family Fun Park, located in this town across the river from Fort Myers.

⑥ **Manatee Park** In winter, watch snout-faced manatees in the warm waters of this park from the observation decks, or kayak among them for a whole new experience.

① **Edison and Ford Winter Estates** Edison built two homes and a lab on the river and his friend Henry Ford of Ford Motors later moved in next door. Tour a museum, botanical gardens, and the homes.

② **Southwest Florida Museum of History** Learn about the Calusa tribesmen and cow-hunters, visit a Cracker shack, and see a private Pullman railcar at this museum.

③ **Imaginarium Science Center** Children will delight in seeing the local marine life (including sharks), feeling the force of a hurricane, or even touching a cloud.

⑦ **Calusa Nature Center and Planetarium** Meet fascinating creatures from southwest Florida, then head to the planetarium to view the heavens.

The Lowdown

🌐 **Map reference** 7 C5
Address Edison and Ford Winter Estates: 2350 McGregor Blvd, 33901; edisonfordwinterestates.org. Southwest Florida Museum of History: 2031 Jackson St, 33901; swflmuseumofhistory.com. Imaginarium Science Center: 2000 Cranford Ave, 33902; imaginariumfortmyers.com. Art of the Olympians Museum: 1300 Hendry St, 33901; artoftheolympians.org. Manatee Park: 10901 State Rd 80, Palm Beach Blvd, 33905; www.leeparks.org. Calusa Nature Center and Planetarium: 3450 Ortiz Ave, 33905; calusanature.org

🚗 **Bus** LeeTran buses (www.rideleetran.com) to most sights

ℹ️ **Visitor information** Lee County Visitor & Convention Bureau, 2201 2nd St, 6th floor, 33901; www.fortmyers-sanibel.com

🕐 **Open** Edison and Ford Winter Estates: 9am–5:30pm. Southwest Florida Museum of History: 10am–5pm Tue–Sat. Imaginarium Science Center: 10am–5pm Mon–Sat, noon–5pm Sun. Art of the Olympians: 10am–4pm Tue–Sat. Manatee Park: 8am–sunset. Calusa Nature Center and Planetarium: 10am–5pm Mon–Sat, 11am–5pm Sun

💲 **Prices** Edison and Ford Winter Estates: $62–80; under 5s free. Southwest Florida Museum of History & Calusa Nature Center and Planetarium: $30–40; under 3s free. Imaginarium Science Center: $40–50; under 2s free. Art of the Olympians: $10–20; under 12s free. Manatee Park: $1 per car per hour or $5 per day

👪 **Cutting the line** Arrive early, as parking lots fill up quickly.

👉 **Guided tours** Admission to the Edison & Ford Winter Estates is by guided or self-guided audio tour. There is also an extensive Behind the Scenes tour.

Prices given are for a family of four

Letting off steam

Get some fresh air and playtime at **Centennial Park** (*2000 W 1st St; 239 321 7530*), which overlooks the Caloosahatchee River in the River District. A fishing pier, picnic tables, and lots of benches for overlooking the river give the park an old-world charm.

Uncommon Friends by D.J. Wilkins in Centennial Park

Eat and drink

Picnic: under $25; Snacks: $25–50; Real meal: $50–80; Family treat: over $80 (based on a family of four)

PICNIC Publix Delis (*13401 Summerlin Rd, 33919; 239 481 2242; www.publix.com*) has great subs, salads, and chicken wings. Picnic at **Lakes Regional Park** (*7330 Gladiolus Dr, 33908; www.leeparks. org*), a 20-minute drive on the highway, where kids can ride a mini-train, or cool off in the fountain.
SNACKS Rene's (*12731 McGregor Blvd, 33919; 239 489 0833; www. reneslunch.com*) offers some of the best sandwiches and salads in town.

🧑‍🤝‍🧑 **Age range** 2 plus for most sights; 6 plus for Edison and Ford Winter Estates and Southwest Florida Museum of History

🏃 **Activities** Edison and Ford Young Inventors family tours at 11am on Sat

⏱ **Allow** 3 days or more

🚻 **Restrooms** In all the sights

Good family value?

Fort Myers Beach is known for its affordable accommodations and restaurants. Cape Coral, too, offers good value for families who don't mind a drive to the beach.

In addition, there are soups, wraps, pitas, and croissants on the menu. Do try their awesome carrot cake.
REAL MEAL The Edison (*3583 McGregor Blvd, 33901; 239 936 9349; www.edisonfl.com*) is perfect before or after visiting Edison's digs. There are soups, pizza, pasta, and seafood. Kids eat free on Mondays.
FAMILY TREAT Bayfront Bistro (*4761 Estero Blvd, 33931; 239 463 3663; www.bayfrontbistro.com*) offers seafood quesadillas, fish tacos, and fish sandwiches. Sit on the porch overlooking the marina for the view.

Shopping

Look for bargains at flea markets in Fort Myers, such as Fleamasters (*4135 Dr. M. L. King Jr Blvd; 239 334 7001; www.fleamall.com*). Downtown's **Franklin Shops** (*2200 1st St; 239 333 3130; www.the franklinshops.com*) have everything from apparel and jewelry to fine art within a historic building.

Find out more

DIGITAL Visit the Young Inventors page at *www.edisonfordwinter estates.org* and find coloring sheets and a detective game to play.
FILM The movie *Hoot* (2006), based on the book of the same name, is set in a fictional town based on Cape Coral and its burrowing owl population. Much of the filming was done in this area.

Relaxing at tranquil Bowditch Point Park, Fort Myers Beach

Next stop...

FORT MYERS BEACH Take a LeeTran bus 16 miles (26 km) southwest to Fort Myers Beach, a favorite with families. Visit its Lynn Hall Memorial Park beach, which has a cool playground, a fishing pier, and a pedestrian mall. Hit Bowditch Point Park for a quieter, more natural beach experience.

② Sanibel and Captiva Islands

Shell-bent and water-bound

These two barrier islands, attached by a short bridge, boast a reputation for shelling, and also for wildlife and watersports. The islands have given rise to the expressions Sanibel Stoop and Captiva Crouch, which refer to the posture shell-seekers habitually assume while hunting on the shell-blanketed beaches.

A causeway from the mainland brings visitors to Sanibel Island, more than half of which is a protected wildlife refuge. The **Sanibel Historical Museum and Village** exhibits historic island homes and buildings. At Sanibel's **Lighthouse Beach**, there is lots to do – from fishing off the pier to exploring the historic lighthouse and the nature trails. Along the island's "conservation corridor,"

Vacationers at one of Sanibel Island's beautiful beaches

nature-lovers can learn how the **Clinic for the Rehabilitation of Wildlife (CROW)** administers to sick and orphaned animals. Visit a butterfly house, climb an observation tower for fine views, and hike trails at the **Sanibel-Captiva Conservation Foundation (SCCF).**

Farther north, Captiva Island has an off-the-beaten-path vibe. Rent a boat or kayak at one of the marinas to fish, or to explore the upper islands. Charter and tour boats customize tours for shelling, fishing, and dolphin-watching.

Kids learning about shells at the Bailey-Matthews Shell Museum, Sanibel Island

Take cover

Head for Sanibel's **Bailey-Matthews Shell Museum** (3075 Sanibel-Captiva Rd, 33957; www.shellmuseum.org), to identify beach findings and admire seashells, or take part in shell scavenger hunts.

③ Upper Islands

Adrift from the mainland

North of Captiva Island are a set of islands with no bridges to the mainland, and no means of access other than by boat. Closest to Captiva, North Captiva Island broke

The Lowdown

🌐 **Map reference** 7 C6

Address Sanibel Historical Museum and Village: 950 Dunlop Rd, 33957; www.sanibelmuseum. org. Lighthouse Beach: East end of Periwinkle Way, 33931; 239 472 3700. CROW: 3883 Sanibel-Captiva Rd, 33957; www.crow clinic.org. SCCF: 3333 Sanibel-Captiva Rd, 33957; www.sccf.org

🚗 **Car** Rent a car from Fort Myers.

ℹ️ **Visitor information** Sanibel Island & Captiva Island Chamber of Commerce, 1159 Causeway Rd, 33957–3709; 239 472 1080; www.sanibel-captiva.org

🕑 **Open** Sanibel Historical Museum and Village: Wed–Sat. SCCF: Mon–Fri (Dec–Apr: also Sat & Jun–Sep: till 3pm Mon–Fri)

💲 **Prices** Sanibel Historical Museum and Village & SCCF: $10–20; under 18s free. CROW: $15–25; under 13s free

👫 **Cutting the line** Sanibel's sights are not usually crowded, except when school groups visit them.

🚩 **Guided tours** SCCF runs guided nature and beach walks and butterfly house tours seasonally.

🕑 **Allow** At least a day

🍴 **Eat and drink** SNACKS Hungry Heron (2330 Palm Ridge Rd, 33957; www.hungryheron.com) has 36 kids' items on its extensive menu. REAL MEAL Jerry's Foods Family Restaurant (1700 Periwinkle Way, 33957; www.jerrysfoods.com) serves a range of cuisine all day.

The Lowdown

🌐 **Map reference** 7 C5

Address Cayo Costa State Park: Boca Grande, 33921; 941 964 0375; www.floridastateparks.org

🚗 **Boat** Water taxi from Jensen's Marina (www.gocaptiva.com) on Captiva Island to the Upper Islands. Captiva Cruises (www. captivacruises.com) does lunch excursions to Cabbage Key.

ℹ️ **Visitor information** Sanibel Island & Captiva Island Chamber of Commerce, 1159 Causeway Rd, Sanibel Island, 33957; 239 472 1080; www.sanibel-captiva.org

🕑 **Open** Cayo Costa State Park: 8am–sunset daily

💲 **Price** Cayo Costa State Park: $8–18

👫 **Cutting the line** Avoid Cabbage Key when the Captiva Cruises lunch excursion is on the island.

👫 **Age range** 3 plus

🕑 **Allow** Half a day or more

🍴 **Eat and drink** REAL MEAL Barnacle Phil's Harbor Restaurant (North Captiva, 33924; 239 472 1200; barnaclephilsrestaurant.word press.com) is famous for its black beans and rice. REAL MEAL Cabbage Key Inn (Cabbage Key, 33922; 239 283 2278; www. cabbagekey.com) is where diners write their family name on a dollar bill and tape it to the wall before digging into burgers, grilled cheese sandwiches, and seafood.

off from its parent island during a hurricane in the 1920s. Private and vacation rental homes, a grassy airstrip, and a club occupy the quiet, 5-mile (8-km) long island, along with superb beaches and restaurants. Walk or rent a golf cart to get around the island.

Farther north, Cayo Costa Island is mostly occupied by the **Cayo Costa State Park**, where visitors can swim, collect shells, hike, and camp or rent cabins. Look out for the pioneer cemetery along one of several nature trails.

Between Cayo Costa and the mainland, Cabbage Key has no beaches, but its rustic 1920s Cabbage Key Inn is a great attraction for the island-hopping lunch crowd. Have a bite to eat, and then walk it off along a short nature trail. Visitors can also spend the night at the inn, or in one of its cottages.

Letting off steam

Head to the uninhabited **Picnic Island**, near Sanibel Island, for a picnic on its beach park. Be sure to bring along essential supplies. Adventures in Paradise (www. adventureinparadiseinc.com) runs tours to the island, which include netting and identifying sea life.

Boating off a beach at Cayo Costa State Park

④ J. N. "Ding" Darling National Wildlife Refuge

Into the wild

Named for Jay Norwood, a Pulitzer-Prize-winning American cartoonist, and covering more than half of Sanibel Island, "Ding" gives the island its reputation among wildlife-lovers, especially birders. It counts about 230 species of birds among its resident and migrating populations, including the bald eagle, the roseate spoonbill, and the mangrove cuckoo.

At its main campus along Sanibel-Captiva Road, the refuge has an Education Center, a 4-mile (6-km) Wildlife Drive through wetlands, an observation tower, and several trails. Nearby, Bailey Tract protects a different freshwater habitat, which alligators and nocturnal bobcats frequent.

Horseshoe crab in J.N. "Ding" Darling National Wildlife Refuge, Sanibel Island

Take cover

The **"Ding" Darling Education Center** in the refuge has various interactive exhibits. Check out the eBird computer, habitat vignettes, a Kids' Corner, and the nature store with games, books, and toys.

The Lowdown

🌐 **Map reference** 7 C6
Address 1 Wildlife Dr, Sanibel Island, 33957; 239 472 1100; www.fws.gov/dingdarling

🚗 **Car** Rent a car from Fort Myers.

ℹ️ **Visitor information** Sanibel Island & Captiva Island Chamber of Commerce, 1159 Causeway Rd, 33957; 239 472 1080; www.sanibel-captiva.org

🕐 **Open** 7am–sunset Sat–Thu

💲 **Price** $5 per vehicle & $1 per cyclist or pedestrian

🚶 **Guided tours** For a narrated tour of Wildlife Drive, hop aboard the refuge tram (239 472 8900). The Sealife Nature Tour at Tarpon Bay Recreation Area (www.tarponbay explorers.com), located south of the refuge, includes a touch tank presentation.

👫 **Age range** 3 plus

🏃 **Activities** Ask at the Education Center desk about Junior Ranger and Earth Caching activities, as well as reading-and-crafts programs for kids. At the Tarpon Bay Recreation Area, kayak, nature and sea life, and sunset boat tours take visitors into the area's preserved rookeries, or along a mangrove estuary trail.

⏱️ **Allow** At least half a day

☕ **Eat and drink** SNACKS Lazy Flamingo (6520-C Pine Ave, 33957; 239 472 5353; www.lazy flamingo.com) offers reasonably priced sandwiches and seafood. REAL MEAL Doc Ford's Sanibel (975 Rabbit Rd, 33957; 239 472 8311; www.docfordssanibel.com) tempts with family favorites such as fish fingers and beach bread.

⑤ Corkscrew Swamp Sanctuary

A big bird's nest and age-old trees

Some 20 miles (32 km) from Bonita Beach lies a whole different brand of water wonderland – the swamp. The Corkscrew Swamp Sanctuary is the regional headquarters of the Great Florida Birding Trail, and here nature-lovers can wander a 2-mile (4-km) boardwalk to explore a rich habitat where alligators, bobcats, black bears, and white-tailed deer cavort. Perhaps the sanctuary's most important creature, however, is the wood stork. These big white-and-black birds come to nest in the 500-year-old bald cypress trees. The towering trees, with their protruding "knees," constitute the species' largest old-growth stand in the country. The wood stork is only one of the 200 or so species that visit the sanctuary – others include wading birds, songbirds, raptors, the tricolored heron, and the fabulous painted bunting.

Black crowned night heron in the Corkscrew Swamp Sanctuary

Take cover

After exploring the Corkscrew trail, visit the **Blair Audubon Center** (on site) and learn about the sanctuary's ecology. Kids will love the Swamp Theater, which re-creates a day in the swamp with sound and light, and the cool nature store.

⑥ Naples

A little Italy, Florida-style

The hardy pioneers who settled south of Florida's west coast compared the area's beaches and waterways to those of Italy, and so they named their settlement Naples-on-the-Gulf. Today, the city's architecture and cuisine have an Italian flavor.

Once a rough-and-tumble Indian trading post, Naples has evolved into a haven for vacationers seeking golf, shopping, and fine dining. The heart of downtown, known as Old Naples, has two fashionable streets – Fifth Avenue South and Third Street South. Most of the town's superb restaurants are located here. Near Third Street South, the Naples Pier stretches into the Gulf of Mexico from the beach's soft white sands.

Northeast of the downtown area, the **Children's Museum of Naples** is located in North Collier Regional Park, also home to the **Sun-n-Fun Lagoon** water park. In the museum, kids can drive a facsimile of the Naples Trolley, climb up to a tree house, walk into a seashell, and chill out in an igloo.

With the Everglades at its back door, Naples sees plenty of wildlife. However, the easiest way to spot animals – local and from as far away as Madagascar – is to head to **Naples Zoo**. Special animal shows, giraffe hand-feeding, and a boat excursion to Primate Island add adventure to a visit.

The Lowdown

🌐 **Map reference** 9 D1
Address 375 Sanctuary Rd, 34120; 239 348 9151; www.corkscrewsanctuary.org

🚗 **Car** Rent a car from Fort Myers.

ℹ️ **Visitor information** Greater Naples Marco Everglades Convention & Visitors Bureau, 2800 N Horseshoe Blvd, 34104; www.paradisecoast.com

🕐 **Open** Apr 11–Sep 30: 7am–7:30pm & Oct 1–Apr 10: 7am–5:30pm (last adm 1 hour before closing)

💲 **Price** $28–40; under 6s free

👫 **Cutting the line** Call ahead to see if any school or youth groups will be visiting that day.

🚩 **Guided tours** The education staff leads tours early morning, at sunset, and at night in season. Check website for dates and timings.

👫 **Age range** 5 plus

⏱️ **Allow** 2 hours

☕ **Eat and drink** PICNIC Publix (12900 Trade Way Four, Bonita Springs, 34135; 239 992 2159; www.publix.com) sells salads, sandwiches, and drinks. There is a picnic area across the parking lot.

The Lowdown

🌐 **Map reference** 9 C1
Address Children's Museum of Naples: 15080 Livingston Rd, 34109; www.cmon.org. Sun-n-Fun Lagoon: 15000 Livingston Rd, 34109; www.collierparks.com. Naples Zoo: 1590 Goodlette-Frank Rd, 34102; www.napleszoo.com

🚗 **Car** Rent a car from Fort Myers.

ℹ️ **Visitor information** Greater Naples Marco Everglades Convention & Visitors Bureau, 2800 N Horseshoe Blvd, 34104; 239 252 2384; www.paradisecoast.com

🕐 **Open** Children's Museum of Naples: 10am–5pm Tue–Sat, 11am–4pm Sun. Sun-n-Fun Lagoon: hours vary, check website for timings. Naples Zoo: 9am–5pm daily

💲 **Prices** Children's Museum of Naples: $40–50; under 1s free. Sun-n-Fun Lagoon: $35–48; under 4s free. Naples Zoo: $66–80; under 3s free

🚩 **Guided tours** The Naples Trolley (www.naplestrolleytours.com) runs tours of the town from Old Naples north to Vanderbilt Beach.

⏱️ **Allow** A day

☕ **Eat and drink** SNACKS Aurelio's Is Pizza (590 N Tamiami Trail, 34102; 239 403 8882; www.aureliosofnaples.com) offers tasty pizza, pasta, and sandwiches. REAL MEAL Dock at Crayton Cove (845 12th Ave S, 34102; 239 263 9940; www.dockcraytoncove.com) is an old fishhouse-style place on the water with a kids' menu.

Kids enjoying a guided camel ride in Naples Zoo

Letting off steam

Head north of Naples to **Delnor-Wiggins Pass State Park** (11135 Gulf Shore Dr N, 34108; 239 597 6196; www.floridastateparks.org/delnor-wiggins) on Vanderbilt Beach.

Vanderbilt Beach, a popular white-sand beach in Naples

Families can soak up the sun, climb the observation tower, fish in the pass, kayak, and, in summer, follow a ranger on a sea turtle walk.

7 Marco Island

Indians, fishermen, and one cool cat

The jumping-off point for Ten Thousand Islands, a maze of protected islands to the south, Marco Island prides itself on its fishing and boating. Rent or charter a boat from one of the island's marinas and get out on the water. At its east end, the fishing town of Goodland retains the salty character of old-time fishing communities.

The Calusa Indians fished these waters for 1,500 years, until they were wiped out by European invaders. They built one center of their kingdom on Marco Island, as revealed by archaeological excavations in 1895. One important find, a carved wood effigy known as the Key Marco Cat, now resides in the Smithsonian Institution in Washington D.C. Families can drive over the top of one 58-ft (18-m) ancient shell mound and follow trails along another at the **Otter Mound Preserve**.

Two public beach accesses welcome visitors to Marco's wide beaches. **Tigertail Beach** has playgrounds and a sheltered lagoon that draws lots of birds, especially in winter.

Take cover

Go to the **Marco Island Historical Museum** (*180 Heathwood Dr, 34145; 239 642 1440; www.themihs. org*), which was built to look like a Calusa Indian village on the outside. The museum has displays that tell the local history. Replicas of the Key Marco Cat can be seen and purchased in the museum's store.

The Lowdown

- 🌐 **Map reference** 9 D2
- 📍 **Address** Otter Mound Preserve: 1831 Addison Ct, 34145; *www. colliergov.net*. Tigertail Beach: 430 Hernando Dr, 34145; *www.collierparks.com*
- 🚗 **Car** Rent a car from Naples.
- ℹ️ **Visitor information** Greater Naples Marco Everglades Convention & Visitors Bureau, 2800 N Horseshoe Blvd, 34104; *www.paradisecoast.com*
- 🕐 **Open** Otter Mound Preserve: daily. Tigertail Beach: 8am–sunset
- 💲 **Price** Otter Mound Preserve: free
- 👫 **Cutting the line** Arrive early as Tigertail Beach's parking lot fills quickly in season, and on weekends.
- 🚩 **Guided tours** Check the website of the Conservancy of Southwest Florida (*www.conservancy.org*) for tours.
- 👫 **Age range** All ages
- ⏱️ **Allow** A day
- 🍴 **Eat and drink** SNACKS Old Marco Lodge Crab House (*401 Papaya St, Goodland, 34140; 239 642 7227; www.oldmarcolodge.com*) is a historic place with outdoor porch seating and live entertainment. It serves crab cakes, chicken quesadillas, and salads. REAL MEAL Snook Inn (*1215 Bald Eagle Dr, 34145; www.snookinn.com*) overlooks the Marco River outside, under a thatched tiki roof; inside an aquarium and salad bar dominate. The menu offers many seafood and meat dishes.

⑧ Everglades National Park
Florida's land down under

Displaced Native Americans and outlaws were among the first to settle in this forbidding land riddled with swamps at the very bottom of Florida. Later came slick developers who wanted to drain the precious wetland in favor of building. Luckily, Marjory Douglas Stoneman stepped up in the 1940s to make sure that this special territory would forever be protected as the Everglades National Park. Today, the park safeguards 2,200 sq miles (3,540 sq km), and more than 1,000 species of fish, birds, reptiles, amphibians, and mammals.

View from the observation tower

Key Sights

① Flamingo Visitor Center See the exhibits and pick up maps for exploring trails and waterways. Besides a marina and store, the center also has a campground on Florida Bay.

② Trails along the drive to Flamingo The 38-mile (60-km) Main Park Road passes four major trailheads for short hikes: Pinelands Trail, Pa-hay-okee Overlook, Mahogany Hammock Trail, and West Lake.

③ Long Pine Key Arguably the prettiest spot in the Everglades, this area's forest of pine trees is perfect for picnicking, or an overnight stay in the well-kept campground.

④ Royal Palm Visitor Center The first stop along the Main Park Road to Flamingo, this is one of the best places to spot wildlife. The popular Anhinga and Gumbo Limbo trails begin here.

⑤ Ernest Coe Visitor Center/ Main Entrance This center lies outside the park gates and its interactive exhibits make a good introduction to the park.

⑥ Shark Valley Entrance/ Visitor Center Hike, bike, or take the tram tour from here around the 15-mile (24-km) loop trail. Climb the observation tower for fine views.

⑦ Gulf Coast Entrance/ Visitor Center Hiking, boating, kayaking, and biking tours depart from this west coast gateway in the historic fishing town of Everglades City.

Letting off steam

Stop over at one of the Everglades' more remote accesses, **Chekika** (24200 SW 160th St, Miami, 33194; Dec–Apr), north of Homestead. A short boardwalk trail passes sawgrass wetlands, a hammock, and a gator hole before reaching a nice green lawn for picnicking.

Eat and drink

Picnic: under $25; Snacks: $25–50; Real meal: $50–80; Family treat: over $80 (based on a family of four)

PICNIC Robert Is Here Fruit Stand (19200 SW 344th St, Homestead, 33034; 305 246 1592; www.robert

Prices given are for a family of four

ishere.com) offers fruit smoothies and snacks. Picnic in the grounds near the free petting farm and splash pool.

SNACKS Buttonwood Café (Flamingo Visitor Center; 239 695 3101; tinyurl.com/7d5bjne) operates

Fresh produce for sale at the Robert Is Here Fruit Stand, Homestead

in the winter–spring season. It has hot dogs, burgers, steaks, and a kids' menu. It also cooks guests' fish catches for a nominal charge.

REAL MEAL Oyster House Restaurant (Hwy 29 S, Everglades City, 34139; 239 695 2073; www.oysterhouserestaurant.com) keeps families entertained with its mounted animals and other crazy memorabilia. Start off with an order of fried gator or frog legs.

FAMILY TREAT Capri Restaurant (935 N Krome Ave, Florida City, 33034; 305 247 1542; www.dinecapri.com) offers a menu that covers everything from sandwiches and entrée salads to pizza and pasta.

The Lowdown

Map reference 9 F3
Address Flamingo Visitor Center: 38 miles (61 km) past entrance on Main Park Rd; 239 695 2945. Royal Palm Visitor Center: 2 miles (3 km) past entrance on Royal Palm Rd; 305 242 7700. Ernest Coe Visitor Center: 40001 State Rd 9336, Homestead, 33034–6733; 305 242 7700. Shark Valley Visitor Center: 36000 SW 8th St, Miami, 33194; 305 221 8776. Gulf Coast Visitor Center: 815 Oyster Bar Lane, Everglades City, 34139; 239 695 3311

Car Rent a car from Homestead for the Main Entrance; Miami airport for the Shark Valley Entrance, and Naples airport for the Gulf Coast Entrance.

Open Everglades National Park & trails: daily. Flamingo Visitor Center: 9am–4:30pm daily (lobby: all day). Royal Palm Visitor Center: 8am–4:15pm daily. Ernest Coe Visitor Center: mid-Apr–mid-Dec: 9am–5pm daily; rest of the year 8am–5pm daily (main entrance daily). Shark Valley Visitor Center: 9:15am–5:15pm; also check website. Gulf Coast Visitor Center: 8:30am–4:30pm daily in season (Dec–Apr); shorter hours rest of the year

Prices Everglades National Park Main: $10 per vehicle; $5 per pedestrian or cyclist, under 17s free. Shark Valley: $76–86, under 3s free. Other entrances and visitor centers: free

Cutting the line The Everglades' two seasons are dry (winter) and wet (summer). Low risk of flooding and fewer mosquitoes make winter the most popular time to visit. Be sure to carry bug repellent, especially in the wet season.

Guided tours Go for a two-hour tram tour at Shark Valley (www.sharkvalleytramtours.com). Boat tours depart from the Flamingo marina and Gulf Coast entrance; call the visitor centers for schedule and prices.

Age range 6 plus

Activities Download the Junior Ranger Book at www.nps.gov/ever/forkids/beajuniorranger.htm, or ask for it at the visitor centers.

Allow At least 2 days

Café Buttonwood Café in the Flamingo Visitor Center (see p242)

Restrooms In all visitor centers and campgrounds

Good family value?

The Everglades offers year-round outdoor fun, with amazing wildlife to see and great trails to explore. The prices suit all budgets.

Shopping

Drop in to the **Gift Shop** (at most visitor centers) and support conservation efforts. Choose from rubber snakes, plush birds, wildlife puzzles, books, and T-shirts.

Find out more

DIGITAL Check out the kids' pages on www.nps.gov/ever/forkids/learning-about-the-everglades.htm.

Take cover

The **Museum of the Everglades** (www.colliermuseums.com), in Everglades City, focuses on the huge feat of blazing a road through the swampy Everglades and on the region's Calusa Indian and fishing heritage.

Next stop...

WILDER WILDERNESS Head 73 miles (117 km) northwest to explore the **Rookery Bay National Estuarine Research Reserve** (www.rookerybay.org), an unspoiled mangrove estuary. The learning center here has a huge aquarium and interactive exhibits about the park's history. The **Ten Thousand Islands National Wildlife Refuge** (www.fws.gov) offers fishing and a chance to observe wildlife.

Mangroves in Rookery Bay National Reserve

KIDS' CORNER

Croc or gator?

How can you tell a crocodile from an alligator? Luckily, you don't have to get too close to distinguish one from the other!

1 The American alligator has dark skin and a wide snout for cracking turtle shells.
2 A croc is lighter in color than a gator, with a narrower, pointier snout and a flatter profile in the water.
3 When a gator closes its mouth, the teeth in its top jaw are the only ones visible. When a croc closes its mouth, you can see its distinctive overbite: the teeth of both jaws are visible.

HOW DO YOU SPELL "EVERGLADES"?

Write out Everglades National Park, leaving spaces between the letters. For each letter in the park's name, think of something you saw or learned about that starts with that letter. Write them down, until you've used up all 22 letters with no repeated words.

Collecting birds

Serious birders keep what they call a life list – a record of every species of bird they have seen in the wilds during their lifetime. The Everglades, with 366 species, is the best place to start your Florida life list.

With the help of a ranger, see how many birds you can spot. Print the Florida bird list at fl.audubon.org/PDFs/birds_checklist.pdf, and check off all the birds you saw.

⑨ Biscayne National Park

Water, water, everywhere

This vast, mostly underwater refuge encompasses the third-longest stretch of coral reef in the world. Geographically, the park kicks off the Florida Keys, and, for outdoor enthusiasts, it has it all – boating, kayaking, snorkeling, scuba diving, hiking, camping, and also a slice of history dating back to the Tequesta Indians. However, it takes some effort to enjoy what's best about the park, namely what's under and out on the water. Biscayne's two main islands – Boca Chita and Elliott Key – are accessible only by boat, but worth the trip to learn about some quirky elements of local history, hike trails, go fishing, and camp overnight.

Take cover

Overlooking the marina at Biscayne National Park, the **Dante Fascell Visitor Center** (9700 SW 328th St, Homestead, 33033; 305 230 7275; www.nps.gov/bisc) houses artistic exhibits representing the park's

Palmetto dolls and beadwork for sale in the Miccosukee Indian Village

different maritime habitats. In the auditorium, rotating exhibits show the Biscayne-related art of local painters.

⑩ Miccosukee Indian Village

Going native

The Miccosukee Indian tribe has lived at the edge of the Everglades on a narrow strip of land since the Seminole Wars chased them from their homeland, Tallahassee, in the 1800s. Today, visitors can experience their way of life and learn about their beliefs at this village. Guided and self-guided tours of the superb museum and its grounds explore the history of the Miccosukee and their thatched huts, or chickee, with elevated floors. Members of the tribe give daring alligator presentations and demonstrate native crafts all day.

Letting off steam

Hop aboard an airboat tour from the Miccosukee Village to visit a Native American clan camp. A former tribal chief takes visitors out on a cultural experience with **Buffalo Tiger's Airboat Tours** (www.buffalotigers airboattours.com).

⑪ Big Cypress National Preserve

Bald cypresses, furry critters, and feathered friends

The US government legislated the creation of Big Cypress to put an end to logging operations that were depleting the forest of its tall, beautiful, bald cypress trees. The preserve provides a number of options for adventure enthusiasts. Begin at the **Oasis Visitor Center** or **Big Cypress Swamp Welcome Center**. The Oasis' boardwalk is a great place to see gators swimming down below. Walk the boardwalk at the Welcome Center and listen to the manatees blow as they surface for a breath of air. Pick up a map

Young visitors at the Big Cypress Swamp Welcome Center

The Lowdown

🌐 **Map reference** 10 H3

🚗 **Car** Rent a car from Homestead. The park provides boats to the main islands (305 230 1100).

ℹ️ **Visitor information** Tropical Everglades Visitor Center, 160 US Hwy 1, Florida City, 33034; 305 245 9180; www.tropical everglades.com

🕐 **Open** Visitor center: 9am–5pm daily; grounds: 7am–5:30pm daily

💲 **Price** Free

🚩 **Guided tours** The park conducts snorkeling, scuba, and glass-bottom boat tours in winter and spring. Rangers run programs during the same season.

👫 **Age range** 5 plus

👪 **Activities** Pick up a Junior Ranger activity booklet at the visitor center.

⏱️ **Allow** 1–2 days

🍴 **Eat and drink** PICNIC The visitor center (on site; 305 230 1100) sells cold sandwiches, snacks, and beverages. REAL MEAL Mutineer Restaurant (11 SE 1st Ave, Florida City, 33034; 305 245 3377; www.mutineer.biz) has an extensive menu of local dishes and seafood on offer.

The Lowdown

🌐 **Map reference** 10 F2

🏠 **Address** MM 70, Tamiami Trail, Miami, 33194; 1 877 242 6464; www.miccosukee.com/indian_village

🚗 **Car** Rent a car from Miami airport.

ℹ️ **Visitor information** Tropical Everglades Visitor Center, 160 US 1, Florida City, 33034; 305 245 9180; www.tropicaleverglades.com

🕐 **Open** 9am–4pm daily

💲 **Price** $32–42; under 5s free

🚩 **Guided tours** Museum and airboat tours run all day.

👫 **Age range** 5 plus

⏱️ **Allow** Half a day

🍴 **Eat and drink** SNACKS Everglades Gator Park (24050 SW 8th St, Miami 33194; 305 559 2255; www.gatorpark.com) offers local delicacies such as gator tail, gator sausage, and catfish sandwiches. REAL MEAL Miccosukee Restaurant (on site; 305 894 2374) serves frog legs, pumpkin bread, and other Native American dishes, as well as burgers and salads.

The Lowdown

🌐 **Map reference** 10 E2

Address Ochopee 34141.
Big Cypress National Preserve:
33100 Tamiami Trail E; 239 695
2000; www.nps.gov/bicy. Big
Cypress Swamp Welcome Center:
33000 Tamiami Trail E; 239 695
4758. Oasis Visitor Center: 52105
Tamiami Trail E; 239 695 1201

🚗 **Car** Rent a car from Shark Valley.

ℹ️ **Visitor information** Greater
Naples Marco Everglades
Convention & Visitors Bureau,
2800 N Horseshoe Blvd, Naples,
34104; 239 252 2384; www.
paradisecoast.com

🕐 **Open** Oasis Visitor Center & Big
Cypress Swamp Welcome Center:
9am–4:30pm daily

💲 **Price** Free

🚩 **Guided tours** Free ranger-led
tours in winter and spring.

👫 **Age range** 6 plus

👫 **Activities** Ask for a Junior Ranger
activity booklet at either center.

⏱️ **Allow** Half a day to a full day

🍽️ **Eat and drink** SNACKS Coopertown
(22700 SW 8th St, Miami; 305 226
6048; www.coopertownairboats.
com) sells sandwiches and frog
legs. REAL MEAL Joanie's Blue
Crab Café (39395 Hwy 41,
34141; 239 695 2682) serves
authentic Everglades cuisine.

at either center and rent a kayak in
Everglades City to paddle trails, or
hike on part of the statewide Florida
Trail. In the dry season, following one
of the scenic drives is a good idea.

Take cover
Visit the **Big Cypress Swamp
Welcome Center** to learn about
Florida's wildlife and watersheds,
using games and hands-on devices.

⑫ Everglades City
Gateway to the Gulf Coast

Located at the western entrance to
the Everglades National Park, this
sleepy little town offers opportunities
for fishing, kayaking, and airboat
rides. Nearby, there are attractions
that introduce families to the
Everglades' unique plant and animal
life. The **Fakahatchee Strand State
Preserve**, 5 miles (8 km) north of
town, is known for its wild orchids.
Located 15 miles (24 km) to the
northwest, the **Collier-Seminole
State Park** is the place for biking,
hiking, and camping. Head for

*Bald cypress trees in Fakahatchee
Strand State Preserve*

Wooten's Airboat Tours, 6 miles
(9 km) to the northeast, where a gator
pond and animal exhibits, as well
as shows, supplement tours.

Take cover
Across a causeway from Everglades
City, Chokoloskee Island is home to
the **Historic Smallwood Store &
Museum** (www.smallwoodstore.
com), an old Indian trading post on
the bay that still holds some vintage
products and historic exhibits.

The Lowdown

🌐 **Map reference** 10 E2

Address Fakahatchee Strand
State Preserve: 137 Coastline Dr,
Copeland, 34137; www.florida
stateparks.org. Collier-Seminole
State Park: 20200 E Tamiami Trail,
Naples, 34114; www.floridastate
parks.org. Wooten's Airboat Tours:
32330 Tamiami Trail, Ochopee,
34141; wootensairboats.com

🚗 **Car** Rent a car from Miami airport.

ℹ️ **Visitor information** Visitors
Bureau, 2800 N Horseshoe Blvd,
Naples, 34104; 239 252 2384;
www.paradisecoast.com

🕐 **Open** Fakahatchee Strand State
Preserve, Collier-Seminole Park
& Wooten's Airboat Tours: daily

💲 **Price** Collier-Seminole State Park:
$5 per vehicle

🚩 **Guided tours** Seasonal tours at
Fakahatchee and Collier-Seminole.

🍽️ **Eat and drink** SNACKS City Seafood
(702 Begonia St, Everglades City,
34139; 239 695 4700) serves half
portions for kids. REAL MEAL The
Rod & Gun Club (200 Riverside
Dr, Everglades City, 34139; 239
695 2101) has fried gator. Try the
chocolate peanut butter pie.

KIDS' CORNER

'Glades vocab
1 'Glades: Long before
Everglades National Park
existed, the name Everglades
was applied to the region and
its ecology. "Ever" comes from
the word "forever" and "glades"
means a forest clearing. Locals
call it 'Glades for short.

2 Seminoles: The US
government gave this name,
which means "runaway," to the
almost 20 different tribes that
migrated to Florida in its early
days before
statehood.

3 Airboat:
Specially made
for Everglades
travel by frog
hunters, this
noisy, jet-propelled craft
practically flies across the
local shallows.

4 Swamp buggy: Engineered
specifically for traveling across
Everglades wetlands, its big
tires and elevated bed make
for high-and-dry touring.

PLANT A TREE
When paddling among the
saltwater mangroves, look out
for long, green, bean-like seeds
bobbing in the water. Known as
props (short for propagules), they
drop off of mangrove trees.
If you find one, stick the
sprouting end into
mud to give life
to another tree.

Sharp spotter
On the drive across the Tamiami
Trail, you will see lots of alligators
alongside the parallel-running
waterway. A little tricky to spot,
they may be on the bank sunning
themselves, or in the water.
Take a close look
at what appears to
be a log. If you can
see a snout and what
looks like tire tread,
you've got yourself
a gator!

Picnic under $25; **Snacks** $25–50; **Real meal** $50–80; **Family treat** over $80 (based on a family of four)

⑬ Key West
Pirates, shipwrecks, and treasure

Ever seen a six-toed cat or a man riding a bike with an iguana on his shoulder? Both sights are likely in Key West, the most popular destination in the Florida Keys. The Old Town, the city's downtown core, is known for its party vibe. Nonetheless, a wealth of attractions and a history dating back to 19th-century pirates makes it a huge draw for families. It lies at the end of a necklace of keys (small islands) where wildlife encounters, beaches, parks, and watersports fill mellow days.

Entrance to Mallory Square

Key Sights

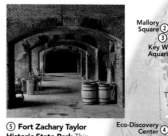

Historic Seaport at Key West Bight ①
Mallory Square ②
③
Key West Aquarium
i
Eco-Discovery Center ④
Key West Lighthouse Museum ⑥
⑤
Fort Zachary Taylor Historic State Park
Ernest Hemingway Home and Museum ⑦
Key West Butterfly and Nature Conservatory ⑧
OLD TOWN
TRUMAN ANNEX
Southernmost Point

0 metres 600
0 yards 600

① Historic Seaport at Key West Bight This restored neighborhood and its Harborwalk forms the new, earthy heart of Old Town, filled with activity, shopping, dining, and watersports charters.

② Mallory Square Celebrate sunset every night at this cruise ship dock, with musicians and magicians, and conch fritter and margarita vendors.

③ Key West Aquarium Built in 1934, this was the world's first open-air aquarium, though it is now mostly enclosed. Take a tour to watch the guides feed sharks, stingrays, and sea turtles.

④ Eco-Discovery Center This attraction shows off the Keys' natural treasures – their valuable coral reef and ecosystems. Kids will like the walk-through model of an underwater ocean lab.

⑤ Fort Zachary Taylor Historic State Park This Civil War-era fort sits on prime beachfront. Follow a fort tour with a dip and a nature hike.

⑥ Key West Lighthouse Museum Climb the 88 steps to the top of the 92-ft (28-m) tower here built in 1844, for fine views. Go to the adjacent lighthouse-keeper's home, where historic exhibits tell the story of the keepers.

⑦ Ernest Hemingway Home and Museum Find about 50 six-toed cats snoozing around this house, where famous novelist Ernest Hemingway lived and wrote from 1931 to 1942.

⑧ Key West Butterfly and Nature Conservatory Walk into a glass bubble that encases more than 40 species of butterflies, plus birds, waterfalls, and lush vegetation. The gift shop is also a must-visit.

The Lowdown

🌐 **Map reference** 9 D6
Address Key West 33040. Historic Seaport at Key West Bight: off Front St; 305 809 3801. Mallory Square: off Wall St; *www.mallorysquare.com.* Key West Aquarium: 1 Whitehead St; *www.keywestaquarium.com.* Eco-Discovery Center: 35 E Quay Rd; *floridakeys.noaa.gov/eco_discovery.html.* Fort Zachary Taylor Historic State Park: 601 Howard English Way; *www.floridastateparks.org/fort taylor.* Ernest Hemingway Home and Museum: 907 Whitehead St;

www.hemingwayhome.com. Key West Lighthouse Museum: 938 Whitehead St; *www.kwahs.com.* Key West Butterfly and Nature Conservatory: 1316 Duval St; *www.keywestbutterfly.com*

🚗 **Bus** From Marathon (*www.kw transit.com*). **Car** Park at 300 Grinnell St, and take a hop-on hop-off trolley tour. **Ferry** From Fort Myers (*seakeywestexpress.com*)

ℹ **Visitor information** Greater Key West Chamber of Commerce, 510 Greene St, 33040; 305 294 2587; *www.keywestchamber.org*

🕐 **Open** Most sights are open daily; check websites for timings.

💲 **Prices** Key West Aquarium: $45–60. Eco-Discovery Center: free. Fort Zachary Taylor Historic State Park: $8–18. Ernest Hemingway Home and Museum: $38–50. Key West Lighthouse Museum: $30–40. Key West Butterfly and Nature Conservatory: $30–40. Most sights are free for under 6s.

👥 **Cutting the line** The sights are busiest during the spring break, Fantasy Fest (Oct), and when cruise ships are in port.

Prices given are for a family of four

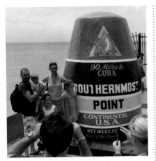

Posing for photos at the marker denoting the Southernmost Point

Letting off steam

After visiting the Hemingway Home and the lighthouse across the street, walk to the **Southernmost Point** (South St, 33040; 305 292 1880). Taking photos at the US's most southerly mainland spot is de rigueur. While grown-ups read the historic markers, kids can run along the waterfront plaza.

Eat and drink

Picnic: under $25; Snacks: $25–50; Real meal: $50–80; Family treat: over $80 (based on a family of four)

PICNIC Lobo's Mixed Grill (5 Key Lime Square, 33040; 305 296 5303; www.loboskw.com) is tricky to find, but worth a visit for its long list of burgers, wraps, and salads. Choose fixings for a picnic, then head to Higgs Beach-Astro Park for sun, sand, and a playground.
SNACKS B.O's Fish Wagon (801 Caroline St, 33040; 305 294 9272) serves up a true taste of Key West in a funky setting at the Historic Seaport. Grouper sandwiches with Key lime sauce are the specialty.

Guided tours Check www.conch train.com and www.cityview trolleys.com for details.

Age range 5 plus

Allow 3–5 days

Restrooms In most sights

Good family value?
Online discounts make Key West's sights affordable. At the beaches, the only charge is for parking.

REAL MEAL Croissants de France (816 Duval St, 33040; 305 294 2624; www.croissantsdefrance.com) offers baked goodies and sweet and savory crêpes. The less adventurous can order a croque monsieur (grilled ham and cheese sandwich).
FAMILY TREAT Latitudes (245 Front St, 33040; 305 292 5394) serves fish tacos, burgers, and other kid-pleasers. Its outdoor dining room overlooks the Gulf of Mexico. A meal here means taking the free ferry ride to Sunset Key to reach the restaurant.

Shopping

Walk along Duval Street, in the Old Town, where merchandise ranges from tacky T-shirts to fine art glass. **Cayo Hueso y Habana** (410 Wall St, Mallory Square, 33040; 305 293 7260) is a part-museum part-mall, with souvenirs, such as rooster mementos and hand-rolled cigars.

Find out more

FILM Originally built as a filming site for Flipper (1963), the Dolphin Research Center in Marathon is home to about 20 dolphins. Some of these are the descendants of the five "stars" that played the film's title role.

Outdoor seating at Croissants de France, Key West

Next stop...

DRY TORTUGAS NATIONAL PARK Board the Yankee Freedom II fast ferry (www.yankeefreedom.com) for a day trip to the Dry Tortugas National Park (www.nps.gov/drto), located 68 miles (109 km) west of Key West. The Dry Tortugas comprise seven reef islands, of which Garden Key is the most visited. The islands are a treat for birdwatchers, especially between March and October. Besides awesome coral reefs, families can explore the 19th-century **Fort Jefferson** (www.fortjefferson.com), the largest brick fortification in the US.

⑭ Big Pine Key
Home of the Key deer

Just over the bridge from downtown Key West, there is a distinct change of pace as the Overseas Highway takes visitors to a slower, more relaxed part of Florida.

Look out for Mile Markers, the small green rectangular signs that mark the miles and give directions in the Keys. Around about MM 32, signs caution drivers to slow down to protect the endangered Key deer population of Big Pine Key. The best place to spot these undersized deer, fewer than 800 of which remain, is the **National Key Deer Refuge** at No Name Key. While in the refuge, visit the Blue Hole, an old quarry filled with water that is home to one resident alligator, as well as other wildlife, and then hike the easy trails.

Big Pine Key is also known for fishing and kayaking. Paddling trails lead into refuge waters that look like a maze of mangrove islands. Follow a tour to avoid getting lost.

The Lowdown

🌐 **Map reference** 10 E6
📍 **Address** National Key Deer Refuge: 179 Key Deer Blvd, 33043; 305 872 2239; www.fws.gov/nationalkeydeer
🚌 **Bus** Key West Transit (www.kw transit.com) runs buses from Key West to Marathon daily.
ℹ️ **Visitor information** Lower Keys Chamber of Commerce, 31020 Overseas Hwy (MM 31), Big Pine Key, 33043; 800 872 3722; www.lowerkeyschamber.com
🕐 **Open** National Key Deer Refuge: sunrise–sunset daily
💲 **Price** National Key Deer Refuge: free
🚩 **Guided tours** Visit www.fws.gov/nationalkeydeer for free ranger-guided trail walks in season. Big Pine Key Kayaking Adventures (www.keyskayaktours.com) takes tours into the refuge.
👫 **Age range** 5 plus
⏱️ **Allow** Half a day for the refuge, a full day if kayaking
🍽️ **Eat and drink** SNACKS No Name Pub (N. Watson Blvd, 33043; 305 872 9115; www.nonamepub.com) has a full menu of favorites, including pizza. REAL MEAL Hogfish Bar & Grill (6810 Front St, Stock Island, 33040; 305 293 4041; www.hogfishbar.com) offers fresh seafood. Try the hog snapper.

Take cover

Head for the small **visitor center** at the **National Key Deer Refuge**, located within the Big Pine Key Shopping Plaza. It has indoor displays that help visitors discover the local habitat and wildlife.

An alligator in the Blue Hole, a flooded limestone quarry in Big Pine Key

⑮ Bahia Honda State Park
Great beaches and a really long bridge

Often seen on America's best beaches lists, Bahia Honda's white sands, turquoise waters, multihued coral reefs, and well-stocked marina make it great for families. Swimming and snorkeling are the most popular activities, but the marina also rents kayaks. It is possible to explore the offshore reef on a snorkeling cruise that the marina offers twice a day. Rangers lead hikes and host talks year-round; consider hiking the beautiful Silver Palm Nature Trail.

At the end of Bahia Honda Key, at MM 40, the Overseas Highway reaches one of the world's longest segmental bridges – the famed Seven-Mile Bridge. This railroad bridge is now disused but was considered an engineering marvel when it was completed in 1912 and is listed on the National Register of Historic Places. It is possible to walk or bike along the old bridge, and fish from the northernmost 2-mile (3-km) section, which is accessible from Marathon.

Take cover

The park's **Sand and Sea Nature Center** introduces visitors to local sea life, with exhibits and an aquarium. Learn about the park's six different habitats, play games, watch one of 30 nature videos, and guess what is in the Mystery Boxes.

The Lowdown

🌐 **Map reference** 10 E6
📍 **Address** 36850 Overseas Hwy (MM 37), 33043; 305 872 2353; www.floridastateparks.org
🚌 **Bus** Key West Transit runs buses from Key West to the park's entrance daily.
ℹ️ **Visitor information** Lower Keys Chamber of Commerce, 31020 Overseas Highway (MM 31), Big Pine Key, 33043; 800 872 3722; www.lowerkeyschamber.com
🕐 **Open** 8am–sunset daily
💲 **Price** $10–20
👫 **Cutting the line** Arrive early in spring and summer months, to avoid long lines at park entrance.
👫 **Age range** 2 plus
👫 **Activities** Ranger-led Beach Walks at 9am on Wednesdays
⏱️ **Allow** At least half a day
🍽️ **Eat and drink** SNACKS The park concession stand (305 872 3210) sells hot dogs, sandwiches, and nachos. REAL MEAL Head south to Big Pine Key or north to Marathon for restaurants.

Old Bahia Honda Bridge, seen at sunset from Bahia Honda State Park

Prices given are for a family of four

Visitors at a dolphin show at the Dolphin Research Center, Grassy Key

⑯ Marathon

Dolphins and pirates

Outside of Key West, the town of Marathon holds most of the Keys' historic and natural attractions. The neighboring Grassy and Duck keys boast two dolphin encounter operations – the **Dolphin Research Center** and **Dolphin Connection** – where visitors can pet a dolphin and also paint with one.

Another type of Keys sea life can be seen on the mend at **Turtle Hospital**. In summer, the possibility of seeing sea turtle hatchlings adds more excitement to visiting and feeding the mammoth adults.

Crane Point combines nature and history in extensive waterfront woods. There is a natural history museum, a pirate dress-up ship for kids, the Wild Bird Center, a historic home, and nature trails.

Marathon was named for the breakneck speed at which the railroad was built. Below the Seven-Mile Bridge, **Pigeon Key** was home to the construction workers. Board a ferry *(305 743 5999)* at Marathon's southern end to tour the old village and its railroad museum.

The preserved village of Pigeon Key beside the Seven-Mile Bridge

Letting off steam

Head south to **Sombrero Beach** *(521 23rd St, MM 50; 305 743 0033)*, which offers plenty of room to play, as well as barbecue grills, picnic tables, and a playground.

The Lowdown

🌐 **Map reference** 10 E6
Address Marathon 33050. Dolphin Research Center: 58901 Overseas Hwy (MM 59); *www. dolphins.org*. Dolphin Connection: 61 Hawks Cay Blvd (MM 61) at Hawks Cay Resort; *www.dolphin connection.com*. Turtle Hospital: 2396 Overseas Hwy (MM 48.5); *www.turtlehospital.org*. Crane Point: 5550 Overseas Hwy (MM 50.5); *www.cranepoint.net*. Pigeon Key: 1 Knights Key Blvd (MM 45); *www.pigeonkey.net*

🚌 **Bus** Key West Transit runs buses from Key West to Marathon daily.

ℹ️ **Visitor information** Greater Marathon Chamber of Commerce, 12222 Overseas Hwy (MM 53.5); *www.floridakeysmarathon.com*

🕐 **Open** Dolphin Research Center & Crane Point: daily. Dolphin Connection: call 1 888 251 3674 to reserve. Turtle Hospital: 9am–6pm (educational center). Pigeon Key: daily (visitor center)

💲 **Prices** Dolphin Research Center: $70–80; under 4s free. Dolphin Connection: prices differ with programs; check website. Turtle Hospital: $45–55; under 4s free. Crane Point: $42–52; under 5s free

👫 **Age range** 4 plus

⏱️ **Allow** At least a day

🍴 **Eat and drink** SNACKS Herbie's *(6350 Overseas Hwy MM 50.5; 305 743 6373)* serves seafood and cheeseburgers. *REAL MEAL* Keys Fisheries Market *(3502 Gulfview Ave, 33050; www.keysfisheries. com)* has fresh seafood.

KIDS' CORNER

Did you know...

1 The Key deer is a subspecies of the Virginia white-tailed deer.

2 The male Key deer is less than 32 inches (81 cm) high at the shoulder and weighs around 36 kg (80 lb).

3 By 1927, hunters had decimated key deer numbers to fewer than 30.

4 Key deer are mostly found in Big Pine Key, but they range around the Lower Keys and even swim to some islands not connected by roads.

TURN OVER A NEW LEAF

Crane Point's Hammock Loop Trail identifies the types of trees you will see throughout the site. Carry a notepad and pencil to make a sketch of each tree and its leaves, to help you spot them along the way.

Snorkel scavenge

To preserve reefs, you should avoid touching the coral and collecting shells or other sea life. But after you've surfaced, see who can tally up the most points for having spotted these reef and seagrass meadow inhabitants:

- Tubed Sponge (1 point)
- Sergeant Major Fish (1 point)
- Conch Shell (1 point)
- Angelfish (1 point)
- Sea Fan (1 point)
- Fire Coral (2 points)
- Sea Urchin (2 points)
- Sea Cucumber (3 points)
- Spiny Lobster (4 points)
- Sea Turtle (5 points)
- Octopus (5 points)
- Sea horse (5 points)

Picnic under $25; **Snacks** $25–50; **Real meal** $50–80; **Family treat** over $80 (based on a family of four)

Kayak Shack at Robbie's Marina selling a variety of merchandise, Islamorada

⑰ Islamorada

Fighting fish, hungry tarpon, and the tree of life

Known as the sport-fishing capital of the world, Islamorada is a 20-mile (32-km) strip of seven separate islands. A good place to start exploring Islamorada's rich sea world is **Robbie's Marina**, located at the southern end of the chain of keys. Buy a bucket of bait to feed the powerful tarpon at the dock, shop the crafts booths, and sign up for a boat ride to **Indian Key State Park** and **Lignumvitae Key Botanical State Park**. Alternatively, rent a kayak from Robbie's Marina and paddle out to Indian Key State Park. Be sure to bring along snorkeling equipment.

Visit the **History of Diving Museum** to discover more about underwater exploration. The museum has exhibits on sunken treasure, the filming of *20,000 Leagues Under the Sea*, and early diving gear. Children will enjoy the **Theater of the Sea**, where they can interact with dolphins, sea lions, and stingrays, or ride a glass-bottom boat to see what lies under water.

Letting off steam

For young kids who are not yet comfortable swimming in the sea, the pool at **Founder's Park** *(87000 Overseas Hwy, MM 87)* is a good option. The park also has a beach, a skate park, and a tennis court.

⑱ Key Largo

Underwater capital of the world

One of the most popular destinations for snorkeling in the world, Key Largo is also where two Humphrey Bogart movies were filmed: *Key Largo*

(1948) and *The African Queen* (1952). See the original steamboat that starred in the latter at the marina next to the Holiday Inn at MM 100 – it does cruise tours. There is also a glass-bottom boat here, the *Key Largo Princess* (*www.keylargo princess.com*), which offers tours of the region's legendary coral reefs.

Created in 1990, the **Florida Keys National Marine Sanctuary** protects 2,900 sq nautical miles (9,947 sq km) of waters surrounding the Florida Keys and more than 6,000 marine species. Just step into the water to reach the sanctuary, or explore the vibrant, colorful world of coral and fish by snorkeling or scuba diving. Charters also take visitors under water to see the submerged 9-ft (3-m) statue, *Christ of the Deep*. Alternatively, two dolphin encounter operations – **Dolphin Cove** and **Dolphins Plus** – in Key Largo offer educational and interactive programs, while Dolphins Plus also has a sea lion swim.

Colorful corals in Key Largo, with the Christ of the Deep in the background

Take cover

If inclement weather threatens, head to **Shellworld** *(97600 Overseas Hwy MM 101.9)*, which has a wide variety of merchandise, from specimen shells and plush toys to Key Lime products.

⑲ John Pennekamp Coral Reef State Park

Nature meets history

The first undersea park in the US, the John Pennekamp Coral Reef State Park is located close to the Florida Keys National Marine Sanctuary. The visitor center has a massive reef aquarium, and the park's concessions provide diving, snorkeling, and glass-bottom boat excursions, and rent out equipment. Snorkelers off Cannon Beach can see the ruins of a Spanish ship just 100 ft (30 m) from shore. Families can rent kayaks, canoes, and powerboats, or hike the short trails and then picnic at one of the two beaches in the park. Pretty,

palm-fringed Far Beach is ideal for a relaxing day spent sunbathing or splashing around in the water.

Take cover

Besides the 30,000-gallon (113,562-liter) aquarium, the park's visitor center houses six other aquaria that display the local sea fauna. Listen to rangers at the center explain how they are re-growing damaged coral. The center's theater screens videos about the park, and natural history exhibits interpret the different habitats of corals.

The Lowdown

- 🌐 **Map reference** 10 G4
- 📍 **Address** 102601 Overseas Hwy (MM 102.5); www.florida stateparks.org/pennekamp
- 🚗 **Car** Rent a car from Key West.
- ℹ️ **Visitor information** Key Largo Chamber of Commerce, 106000 Overseas Hwy (MM 106); www.keylargochamber.org
- 🕐 **Open** Park: 8am–sunset. Visitor Center: 8am–5pm
- 💲 **Price** $10–20
- 🧍 **Cutting the line** Arrive early in the day to avoid long queues.
- 🌴 **Guided tours** The 2½-hour snorkeling tours start at 9am, noon & 3pm daily; equipment rental extra. The 2½-hour glass-bottom boat tours begin at 9:15am, 12:15pm & 3:15pm daily.
- 👫 **Age range** All ages
- ⏱️ **Allow** Half a day to a full day
- 🍔 **Eat and drink** SNACKS A food counter and snack bar *(on site)* serves breakfast and lunch. REAL MEAL Sundowners *(103900 Overseas Hwy; MM 104; 305 451 4502; sundownerskeylargo.com)* is a sit-down restaurant that serves fresh seafood. It has starters, salads, sandwiches, steaks, and beverages.

Far Beach, a scenic strip of sand in John Pennekamp Coral Reef State Park

Picnic under $25; **Snacks** $25–50; **Real meal** $50–80; **Family treat** over $80 (based on a family of four)

Where to Stay in the Lower Gulf Coast, Everglades, and Keys

From waterfront campgrounds and chain hotels to vacation homes and grand resorts, this region has it all. While Key West is renowned for its B&Bs, camping is part of the Everglades experience. For exploring the Everglades and the Keys, staying at a chain hotel in Homestead and Florida City is the best option.

AGENCIES

Rent Key West
www.rentkeywest.com
This website offers weekly and monthly rentals, from historic downtown bungalows to waterside homes with their own pool.

Sanibel & Captiva Accommodations
www.sanibelaccom.com
The catalog lists by-the-month home rentals, and condos that can be rented for shorter periods.

A bedroom at Port of the Islands Everglades Adventure Resort

Everglades National Park
Map 10 F3

SELF-CATERING
Port of the Islands Everglades Adventure Resort
25000 Tamiami Trail E, Naples, 34114; 239 394 3005; poiresort.com
Located near the Gulf Coast entrance to the Everglades National Park this pleasant place packages adventure excursions with lodgings. It is the resort nearest to the national park.
🐿 🐾 P ☺ $$

CAMPING
Big Cypress National Preserve Campgrounds
Tamiami Trail; 239 695 1201; www.nps.gov/bicy
These four free, quite basic campgrounds, and two fee-paying parks with RV lodging, are located

off the Tamiami Trail. The campgrounds have no showers or restrooms, and sites are available on a first-come, first-served basis. Some sites are inaccessible in summer due to flooding.
🐿 P $

Flamingo Campground
Flamingo; 305 242 7700 (park) and 877 444 6777 (reservations); www.nps.gov/ever
This campground sits on the shores of Florida Bay, and more than 60 of the sites offer great bay views. Most of the sites are drive-in, but some are walk-in. Close to the marina, the campground affords easy access to paddlecraft rentals and boating tours.
🐾 ☺ $

Fort Myers
Map 7 C5

RESORT
Sanibel Harbour Marriott
17260 Harbour Pointe Dr, 33908; 239 466 4000 or 800 767 7777; www.sanibel-resort.com
An award-winning destination resort just east of the Sanibel Causeway, this is known for its full complement of facilities and kids' programs. Choose from rooms and one-bedroom suites. Families can also book boating excursions. A shuttle bus takes guests to Sanibel Island.
🐿 🍴 P ☺ $$$

Fort Myers Beach
Map 7 C6

RESORT
Outrigger Beach Resort
6200 Estero Blvd, 33931; 239 463 3131 or 800 657 5659; www.outriggerfmb.com
At the southern end of the island, this resort offers a peaceful respite from the party atmosphere around Times Square. It offers simple

accommodations with an old Florida feel. Some of the rooms come with kitchens. The wide stretch of white sands, a lively pool deck, and a tiki bar area add to the family-holiday air.
🐾 🍴 P ☺ ☺ $$

Key Largo
Map 10 G5

RESORT
Key Largo Grande Resort
97000 Overseas Hwy (MM 97), 33037; 305 852 5553 or 888 871 3437; www.keylargogrande.com
With its cool "Scout About" family discovery program, lovely beach, gorgeous forested grounds, and two pools, this full-service resort is good for families. It feels safer than some of the other resorts because it is set back from the main road.
🐿 🛎 🍴 P ☺ $$

CAMPING
John Pennekamp Coral Reef State Park
Map 10 G4
102601 Overseas Hwy (MM 102.5), 33037; 305 451 1202 (park); www.floridastateparks.org/pennekamp
RV and tent sites are tucked into this park's shady grounds, out of the way of day visitors. A variety of activities sure to keep the kids happily occupied are available here,

An RV parked at John Pennekamp Coral Reef State Park

with beaches and glass-bottom boat tours, plus woods to explore. Call well in advance for reservations.

  🎱 🕐 P 🚲 $

Key West
Map 9 D6

RESORTS
Hyatt Key West Resort
601 Front St, 33040; 305 809 1234; www.keywest.hyatt.com
Near the Historic Seaport, the Hyatt has its own small beach, lots of options for watersports, and a spa. Close enough to all the action in the Old Town, yet away from its noise and crowds.

🐟 🍽 P 🚫 $$$

The artificial lagoon at Hawks Cay Resort, fringed with coral reefs

Ocean Key Resort
Zero Duval St, 33040; 305 296 7701, 800 328 9815; www.oceankey.com
Families who love being in the thick of the action will love this full-service resort's location next to Mallory Square. Enjoy hanging out at its pool and Sunset Deck restaurant. Ask for a suite with a sleeper sofa or adjoining rooms.

🍽 🚀 🏨 P 🚫 $$$

BED & BREAKFAST
Ambrosia Key West
615, 618, 622 Fleming St, 33040; 305 296 9838 or 800-535-9838; www.ambrosiakeywest.com
One of the few B&Bs in Key West that welcome kids, this one spreads down a city block with rooms, town houses, suites, and a cottage. Some pets are also allowed.

🎱 🐟 P 🚫 $$$

Island City House Hotel
411 William St, 33040; 305 294 5702; www.islandcityhouse.com
Another family-friendly B&B, this property's suites occupy a former cigar factory complex. There are resident cats for the kids to play with.

🎱 🐟 P 🚫 $$$

Marathon/Big Pine Key
Map 10 E6

RESORTS
Gulf View Waterfront Resort
58743 Overseas Hwy (MM 58.5), Marathon, 33050; 305 289 1414 or 877 289 0111; www.gulfviewwaterfrontresort.com
Right next door to the Dolphin Research Center, this resort offers discount vouchers to the sealife-

encounter attraction, and also has its own small menagerie of critters. Rooms are simple, but families will spend most time on the beach, in the pool, or paddling in the Gulf.

🎱 🐟 P 🚫 $$

Hawks Cay Resort
Hawks Cay Blvd (MM 61), Duck Key, 33050; 305 743 7000 or 888 432 2242; wwww.hawkscay.com
Something of its own little village, this resort caters to families with its on-site Dolphin Connection interaction operation, a kids' club with a fun pirate ship-themed pool and games, supervised programs, and watersports concessions at the marina.

🐟 🍽 P 🚫 $$$

CAMPING
Bahia Honda State Park
36850 Overseas Hwy, Big Pine Key, 33043; 305 872 2353 (park) or 800 326 3521 (reservations); www.floridastateparks.org/bahiahonda
Choose from waterfront cabins or RV and tent campsites close to the most beautiful beaches in the Keys. Guests have access to the park's additional facilities: snorkeling, beaches, nature trails, and educational programs. Reserve well in advance.

🎱 🍴 P 🚫 $$$

Naples
Map 9 C1

HOTEL
Naples Beach Hotel
851 Gulf Shore Blvd N, 34102; 239 261 2222 or 800 237 7600; www.naplesbeachhotel.com
Naples' first hotel, and one of its most popular with families, this place is loaded with family-friendly

features. Kids will love the pool, beach, and Kids' Klub; grown-ups will like the fine spa and 18-hole golf course. The hotel offers several dining options, including a pool bar and grill where all gather for sunset.

🐟 🍽 P 🚫 🚲 $$$

Sanibel and Captiva Islands
Map 7 C6

RESORT
South Seas Island Resort
5400 Plantation Rd, Captiva Island, 33924; 239 472 5111 or 800 965 7772; www.southseas.com
One of Florida's first and largest gated destination resorts, this offers accommodations ranging from guestrooms to rental homes. There is a mini-waterpark, lots of beaches, nine holes of golf, top-rated kids' programs, and a nature center.

🐟 🍽 🚀 🚫 🚲 $$$

HOTEL
Gulf Breeze Cottages & Motel
1081 Shell Basket Lane, Sanibel Island, 33957; 239 472 1626 or 800 388 2842; www.gbreeze.com
Cozy and family-friendly, this hotel's cottages and duplexes sit right on the beach, and the owners provide beach toys. There is a fairy-tale quality to its gingerbread detailing and lush gardens.

🚀 🍴 P 🚲 $$$

Price Guide
The following price ranges are based on one night's accommodation in high season for a family of four, inclusive of service charges and additional taxes.

$ Under $150 **$$** $150–300 **$$$** over $300

Key to symbols *see back cover flap*

Miami's skyscrapers and the MacArthur
Causeway, seen from the air, above
Palm Island

Florida

MAPS

Florida Maps

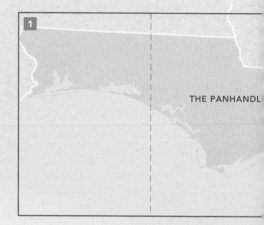

THE PANHANDL

KEY TO MAPS 11–16

⬛	Major sight	— Railroad line	
▨	Place of interest	— Metromover line	
▨	Other building	⬜ Beach	
🚉	Railway station		
Ⓜ	Metromover station		
ℹ	Visitor information		
👫	Playground		
🚓	Police station		
⋯	Pedestrian street		

Maps 11–16

0 km   2

0 miles   2

Miami

15 16

MIAMI
BEACH

13   DOWNTOWN 14

LITTLE
HAVANA

11   12

CORAL   COCONUT
GABLES   GROVE

KEY
BISCAYNE

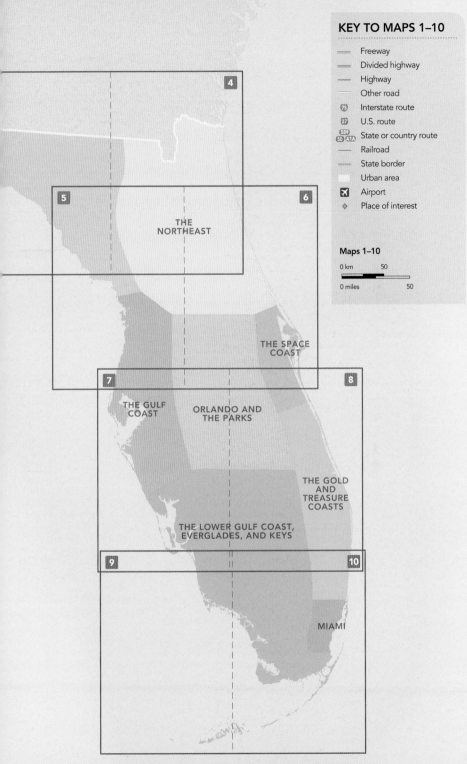

KEY TO MAPS 1–10

Freeway
Divided highway
Highway
Other road
🚲 Interstate route
㉗ U.S. route
State or country route
Railroad
State border
Urban area
✈ Airport
◇ Place of interest

Maps 1–10

0 km   50

0 miles   50

THE NORTHEAST

THE SPACE COAST

THE GULF COAST

ORLANDO AND THE PARKS

THE GOLD AND TREASURE COASTS

THE LOWER GULF COAST, EVERGLADES, AND KEYS

MIAMI

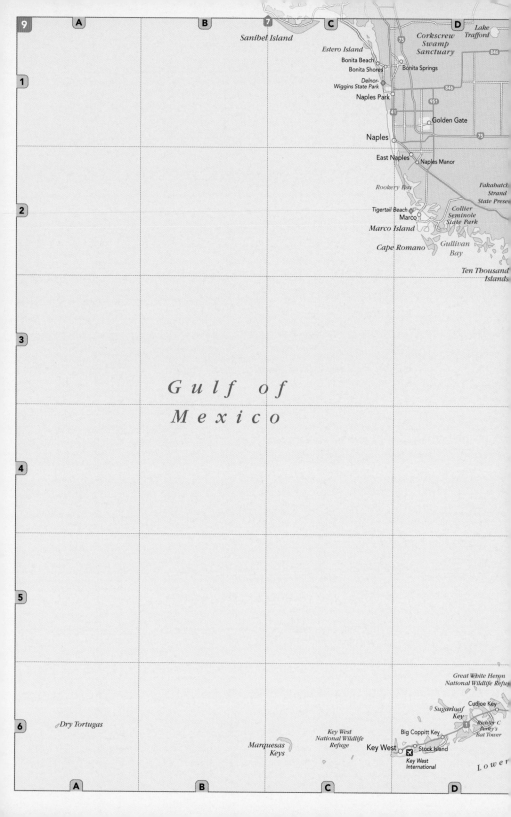

9

A   B   **7**   C   D

Sanibel Island

Estero Island

Bonita Beach
Bonita Shores   Bonita Springs

Delnor-
Wiggins State Park

Naples Park

*Lake
Trafford*

*Corkscrew
Swamp
Sanctuary*

Golden Gate

Naples

East Naples   Naples Manor

Rookery Bay

*Fakahatch
Strand
State Prese*

Tigertail Beach
Marco

Marco Island

*Collier
Seminole
State Park*

Cape Romano

*Gullivan
Bay*

*Ten Thousand
Islands*

*Gulf of
Mexico*

*Great White Heron
National Wildlife Refu*

*Sugarloaf
Key*

Cudjoe Key

*Richtic C
Perky's
Bat Tower*

Dry Tortugas

*Marquesas
Keys*

*Key West
National Wildlife
Refuge*

Big Coppitt Key

Key West   Stock Island

Key West
International

Lower

Selected Florida Town Index

A B C D

1

2

VENETIAN CAUSEWAY (TOLL)

VENETIAN CAUSEWAY (TOLL)

VENETIAN ISLAND

W DI LIDO DRIVE
E DI LIDO DRIVE
W DI LIDO DRIVE
E DI LIDO DRIVE

Miami Children's Museum

Jungle Island

HIBISCUS ISLAND

FLAGLER MEMORIAL ISLAND

N HIBISUCUS DRIVE
S HIBISUCUS DRIVE

3

WATSON ISLAND

MACARTHUR

N COCONUT LANE
S COCONUT LANE

PALM ISLAND

PALM AVENUE

4

CAUSEWAY

PORT BOULEVARD

DODGE ISLAND

AUSTRALIA WAY

PORT BOULEVARD

5

PORT OF MIAMI

14

AUSTRALIA WAY

6

Biscayne Bay

Miami Street Index

Index

Acknowledgments

Dorling Kindersley would like to thank the following people whose help and assistance contributed to the preparation of this book.

Main Contributors

Eleanor Berman is a widely published writer for magazines and newspapers and the author of 14 travel guides. Her books include two other guides for Dorling Kindersley, *Top 10 New York City* and the *Eyewitness Travel Guide: New York City*, which won a Thomas Cook award for best guidebook. She also contributed to *DK Family Guide: New York City* and *Family Guide: Washington, DC.*

Joseph Hayes moves between New York, Italy, Scotland, and his home in Orlando, while writing about travel, food, and art for print and online publications across the world. He is the restaurant critic for *Orlando Magazine* and has worked with DK Eyewitness Travel since 2003. He is also a playwright and a jazz event producer, whose work has been produced in New York, California, Florida, and the United Kingdom. Hayes worked for many years in the publishing field in New York before moving to central Florida to take up writing as a full-time career.

Stephen Keeling has been traveling to Florida since 1991, and covering the state for various travel guides since 2008. He worked as a financial journalist and editor in Asia for seven years before writing his first travel book. Since then he has written for *The Independent*, *The Daily Telegraph*, and various travel publications. He has authored an award-winning family guide to Tuscany and Umbria, and has researched travel guides to Puerto Rico, New England, Mexico, and Canada. Stephen lives in New York City.

Chelle Koster Walton, a travel writer, has written and contributed to 10 guidebooks – two of which won Lowell Thomas Awards – and articles for magazines such as *FamilyFun*, *Caribbean Travel + Life*, *National Geographic Traveler*, *Arthur Frommer's Budget Travel*, *Endless Vacation*, *The New York Post*, and other print and electronic media. She is the co-founder of *www.guidebookwriters.com* and is a member of the Society of American Travel Writers.

Sharon Weightman Hoffmann is a freelance writer and editor based in Atlantic Beach, Florida. Although her primary work is in journalism and marketing, she also provides emerging authors with a range of "book doctor" services. Her first non-fiction book is a biography of blues musician Blind Blake, forthcoming from Blues Images.

Editorial Consultant

Fay Franklin

Additional Photography

Max Alexander; Dave King; Pearson Education: Gideon Carpenter; Rough Guides: Demetrio Carrasco, Angus Oborn, Anthony Pidgeon; Stephen Whitehorn; Linda Whitwam; Peter Wilson.

Design and Editorial

PUBLISHER Vivien Antwi
LIST MANAGER Christine Stroyan
SENIOR DESIGN MANAGER Mabel Chan
SENIOR CARTOGRAPHIC EDITOR Casper Morris
SENIOR EDITOR Georgina Palffy
JACKET DESIGN Shahid Mahmood, Nicole Newman, Tracy Smith
ICON DESIGN Claire-Louise Armitt
SENIOR DTP EDITOR Jason Little
PICTURE RESEARCH Ellen Root, Marta Bescos
PRODUCTION CONTROLLER Kerry Howie
READER Debra Wolter
FACT CHECKER Melinda S. Koster
PROOFREADER Lucilla Watson
INDEXER Hilary Bird

With thanks to Douglas Amrine for his help in developing this series.

Special Assistance

Dorling Kindersley would like to thank the following for their assistance:

Kathy White at The Dalí Museum; David Carson at The Flagler Museum; Julian Ashmore & Martha J. Robinson at Florida Department of Environmental Protection; Kerry Falwell at Glazer Children's Museum; John Kennedy at Kennedy Space Center; Jacqueline Luzunaris at LEGOLAND Florida®; Rene Bell Adams at The Museum of Arts and Sciences; Kristi Ballinger Taylor at Museum of Science & History; Mark Schaub at Orlando Science Center; Brittany Tollerton Baron at Universal Orlando® Resort; Holly Blount at Vizcaya Museum and Gardens.

Photography Permissions

DORLING KINDERSLEY would like to thank all the museums, galleries, churches and other sights that allowed us to photograph at their establishments: Actors' Playhouse at the Miracle Theatre; Air Force Armament Museum; Al's Coffee Shop; The Bailey-Matthews Shell Museum; The Barefoot Cafe; The Bass Museum of Art; Busch Gardens Tampa Bay

& Adventure Island; Cummer Museum of Art & Gardens; The Florida Museum of Natural History; IGFA Fishing Hall of Fame and Museum; Imaginarium: Science Center; Indian River Citrus Museum; Jacksonville Zoo and Gardens; The John and Mable Ringling Museum of Art; The Lightner Museum; Museum of Science & History; National Naval Aviation Museum; Orlando Science Center; Wet 'n Wild; Walt Disney World® Resort.

Works of art have been reproduced with the kind permission of the following copyright holders:

Pink Snail © Cracking Art Group 62br; *Daniyyel* © Boaz Vaadia 66br; *Sword Dance* © Kent Ulberg 83cl; *Trial Scene* © 94tr; *Water-Breathing Dragon Fountain* © Patrick McGee 181cl; *The Indian Heritage Tableau* © Cooley artists Bradley Cooley and Bradley Cooley Jr. 186cl; *The Hallucinogenic Toreador* © Salvador Dalí, Fundació Gala-Salvador Dalí, DACS, 2012 220bl; *Uncommon Friends* © D. J. Wilkins 237cl.

Picture Credits

a = above; b = below/bottom; c = centre; f = far; l = left; r = right; t = top.

The publisher would like to thank the following for their kind permission to reproduce their photographs:

ALAMY IMAGES: AAA Photostock 40cl; Jerry Ballard 154-155, 173tc; Ron Buskirk 29bl, 34bl; Chris A Crumley 232cr; Danita Delimont 141cr; Greg Davis 137tc; Disney Magic 114cla; Dorf 192bc; Furlong Photography 23bl; Susan Gottberg 167tl; Jeff Greenberg 26br, 28br, 29br, 32bc, 46cl, 47br, 225tl; Eric James 23br; Andre Jenny 227tl; JHP Attractions 211tr; JTB Media Creation, Inc. 1c; Kelly Shannon Kelly 172bc; Klaus Lang 222cr; Judie Long 168cr; Dennis MacDonald 27br, 171tl; Rod McLean 233t; MPM Images 134tl; North Wind Picture Archives 39cl; M. Timothy O'Keefe 119tc; Michael Patrick O'Neill 77bl; Philipus 27bl; Peter Ravallo 28bl; James Schwabel 21bl, 22bl, 173bl; Alex Segre 24bl; Jack Sullivan 44-45; Tom & Therisa Stack 12br; Frank Tozier 187bl; Travelshots.com / Peter Phipp 64cla; Gregory Wrona 103t; Zuma Press 35bl,/ The Palm Beach Post / Bill Ingram 20br; Zuma Wire Service 25br; 220bl.

THE BILTMORE HOTEL: 31bc, 72br.

BIRCH PATIO MOTEL: 98c.

THE BREAKERS PALM BEACH: 99bl.

BUSCH GARDENS TAMPA BAY & ADVENTURE ISLAND: 215ca.

COASTAL AND AQUATIC MANAGED AREAS: 171cb.

COLUMBIA RESTAURANT: 32bl.

CORBIS: Bettmann 40tr; Stephen Frink 19clb; National Geographic / Joel Sartore & Joe Stancampiano 21clb; NewSport / Walter G Arce 17br; Patrick Ward 16bc.

THE DALÍ MUSEUM, ST. PETERSBURG: Dana Hoff 220tr, 220cl, 220clb, 220cb; Rixon Photography 34br, 221tl.

DORAL GOLF RESORT & SPA MIAMI: 19t.

DORLING KINDERSLEY: Courtesy of Coral Gables Venetian Pool, Florida / Peter Wilson 52clb.

DREAMSTIME.COM: Apexgs 251tl; Cheryl Casey 184-185; Ivan Cholakov 222tl; Christian De Grandmaison 68c; Diver721 198cl; Drlunatik 213tc; Geraldmarella 212cra; Alex Gorodnitchev 212cl; Gynane 25bl; Jcmeyer72 197c; Wangkun Jia 114tr; Luckynick 240tc; Michael Ludwig 19bl; Mpwood 185cr; Sborisov 47t; Typhoonski 68cr; Wilsilver77 195cl, 245tc.

FLAGLER MUSEUM: 74-75, 90tr, 90cr, 90crb, 91cl, 91cb.

FLORIDA DEPARTMENT OF ENVIRONMENTAL PROTECTION: 19cla, 30bl, 73c, 97bl, 164clb, 177bl, 183c, 193cl, 199c, 205bl, 209br, 219bl, 239cl, 243bc, 252br; Thelma Proctor 18cra.

FLORIDA KEYS NEWSROOM: 14-15bc, 15br.

FLORIDA STATE FAIR: 17bl.

FLORIDAYS RESORT ORLANDO: 136bl.

FLYING HIGH CIRCUS: 36br.

FORT DE SOTO PARK: 229tl.

FOTOLIA: se7enimage 42-43.

GETTY IMAGES: Buena Vista Images 22br; Encyclopaedia Britannica / UIG 38cr; The Image Bank / Claudia Uribe 254-255,/ John Coletti 141t;

Greater Orlando

Lake Apopka

Lake Lotus

Spr. Lak

FOREST CITY ROAD

MAITLAND

LOCKHART

EATONVIL

ORANGE BLOSSOM TRAIL

JOHN YOUNG PARKWAY

APOPKA BOULEVARD

Long Lake

CLARCONA

Lake Orlando

Lake Fairview

LAKEVILLE RD.

APOPKA VINELAND ROAD

OCOEE APOPKA RD.

CLARCONA-OCOEE ROAD

Crooked Lake

PINE HILLS ROAD

HIAWASSEE ROAD

SILVER STAR ROAD

WESTERN BELTWAY

WINTER GARDEN

OCOEE

PINE HILLS

OAKLAND

Florida's Turnpike

EAST PLANT STREET

WEST COLONIAL DRIVE

WEST COLONIAL DRIVE

EAST-WEST EXPRESSWAY

ORLOVISTA

OLD WINTER GARDEN ROAD

WASHIN

Johns Lake

Black Lake

MARSH ROAD

TILDEN ROAD

Lake Mann

Lake Hiawassee

Lake Avalon

AVALON ROAD

HARLEM HEIGHTS

Lake Down

WINDERMERE

CONROY ROAD

Turkey Lake

KIRKMAN ROAD

Clear Lake

VINELAND ROAD

ORANGE BLOSSOM TRAIL

Lake Butler

Lake Speer

FICQUETTE ROAD

Lake Hancock

WINTER GARDEN-VINELAND RD.

Lake Tibet

AMERICANA BLVD.

JOHN YOUNG PARKWAY

Universal Studios Florida®

Universal's Islands of Adventure®

Fun Spot Action Park

Festival Bay Mall

SKY LAKE

OAK RIDGE ROAD

Wet 'n Wild®

Hickorynut Lake

BEAMS ROAD

Lake Mabel

Lake Sheen

Big Sand Lake

INTERNATIONAL DRIVE

TURKEY LAKE ROAD

Ripley's Believe It or Not! Odditorium

Reedy Lake

LAKE HANCOCK ROAD

See Walt Disney World® Resort map right

Magic Kingdom®

Bay Lake

WALT DISNEY WORLD® RESORT

Wonderworks

BEACHLINE

SeaWorld®

Aquatica

CENTRAL FLORIDA PARKWAY

Discovery Cove®

VISTA BOULEVARD

LAKE BUENA VISTA

EPCOT

Epcot®

BUENA VISTA DRIVE

CENTER DRIVE

WORLD DRIVE

Disney's Animal Kingdom®

Disney's Hollywood Studios

OSCEOLA PARKWAY

Lake Bryan

JOHN YOUNG PARKWAY

441

WESTERN BELTWAY

IRLO BRONSON MEMORIAL HIGHWAY

OLD LAKE WILSON DRIVE

OSCEOLA PARKWAY

FLORIDA GREENEWAY

CENTRAL FLORIDA PARKWAY

IRLO BRONSON MEMORIAL HIGHWAY

BERMUDA AVENUE

ORANGE BLOSSOM TRAIL

CELEBRATION

POINCIANA

Kiss

0 km 2

0 miles 2

& Adventure Island; Cummer Museum of Art & Gardens; The Florida Museum of Natural History; IGFA Fishing Hall of Fame and Museum; Imaginarium: Science Center; Indian River Citrus Museum; Jacksonville Zoo and Gardens; The John and Mable Ringling Museum of Art; The Lightner Museum; Museum of Science & History; National Naval Aviation Museum; Orlando Science Center; Wet 'n Wild; Walt Disney World® Resort.

Works of art have been reproduced with the kind permission of the following copyright holders:

Pink Snail © Cracking Art Group 62br; *Daniyyel* © Boaz Vaadia 66br; *Sword Dance* © Kent Ulberg 83cl; *Trial Scene* © 94tr; *Water-Breathing Dragon Fountain* © Patrick McGee 181cl; *The Indian Heritage Tableau* © Cooley artists Bradley Cooley and Bradley Cooley Jr. 186cl; *The Hallucinogenic Toreador* © Salvador Dalí, Fundació Gala-Salvador Dalí, DACS, 2012 220bl; *Uncommon Friends* © D. J. Wilkins 237cl.

Picture Credits

a = above; b = below/bottom; c = centre; f = far; l = left; r = right; t = top.

The publisher would like to thank the following for their kind permission to reproduce their photographs:

ALAMY IMAGES: AAA Photostock 40cl; Jerry Ballard 154-155, 173tc; Ron Buskirk 29bl, 34bl; Chris A Crumley 232cr; Danita Delimont 141cr; Greg Davis 137tc; Disney Magic 114cla; Dorf 192bc; Furlong Photography 23bl; Susan Gottberg 167tl; Jeff Greenberg 26br, 28br, 29br, 32bc, 46cl, 47br, 225tl; Eric James 23br; Andre Jenny 227tl; JHP Attractions 211tr; JTB Media Creation, Inc. 1c; Kelly Shannon Kelly 172bc; Klaus Lang 222cr; Judie Long 168cr; Dennis MacDonald 27br, 171tl; Rod McLean 233t; MPM Images 134tl; North Wind Picture Archives 39cl; M. Timothy O'Keefe 119tc; Michael Patrick O'Neill 77bl; Philipus 27bl; Peter Ravallo 28bl; James Schwabel 21bl, 22bl, 173bl; Alex Segre 24bl; Jack Sullivan 44-45; Tom & Therisa Stack 12br; Frank Tozier 187bl; Travelshots.com / Peter Phipp 64cla; Gregory Wrona 103t; Zuma Press 35bl,/ The Palm Beach Post / Bill Ingram 20br; Zuma Wire Service 25br; 220bl.

THE BILTMORE HOTEL: 31bc, 72br.

BIRCH PATIO MOTEL: 98c.

THE BREAKERS PALM BEACH: 99bl.

BUSCH GARDENS TAMPA BAY & ADVENTURE ISLAND: 215ca.

COASTAL AND AQUATIC MANAGED AREAS: 171cb.

COLUMBIA RESTAURANT: 32bl.

CORBIS: Bettmann 40tr; Stephen Frink 19clb; National Geographic / Joel Sartore & Joe Stancampiano 21clb; NewSport / Walter G Arce 17br; Patrick Ward 16bc.

THE DALÍ MUSEUM, ST. PETERSBURG: Dana Hoff 220tr, 220cl, 220clb, 220cb; Rixon Photography 34br, 221tl.

DORAL GOLF RESORT & SPA MIAMI: 19t.

DORLING KINDERSLEY: Courtesy of Coral Gables Venetian Pool, Florida / Peter Wilson 52clb.

DREAMSTIME.COM: Apexgs 251tl; Cheryl Casey 184-185; Ivan Cholakov 222tl; Christian De Grandmaison 68c; Diver721 198cl; Drlunatik 213tc; Geraldmarella 212cra; Alex Gorodnitchev 212cl; Gynane 25bl; Jcmeyer72 197c; Wangkun Jia 114tr; Luckynick 240tc; Michael Ludwig 19bl; Mpwood 185cr; Sborisov 47t; Typhoonski 68cr; Wilsilver77 195cl, 245tc.

FLAGLER MUSEUM: 74-75, 90tr, 90cr, 90crb, 91cl, 91cb.

FLORIDA DEPARTMENT OF ENVIRONMENTAL PROTECTION: 19cla, 30bl, 73c, 97bl, 164clb, 177bl, 183c, 193cl, 199c, 205bl, 209br, 219bl, 239cl, 243bc, 252br; Thelma Proctor 18cra.

FLORIDA KEYS NEWSROOM: 14-15bc, 15br.

FLORIDA STATE FAIR: 17bl.

FLORIDAYS RESORT ORLANDO: 136bl.

FLYING HIGH CIRCUS: 36br.

FORT DE SOTO PARK: 229tl.

FOTOLIA: se7enimage 42-43.

GETTY IMAGES: Buena Vista Images 22br; Encyclopaedia Britannica / UIG 38cr; The Image Bank / Claudia Uribe 254-255,/ John Coletti 141t;

Lonely Planet Images / Stephen Saks 194cr; Photographer's Choice / Mitchell Funk 13bl; George Rose 229cr McClatchy-Tribune / Miami Herald 133bl.

GLAZER CHILDREN'S MUSEUM: 208cl, 218cr.

GREATER FORT WALTON BEACH CHAMBER OF COMMERCE: 14bl.

HAWKS CAY RESORT: 30-31bc, 253tr.

HILTON HOTELS & RESORTS: 31br, 182br.

INTERNATIONAL PALMS RESORT: 152tc.

INTERNATIONAL POLO CLUB PALM BEACH: 89cl.

JACKSONVILLE ZOO AND GARDENS: 163c, 163bl.

THE JOHNNY ROCKETS GROUP, INC: 33bc.

KATHRYN ABBEY HANNA PARK: 161tl.

KENNEDY SPACE CENTER: 138-139, 140b, 144tr, 144cl, 144clb, 144crb, 144bc, 145tl, 145cl, 145c, 145clb, 145bc, 146tr, 146cl, 146cr.

LEGOLAND FLORIDA®: Merlin Entertainments Group 132cl, 132cr, 134cr, 135cr.

LOEWS DON CESAR HOTEL: 228br.

MASTERFILE: Alberto Biscaro 8-9.

MID-AMERICA FESTIVALS: 14bc.

MOON UNDER WATER: 221cl.

MORIKAMI MUSEUM AND JAPANESE GARDENS: 87bc.

MURDER MYSTERY DINNER TRAIN: 37bl.

MUSEUM OF ARTS AND SCIENCES: 176tr, 176cl, 176cr, 176crb, 177tl.

NAVAL AVIATION MUSEUM FOUNDATION: 196clb.

OLD SALTY DOG CORP: 32-33bc.

ORLANDO SCIENCE CENTER: Frank Weber 128cl, 129cl, 129c.

ORLANDO SHAKESPEARE THEATER: 36bl.

PIZZA AL FRESCO: 88bc.

PORT D'HIVER BED & BREAKFAST: 153bl.

EARL QUENZEL: 16bl.

SANDESTIN GOLF AND BEACH RESORT: 204cl.

SEAWORLD® PARKS & ENTERTAINMENT: 122cl, 123c, 123bl.

SEMINOLE HARD ROCK HOTEL AND CASINO: Costea Photography Inc. 84tl.

SLIDERS SEASIDE GRILL: 164br.

SUNDAY AFTERNOONS OF MUSIC: 37br.

SUNSTREAM HOTELS & RESORTS: 252cl.

© 2012 UNIVERSAL ORLANDO® RESORT. ALL RIGHTS RESERVED: 118ca, 118c, 119c, 120tr, 120cl, 120cra, 120cr, 120bc, 121tl, 121c; Harry Potter characters, names and related indicia are trademarks of and © Warner Bros. Entertainment Inc. Harry Potter Publishing Rights © JKR 118cl.

VIZCAYA MUSEUM AND GARDENS: 60crb, 61c; Bill Sumner 60clb.

WATERSOUNDVACATIONRENTALS.COM: 205tr.

Jacket images: Front: ALAMY IMAGES: Songquan Deng tl; Steven Widoff tc; GETTY IMAGES: Travel Images / UIG tr; SEAWORLD® PARKS & ENTERTAINMENT: b;
Back: ALAMY IMAGES: Travelshots.com / Peter Phipp tl; DORLING KINDERSLEY: Steven Greaves tc; SUPERSTOCK: F1 ONLINE tr;
Spine: DORLING KINDERSLEY: Steven Greaves t.

All other images © Dorling Kindersley.
For further information see: www.dkimages.com.

SPECIAL EDITIONS OF DK TRAVEL GUIDES

DK Travel Guides can be purchased in bulk quantities at discounted prices for use in promotions or as premiums.

We are also able to offer special editions and personalized jackets, corporate imprints, and excerpts from all of our books, tailored specifically to meet your own needs.

To find out more, please contact:
(in the United States) **SpecialSales@dk.com**
(in the UK) **TravelSpecialSales@uk.dk.com**
(in Canada) DK Special Sales at
general@tourmaline.ca
(in Australia) **business.development@pearson. com.au**

Greater Orlando

Lake Apopka

LOCKHART

MAITLAND

EATONVIL

Lake Lotus

Spr. Lak

FOREST CITY ROAD

APOPKA BOULEVARD

OCOEE-APOPKA RD

LAKEVILLE RD

Long Lake

CLARCONA-OCOEE

ROAD

CLARCONA

PINE HILLS ROAD

Crooked Lake

Lake Orlando

Lake Fairview

ORANGE BLOSSOM TRAIL

JOHN YOUNG PARKWAY

LEE ROAD

Lake Edge

SILVER STAR ROAD

WINTER GARDEN

OAKLAND

EAST PLANT STREET

OCOEE

PINE HILLS

HIAWASSEE RD

FLORIDA'S WEST COLONIAL DRIVE

WEST COLONIAL DRIVE

WASHIN

TURNPIKE

EAST-WEST EXPRESSWAY

ORLOVISTA

OLD WINTER GARDEN ROAD

Lake Mann

Clear Lake

Johns Lake

Black Lake

MARSH ROAD

Lake Avalon

Lake Hiawassee

KIRKMAN ROAD

VINELAND ROAD

HARLEM HEIGHTS

TILDEN ROAD

Lake Down

WINDERMERE

CONROY ROAD

Turkey Lake

JOHN YOUNG PARKWAY

AMERICANA BLVD

SKY LAKE

Lake Butler

Lake Speer

FICQUETTE ROAD

OAK RIDGE ROAD

Universal Studios Florida®

Universal's Islands of Adventure®

Fun Spot Action Park

Festival Bay Mall

Lake Hancock

WINTER GARDEN-VINELAND RD

Lake Tibet

APOPKA VINELAND ROAD

TURKEY LAKE ROAD

INTERNATIONAL DRIVE

Wet 'n Wild®

Ripley's Believe It or Not! Odditorium

Hickorynut Lake

LAKE HANCOCK ROAD

REAMS ROAD

Lake Mabel

Lake Sheen

Big Sand Lake

ℹ

Wonderworks

Reedy Lake

Magic Kingdom®

Bay Lake

See Walt Disney World® Resort map right

BEACHLINE

Reedy Lake

WALT DISNEY WORLD® RESORT

VISTA BOULEVARD

LAKE BUENA VISTA

SeaWorld®

Aquatica

CENTRAL FLORIDA PARKWAY

Discovery Cove®

JOHN YOUNG PARKWAY

ORANGE BLOSSOM TRAIL

AVALON ROAD

WESTERN BELTWAY

WORLD DRIVE

EPCOT CENTER DRIVE

Epcot®

BUENA VISTA DRIVE

Lake Bryan

4

Disney's Animal Kingdom®

Disney's Hollywood Studios®

OSCEOLA PARKWAY

FLORIDA GREENEWAY

BERMUDA AVENUE

IRLO BRONSON MEMORIAL HIGHWAY

OLD LAKE WILSON DRIVE

OSCEOLA PARKWAY

CENTRAL FLORIDA PARKWAY

IRLO BRONSON MEMORIAL HIGHWAY

OSCEOLA PARKWAY

POINCIANA ROAD

CELEBRATION

0 km 2

0 miles 2

Kiss